CHINA'S NATIONAL SECURITY

All states are challenged by the need to protect national security while maintaining the rule of law, but the issue is particularly complex in the China–Hong Kong context.

This timely and important book explores how China conceives of its national security and the position of Hong Kong. It considers the risks of introducing national security legislation in Hong Kong, and Hong Kong's sources of resilience against encroachments on its rule of law that may come under the guise of national security. It points to what may be needed to maintain Hong Kong's rule of law once China's 50-year commitment to its autonomy ends in 2047.

The contributors to this book include world-renowned scholars in comparative public law and national security law. The collection covers a variety of disciplines and jurisdictions, and both scholarly and practical perspectives to present a forward-looking analysis on the rule of law in Hong Kong. It illustrates how Hong Kong may succeed in resisting pressure to advance China's security interests through repressive law. Given China's growing international stature, the collection's reflections on China's approach to security have much to tell us about its potential impact on the global political, security, and economic order.

China's National Security

Endangering Hong Kong's Rule of Law?

Edited by
Cora Chan
and
Fiona de Londras

•HART•
OXFORD • LONDON • NEW YORK • NEW DELHI • SYDNEY

HART PUBLISHING
Bloomsbury Publishing Plc
Kemp House, Chawley Park, Cumnor Hill, Oxford, OX2 9PH, UK
1385 Broadway, New York, NY 10018, USA

HART PUBLISHING, the Hart/Stag logo, BLOOMSBURY and the Diana logo are trademarks of Bloomsbury Publishing Plc

First published in Great Britain 2020

A catalogue record for this book is available from the British Library.

Library of Congress Cataloging-in-Publication data

Names: Chan, Cora, editor. | De Londras, Fiona, editor.

Title: China's national security : endangering Hong Kong's rule of law? / [edited by] Cora Chan, Fiona de Londras.

Description: Chicago : Hart Publishing, an imprint of Bloomsbury Publishing, 2020. | Includes bibliographical references and index.

Identifiers: LCCN 2019044317 (print) | LCCN 2019044318 (ebook) | ISBN 9781509928156 (hardback) | ISBN 9781509928163 (Epub)

Subjects: LCSH: National security—Law and legislation—China—Hong Kong. | Internal security—Law and legislation—China—Hong Kong. | Rule of law—China—Hong Kong. | National security—Law and legislation—China.

Classification: LCC KNQ9347.3 .C45 2020 (print) | LCC KNQ9347.3 (ebook) | DDC 340/.11—dc23

LC record available at https://lccn.loc.gov/2019044317

LC ebook record available at https://lccn.loc.gov/2019044318

ISBN: HB: 978-1-50992-815-6
ePDF: 978-1-50992-817-0
ePub: 978-1-50992-816-3

Typeset by Compuscript Ltd, Shannon

ACKNOWLEDGEMENTS

This book emerges from a series of workshops held in the Faculty of Law at the University of Hong Kong, funded by the University of Hong Kong's Faculty of Law and Centre for Comparative and Public Law, the British Academy/Leverhulme Small Grants Programme, and the University of Hong Kong Faculty of Law's Cheng Chan Lan Yue Endowment Fund. We are grateful to all of those who supported the work through funding, as well as the Centre for Comparative and Public Law, the Faculty of Law at the University of Hong Kong, and the College of Arts and Law at the University of Birmingham for their logistical and organisational support.

We are indebted to the participants of the roundtable and conference, including Amy Barrow, Eric Cheung, Fergal Davis, Denis Halis, Mingtao Huang, Eric Ip, Malik Imtiaz Sarwar, Carol Jones, Puja Kapai, Benny Tai and Doreen Weisenhaus.

We are thankful to the Global Legal Studies group at Birmingham Law School where some of the ideas underpinning the book were presented. Thanks also go to David Law and Po Jen Yap for their advice.

We thank Michael Hor, Kelley Loper and Victor Ramraj for their support of this project. Finally, we are grateful to Matthew Luke Bucki-Smith, Chan Chi Hang, Kristine Chan, Chan Pui Yu, Francis Chung, Brian Fan, Hung Wing Ki, Jiang Zixin, Stephen Ku, Hugo Lai, Lam Lai Fong, Erica Li, Harrods Wong, Timothy Wong, Julius Yam and Cedric Yeung, for their research assistance, and to the team at Hart for their editorial advice and support.

In the main, the text of this collection was finalised before the events of June 2019 when the largest demonstrations in the history of post-handover Hong Kong occurred, in protest against a proposed extradition law between Hong Kong and China.

TABLE OF CONTENTS

LIST OF CONTRIBUTORS

Paulo Cardinal is a guest teacher at the Faculty of Law of the University of Macau and former Chief Legal Adviser at the Macau Legislative Assembly.

Cora Chan is an Associate Professor at the Faculty of Law of the University of Hong Kong.

Johannes Chan is Chair Professor at the Faculty of Law of the University of Hong Kong and an honorary Senior Counsel in Hong Kong.

Albert HY Chen is Cheng Chan Lan Yue Professor in Constitutional Law at the Faculty of Law of the University of Hong Kong.

Surabhi Chopra is an Associate Professor at the Faculty of Law of Chinese University of Hong Kong.

Michael C Davis is Professor of Law and International Affairs at OP Jindal Global University and Senior Residential Fellow at Woodrow Wilson International Center for Scholars, Washington, DC.

Fiona de Londras is Professor of Global Legal Studies at Birmingham Law School of University of Birmingham.

Hualing Fu is Warren Chan Professor in Human Rights and Responsibilities and Interim Dean at the Faculty of Law of the University of Hong Kong.

Jill Cottrell Ghai is a founder and board member of Katiba Institute in Kenya.

Yash Ghai is an Emeritus Professor at the Faculty of Law of the University of Hong Kong and a founder and board member of Katiba Institute in Kenya.

Danny Gittings is an Associate Professor at the College of Humanities and Law, School of Professional and Continuing Education at the University of Hong Kong.

Swati Jhaveri is an Assistant Professor at the Faculty of Law of National University of Singapore.

Wai-Man Lam is Honorary Associate Fellow at the Centre for Civil Society and Governance of the Faculty of Social Sciences at the University of Hong Kong and Associate Professor at the School of Arts and Social Sciences of Open University of Hong Kong.

Lin Feng is Professor and Associate Dean and Director of the Centre for Judicial Education and Research at the School of Law of City University of Hong Kong.

Pui-Yin Lo is a barrister-at-law (England and Wales, Hong Kong) and Visiting Fellow at the Centre for Comparative and Public Law of the Faculty of Law of the University of Hong Kong.

Margaret Ng is a barrister-at-law (Hong Kong) and a former member of the Hong Kong Legislative Council.

Carole J Petersen is a Professor at the William S Richardson School of Law and Graduate Chair of Matsunaga Institute for Peace at the University of Hawai'i at Mānoa.

Simon NM Young is Professor and Associate Dean (Research) at the Faculty of Law of the University of Hong Kong and barrister-at-law (Hong Kong).

LIST OF ABBREVIATIONS

BRI	Belt and Road Initiative
CA	Hong Kong Court of Appeal
CCP	Communist Party of China
CFA	Hong Kong Court of Final Appeal
CFI	Hong Kong Court of First Instance
ECtHR	European Court of Human Rights
HKBA	Hong Kong Bar Association
HKLRC	Hong Kong Law Reform Commission
HKNP	Hong Kong National Party
HKSAR	Hong Kong Special Administrative Region
ICCPR	International Covenant on Civil and Political Rights
ICESCR	International Covenant on Economic, Social and Cultural Rights
ICJ	International Court of Justice
JORC	Judicial Officers Recommendation Commission of Hong Kong
LegCo	Hong Kong Legislative Council
LSHK	Law Society of Hong Kong
NGO	Non-governmental organisation
NPC	National People's Congress
NPCSC	Standing Committee of the National People's Congress
NPJ	Non-Permanent Judge of the Hong Kong Court of Final Appeal
NSC	National Security Commission of China
POAS	Principal Officials Accountability System
PRC	People's Republic of China
SAR	Special Administrative Region

SCO	Shanghai Cooperation Organisation
UK	United Kingdom
UN	United Nations
UNHCR	United Nations High Commissioner for Refugees
UPR	Universal Periodic Review
US	United States of America

1

Introduction: China's National Security in Hong Kong

A Challenge for Constitutionalism, Autonomy and the Rule of Law

CORA CHAN AND FIONA DE LONDRAS

For 30 years now, the Hong Kong people have persevered in holding an annual candlelight vigil on 4 June to commemorate the 1989 Tiananmen Square Massacre, urging the Chinese Government to admit it was wrong to perpetrate the massacre and to end one-party rule. Hong Kong is the only jurisdiction in China in which such a demonstration could openly take place. A former British colony and now a Special Administrative Region (SAR) of the People's Republic of China (PRC or China), since its return to Chinese sovereignty in 1997 Hong Kong has been governed under the framework of 'one country, two systems', which allows it to practice separate economic, legal and political systems from those on the mainland. The framework's aim is to preserve Hong Kong's distinctiveness vis-à-vis China, including its liberal rule of law tradition, which remains strong after more than two decades of Chinese rule. Yet, given China's intensifying national security advances and rising economic stature, real questions arise about how much longer, and by what means, this tradition can persist.

In this book we aim to explore those questions, understanding them through the prism of the query suggested by its title – *Does China's national security endanger Hong Kong's rule of law?* – by investigating whether, and if so how, China's national security can be protected without jeopardising the rule of law in Hong Kong. From the perspective of both China and Hong Kong this is a vitally important question, not least because it goes to the heart of whether 'one country, two systems' is a viable model for governing the constitutional relationship between them in the long run. Although the opening up of China's economy has rendered the economic differences between China and Hong Kong much less apparent than when that governing model was first conceived, their legal traditions remain highly divergent. For many Hong Kong people the biggest challenge in implementing 'one country, two systems' has been maintaining Hong Kong's vibrant common law system, with its respect for human rights and the separation of powers, within the envelope of China's Leninist legal system. A solution to that challenge would resolve the broader question of how to make this constitutional model work. This is of wider significance for China: from its perspective what is at stake is not just the ability to govern Hong Kong and continue utilising the territory to facilitate its market reforms, but also the prospect of reunification with Taiwan, for which the 'one country, two systems' model was originally designed.[1] What is at stake for the seven million inhabitants of Hong Kong is not just the ability to maintain a separate legal system, but the very identity of Hong Kong, which has long defined itself by being what China is not.[2] For Hong Kong people, without the rule of law, the territory seems destined to become 'just another Chinese city'.[3]

When it comes to security, the relationship between China and Hong Kong, and the functioning of 'one country, two systems' are especially challenging; on the one hand, China fears that security risks to the overall state may foment and find operational space in Hong Kong and thus insists that the Hong Kong Government introduce what it considers 'appropriate' security-related laws; on the other, people in Hong Kong fear the imposition of such laws in a way that undermines their civil liberties, including liberties on the basis of which Beijing can be challenged, organised against and subjected to public criticism. Both concerns have purchase; both point towards the very real difficulties of reconciling two fundamentally different dispositions towards law and legality within one overall national legal system.

I. Relevance Beyond Hong Kong

The questions that are considered in this collection are obviously of relevance to Hong Kong and China, but their significance goes beyond the immediate context in which they arise. Hong Kong is the only contemporary example of a truly liberal region within an authoritarian state. Although there is an extensive body of literature on how national security can be reconciled with the rule of law, the question of how a liberal subnational unit's rule of law can be reconciled with an illiberal national unit's conceptions of national security remains underexplored. Thus,

[1] This was recently reiterated in Xi Jinping's speech commemorating the 40th anniversary of Beijing's 'Message to Compatriots in Taiwan'. See J Xi, 'Working Together to Realize Rejuvenation of the Chinese Nation and Advance China's Peaceful Reunification' (2 January 2019), available at www.gov.cn/xinwen/2019-01/02/content_5354209.htm.

[2] See the contribution of Hualing Fu in this collection.

[3] 'Hong Kong is just another Chinese city: Carrie Lam's reaction to US report proves it' *South China Morning Post*, 20 November 2018, available at www.scmp.com/comment/letters/article/2173991/hong-kong-just-another-chinese-city-carrie-lams-reaction-us-report. On the role of the rule of law as a distinguishing feature of Hong Kong vis-a-vis China see, eg, CAG Jones, *Lost in China? Law, Culture and Identity in Post-1997 Hong Kong* (Cambridge, Cambridge University Press, 2015).

the contributions to this book shed light on the prospects for establishing liberal subunits in illiberal states more generally.

Whilst the book will have direct implications for the building of the rule of law in other Chinese regions (including Macau, the only other SAR of China), they also speak indirectly to other asymmetrical political and economic relationships within which the same kinds of pressures are being applied. These relationships need not be formally constituted in terms of unified statehood. Rather, historical and contemporary political and economic ties between, for example, the Russian Federation and some of its neighbour states, and some of the former states of the former USSR, may result in transnational relationships in which the security concerns of the dominant nation are translated into formal or informal demands and pressures on the other state(s) to introduce 'appropriate' security laws. China's national security strategy explicitly acknowledges that 'sovereignty, security and development interests'[4] are intertwined so that the now well-established practice of China investing and lending money, including in very large volumes to support major infrastructure projects in Africa and South Asia, must be understood as being at least in part an instantiation of its broader security agenda.[5] The 'Belt and Road' agenda is spreading; early in 2019 Italy indicated its intention to sign up to it, thus extending China's influence very substantially into the European political space, seemingly in clear tension with the European Union (itself also a security actor). This programme of economic investment does not, of course, create formal constitutional relationships through which security-related demands can be made. In that sense it is clearly not comparable to the Hong Kong–China relationship. However, that relationship and its working out in and beyond the security space remain apposite for our understanding of China's integrated approach to pursuing security alongside and by means of economic activity. That this is so is clear from some states' resistance to banning Huawei, for example, in spite of requests from the United States of America based apparently on security-related concerns due, it appears, to the economic influence that China can exert.

The questions that are raised in this book and, indeed, the reflections offered on China's approach to security and its pursuit generally are also of international and transnational importance. China is an important and emerging actor in the international security field, including transnational counter-terrorism. Of course, its place as one of the permanent members of the United Nations (UN) Security Council already established that, but increasingly China is acting on transnational scales further to develop and to spread its approach to security across other states. Russia and China are, together, engaged in a process that seems to seek to formalise such relationships by their continued leadership

[4] See, eg, Xi Jinping's Report at the 19th National Congress of the CCP: J Xi, 'Secure a Decisive Victory in Building a Moderately Prosperous Society in All Respects and Strive for the Great Success of Socialism with Chinese Characteristics for a New Era' (18 October 2017), available at www.xinhuanet.com/english/download/Xi_Jinping's_report_at_19th_CPC_National_Congress.pdf.

[5] See the contribution of Yash Ghai and Jill Cottrell Ghai in this collection.

and expansion of the Shanghai Cooperation Organisation (SCO); an organisation devoted almost entirely to security, defined almost exclusively by reference to the interests and definitional preferences of Russia and China, and based on a principle of mutuality in which what is a crime in one Member State is expected to be a crime in all of the others. At the time of writing, the SCO was, geographically, the largest regional organisation in the world; its Member States are China, Russia, Kazakhstan, Kyrgyzstan, Tajikistan, Uzbekistan, India and Pakistan. Afghanistan, Belarus, Iran and Mongolia are observer states, and the status of 'dialogue partner' is held by Armenia, Azerbaijan, Cambodia, Nepal, Sri Lanka and Turkey. It is also an acknowledged 'key' partner of international organisations such as the UN Committee on Counter-Terrorism and its Executive Directorate, and appears to have strong relationships with ASEAN, the UN and the Commonwealth of International States, all of which attend its meetings. Through initiatives such as the SCO, China appears to seek not only to exert its influence in the formal institutional settings of the UN but also to develop forums in which it can dominate, its view of security and its demands can become embedded, and gradually the norms and practices that China's conceptualisation of security demand may spread across states and into other international and transnational spaces.[6]

Seen thus, it becomes abundantly clear that China's engagement with Hong Kong, and Hong Kong's response and ability (if eventually demonstrated) to retain the rule of law and its core propositions – including protection of human rights – matter not only for the people of Hong Kong and the other actual and putative SARs of China, but for all of us.

II. Complexity of the Issues

Reconciling China's national security with Hong Kong's rule of law has been and will continue to be difficult. This is not least because the two jurisdictions have legal systems that are rooted in opposing ideologies: Leninist authoritarianism, and liberal constitutionalism. National security and the rule of law thus take on very different meanings in the two jurisdictions, reconciliation of which is extremely difficult. China conceives of national security in very broad terms to encompass its 'sovereignty, security, and development interests',[7] political control over its territory, the Communist Party of China's (CCP) monopoly on power, and the country's economic interests. Security threats can thus take a variety of forms – many of which would not be viewed through a 'security' lens in other political contexts – and, however small, they must be stamped out immediately. This sweeping conception of national security is reconcilable with China's socialist rule

[6] See further F de Londras, 'Transnational Counter-Terrorism: A Problematique' (2019) *Current Legal Problems* (forthcoming).

[7] See, eg, Xi Jinping's Report at the 19th National Congress of the CCP (2017).

of law, according to which rights are state-granted. However, it clashes with Hong Kong's legal tradition under which the protection of national security is subject to international human rights standards and constitutional and common law principles enforceable by an independent judiciary. Hence, unlike the debate on security and the rule of law in the typical liberal democratic context, where reference to a common set of democratic values to resolve the tension is possible, in the China–Hong Kong context there is no such common frame of reference to appeal to.

At the same time, unlike in the typical authoritarian context where normatively appealing solutions may be found in the liberalisation of or secession from the ruling regime, in the China–Hong Kong context there are strong prima facie normative grounds for retaining the 'one country, two systems' framework. That framework expressly mandates that Hong Kong remain liberal (in fact, it envisages Hong Kong becoming even more liberal-democratic under Chinese rule, ie maturing from a partial to full democracy) without altering the Chinese regime's authoritarian nature and sovereign status.[8] If the framework is to be retained – and this book assumes that it should be – then it is necessary to find ways of preserving the differences between socialist and liberal ideologies within one nation; an arrangement that has no precedent. Any solution to the conflict between national security and the rule of law in the 'one country, two systems' context is therefore likely to be autochthonous.

The complexity of the conflict is aggravated by its constitutional dimension. Hong Kong's post-handover constitutional document, the Basic Law, institutionalises the ideological differences between the two jurisdictions and promises to preserve them for at least 50 years, ie the duration of Hong Kong autonomy to which China committed under the Sino–British Joint Declaration, the international treaty underpinning the handover of sovereignty. However, the Basic Law does not fully specify how such vast differences can be sustained without disintegration or assimilation.[9] On the one hand, the document grants Hong Kong extensive autonomous powers, including the final power of adjudication, and the maintenance of its pre-handover systems. In line with liberal constitutionalism, the Basic Law also guarantees an extensive list of individual rights, entrenches the International Covenant on Civil and Political Rights in domestic law, institutes checks and balances including judicial review by an independent judiciary, and promises eventual universal suffrage for Hong Kong's legislature and Chief Executive. On the other hand, in line with the socialist ethos of control, it vests China with important supervisory powers, including the final power to interpret the Basic Law. In addition, Article 23 of the Basic Law – to which a great many of our contributors refer – requires Hong Kong to enact legislation to prevent

[8] C Chan, 'Thirty years from Tiananmen: China, Hong Kong, and the ongoing experiment to preserve liberal values in an authoritarian state' (2019) 17 *International Journal of Constitutional Law* 439, 442.

[9] This and the following two paragraphs are adapted from Chan, 'Thirty years from Tiananmen' (ibid) 442–43, 444–45.

treason, subversion, secession, sedition, the theft of state secrets and ties with foreign organisations opposed to the Chinese Government. Through these and other provisions, the Basic Law seeks to maintain China's conception of its sovereign prerogatives alongside Hong Kong's liberal values, but it is not at all clear on how these tensions can be resolved.

The potential for such ideological differences to result in constitutional conflict is not academic. This can be illustrated by reference to just two such conflicts. The first, in 2003, revolved around the Hong Kong Government's first, and so far only, attempt to introduce legislation to implement Article 23 of the Basic Law.[10] The attempt failed because of widespread public opposition, much of which considered the Bill overly repressive by reference to international rights standards. A 500,000-person demonstration on 1 July 2003 ultimately forced the Government to shelve the Bill, even though the Basic Law arguably required (and continues to require) the introduction of such a law. The second, in 2014, arose out of disputes over what form 'universal suffrage' would take for the 2017 Chief Executive election.[11] Hong Kong's pan-democratic camp insisted on free and fair elections, but Beijing decided to grant only hegemonic elections[12] in which everyone could vote, but only for a select list of candidates approved by a pro-Beijing committee.[13] This decision sparked the 79-day illegal occupation of roads that became known internationally as the Umbrella Movement. China refused to yield, and the prevailing election methods have thus remained unchanged.

The ideological tension between the two sides has also manifested institutionally. The Basic Law divides the power for interpreting it between the Standing Committee of the National People's Congress (NPCSC) and the Hong Kong courts. Whilst the former enjoys the final, plenary power of interpretation, the latter have authority to interpret the Basic Law in the course of adjudication, subject to a duty to refer provisions on Chinese prerogatives to the NPCSC.[14] The two organs are poles apart in interpretative methods. The text plays a central role in Hong Kong's interpretative tradition, whilst the NPCSC's interpretations may in practice amend legislation. These differences reflect opposing conceptions of the law. In the liberal tradition, the purposes that the law serves are predicated upon the law's ability

[10] National Security (Legislative Provisions) Bill 2003. See generally, HKSAR Government, 'Proposals to implement Article 23 of the BASIC LAW', available at www.basiclaw23.gov.hk/english.

[11] In 2007, the NPCSC determined that universal suffrage for the Chief Executive election could be introduced in 2017.

[12] See, eg, L Diamond, 'Thinking about Hybrid Regimes' (2002) 13 *Journal of Democracy* 21; S Levitsky and LA Way, *Competitive Authoritarianism: Hybrid Regimes after the Cold War* (Cambridge, Cambridge University Press, 2010) 7.

[13] NPCSC, 'Decision of the Standing Committee of the National People's Congress on Issues Relating to the Selection of the Chief Executive of Hong Kong by Universal Suffrage and on the Method for Forming the Legislative Council in Hong Kong in the Year 2016' (adopted at the Tenth Session of the Standing Committee of the Twelfth National People's Congress, 31 August 2014).

[14] This arrangement is inspired by the European Union's preliminary reference procedure. See C Chan, 'Implementing China and Hong Kong's Preliminary Reference System: Transposability of Article 267 TFEU Principles' [2014] *Public Law* 642.

to guide. Legal certainty is important. The courts cannot change the meaning of a law retrospectively in the name of interpretation. However, notwithstanding its recent emphasis on 'law-based governance',[15] for Beijing the law remains chiefly a political tool. Legal certainty is less important than the flexibility required to adapt to political exigencies,[16] illustrating a clear difference between the NPCSC and Hong Kong courts, which has played out in clashes on questions such as the binding scope of an NPCSC interpretation and what material ought to be admissible as an interpretative aid.[17]

III. Developments Since 2003

The question of how China's national security can be reconciled with Hong Kong's rule of law has already been explored in depth in the context of evaluating the 2003 Article 23 Bill.[18] Yet there have been important developments since 2003 that call for a revisiting of the question beyond the Article 23 context. As explained below, these developments suggest that China's imperatives for regulating national security in Hong Kong have increased, whilst Hong Kong's ability to maintain its rule of law has decreased. More generally, we are now almost mid-way through China's 50-year commitment to Hong Kong's autonomy under the Joint Declaration. At the end of the 50-year period in 2047, China is arguably free to depart from its basic policy on segregation of systems, stated as unamendable in the Basic Law. If that policy is to persist beyond 2047 – and it is widely considered to be in the best interests of both jurisdictions that it do so – now would be a timely juncture for reflecting on what constitutional design, institutions, practices and socioeconomic conditions are needed to ensure its long-term viability.[19]

IV. China's Increased Imperatives for Controlling Hong Kong

There are at least three reasons for China's tightened policy over Hong Kong in recent years. First, it is likely part and parcel of Xi Jinping's overall plan to securitise the state, manifested in, for example, the enactment of the PRC National

[15] See, eg, Xi Jinping's Report at the 19th National Congress of the CCP (n 4).

[16] See Y Ghai, *Hong Kong's New Constitutional Order: The Resumption of Chinese Sovereignty and the Basic Law*, 2nd edn (Hong Kong, Hong Kong University Press, 1999) 212–13; C Chan, 'The Legal Limits on Beijing's Powers of Interpreting the Basic Law' (HKU Legal Scholarship blog, 3 November 2016), available at www.researchblog.law.hku.hk/2016/11/cora-chan-on-legal-limits-of-beijings.html.

[17] See *Director of Immigration v Chong Fung Yuen* (2001) 4 HKCFAR 211.

[18] H Fu, CJ Petersen and SNM Young (eds), *National Security and Fundamental Freedoms: Hong Kong's Article 23 under Scrutiny* (Hong Kong, Hong Kong University Press, 2005).

[19] This paragraph is adapted from Chan, 'Thirty years from Tiananmen' (2019) 450–51.

Security Law, the CCP's latest 'retraining' policy for the Uighurs in Xinjiang, the country's ongoing persecution of human rights advocates and lawyers since 2015, and its bold use of technology as a tool for control. Second, recent developments in Hong Kong seem to have convinced Beijing that the territory now poses real security threats that warrant a heavier hand. The large-scale demonstration that led to the failed attempt to enact Article 23 legislation in 2003[20] indicated to Beijing that Hong Kong might spiral out of (its) control if granted genuine democracy. Hence, shortly thereafter, the NPCSC issued an interpretation granting itself additional power to control the pace of democratic reform in Hong Kong.[21] In 2014, civil society engaged in heated debate over the launch of a large-scale Occupy Central movement should Beijing refuse to grant genuine democracy. Amongst Beijing's responses to this debate was a white paper pronouncing that it had 'comprehensive jurisdiction' over Hong Kong, a position that apparently contradicts the Joint Declaration's promise of a high degree of autonomy,[22] and the aforementioned imposition of hegemonic elections. The moves were indicative of China's strong resolve to prevent any possibility of Hong Kong becoming a base for subversion.

Occupy Central did indeed take place, but the failure of the movement to achieve democratisation prompted calls for Hong Kong's disconnection from China, self-determination and even secession.[23] Although these calls have never been widespread, and none of the activities associated with them thus far constitutes a genuine threat to national security or comes close to being a public emergency by international human rights standards, China considers them a threat and has responded resolutely. In 2016, through an interpretation of the Basic Law (the 'oath-taking interpretation'),[24] the NPCSC transformed a provision whose original formulation simply required major officers to swear an oath of allegiance to the Basic Law before assuming office into a formal political screening mechanism: individuals who wish to run for or assume office must be 'sincere' in upholding the Basic Law, including its stipulation of Chinese sovereignty. Anyone who has advocated, or even displayed mild sympathy for, secession or self-determination cannot be sincere, and is thus disqualified. At the time of writing, 13 elected or would-be legislators have been disqualified on this ground.

Furthermore, in 2018, in an unprecedented move the Hong Kong Government used local law to ban a pro-independence political party. It publicised a letter from the Chinese Government expressing support for its decision to ban the party and subsequently submitted a report to the latter on the ban. At the same

[20] J Cheng, 'The Story of a New Policy' (Fall 2009) 15 *Hong Kong Journal*.

[21] NPCSC, 'The Interpretation by the Standing Committee of the National People's Congress of Article 7 of Annex I and Article III of Annex II to the Basic Law' (Adopted at the Eighth Session of the Standing Committee of the Tenth National People's Congress, 6 April 2004). See also Chan (n 8) 445.

[22] Information Office of the State Council of the PRC, 'The Practice of the "One Country, Two Systems" Policy in the Hong Kong Special Administrative Region' (10 June 2014).

[23] This paragraph is adapted from Chan (n 8) 445.

[24] NPCSC, 'Interpretation by the Standing Committee of the National People's Congress of Article 104 of the Basic Law' (Adopted by the Standing Committee of the Twelfth National People's Congress at its Twenty-fourth Session, 7 November 2016).

time, the push for secession has prompted renewed calls from pro-China sections of society for the Hong Kong Government to reintroduce legislation to implement Article 23. All of these events clearly demonstrate Beijing's will to stamp out pro-self-determination or pro-independence moves in Hong Kong, however unpromising they may be. Any Article 23 law introduced in this context is likely to be draconian, and more repressive towards rights than the 2003 Bill was, targeting not just acts that pose a genuine threat to territorial integrity or are likely to incite imminent violence, but also the mere advocacy of anything Beijing perceives to be a threat.

Third, increasing economic, social and cultural integration between China and Hong Kong, coupled with the widening power imbalance between the two jurisdictions, has given China new incentives (and weakened disincentives) to assimilate the two legal systems.[25] A good illustration of these dynamics at work is the controversy over China's 'co-location arrangement' for a train station in Hong Kong that links the territory to China's high-speed railway network. Under the arrangement, both Chinese and Hong Kong checkpoints are located in Hong Kong, leading to the application of Chinese law and jurisdiction (including criminal jurisdiction) to a part of Hong Kong. However, the Basic Law's mechanism for such application was bypassed; instead, Beijing sought to legitimise the arrangement through a mere 'decision' issued outside the Basic Law framework.[26] Despite the far-reaching constitutional implications of the arrangement, many in Hong Kong seem to have accepted it as a necessary, and not particularly significant, trade-off for securing the vast potential economic benefits of integration with the national railway network and the placation of Beijing. In the end, the arrangement was approved by the Legislative Council.

This controversy reveals that, first, economic integration can drive legal integration and, second, as China's economic power grows, the incentives to retain (and disincentives to dismantle) Hong Kong's distinctiveness are dwindling. Three decades ago when the 'one country, two systems' model was first conceived, China's economy was just beginning to open up, whereas Hong Kong was already a thriving capitalist economy. The means to economic prosperity for both was thus segregated systems. Three decades on, however, China has become the world's second largest economy and is projected to become the largest by 2032.[27] The country no longer needs a distinct Hong Kong in the way that it used to and, for Hong Kong, the means to achieve continued prosperity may no longer be segregation but rather integration with the Chinese economy and the securing of Beijing's

[25] This and the following paragraph is adapted from Chan (n 8) 449–50.

[26] NPCSC, 'Decision of the Standing Committee of the National People's Congress on Approving the Co-Operation Arrangement Between the Mainland and the Hong Kong Special Administrative Region on the Establishment of the Port At the West Kowloon Station of the Guangzhou-Shenzhen-Hong Kong Express Rail Link For Implementing Co-Location Arrangement' (Adopted at the Thirty-first Session of the Standing Committee of the Twelfth National People's Congress, 27 December 2017).

[27] Centre for Economics and Business Research, *World Economic League Table 2019* (2018), available at cebr.com/welt-2019.

patronage. The economic incentives for assimilation have seemed to embolden an ever more interventionist China. Those imperatives will only be reinforced, and the choice between economic prosperity and the rule of law that Hong Kong faces starker, as the two economies integrate further as part of the Greater Bay Area project and as China trundles towards becoming 'a global leader in terms of composite national strength and international influence' by its centenary in 2049.[28]

All of this suggests that the scene is set for a Hong Kong debate on national security. Certainly, such a debate seems timelier and more likely now than it was in 2003 when the Hong Kong Government first attempted to pass an Article 23 law. While the prospect of an Article 23 law being introduced is very real, the evolving understanding of security in China and the developing political situation in Hong Kong point towards the relevance of far more contexts than 'merely' Article 23 for questions relating to security and the rule of law. The NPCSC's oath-taking interpretation demonstrates that China can export its security concepts by issuing an interpretation of the Basic Law. The co-location controversy illustrates that the NPCSC may even be able to achieve the effects of such interpretation without following the Basic Law's procedure for issuing one.[29] Beijing seems able to enforce its desired security measures through the Hong Kong Government, as shown by the latter's active disqualification of legislators and candidates and, most recently, the attempt (met with substantial civil resistance) to introduce legislative amendments that would allow for surrender of fugitives in Hong Kong to mainland China.[30] Finally, if it is true that (as some suspect) the Chinese Government abducted the owners of Causeway Bay Books in 2016, took them to mainland China, and coerced them to admit their guilt, then it seems that Beijing is ready to quench its national security concerns even extra-constitutionally. Hence, whilst Article 23 continues to be a core focus of scholarly and political debate about national security and the rule of law in Hong Kong, it is by no means the only issue that requires urgent attention.

V. Democratic Backsliding in Hong Kong[31]

Just as China's imperatives to regulate national security in Hong Kong are intensifying, the institutions and culture needed to maintain Hong Kong's rule of law are waning. Some of the means used to erode those institutions and culture are similar to those adopted by popularly elected rulers in other jurisdictions experiencing

[28] See, eg, Xi Jinping's Report at the 19th National Congress of the CCP (n 4).

[29] Chan (n 8) 445.

[30] Fugitive Offenders and Mutual Legal Assistance in Criminal Matters Legislation (Amendment) Bill 2019. On 15 June 2019, in response to widespread opposition, the Hong Kong Government announced that legislative proceedings on the Bill would be suspended.

[31] This section is adapted from Chan (n 8) 443–49.

democratic backsliding.[32] As a polity with a strong rule of law tradition within an authoritarian state, Hong Kong has seen sophisticated uses of the law by both Beijing and the Hong Kong Government that tend towards eroding its liberal foundations.[33]

First, the Basic Law has been weakened as a framework for guaranteeing the rule of law in Hong Kong. Although it is not clear from the Basic Law's wording that the NPCSC can issue an interpretation on any provision on its own volition, or that it can use an interpretation to change the prevalent understanding of the Basic Law, the NPCSC has since 2003 used its interpretative powers in these ways. The way in which Beijing pushed through the co-location arrangement suggests that it may even be able to circumvent the formal procedure for issuing an interpretation altogether. The result is that the Basic Law's guarantees – extensive though they may seem – can be delivered only at China's grace,[34] calling into question the constitutional character of the document in respect of individuals' and society's relationship with China, and arguably also with the Hong Kong Government.

Second, the courts have become less muscular in checking Chinese actions that may intrude upon Hong Kong's autonomy and the freedoms of its population. Back in 1999, the Hong Kong courts were bold enough to assert jurisdiction to strike down Chinese acts that did not comply with the Basic Law[35] and, in 1999–2001, to use the common law distinction between obiter and *ratio* to render non-binding a certain part of an NPCSC interpretation.[36] Recently, however, they have become much less ready to challenge Chinese decisions. In a 2017 case, for example, the courts refused to examine whether the NPCSC's oath-taking interpretation added so much content that it exceeded the boundaries of an interpretation allowed by the Basic Law.[37] In 2018, when faced with a decision issued by the NPCSC outside the Basic Law's framework, the Court of First Instance (CFI) held that the NPCSC could act outside the Basic Law, that the courts had no power to challenge such an act, and that the NPCSC decision at stake attracted conclusive weight.[38] In another case, the CFI refused to use common law methods to read down an NPCSC interpretation.[39]

[32] See eg MA Graber, S Levinson and M Tushnet (eds), *Constitutional Democracy in Crisis?* (Oxford, Oxford University Press, 2018); D Landau, 'Abusive Constitutionalism' (2013) 47 *UC Davis Law Review* 189; OO Varol, 'Stealth Authoritarianism' (2015) 100 *Iowa Law Review* 1673.

[33] See, eg, A Cheung, '"For My Enemies, The Law": Abusive Legalism' (2018 International Society of Public Law Conference, University of Hong Kong, 2018).

[34] Chan, 'The Legal Limits on Beijing's Powers' (2016).

[35] *Ng Ka Ling v Director of Immigration* (1999) 2 HKCFAR 4, 26A–B.

[36] *Chong Fung Yuen v Director of Immigration* [2000] 1 HKC 359 (CFI) 382E–83D; [2000] 3 HKLRD 661 (CA) 675D–E, 679D–F, 680C–F, 686E–F; (2001) 4 HKCFAR 211 (CFA) section 6.2.

[37] *Chief Executive of HKSAR v President of The Legislative Council* [2017] 1 HKLRD 460 (CA) [55]–[58]; sub nom *Yau Wai Ching v Chief Executive of HKSAR* (2017) 20 HKCFAR 390 (CFA) [35]–[36].

[38] *Leung Chung Hang, Sixtus v President of Legislative Council and Secretary for Justice* [2019] 1 HKLRD 292 [53]–[76].

[39] *Chan Ho Tin v Lo Ying-Ki Alan and others* [2018] 2 HKLRD 7 [46]–[49].

The cumulative effect of these recent cases is that the courts are giving Chinese actions full force in Hong Kong, regardless of whether they comply with the substantive or procedural requirements of the Basic Law. The courts' changing attitudes did not arise from formal changes in the structure or competences of the courts or from direct political pressure. There have been no attempts to pack the courts in Hong Kong or to oust their jurisdiction, and nor is there any evidence of direct threats to judges. Rather, the pressure seems more subtle, indicating perhaps that, as Ghai has put it, the Chinese legal system has 'triumphed' over common law in Hong Kong because of its 'predominant political power'.[40]

Third, the legislature's role in curbing abuses of power has also waned. The Government's disqualification of candidates and legislators (2016) and changes in procedural rules (2017), and the increasing success of pro-China candidates in direct elections since the handover have diminished the legislature's ability to check repressive laws. The passing of the co-location bill in 2018 is a case in point, illustrating its compliant attitude even in the face of proposals that blatantly violate the Basic Law.

Although China's increased intervention and the Hong Kong Government's full cooperation in implementing China's will (and at times even exceeding it) have sparked social movements that have strengthened civil society in Hong Kong, they have also served to undermine civil society. To name but a few examples of local government measures to restrict civil society action, the Government criticised a university publication for advocating Hong Kong independence; denied an international journalist who had hosted a talk by the leader of a pro-independence political party entry to Hong Kong as well as subsequently banning that party; and disqualified a pro-self-determination candidate from standing in village elections, which fall outside the scope of the NPCSC oath-taking interpretation. These measures, amongst others, have directly impaired, or exerted chilling effects upon, political rights and freedoms of speech, association and the press, handicapping civil society's capacity to mobilise against repressive measures. Most recently, the Hong Kong Government proposed a law that criminalises expressions of disrespect for the national anthem[41] and legislative amendments that would lift the restriction on surrender of fugitives to China,[42] both of which, if passed, would have serious chilling effects on civil liberties. At the time of finalising this Introduction (June 2019), the Hong Kong Government has suspended the legislative proceedings on the latter due to widespread opposition,[43] but it is not yet clear

[40] See Y Ghai, 'The Intersection of Chinese Law and the Common Law in the Hong Kong Special Administrative Region: Question of Technique or Politics?' (2007) 37 *Hong Kong Law Journal* 363, 403–05.

[41] National Anthem Bill.

[42] Fugitive Offenders and Mutual Legal Assistance in Criminal Matters Legislation (Amendment) Bill 2019. On 15 June 2019, the Hong Kong Government announced that legislative proceedings on the Bill would be suspended, in response to widespread opposition thereto.

[43] 'As it happened: Carrie Lam backs down and "suspends" Hong Kong extradition bill, sets no new time frame', *South China Morning Post*, 15 June 2019, available at www.scmp.com/news/hong-kong/politics/article/3014638/hong-kong-extradition-bill-carrie-lam-hit-pause-button. See also text to n 49 below.

whether and in what form it will be reintroduced. There are numerous signs of self-censorship by the media.[44] Indeed, the latest survey by the Public Opinion Programme of the University of Hong Kong shows that 'the freedoms of "academic research", "speech", "press", "publication" and "association" have dropped to their record lows since the questions were first asked in August 1997'.[45]

Finally, China's formidable economic power poses a key obstacle to the mobilisation of civil society to resist China's authoritarian advances. A substantial portion of the Hong Kong population has become willing to succumb to Chinese pressure in return for economic patronage, as reflected in the relatively muted response to China's co-location arrangement. The ability of the territory to remain liberal ultimately depends on a general desire to safeguard Hong Kong's liberal character, as without such a desire even 'the best institutional and constitutional design in the world will likely be for naught'.[46] At the time of finalising this Introduction (June 2019), large-scale protests forced the Hong Kong Government to suspend its proposed legislative amendments that would allow Hong Kong to surrender fugitives to China. These protests are the largest that Hong Kong has seen since the 2003 demonstration against the National Security Bill and the 2014 occupy movement on democratic reform. According to the organisers, the protest on 9 June 2019 drew over a million people; the one on 16 June 2019 nearly two million.[47] This turn of events suggests that a significant portion of the general public in Hong Kong are still willing to stand up to guard Hong Kong's rule of law. However, the point being made here remains true: that the rising economic stature of China is an incentive for many in Hong Kong to forego liberal values. The power imbalance between the two jurisdictions will remain the key impediment to safeguarding liberal values in Hong Kong.

VI. Organisation of the Book

These developments do not bode well for Hong Kong's rule of law. Indeed, the first two parts of this book do not appear to counsel optimism. The chapters in Part I suggest that a clash is inevitable. Chen explains why legislating for national security in Hong Kong is one of the most difficult challenges facing the China–Hong Kong

[44] See eg Hong Kong Journalists Association, 2018 Annual Report, 'Candle in the wind: national security law looms over diminishing freedoms', available at www.hkja.org.hk/ebook/e_Annual_report_2018/files/downloads/HKJA%20Annual%20Report%202018.pdf, ch 3.

[45] Public Opinion Programme of the University of Hong Kong, 'HKU POP releases its final round of social indicators' (21 May 2019), available at www.hkupop.hku.hk/english/release/release1588.html.

[46] T Ginsburg and AZ Huq, *How to Save a Constitutional Democracy* (Chicago, The University of Chicago Press, 2018) 245.

[47] 'Hong Kong protest: 'Nearly two million' join demonstration' BBC News (17 June 2019), available at www.bbc.com/news/world-asia-china-48656471; 'Hong Kong extradition protests leave city in shock' BBC News (13 June 2019), available at www.bbc.com/news/world-asia-china-48618484; 'Violent clashes mar protest after "more than a million" Hongkongers of all ages and backgrounds march against controversial extradition bill' *South China Morning Post*, 10 June 2019, available at www.scmp.com/news/hong-kong/politics/article/3013757/violent-clashes-mar-protest-after-more-million-hongkongers.

relationship. That explanation is followed by Fu's chapter, which elaborates China's approach to national security and the role that Hong Kong plays in China's security order. Lam then analyses the relationship between the rule of law and such concepts as national identity and highlights the implications of her findings for the introduction of national security measures in Hong Kong. Cardinal, offering a comparative perspective from Macau, which passed the equivalent of Article 23 legislation in 2009, suggests that Hong Kong is now converging with Macau in terms of its (lack of) resilience against Chinese pressure. In his critical reflection on these chapters, Lin argues that at a fundamental level the existence not only of two systems but of two *national security* systems within what is one country explains the difficulties posed by and to the passage of an Article 23 law in Hong Kong. In doing so he develops his argument that in the absence of Article 23 legislation in Hong Kong the likelihood is that the Central Government will take action either by applying national security law from mainland China to Hong Kong or by issuing an interpretation of the Basic Law and that, in either case, such a development may effectively dismantle the commitment to two systems. This highlights what might be said to be Hong Kong's Article 23 predicament: if Hong Kong law on Article 23 is undesirable from a rule of law perspective but nevertheless preferable to law developed by China, what should be done and, if Article 23 law is to be passed, is there any way in which to bolster the rule of law in Hong Kong regardless?

Part II of the book then explores what sources of resilience Hong Kong has for resisting encroachments on the rule of law that come in the guise of national security. At first reading, these chapters suggest that these sources are either waning or insignificant. Jhaveri suggests that the Hong Kong courts have some space in administrative law to safeguard rights. That space is described as modest, however, because the NPCSC can ultimately restrict it via an interpretation of the Basic Law. The following chapters then analyse the weakening of various institutions' ability to defend the rule of law: the judiciary and legal profession (Lo), the legislature (Ng) and civil society (Davis). A closer reading, however, reveals that these authors all believe that there is much that the people and institutions of Hong Kong can still do to strengthen their resilience. A common message is that Hong Kong is well-endowed with constitutional arrangements (extensive autonomous powers and guarantees of eventual universal suffrage), institutions (impartial courts, a clean election system), traditions (a fine judiciary and legal profession, vibrant judicial review), culture (strong civil society, high esteem for the rule of law) and geo-political status (an international financial centre that attracts international attention) that could help to sustain the rule of law if properly utilised. In her commentary on Part II Chopra offers a sobering analysis of the limitations of the Basic Law as a source of resilience in the face of national security logics and legislation. She subtly but powerfully questions whether reliance on the Basic Law – especially without further institutional strengthening and innovation, and without a continued commitment to Hong Kong's openness and transnationalism – is sufficient, or whether Hong Kong people committed to the rule of law need better to 'transcend liberal blind spots', as she puts it, through a 'critical, creative, heterodox engagement with the law'.

The message that it is possible to strengthen Hong Kong's resilience becomes even clearer in Part III of the book, the contributors to which propose ways of strengthening Hong Kong's sources of resilience. The chapters therein suggest that much lies in the hands of the territory's people and institutions at all three key stages of the security law's lifecycle: drafting, enforcement and adjudication. Young sketches the principles that Hong Kong law-makers should follow in drafting any Article 23 legislation to ensure respect for the rule of law. Petersen proposes a role for international law and institutions in monitoring Hong Kong's liberal status. Johannes Chan then demonstrates how the proper application of common law principles could limit the undue import of expansive national security concepts into Hong Kong's legal system, how the independence of the judiciary could be enhanced, and how best to maintain open justice while respecting the need for secrecy in national security cases. This chapter is followed by Cora Chan and de Londras's chapter proposing new arrangements for monitoring the excesses of national security measures, including the establishment of an Independent Reviewer, the enactment of an access to information law and archives law, and the use of sunset clauses. Hitting a pragmatic and realistic tone, however, Gittings concludes Part III with a critical reflection that considers the costs and likely success of the proposals in the preceding chapters, showing keenly the ways in which local, national and geopolitical realities may well conspire to limit the possible impact and feasibility of the other authors' proposals.

Expanding our lens somewhat to place the China–Hong Kong relationship into broader perspective, Yash Ghai and Jill Cottrell Ghai conclude the book by highlighting the increasing influence that China has over security, economy and politics in other parts of the world, particularly through the Belt and Road Initiative. For Ghai and Cottrell Ghai the implications of this for Hong Kong are significant, not least because China's growing economic influence may well lead to a decline in solidarity from other states on which Hong Kong may find itself reliant to sustain its autonomy in the longer term.

The answer this book offers to the question of whether China's national security endangers Hong Kong's rule of law is, thus, 'not necessarily'. China's conceptions of national security are inherently incompatible with Hong Kong's conception of the rule of law. However, the timely, wise and creative use of sources of resilience by the people and institutions of Hong Kong could ensure that the territory's rule of law continues to flourish in China's authoritarian shadow. As one of us has argued elsewhere:

> [S]uch tension [between the two systems] is precisely the beauty of 'one country, two systems'. The crux of this governing framework is tension, not harmony. It is through the solemn ping-ponging between institutions in the two systems that such divergent systems continue to survive side by side.[48]

[48] C Chan, 'How Hong Kong's courts interpret Beijing's interpretation of the Basic Law may yet surprise' *South China Morning Post*, 9 November 2016, available at www.scmp.com/comment/insight-opinion/article/2044385/how-hong-kongs-courts-interpret-beijings-interpretation.

PART I

China v Hong Kong: National Security v the Rule of Law?

2

Hong Kong in China: The Project of 'One Country, Two Systems' and the Question of National Security

ALBERT HY CHEN*

In July 2017, Hong Kong celebrated the 20th anniversary of the establishment of the Hong Kong Special Administrative Region (HKSAR) of the People's Republic of China (PRC). In October 2017, the 19th National Congress of the Chinese Communist Party was convened, at which General Secretary Xi Jinping outlined a grand vision for China's strategic development all the way up to the middle of the twenty-first century. The vision was termed 'socialism with Chinese characteristics for the new age'.[1] It consists of 14 policy components, and the 'one country, two systems' policy is one of them. What was this policy originally and how has it been implemented in the case of Hong Kong? What is the status of Hong Kong as a special administrative region (SAR) of the PRC? What is the nature of Hong Kong's 'high degree of autonomy' – a term used in both the Sino–British Joint Declaration on the Question of Hong Kong (1984) and the Basic Law of the HKSAR of the PRC (1990)? How does the Basic Law seek to protect China's national security and limit Hong Kong's autonomy for this purpose? This chapter explores these questions.

Although the HKSAR is our focus, it should be borne in mind that Hong Kong is one of the two SARs of the PRC, and the other SAR is Macau.[2] Following the reunification of Hong Kong and Macau with China in 1997 and 1999 respectively, the structure of the PRC consists of a national or central government, and, at the

* Cheng Chan Lan Yue Professor in Constitutional Law, Faculty of Law, University of Hong Kong. The author is grateful to the editors for their helpful comments on the draft of this chapter. This chapter draws on the author's chapter on 'The Autonomy of Hong Kong under "One Country, Two Systems"' in TL Lui, SWK Chiu and R Yap, (eds), *Routledge Handbook of Contemporary Hong Kong* (Abingdon, Routledge, 2019) ch 1.

[1] For the English translation of the full text of Xi's report at the 19th congress, see J Xi, 'Secure a Decisive Victory in Building a Moderately Prosperous Society in All Respects and Strive for the Great Success of Socialism with Chinese Characteristics for a New Era', 18 October 2017, available at www.chinadaily.com.cn/china/19thcpcnationalcongress/2017-11/04/content_34115212.htm.

[2] See also the contribution of Paulo Cardinal in this collection.

level directly below it, 27 provincial governments (including the governments of five autonomous regions but excluding Taiwan), four governments of municipalities directly under the Central Government, and two governments of SARs (Hong Kong and Macau).

Chinese scholars have always stressed that the PRC is a unitary state.[3] It is not a federal system; there is nothing in the PRC Constitution that provides for a formal division of power between the national Government and the provincial, municipal, and SAR governments. That is, there is no *constitutional* limitation on the capacity of the national Government to exercise power with regard to any matter within any province, city or SAR of the PRC. However, since the enactment of the Basic Laws of the SARs of Hong Kong and Macau, the powers that the Central Government may exercise with regard to the SARs have been constrained by the Basic Laws. It can be argued that the concept of an SAR within the PRC with a high degree of autonomy, and the related policy of 'one country, two systems', represent a substantial modification of the original model of a highly centralised unitary state.[4]

I. The Origins of 'One Country, Two Systems'

The concept of 'one country, two systems' was originally developed as a new cornerstone of the PRC's policy towards Taiwan in the late 1970s,[5] although the full elaboration of the concept took place during the Sino–British negotiations in 1982–84 on the status of the British colony of Hong Kong after 1997. The PRC's original position vis-à-vis Taiwan since the establishment of the PRC in 1949 was that the 'liberation of Taiwan' should be pursued, 'liberation' referring, of course, to liberation from the evils of capitalism and imperialism, and the revolutionary introduction of communism.

The new Taiwan policy, in which we find the origins of 'one country, two systems', was revealed in several official statements published since 1979, the most important of which was the nine-point proposal of Ye Jianying, then Chairman of the Standing Committee of the National People's Congress (NPCSC), published in September 1981.[6] The proposal envisaged the peaceful reunification of China,

[3] S Wang (ed), *Introduction to the Basic Law of the Hong Kong Special Administrative Region* (Beijing, Law Press, 2000) 57–62, 67.

[4] See generally G Zhu, 'The composite state of China under "One Country, Multiple Systems"' (2012) 10 *I-CON* 272.

[5] See generally YJ Ma, 'Policy towards the Chinese Mainland: Taipei's view' in Steve Tsang (ed), *In the Shadow of China: Political Developments in Taiwan Since 1949* (Hong Kong, Hong Kong University Press, 1993); HH Wu, *Bridging the Strait: Taiwan, China, and the Prospects for Reunification* (New York, Oxford University Press, 1994).

[6] See generally C Zhao (ed), *Yiguo liangzhi gailun* (General Principles of 'One Country, Two Systems') (Jilin, Jilin daxue chubanshe, 1988); Editorial Department of the Overseas Edition of Liaowang Weekly (ed), *'Yiguo liangzhi' yu zuguo tongyi* ('One Country, Two Systems' and China's Unification) (Beijing, Liaowang Weekly, 1988).

with Taiwan being given the status of an SAR of the PRC. As such it would retain its existing social and economic systems after unification and enjoy a high degree of autonomy; it could enter into external economic and cultural relations with other countries, and even maintain its own armed forces.[7]

In January 1982, elder statesman Deng Xiaoping coined the expression 'one country, two systems' and said that this was the essence of Ye Jianying's 1981 statement: that there was to be one China, but two systems – the socialist system on the mainland, and the capitalist system in Taiwan. In December 1982, a new Constitution of the PRC was enacted. Reflecting this thinking, Article 31 of this Constitution provides that 'The State may establish special administrative regions when necessary. The systems to be instituted in special administrative regions shall be prescribed by law enacted by the National People's Congress in the light of specific conditions.' At the time, it was generally believed that in the future, SARs might practise social systems different from those in other parts of China.

In September 1982, British Prime Minister Margaret Thatcher visited Beijing, seeking a solution to the question of Hong Kong's constitutional status after 1997. The British Government was concerned that there was no legal basis for its continued governance of the New Territories after 1997, the New Territories being that part of the Hong Kong colony which was leased by the Qing Dynasty Government in China to Britain for 99 years in 1898, unlike Hong Kong Island and the Kowloon Peninsula, which were permanently ceded to Britain in 1842 and 1860 respectively. High-level negotiations between the two governments started after Thatcher's visit. Two years of hard bargaining and strenuous work finally produced the Sino–British Joint Declaration on the Question of Hong Kong in September 1984 in which the 'one country, two systems' concept was enshrined and applied to post-1997 Hong Kong, with similar wording then being used for Macau in the 1987 Sino–Portuguese Joint Declaration.[8]

II. The Basic Law and the Autonomy of the HKSAR

As applied to Hong Kong, 'one country, two systems' was concretised and codified in the Basic Law of the HKSAR, which is a law enacted in 1990 by the national legislature, the National People's Congress (NPC), in pursuance of Article 31 of

[7] As of 2019, 'one country, two systems' is still the PRC's official policy on the reunification of Taiwan with the mainland. See J Xi, 'Working Together to Realize Rejuvenation of the Chinese Nation and Advance China's Peaceful Reunification' (Speech at the Meeting Marking the 40th Anniversary of the Issuance of the Message to Compatriots in Taiwan, Beijing, 2 January 2019), English translation available at www.gwytb.gov.cn/wyly/201904/t20190412_12155687.htm.

[8] P Cardinal, 'Macau: Transformations of an Historic Autonomy' in Y Ghai and S Woodman (eds), *Practising Self-Government: A Comparative Study of Autonomous Regions* (Cambridge, Cambridge University Press, 2013).

the PRC Constitution and the Sino–British Joint Declaration.[9] The Basic Law came into effect in Hong Kong on 1 July 1997, upon the establishment of the HKSAR. This law provides for the modes of formation and operation of the government of the SAR, defines its relationship with the Central Government and the scope of its autonomous powers, identifies the sources of law in the SAR, guarantees the human rights of its residents, and stipulates the social and economic systems and policies to be practised in the SAR.

Under the Basic Law, the HKSAR Government (including its executive, legislative and judicial branches) enjoys broad autonomy in terms of the subject matters over which the Hong Kong Government may exercise jurisdiction. The scope of this autonomy is arguably much larger than that enjoyed by member states of federal states.[10] Essentially, all governmental affairs in the SAR other than defence, foreign affairs and constitutional change in the electoral system are within the jurisdiction of the SAR Government. Instead of listing here all the powers of the SAR, the following examples of its powers may be noted:

(1) More than 99 per cent of the laws enacted by the national legislature (the NPC and its Standing Committee) are not applicable to the SAR, in which the pre-existing common law system is preserved.[11] The only national laws that apply to Hong Kong are those listed in Annex III to the Basic Law, and there are currently 13 such laws, including the Nationality Law, National Flag Law, National Anthem Law, Law on the Territorial Sea, Law on the Garrisoning of the HKSAR, Regulations on Diplomatic Privileges and Immunities, etc.[12]

(2) Cases litigated before the Hong Kong courts are dealt with entirely within the Hong Kong court system, with the Hong Kong Court of Final Appeal (CFA) being the highest appellate court.[13] No appeal lies from a Hong Kong court to any court or institution in mainland China. The Basic Law requires the CFA to refer relevant provisions of the Basic Law to the NPCSC for interpretation in certain circumstances.[14] However, interpretations made by the NPCSC

[9] See PY Lo, *The Hong Kong Basic Law* (Hong Kong, LexisNexis, 2011). A similar Basic Law of the Macau SAR was enacted in 1993.

[10] H Hannum, *Autonomy, Sovereignty and Self-Determination: The Accommodation of Conflicting Rights*, rev edn, (Philadelphia, University of Pennsylvania Press, 1996) 137–49; Y Ghai, 'Hong Kong's autonomy: dialects of powers and institutions' in Ghai and Woodman, *Practising Self-Government* (2013) 335–36.

[11] Basic Law, Arts 8, 18 and 160.

[12] See Basic Law, Art 18. Annex III has been amended four times after the Basic Law was enacted in 1990. On 1 July 1997, the NPCSC added to it five new laws enacted between 1990 and 1997: the Law on the Garrisoning of the HKSAR; the National Flag Law; the National Emblem Law; and two other laws on the territorial sea and consular privileges. After 1 July 1997, only three laws have been added: the Law on the Exclusive Economic Zone and the Continental Shelf was added to Annex III in December 1998; the Law on Judicial Immunity from Compulsory Measures Concerning the Property of Foreign Central Banks was added in October 2005; the National Anthem Law was added in November 2017.

[13] Basic Law, Arts 2, 19, 80 and 81.

[14] The circumstances are specified in Basic Law, Art 158(3).

cannot have the effect of overturning a final court judgment previously rendered: for example, litigants in a case that the CFA has already decided would not be affected by a subsequent NPCSC interpretation.[15]

(3) Hong Kong residents do not have to pay any tax to the Central Government, and the tax that they pay to the SAR Government will be used for the SAR exclusively; no part of it has to be handed over to the Central Government.[16]
(4) The SAR can continue to have and issue its own currency, the Hong Kong dollar.[17]
(5) The SAR can control and regulate entry and exit of persons into and out of the SAR.[18]
(6) The SAR is a customs territory separate from other parts of China.[19]
(7) The SAR, using the name of 'Hong Kong, China', enters into economic and cultural relations with other countries and participates in some international organisations (such as the World Trade Organisation) whose membership is not restricted to sovereign states.[20] The Basic Law authorises the SAR Government to handle certain 'external affairs' even though, generally speaking, 'foreign affairs' are within the power of the Central Government.[21]

The degree of autonomy which the HKSAR has enjoyed since 1997 is certainly not less than what it had under British colonial rule. Indeed, whereas Hong Kong's autonomy in the colonial era was largely a product of unwritten practices and constitutional conventions, the Basic Law now expressly guarantees the SAR's autonomy in many domains.[22]

III. The Powers of the Central Authorities

The Basic Law confers various powers that the Central Government may exercise over the HKSAR. These powers may be considered limitations on the SAR's autonomy as, generally speaking, the more extensive are the powers of the Central Government, the lesser is the regional unit's scope of autonomy. The Central Authorities' powers are provided for in Articles 17 (invalidation of

[15] See Basic Law, Art 158(3). See below for further discussion.
[16] Basic Law, Arts 106 and 108.
[17] Basic Law, Art 111.
[18] Basic Law, Arts 154(2) and 22(4).
[19] Basic Law, Art 116.
[20] Basic Law, Arts 116, 151 and 152. See R Mushkat, *One Country, Two International Legal Personalities: The Case of Hong Kong* (Hong Kong, Hong Kong University Press, 1997); R Mushkat, 'Hong Kong's Exercise of External Autonomy: A Multi-faceted Appraisal' (2006) 55 *International & Comparative Law Quarterly* 945.
[21] See Basic Law, Art 13 and Ch 7.
[22] AHY Chen, 'From Colony to Special Administrative Region: Hong Kong's Constitutional Journey' in Raymond Wacks (ed), *The Future of the Law in Hong Kong* (Hong Kong, Oxford University Press, 1989) 112–15.

Hong Kong legislation), 18 (application of national laws to Hong Kong), 158 (interpretation of the Basic Law) and 159 (amendment of the Basic Law) of the Basic Law. In practice, the NPCSC's power to interpret the Basic Law is the most potent and more frequently exercised one.

As mentioned above, where certain conditions are satisfied (ie a case concerns the interpretation of one or more Basic Law provisions that relate to matters within the Central Government's 'responsibility' or the Central–SAR relationship), the CFA is obliged by Article 158(3) to refer the relevant provision to the NPCSC for interpretation. Since 1999, it has been established that even if no reference has been made by the CFA to the NPCSC, the latter has the power to promulgate an interpretation under Article 158(1) on its own initiative or upon the request of the Chief Executive of the SAR.

As of the time of writing (April 2019), a total of five interpretations of the Basic Law have been issued by the NPCSC. The first interpretation, in 1999, was issued on Articles 22 and 24 of the Basic Law relating to the right of abode in the SAR of children born in the mainland of Hong Kong permanent residents. This interpretation was issued because the SAR Government submitted to the Central Government a request for interpretation after the CFA rendered its decisions in early 1999 in the cases of *Ng Ka Ling & Ors v Director of Immigration*[23] and *Chan Kam Nga & Ors v Director of Immigration*.[24] The CFA had held that mainland-born children of Hong Kong permanent residents qualified for the right of abode in Hong Kong, irrespective of whether, at the time of the child's birth, either of his or her parents was a Hong Kong permanent resident. The Government estimated that the CFA's interpretation of the relevant Basic Law provisions would result in 1.67 million mainland residents being entitled to migrate to Hong Kong in the following 10 years. Responding to the Chief Executive's request for interpretation, the NPCSC issued its interpretation in June 1999, overruling the CFA's interpretation.

The NPCSC's interpretation was extremely controversial,[25] as there is no express provision in the Basic Law on whether, and, if so, under what circumstances, the NPCSC may interpret the Basic Law in the absence of a reference by the CFA, nor on the Chief Executive's power or right to request the NPCSC to make an interpretation. The precise effect of the interpretation needed to be determined. As already mentioned,[26] under Article 158(3) of the Basic Law, the NPCSC's interpretation did not have the effect of reversing the CFA's judgments and orders concerning the litigants in the *Ng* and *Chan* cases; it only meant that Hong Kong courts in future cases must follow the NPCSC's interpretation instead of the CFA's interpretation of the relevant Basic Law provisions. In *Lau Kong Yung & Ors v Director of Immigration*,[27] the CFA considered the effect of the NPCSC

[23] *Ng Ka Ling & Ors v Director of Immigration (No 1)* (1999) 2 HKCFAR 4.

[24] *Chan Kam Nga & Ors v Director of Immigration* (1999) 2 HKCFAR 82.

[25] See generally JMM Chan, HL Fu and Y Ghai (eds), *Hong Kong's Constitutional Debate* (Hong Kong, Hong Kong University Press, 2000).

[26] See text to n 15.

[27] *Lau Kong Yung & Ors v Director of Immigration* (1999) 2 HKCFAR 300.

interpretation and recognised its binding force. The court also accepted that the NPCSC's power to interpret the Basic Law is a 'free-standing' one, in the sense that it may exercise this power on its own initiative without being requested by the court to do so.

Since 1999, the NPCSC has exercised the power of Basic Law interpretation on four other occasions. In 2004, acting on its own initiative (instead of at the request of the Chief Executive of the HKSAR), the NPCSC issued an interpretation of the Basic Law provisions relating to the procedure for electoral reform.[28] In 2005, upon the request of the Acting Chief Executive of the HKSAR, the NPCSC issued an interpretation to clarify the term of office of a Chief Executive who succeeds one who resigns before completing his term of office.[29] In 2011, the CFA in *Democratic Republic of the Congo v FG Hemisphere Associates LLC (No 1)*[30] used for the first time the reference procedure in Article 158(3) of the Basic Law to refer certain Basic Law provisions relating to foreign affairs and 'acts of state' to the NPCSC for interpretation.[31] This *Congo* case concerned whether the applicable law of foreign sovereign immunity in the HKSAR was the same as that in the mainland. In November 2016, the NPCSC, acting on its own initiative, issued an interpretation of Article 104 of the Basic Law, which relates to the oath-taking requirements applicable to officials, judges and members of the Legislative and Executive Councils. This interpretation was particularly controversial, as it was issued three days after Hong Kong's High Court heard a case on oath-taking and before the court delivered judgment in that case. In this case,[32] the Government argued that two pro-'Hong Kong independence' Legislative Councillors had been disqualified by reason of their failure to comply with the oath-taking requirements stipulated in Article 104 of the Basic Law and other Hong Kong legislation.

As regards other powers that the Central Authorities have under the Basic Law, it seems that the Central Authorities have exercised some degree of self-restraint in the exercise of these powers.[33] For example, under Article 17, the NPCSC has the power to nullify SAR laws that exceed the scope of the SAR's autonomy.

[28] AHY Chen, 'The Constitutional Controversy of Spring 2004' (2004) 34 *Hong Kong Law Journal* 215.

[29] AHY Chen, 'The NPCSC's Interpretation in Spring 2005' (2005) 35 *Hong Kong Law Journal* 255.

[30] *Democratic Republic of the Congo v FG Hemisphere Associates LLC (No 1)* (2011) 14 HKCFAR 95, 395.

[31] AHY Chen, 'The *Congo* Case' (2011) 41 *Hong Kong Law Journal* 369. For a discussion of acts of state, see the contribution of Johannes Chan in this collection.

[32] *Chief Executive of the HKSAR v President of the Legislative Council and Leung Chung Hang Sixtus* (unreported, HCAL 185/2016, 15 November 2016) (CFI); [2017] 1 HKLRD 460 (CA); (2017) 20 HKCFAR 390 (leave to appeal rejected by the CFA). The two Legislative Councillors were disqualified. Four other Legislative Councillors were subsequently also disqualified on the ground of failure to take their oaths properly: *Nathan Law Kwun Chung* [2017] 4 HKLRD 115 (CFI), *Leung Kwok Hung* [2019] HKCA 173. For an analysis, see H Zhu and AHY Chen, 'The Oath-taking Cases and the NPCSC Interpretation of 2016' (2019) 49 *Hong Kong Law Journal* 381.

[33] See J Chan, 'Asymmetry in the Face of Heavily Disproportionate Power Relations: Hong Kong' in M Weller and K Nobbs (eds), *Asymmetric Autonomy and the Settlement of Ethnic Conflicts* (Philadelphia, University of Pennsylvania Press, 2010) 140; A Mason, 'The Rule of Law in the Shadow of the Giant: The Hong Kong Experience' (2011) 33 *Sydney Law Review* 623.

However, since the HKSAR was established in 1997, the Central Government has never exercised this power to nullify an SAR law. Under Article 18, national laws may be applied to the SAR, but only three national laws have been applied in this way since 1 July 1997,[34] and the NPC's power to amend the Basic Law has never been exercised.[35]

To conclude, it may be said that that HKSAR enjoys a fairly large scope of autonomy both in law and in practice, but the judicial autonomy of the SAR courts to interpret the Basic Law is subject to the overriding power of the NPCSC to promulgate an interpretation of the Basic Law upon or without a reference by the CFA to the NPCSC. As discussed in the next section, the Central Government's power to appoint the Chief Executive and principal officials of the HKSAR, and the policy rationale behind such institutional design, also have far-reaching implications for, and may be considered limitations on, the autonomy of the HKSAR.

IV. Hong Kong's Political System

Regional autonomy is usually taken to imply that the government of the regional unit is democratically constituted by the people of the region. In the case of the HKSAR, apart from the above-identified powers of the Chinese Central Government that circumscribe Hong Kong's autonomy, it is noteworthy that the domestic political system of the HKSAR falls short of international or Western standards of liberal democracy, and there are limits to it being reformed towards that direction.[36]

First, the methods of selecting the Chief Executive and legislature do not satisfy such standards. The first Chief Executive of the SAR was elected by a 400-member Selection Committee, which was in turn elected on the basis of business, occupational and community groupings in various social sectors, by the SAR Preparatory Committee appointed by Beijing. The second- and third-term Chief Executives were elected by an 800-member Election Committee itself elected by groups from business, professional and other social sectors. In 2012 and 2017, the fourth- and fifth-term Chief Executives were each elected by an Election Committee of 1,200 members constituted by the same social sectors. After each election, the elected candidate does not become Chief Executive until and unless the Central People's Government exercises the power to appoint him or her to that office.[37]

Under the Basic Law, the Central Government not only has the power to appoint the Chief Executive, but principal officials of the SAR are also appointable

[34] See text to n 12.

[35] The amendment of the Basic Law is governed by Art 159 of the Basic Law. The amendment of Annex I and Annex II to the Basic Law is separately provided for in these Annexes, and involves, among other steps, an act of the LegCo of the HKSAR. The Annexes were amended once in 2010.

[36] Ghai, 'Hong Kong's autonomy' (2013).

[37] See Basic Law, Art 45.

by the Central People's Government upon the Chief Executive's nomination.[38] This aspect of the institutional design of the Basic Law is explicable with reference to Deng Xiaoping's idea, which he developed in the 1980s, that 'Hong Kong people ruling Hong Kong' (instead of mainland officials ruling Hong Kong) meant 'patriots ruling Hong Kong':[39] the Hong Kong people who hold key governmental posts in Hong Kong must be people whom Beijing considers acceptable and trustworthy for this purpose. Mainland scholars and officials have stressed that the power of appointment of the Chief Executive, who under the Basic Law is accountable both to the Central People's Government and the HKSAR, is substantive and not merely formal or ceremonial.[40] Wang Guangya, Director of the Hong Kong and Macau Affairs Office of the State Council, publicly stated a few months before the Chief Executive election in March 2017 that the Chief Executive should meet four criteria: loving the nation and loving Hong Kong; being trusted by the Central Government; being capable of governing Hong Kong; and enjoying the support of Hong Kong people.[41]

As regards the legislature, in each of the first four terms of office of the Legislative Council (LegCo) of the HKSAR (other than the 'Provisional Legislative Council' of 1997–98), not more than half of the members were directly elected by universal suffrage, the others being elected mainly or wholly by 'functional constituencies' based on business, professional and other social groupings.[42] As from 2012, the number of members of LegCo was increased from 60 to 70, half of whom are elected by universal suffrage, and half by functional constituencies, including five District Councillors elected by 'quasi' universal suffrage in the 'super District Councils' functional constituency.[43]

Second, the NPCSC has control over the substance and speed of democratisation in Hong Kong. Such control is based on the text of the Basic Law, which requires electoral reform relating to the Chief Executive to be approved by the NPCSC,[44] and partly on the 2004 interpretation of the NPCSC, which provides that the SAR Government may only proceed with political reform if the NPCSC, upon

[38] See Basic Law, Arts 15 and 48(5).

[39] Deng's speeches on 'one country, two systems' in the 1980s were republished in Hong Kong in 2004 in the midst of the debate on political reform in Hong Kong at that time. The English translation of the book is *Deng Xiaoping on 'One Country, Two Systems'* (Hong Kong, Joint Publishing, 2004). See particularly the speeches at pp 13, 23 and 67.

[40] Wang, 'Introduction to the Basic Law' (2000) 364–65; R Yep, '"One Country, Two Systems" and Special Administrative Regions: The Case of Hong Kong' in JH Chung and TC Lam (eds), *China's Local Administration: Traditions and Changes in the Sub-national Hierarchy* (London, Routledge, 2010) 98.

[41] J Ng and T Cheung, 'Beijing not ready to show its hand on Hong Kong chief executive preference, top official hints' *South China Morning Post*, 31 December 2016; G Cheung, 'Crucial for next Hong Kong leader to have central government's trust, according to Beijing official' *South China Morning Post*, 17 February 2017.

[42] See Basic Law, Annex II; the Legislative Council Ordinance (Cap 542).

[43] AHY Chen, 'An Unexpected Breakthrough in Hong Kong's Constitutional Reform' (2010) *Hong Kong Law Journal* 259; N Ma, 'Negotiating Democracy and "High Autonomy": The 2010 Political Reform' in R Yep (ed), *Negotiating Autonomy in Greater China: Hong Kong and its Sovereign before and after 1997* (Copenhagen, Nordic Institute of Asian Studies Press, 2013).

[44] See Basic Law, Annex I, para 7.

consideration of the Chief Executive's report, agrees that there is a need for such reform.[45] In practice, the NPCSC has, in its decisions on the Chief Executive's reports, also stipulated the scope of permissible reform and even the timetable of reform.[46] The Basic Law itself affirms the possibility of further democratisation of the SAR and stipulates the destination of political reform. As regards LegCo, Article 68 stipulates that the 'ultimate aim' is the election of all legislators by universal suffrage. As regards the Chief Executive, Article 45 also stipulates that the 'ultimate aim' is selected by universal suffrage 'upon nomination by a broadly representative nominating committee'. In 2014, the NPCSC handed down a decision that would effectively enable the nominating committee to become a 'screening' stage to screen out persons not acceptable to Beijing. This, together with the reservation to the Central Government of the power to appoint the Chief Executive, was apparently intended to ensure that the HKSAR would not be governed by anyone who is not considered trustworthy and acceptable by the Central Government.[47] The rejection in 2015 by more than one-third of Legislative Councillors (from the camp of 'pan-democrats') of such 'screening' mechanism proposed by Beijing led to the failure of the SAR Government's attempt to introduce universal suffrage for the election of the Chief Executive in 2017.[48]

To conclude this section, it may be said that the political system established by the Basic Law is a 'hybrid regime', a 'semi-democracy' or a 'liberal authoritarian regime'.[49] The Basic Law promises the people of Hong Kong 'a democracy that might never come'.[50]

V. Hong Kong's Political Landscape

To understand the political and constitutional dynamics in Hong Kong, it is necessary to have an idea of the political landscape of the jurisdiction. Hong Kong's political forces are broadly divided between pro-China forces (also

[45] Chen, 'The Constitutional Controversy' (2004).

[46] See the NPCSC's decisions in 2004, 2007 and 2014 on political reform in Hong Kong. The binding effect in Hong Kong of the 2014 decision was challenged and discussed in *Leung Lai Kwok Yvonne v Chief Secretary for Administration* (unreported, HCAL 31/2015, 5 June 2015).

[47] The composition of the nominating committee and the procedure of nomination were subsequently specified in the NPCSC's Decision on Issues Relating to the Selection of the Chief Executive of the HKSAR by Universal Suffrage and on the Method for Forming the Legislative Council of the HKSAR in the Year 2016, promulgated on 31 August 2014.

[48] AHY Chen, 'The Law and Politics of the Struggle for Universal Suffrage in Hong Kong, 2013–15' (2016) 3 *Asian Journal of Law and Society* 189; C Chan, 'Legalizing Politics: An Evaluation of Hong Kong's Recent Attempt at Democratization' (2017) 16 *Election Law Journal* 296.

[49] AHY Chen, 'Development of Representative Government' in J Chan and CL Lim (eds), *Law of the Hong Kong Constitution*, 2nd edn (Hong Kong, Sweet and Maxwell, 2015) ch 8, 265–67; S Lau, *Huiguihou Xianggang de dute zhengzhi xingtai* (The Unique Political Form of Post-Handover Hong Kong) (Hong Kong, Commercial Press, 2017); BYT Tai, 'Hong Kong No More: From Semi-democracy to Semi-authoritarianism' (2018) 4 *Contemporary Chinese Political Economy and Strategic Relations* 395.

[50] N Ma, *Political Development in Hong Kong* (Hong Kong, Hong Kong University Press, 2007) 225.

known as 'pro-establishment' forces or 'patriots') and pro-democracy forces (the 'pan-democrats').[51] The pro-China camp supports the policies of the PRC Government towards Hong Kong, including its cautious and gradualist approach to Hong Kong's democratisation. That camp also supports, or at least does not question, one-party rule in mainland China, and generally refrains from criticising the PRC's human rights record. On the other hand, the pan-democrats advocate Western-style liberal democracy for Hong Kong, and are critical of authoritarian one-party rule in China and its human rights record.

Since the pro-democracy camp came into existence in the 1980s, it has consistently enjoyed significant support from civil society and the electorate in Hong Kong. It is noteworthy that since direct election by universal suffrage to a portion of LegCo seats was introduced in Hong Kong in 1991, pro-democracy politicians have consistently succeeded in capturing approximately 55 to 60 per cent of the popular votes for that portion of LegCo seats.[52] It is believed that Beijing has been concerned that if entirely free and unrestricted elections by universal suffrage were introduced in Hong Kong, and the Chief Executive and all LegCo seats were elected by universal suffrage, the office of the Chief Executive and the majority of LegCo seats would be captured by members of the pro-democratic camp. This may explain why Beijing sought to introduce a 'screening' mechanism for the nomination of candidates for election of the Chief Executive by universal suffrage, and the retention of the system of functional constituencies in LegCo elections in which the majority of functional constituencies' seats has always been held by members of the pro-establishment camp.

Since the establishment of the HKSAR, the effectiveness of the 'executive-led' Government in Hong Kong has depended on the support of the pro-China camp in the legislature, which occupied the majority of seats in LegCo.[53] But the coalition of legislators in this camp is loose, and its effectiveness varies depending on the issues and context concerned. There has never been any ruling party in the HKSAR. No single political party has ever occupied the majority of, or any number close to half of, the seats in LegCo. As explained above, the Chief Executive is elected independently of LegCo by an Election Committee that has never been dominated by political parties, but the majority of which is generally considered 'pro-China'. Members of the pro-China camp in LegCo are generally supportive of the Chief Executive and his administration, although such support cannot be guaranteed for every policy, bill or item of financial expenditure because these elected legislators have to be answerable to their own constituencies. This is part of the context for understanding why the attempt to introduce Article 23

[51] N Ma, 'The Rise of "Anti-China" Sentiments in Hong Kong and the 2012 Legislative Council Elections' (2015) 15 *China Review* 39; J Jang, 'Competing Political Visions in the Legislative Council of Hong Kong' (2016) 21 *Journal of Chinese Political Science* 89.

[52] Ma, *Political Development* (2007) 154, 223; Ma 'The Rise of "Anti-China" Sentiments' (ibid) 58, 62.

[53] PLT Lui, 'The Legislature' in WM Lam et al (eds), *Contemporary Hong Kong Government and Politics*, 2nd edn (Hong Kong, Hong Kong University Press, 2012).

legislation failed in 2003.[54] In practice, the Central Government in Beijing and its Liaison Office in Hong Kong[55] have played a significant role – informal rather than constitutional ordained – in promoting, coordinating and supporting this pro-China camp of politicians in Hong Kong.[56]

VI. Evolution of the 'One Country, Two Systems' Policy

As applied to Hong Kong, 'one country, two systems' was a pragmatic compromise. It allows a capitalist system with significant elements of Western-style liberal democracy to exist in Hong Kong as an SAR of the PRC, but it has faced major challenges since it was fully put into practice in 1997. Thus a dynamic 'crisis-transformation perspective'[57] should be adopted so as to understand the evolution of Chinese policies towards the HKSAR as various events – such as the march of half a million demonstrators on 1 July 2003 and the Occupy Central movement of 2014 – unfolded in a manner not previously envisaged.

It is well-known that the first watershed in post-1997 Chinese policy towards the HKSAR was the march of half a million people on 1 July 2003 against the National Security Bill to implement Article 23 of the Basic Law.[58] Until then the Central Government had been content to leave the governance of the SAR almost completely to the Chief Executive and his Government. The turmoil of 2003 and the rise of the democracy movement at that time made Beijing realise that the situation in Hong Kong might be getting out of control. Hence the previous laissez-faire policy, epitomised by Jiang Zemin's saying that 'the well water does not interfere with the river water', was replaced by a new policy of 'engagement and involvement in Hong Kong's political development'.[59] This was the context in which it has been suggested that there were two 'governing teams' for the HKSAR – the HKSAR Government itself, and officials of the Central Government (in Beijing and at the

[54] See generally H Fu, CJ Petersen and SNM Young (eds), *National Security and Fundamental Freedoms: Hong Kong's Article 23 under Scrutiny* (Hong Kong, Hong Kong University Press, 2005). See also the contribution of Margaret Ng in this collection.

[55] Yep, 'One Country, Two Systems' (2010) 100.

[56] AHY Chen, 'The Autonomy of Hong Kong under "One Country, Two Systems"' in TL Lui et al (eds), *Routledge Handbook of Contemporary Hong Kong* (2019) ch 1, 44–45; SSH Lo, *The Dynamics of Beijing-Hong Kong Relations* (Hong Kong, Hong Kong University Press 2008) 10–11, 18–19; M Sing, 'Hong Kong's Democrats Hold Their Own' (2009) 20 *Journal of Democracy* 98, 107–11; PTY Cheung, 'The Changing Relations between Hong Kong and the Mainland since 2003' in Lam et al, *Contemporary Hong Kong Government* (2012) 325, 329; Ma, 'The Rise of "Anti-China" Sentiments' (n 51) 52; BCH Fong, 'One Country, Two Nationalisms: Center-periphery Relations between Mainland China and Hong Kong, 1997–2016' (2017) 43 *Modern China* 523, 531.

[57] AY So, '"One Country, Two Systems" and Hong Kong-China National Integration: A Crisis-transformation Perspective' (2011) 41 *Journal of Contemporary Asia* 99.

[58] See eg the contribution of Michael C Davis in this collection.

[59] J Cheng, 'The Story of a New Policy' (2009) 15 *Hong Kong Journal*, available at www.hkbasiclaw.com/Hong%20Kong%20Journal/Cheng%20Jie%20article.htm.

Central People's Government's liaison office in Hong Kong) with responsibilities for Hong Kong.[60] The latter team would be the one that implements the Central Government's policy of 'engagement and involvement' in the HKSAR.

The gradual adaptation or modification of the 'one country, two systems' policy to the changing circumstances of the HKSAR may be observed by examining the discourse or official statements of the Central Authorities regarding the policy. It is noteworthy that several key expressions and concepts subsequently came into use, which were neither expressly mentioned in the Basic Law nor the speech to the NPC in 1990 by Ji Pengfei, chairman of the Basic Law Drafting Committee, explaining the draft Basic Law to the NPC.

For example, 'executive-led government' was not mentioned in the Basic Law nor in Ji's speech. However, since the 1990s, Chinese scholars and officials have stressed that the HKSAR's system of government is an 'executive-led' system and must not be allowed to become a 'legislative-led' one.[61] This emphasis on 'executive-led' government may be understood in the light of the fact that it is the executive (including the Chief Executive and the principal officials) and not the legislature that is appointed by Beijing and thus enjoys the confidence and trust of Beijing, and derives powers and authority from it.[62]

The Basic Law refers to the objectives of 'upholding national unity and territorial integrity, maintaining the prosperity and stability of Hong Kong',[63] but in recent years it has been stressed that 'one country, two systems' must serve China's 'sovereignty, security and development interests'. And the term and concept of the Central Authorities having 'comprehensive jurisdiction' over Hong Kong was developed in the White Paper on 'one country, two systems' issued by the Information Office of the State Council in 2014[64] in the midst of the debate on universal suffrage for the election of the Chief Executive in Hong Kong. The latest official formulation of the policy was summarised in two speeches given by Xi Jinping in 2017.

[60] This was suggested by Cao Erbao in a Chinese article published in *Xuexi shibao* (*Study Times*) (a publication of the Chinese Communist Party's Central Party School). The article was entitled '"一國兩制"條件下香港的管治力量' (Hong Kong's Governing Forces under the Conditions of 'One Country, Two Systems'), available at www.china.com.cn/xxsb/txt/2008-01/29/content_9610867.htm, or www.legco.gov.hk/yr08-09/chinese/panels/ca/papers/ca0420cb2-1389-2-c.pdf. Cao was at the time the director of the Research Division of the Liaison Office of the Central People's Government in Hong Kong.

[61] Wang, 'Introduction to the Basic Law' (n 3) 346–49; PK Li, 'The executive', in Lam et al, *Contemporary Hong Kong Government* (n 53) 27–44; PY Lo and AHY Chen, 'The Judicial Perspective of "Separation of Powers" in the Hong Kong Special Administrative Region of the People's Republic of China' (2018) 5 *Journal of International and Comparative Law* 337, 355–59.

[62] See also the contribution of Margaret Ng in this collection.

[63] See Basic Law, Preamble, para 2.

[64] Information Office of the State Council of the PRC, 'The Practice of the "One Country, Two Systems" Policy in the Hong Kong Special Administrative Region' (10 June 2014), English version available at www.scio.gov.cn/zfbps/ndhf/2014/Document/1373163/1373163.htm (White Paper).

In his speech in Hong Kong on 1 July 2017 at the ceremony to celebrate the 20th anniversary of the HKSAR, President Xi said:[65]

> [I]t is imperative to have a correct understanding of the relationship between 'one country' and 'two systems'. 'One country' is like the roots of a tree. … Now that Hong Kong has returned to China, it is all the more important for us to firmly uphold China's sovereignty, security and development interests. … Any attempt to endanger China's sovereignty and security, challenge the power of the central government and the authority of the Basic Law of the HKSAR or use Hong Kong to carry out infiltration and sabotage activities against the mainland is an act that crosses the red line, and is absolutely impermissible. On the other hand, on the basis of 'one country', the 'two systems' should – and have every reason to – stay in harmony and reinforce each other. We must both adhere to the 'one country' principle and respect the differences of the 'two systems', both uphold the power of the central government and ensure a high degree of autonomy in the HKSAR, both give play to the role of the mainland as a staunch supporter of Hong Kong and enhance Hong Kong's own competitiveness.

In his speech on 18 October 2017 at the opening of the 19th National Congress of the Chinese Communist Party, Xi also said:[66]

> We must organically integrate the comprehensive jurisdiction (*quanmian guanzhi quan*) of the Central Authorities with regard to the Special Administrative Regions of Hong Kong and Macau, and the protection of the high degree of autonomy of the Special Administrative Regions.

The emphasis on China's 'sovereignty, security and development interests', on the 'one country' principle as the basis of the 'two systems', and on the Central Authorities' 'comprehensive jurisdiction' over the HKSAR, reflects the Central Authorities' concern about the developing political trend in Hong Kong as evidenced by the Occupy Central movement in 2014 – perceived by Beijing as a popular challenge to the authority of the Central Government over Hong Kong – and the rise of 'peripheral nationalism'[67] or movements of self-determination or independence. This trend is, from the Central Government's perspective, probably the gravest single threat to the continued viability of the practice of 'one country, two systems' in the HKSAR. The Central Government is concerned that if such a negative trend is not reversed, Hong Kong might become a liability, rather than an asset, to the PRC's longer-term stability and development.

According to one study, the rise in anti-mainland Chinese sentiments was already evident in the 2012 LegCo election.[68] Since then, there has been a 'localist'

[65] J Xi, 'Address at the Meeting Celebrating the 20th Anniversary of Hong Kong's Return to the Motherland and the Inaugural Ceremony of The Fifth-Term Government of the Hong Kong Special Administrative Region' (Hong Kong, 1 July 2017), available at www.locpg.hk/2017-07/01/c_129645318.htm.

[66] See Xi, 'Secure a Decisive Victory' (2017).

[67] Fong, 'One Country, Two Nationalisms' (2017).

[68] Ma, 'The Rise of "Anti-China" Sentiments' (n 51).

turn in Hong Kong politics,[69] with the emergence of radical 'localists' who are dissatisfied with the traditional thinking and strategy of the mainstream pan-democrats. The 'localists' advocate self-determination or even independence for Hong Kong. Some of them were barred from participating in the LegCo election of September 2016[70] – a controversial move which revealed the limits of Beijing's toleration of autonomy in the HKSAR. Despite this move, a total of six 'localists' were elected into the LegCo in this election, collectively capturing 19 per cent of the popular votes.[71]

The success of the 'localists' proved to be short-lived, as some of them were subsequently stripped of their LegCo seats by the court on the ground of their failure to comply with the oath-taking requirement in the Basic Law and other legislation.[72] The pro-independence Hong Kong National Party, founded by Chan Ho Tin Andy, one of the 'localists' barred from participating as a candidate in the 2016 LegCo election,[73] was banned by the Secretary for Security as an 'unlawful society' under the Societies Ordinance on 24 September 2018.[74] The National Party's appeal to the Chief Executive in Council was dismissed on 19 February 2019.[75] On 26 February, the Central People's Government issued an 'official letter' (*gonghan*) to the Chief Executive expressing support for the decision to ban the National Party, affirming that it was the constitutional duty of the HKSAR to 'safeguard national security in accordance with law', and requiring the Chief Executive to submit a report on the matter.[76]

From a historical perspective, the Occupy Central movement[77] marked the culmination of the conflict between the 'pan-democrats' on the one hand and the

[69] See JYS Cheng (ed), *New Trends of Political Participation in Hong Kong* (Hong Kong, City University of Hong Kong Press, 2014).

[70] See Hong Kong newspapers of 3 August 2016, eg, J Ng, T Cheung and O Fung, 'Protests shut down electoral commission briefing as "Hong Kong Indigenous" Edward Leung disqualified from Legco elections' *South China Morning Post*, 2 August 2016; J Lam, 'Hong Kong's returning officers' power to dismiss potential Legco candidates called into question' *South China Morning Post*, 2 August 2016.

[71] 'Localists and self-determination activists capture 6 seats, LegCo divided into 3 factions' and 'Localist self-determination politicians capture 400,000 votes' *Ming Pao*, 6 September 2016 (in Chinese); CK Choy and JM Chan, '*Lifahui xuanju jieguo chubu pingxi* (立法會選舉結果初步評析)' (A preliminary analysis of the outcome of the LegCo election) *Ming Pao*, 6 September 2016.

[72] See cases cited in n 32; Zhu and Chen, 'The Oath-taking Cases' (2019).

[73] Chan subsequently brought an election petition to challenge the returning officer's decision not to allow him to be a candidate, but failed before the Court of First Instance: *Chan Ho Tin v Lo Ying Ki Alan* [2018] HKCFI 345.

[74] See Hong Kong newspapers of 25 September 2018.

[75] A Lum and K Chung, 'Hong Kong National Party ban upheld by panel which says it doesn't trust group not "to resort to violence" in independence bid' *South China Morning Post*, 22 February 2019.

[76] J Lam, T Cheung, LK Sum, K Chung and A Lum, 'Beijing backs city government's ban on Hong Kong National Party, says leader Carrie Lam' *South China Morning Post*, 26 February 2019. For the full Chinese text of the 'official letter', see www.gov.cn/zhengce/content/2019-02/26/content_5368672.htm. The Chief Executive's report was submitted on 16 April 2019: see 'Linzheng jiao Minzudang baogao' (Carrie Lam submits report on National Party) *Ming Pao*, 19 April 2019. For the full Chinese text of the report, see gia.info.gov.hk/general/201904/18/P2019041800415_308614_1_1555572199159.pdf.

[77] See generally BC Jones (ed), *Law and Politics of the Taiwan Sunflower and Hong Kong Umbrella Movements* (London, Routledge, 2017).

Central Government and the 'pro-establishment' camp on the other hand that had been propelled by their divergent visions of how 'one country, two systems' should be practised. From the point of view of the Occupy Central activists, the 'genuine universal suffrage' that they demanded was no more than what was promised in the Basic Law, the realisation of which had been repeatedly delayed since the NPCSC issued its interpretation in 2004 to introduce additional hurdles to the democratisation of Hong Kong. The pan-democrats' vision of universal suffrage and democracy was election of the Chief Executive by universal suffrage in accordance with what they considered to be universally recognised standards and principles of free and fair multi-party elections. In their view, no candidate or political party which has the support of considerable numbers of voters should, either in law or in practice, be barred from participating in the election by the institutional design of the system for nomination of candidates. This, however, was not Beijing's view of universal suffrage in the HKSAR. In Beijing's view, the institutional design of the nominating committee had already been written into the Basic Law when it was first enacted. And in its view, the restrictive nomination process established by the NPCSC decision of 31 August 2014 was consistent with and an application of Deng Xiaoping's original idea of 'patriots ruling Hong Kong'.

After the failure of political reform in 2015, the new generation of political activists who came on the scene[78] distanced themselves from the traditional pan-democrats by abandoning the presupposition that Hong Kong people should strive to realise democracy in and as an SAR of the PRC. Their vision of democracy is no longer the pan-democrats' vision of democracy as part of the 'Hong Kong system' in 'one country, two systems'. As they realised that this would be impossible because the authoritarian PRC regime would not tolerate a true democracy in its SAR, they went one step further to question the assumption that Hong Kong should remain part of the PRC. For them, the question is no longer simply one of democracy, but a more fundamental one of identity. The transition from the quest for democracy to the quest for identity, or from the politics of democratisation to the politics of self-determination, has brought the tension and conflict inherent in the constitutional arrangement of 'one country, two systems' to unprecedented heights.[79] This represents a challenge more fundamental and severe than ever before to the continued viability of 'one country, two systems'.

The nascent movement for Hong Kong's self-determination or independence exemplifies the inherent tension within any constitutional arrangement for the practice of a high degree of autonomy by a regional unit of a state, and the risk of secession that the political dynamics of autonomy might generate. From the perspective of a sovereign state concerned with its territorial integrity and

[78] See generally SSH Lo, 'Ideologies and Factionalism in Beijing-Hong Kong Relations' (2018) 58 *Asian Survey* 392.

[79] See generally PTY Cheung, 'In Beijing's Tightening Grip: Changing Mainland-Hong Kong Relations amid Integration and Confrontation' in BCH Fong and TL Lui (eds), *Hong Kong 20 Years After the Handover* (New York, Palgrave Macmillan, 2018).

the loyalty of its citizens, the practice of territorial autonomy of people within a region of the state can be a double-edged sword. On the one hand, it can strike a good balance between the recognition of regional diversity and the promotion of national unity, and be mutually beneficial to the people of the autonomous region and the people of the state as a whole. On the other hand, the institutions of autonomy might foster or strengthen the sense of collective identity of the people in the autonomous region,[80] which may stand in tension with the original concept of the sovereign state with a fixed, sacred and inalienable territory, a single citizenship and a single allegiance of all to one nation.[81] From the perspective of the Government of the sovereign state, the worst-case scenario is where the people of the autonomous region become dissatisfied with autonomy and begin to clamour for independence. In light of this, Beijing's concern about 'one country, two systems' getting out of hand in Hong Kong is understandable.

VII. The Question of National Security Legislation

We now turn from the general context of 'one country, two systems' to the specific question of national security legislation in Hong Kong. It would be no exaggeration to say that this issue, alternatively known as the 'Article 23 issue', stands at the core of the tension and contradiction between the 'two systems' in 'one country'. What is at stake are questions such as what is the extent to which civil liberties in Hong Kong may and should be restricted in order to protect the 'national security' of the 'one country' of which the HKSAR is a part. Those who cherish civil liberties in Hong Kong are concerned that such liberties might be substantially curtailed by the introduction of national security legislation. This section will set out some preliminary thoughts on the question of national security legislation in the HKSAR.

Article 23 of the Basic Law – probably the single most politically sensitive article among all provisions in the Basic Law – provides as follows:

> The [HKSAR] shall enact laws on its own to prohibit any act of treason, secession, sedition, subversion against the Central People's Government, or theft of state secrets, to prohibit foreign political organizations or bodies from conducting political activities in the Region, and to prohibit political organizations or bodies of the Region from establishing ties with foreign political organizations or bodies.

The original intent behind this Article may be considered benevolent: as part of China, the HKSAR must have laws to protect China's national security. However, it

[80] For the legal and institutional basis of the identity of 'Hongkongers', see STM Ng, 'The Legal Foundation of Hongkonger Identity' (2015) *Hong Kong Journal of Catholic Studies* 111, available at catholic3.crs.cuhk.edu.hk/ch/wp-content/uploads/sites/3/2016/04/Journal_2016-5.pdf.

[81] SJ Henders, *Territoriality, Asymmetry, and Autonomy: Catalonia, Corsica, Hong Kong, and Tibet* (New York, Palgrave Macmillan, 2010) 14, 19–22.

was recognised that national security laws (or laws against counter-revolutionary offences, as they were called in the mainland at the time of enactment of the Basic Law[82]) were relatively draconian in the mainland, and in view of the constitutional framework of 'one country, two systems' it might be too harsh to extend the relevant mainland laws to the HKSAR under Article 18 of the Basic Law. It was therefore decided that the HKSAR may be delegated the power to enact national security laws that presumably will be less draconian and more consistent with other elements of the Hong Kong legal system, such as the protection of human rights and civil liberties.

Despite the fact that the institutional design of Article 23 was well-intentioned, the issue of its implementation has given rise to concerns or even fear since the handover in 1997. Although there were laws in colonial Hong Kong, particularly the provisions of the Crimes Ordinance,[83] that created offences of treason and sedition, such laws had not been used since the 1970s. Indeed, it is arguable that some of such laws, probably being inconsistent with the International Covenant on Civil and Political Rights (ICCPR), may already have been invalidated when the Hong Kong Bill of Rights Ordinance was enacted in 1991 and the Letters Patent – the colonial constitution – was amended at the same time for the purpose of giving legal and constitutional force to the civil liberties enshrined in the ICCPR.[84] The anxiety therefore was that the implementation of Article 23 would curtail the civil liberties which Hong Kong people had enjoyed, at least during the last decade of British colonial rule.

The limb of Article 23 on political organisations was implemented at the time of the handover by the introduction of new provisions into the Societies Ordinance and the Companies Ordinance.[85] In order to implement the other limbs of Article 23, the HKSAR Government introduced into the LegCo the National Security (Legislative Provisions) Bill in 2003.[86] As is well-known, the legislative process on the Bill was aborted after a demonstration of an estimated half a million people on 1 July 2013.[87] Since then, the Government has not made any attempt to legislate on Article 23. In recent years, with the rise of pro-independence activism as mentioned above, there have been occasional calls to implement Article 23. Government officials have repeatedly acknowledged that the HKSAR has the

[82] The PRC Criminal Code of 1979 contained a chapter on 'counter-revolutionary crimes'. When the Code was extensively amended in 1997, this chapter was replaced by one on 'crimes endangering national security'. See AHY Chen, *An Introduction to the Legal System of the People's Republic of China*, rev edn (Hong Kong, Butterworths Asia, 1998) 230–31.

[83] See Crimes Ordinance (Cap 200), ss 2, 3, 9 and 10.

[84] See AHY Chen, 'The Interpretation of the Basic Law' (2000) 30 *Hong Kong Law Journal* 380, 418; *A Solicitor v Law Society of Hong Kong* (2003) 6 HKCFAR 570; *HKSAR v Lam Kwong Wai* (2006) 9 HKCFAR 574.

[85] See the Societies (Amendment) Ordinance (Cap 151), Ord No 118 of 1997 (amending both the Societies Ordinance and the Companies Ordinance).

[86] See generally HKSAR Government, 'Proposals to implement Article 23 of the Basic Law', available at www.basiclaw23.gov.hk/english.

[87] Fu et al, *National Security and Fundamental Freedoms* (2005).

constitutional duty to legislate on Article 23, but has given no indication as regards its timing.[88]

It is arguable that apart from the limb of Article 23 on political organisations which has already been implemented as mentioned above, several other limbs of Article 23 have already been covered by Hong Kong's existing law. For example, the existing Crimes Ordinance provides for the offences of treason and sedition, even though the exacting wording of the provisions creating these offences in the colonial era has not yet been specifically amended by any post-handover law to adapt them to the new constitutional order.[89] In 2016, some members of Hong Kong's legal community expressed the view that advocates of Hong Kong independence may be prosecuted for sedition under the Crimes Ordinance.[90] On the other hand, it may be questioned whether the existing definition of sedition is too draconian and may be held to be a disproportionate and unconstitutional restriction of freedom of speech if litigated before a Hong Kong court.

As the text of Article 23 provides that 'The [HKSAR] *shall* enact laws on its own to prohibit any act of treason' etc. (emphasis added), there is no reasonable doubt that the HKSAR has the constitutional duty to enact the relevant laws. Insofar as the existing law of the HKSAR has not yet achieved the full implementation of the requirements of Article 23, it would appear that the executive authorities of the HKSAR have the constitutional duty to prepare a bill or bills for the introduction of the relevant laws, and to introduce the bill or bills in the LegCo for its deliberation and legislative action. The better view is that this constitutional duty should be performed within a reasonable time after the Basic Law came into effect, because an indefinite delay in the legislative implementation of Article 23 would frustrate the purpose of the Article. When the executive introduces the National Security Bill in LegCo, there is no doubt that each LegCo member has, as in the case of any other Bill, the right to vote in favour of or against the bill as he or she thinks fit. Depending on whether the Bill is passed, the following scenarios may then arise.

The first scenario is that the Bill is rejected by LegCo when put to a vote. This is extremely unlikely to materialise, as the 'pro-establishment' camp has a majority in LegCo and is expected to maintain it in the foreseeable future. Unlike a political reform Bill for amendment of Annex I or II of the Basic Law, when it is proposed the National Security Bill can be passed by a simple majority of LegCo members. The consequences of the unlikely scenario of LegCo rejecting the Bill

[88] At the time of writing, the latest statement on this matter was the speech by Chief Executive Carrie Lam at the 'National Security Day' conference on 15 April 2019. For the full text (in Chinese) of the speech, see *Wen Wei Po*, 16 April 2019, A12.

[89] There do exist some general provisions on the 'construction on and after 1 July 1997 of words and expressions in laws previously in force' in the Hong Kong Reunification Ordinance (Instrument A601, Laws of Hong Kong).

[90] T Chen, '*Falüjie: gangfa ke cheng gangdu, gongkai zhuzhangzhe goucheng shandong zui*' (Lawyers express view that Hong Kong independence advocates may be punished for sedition under Hong Kong law) *Wen Wei Po*, 5 May 2016; '*Liang dazhuang zhi tui gangdu huo chufan shandong zui*' (Two barristers say that advocacy of Hong Kong independence may constitute sedition) *Sing Tao Daily*, 9 August 2016.

may be explored as follows. As Article 23 imposes a constitutional duty on the HKSAR to legislate to implement the requirements of the Article, it is arguable that a failure to perform such duty would give rise to a remedy that can be pursued by the Central Authorities under Article 18 of the Basic Law. It would be inconsistent with the purpose of the Basic Law and of Article 23 for the HKSAR to have a legal vacuum indefinitely on the national security matters covered by Article 23. Thus the Central Authorities are likely to step in by applying to the HKSAR under Article 18 a relevant law or laws made by the NPC or its Standing Committee.

The second scenario is that the National Security Bill introduced by the executive is enacted into law by LegCo. This is the most likely scenario. In theory a question arises as to whether the Central Authorities may consider that the law as enacted fails to meet the requirements of Article 23. This is unlikely, as the executive authorities of the HKSAR would most probably have consulted the Central Authorities and obtained their clearance before the National Security Bill is introduced in LegCo. The capacity of LegCo to amend the Bill against the executive's objections during the legislative process is almost nil, as it is very unlikely that amendments moved by the pan-democrats that are objected to by the SAR and Central Governments will be adopted: amendments to government Bills are subject to the 'separate counting' mechanism in Annex II to the Basic Law and can only be passed by majorities among both legislators elected by functional constituencies and those elected by universal suffrage. In the extremely unlikely scenario that the Bill ultimately enacted by LegCo fails to meet the requirements of Article 23 as understood by the Central Authorities, the NPCSC may exercise its power under Article 17 to return and invalidate the law. In this case, it is arguable that the HKSAR should have a second chance to enact a national security law that does meet the requirements of Article 23 as understood by the Central Authorities, before it is considered to have failed to perform its constitutional obligation under Article 23 – in which case the situation will be analogous to the first scenario above.

A more difficult question is what is the content of a national security law that would satisfy the requirements of Article 23 as understood by the Central Authorities. This in turn raises the question of whether the legislative exercise to implement Article 23 may lead to an NPCSC interpretation on the requirements of Article 23 and its relationship with other provisions in the Basic Law on the protection of civil liberties, particularly Article 39, which incorporates the human rights standards of the ICCPR. For example, the possibility cannot be ruled out that the Central Authorities would take the view that the law on sedition to be enacted under Article 23 should prohibit advocacy of secession even if violence or terrorism is not advocated as a means to achieve the same.[91] If such a law is eventually enacted in the Article 23 legislative exercise, it is foreseeable that its constitutionality will be challenged before the Hong Kong courts. The question

[91] It is noteworthy that the National Security (Legislative Provisions) Bill 2003 did not criminalise peaceful advocacy of secession by peaceful means. See cls 4 and 6 of the Bill.

thus arises as regards whether the NPCSC will promulgate an interpretation that is relevant to this issue *before* the court decides on the matter, as in the case of the LegCo oath-taking controversy in 2016. Even if the NPCSC does not intervene on its own initiative, it is arguable that the CFA may need to refer the relevant questions of interpretation to the NPCSC under Article 158(3) of the Basic Law, as Article 23 is likely to be considered a Basic Law provision that – in the words of Article 158(3) – 'concern[s] the relationship between the Central Authorities and the Region'.

VIII. Concluding Thoughts

The project of 'one country, two systems' is an ambitious one given the vast differences between the 'two systems' that exist within the 'one country'. When 'one country, two systems' was conceived in the early 1980s, the main difference between the 'two systems' was generally understood as being primarily related to economic systems; that is, a difference between 'socialism' on the mainland and 'capitalism' in Hong Kong. Since then, economic reform in China has radically transformed its socialist planned economy into a market economy not much different from the economic system of Hong Kong. Today, the fundamental difference between the 'two systems' is political and legal rather than economic. The legislative implementation of Article 23 of the Basic Law in order to protect China's national security and unity will probably be the single most controversial legal and constitutional issue in the HKSAR in the foreseeable future. It raises the question of the appropriate balance between 'one country' and 'two systems', or to what extent the civil liberties hitherto protected by the legal system of the HKSAR should be restricted by reference to the 'one country' principle. It is hoped that this collection, and this contribution to it, can promote a better understanding of the crossroads we stand at today, and the challenges that face us tomorrow.

3

China's Imperatives for National Security Legislation

HUALING FU

In his speech to celebrate the 20th anniversary of Hong Kong's return to China, President Xi highlighted two national security threats that Hong Kong may pose to China.[1] One is the traditional concern of territorial integrity. While Xi did not specifically mention the emerging secessionist advocacy in Hong Kong, he made it clear that any attempt to harm China's sovereignty will be 'absolutely impermissible'. A second threat concerns the use of Hong Kong as a base to endanger China's security, broadly defined as 'us(ing) Hong Kong to carry out infiltration and sabotage activities against the mainland'.[2] Those two threats in Hong Kong are microcosms of what China has claimed to be the larger national security threat that it faces.

In the eyes of the Central Government, those threats are not imagined. They are real and live issues facing Hong Kong and China. Coinciding with Xi's warning, Hong Kong courts have been handing down decisions on two types of cases: one is the disqualification of members of the Legislative Council (LegCo) from assuming legislative office for, essentially, their advocacy of Hong Kong's independence in violation of the oaths-taking law; and the other is criminal prosecution of individuals for inciting and organising unlawful assembly and its aftermath (ie a democratic movement demanding universal suffrage, widely known as the Occupy Central Movement, and riotous activities that followed it). Regarding both as posing a threat to its national security, China demands effective political and legal action to remove these risk factors.

This security concern is in many ways a subsidiary question to the working of the 'one country, two systems' policy which is considered in detail in other

[1] 'Full text of President Xi Jinping's speech on "one country, two systems" and how China rules Hong Kong' *South China Morning Post*, 1 July 2017, available at www.scmp.com/news/hong-kong/politics/article/2100856/full-text-president-xi-jinpings-speech-one-country-two.

[2] ibid.

contributions to this volume.[3] Xi's warning reflects a long standing and now entrenched fear that Hong Kong's high degree of autonomy, its growing impulse towards democracy, its political stagnation, and (as Beijing puts it) its occasional democratic violence may have turned a historically glorious city that China used to admire into an economic and political liability. As a result, China demands a shift in the balance that underpins 'one country, two systems' to give priority to the concept of sovereignty, central control over Hong Kong affairs, and above all the effective protection of national security and the national interest. At the core of the contention is the demand from the Central Government for Hong Kong to enact national security legislation pursuant to Article 23 of the Basic Law.

This chapter discusses China's new national security regime that includes Hong Kong as an integral part, and its implications for Hong Kong's own domestic security laws. In particular, it will outline China's internal and external security concerns, explain the reason behind China's push for national security legislation in Hong Kong, and explore the critical questions of whether the introduction of a national security legislation in Hong Kong is necessary or sufficient to address prevailing security concerns regarding Hong Kong and China, as well as its potential impact on rights and freedoms that Hong Kong treasures. China's Party State has given priority to stability and security as a development strategy and increasingly sees Hong Kong's democratic aspiration as a threat to China's national security. Since the failed attempt in 2003 to enact national security legislation,[4] the Hong Kong Government has been reluctant to reactivate the legislative process, but how has Hong Kong as a whole and the courts in particular struck a balance between China's national security and Hong Kong's struggle for democracy and maintenance of rule of law? How has this small liberal city engaged in a mega constitutional dialogue with its authoritarian sovereign?

I. China's National Security Concerns

China's two security concerns about Hong Kong correspond to its two principal security concerns: challenges to its territorial integrity, and challenges to its political system. Territorial integrity is a multifaceted issue with ancient roots. For a very long time, forces have existed in China that claim the independence of certain territories, which the Central Government regards as inalienable from China, with intent to effect certain boundary changes, hence a border threat.[5] The boundary risk has the following characteristics.

[3] See the contributions of Albert HY Chen and Michael C Davis in this collection.

[4] See the contributions of Michael C Davis and Simon NM Young in this collection.

[5] For a critical survey of the secessionist challenge in China, see S Kam, 'China' (2015–16) 8 *Counter Terrorist Trends and Analyses* 82.

Firstly, like any other independence movement, the boundary issue often has deep historical roots. Secessionist claims of the Uighurs and the Tibetans date back hundreds of years and involve competing historical facts and narratives. The same is true of Taiwan. While the state policies under the leadership of the Party may have aggravated the independence movements, the conflict predates the Party. In that sense, the Party has inherited a historical burden and managed the problem according to its own political logic. The boundary threat is quintessentially more nationalistic than political. In this respect Hong Kong's independence advocacy comes as a surprise: it lacks cultural support in part because it lacks a historical narrative.

Secondly, like most independence claims, ethnicity, with all the associated differences in language, religion, and customs, among other variables, is at the heart of the conflict. The constitutional identities of the various ethnic groups in China have evolved significantly over the history of the Party, and the current degree of ethnic autonomy represents a significant retreat from the Party's earlier undertakings to offer a special union, federalism, or similarly 'high degree' of autonomy, which has manifestly failed to satisfy the fundamental demands of ethnic minorities to assert their own identity. Even the Taiwanese claim for independence and the embryonic independence movement in Hong Kong have tried to manufacture a different social and cultural identity in their respective societies alongside predominantly political distinctions.[6]

Thirdly, regions that make secessionist demands are geographically located in the periphery reflecting both the historical origins of the claims and the significance of geo-politics. However, the fact that the problem is located at China's periphery does not make the issue per se peripheral. Like elsewhere, independence claims in China are often powerful and resilient. They can be temporarily suppressed but not eliminated. Under certain circumstances, they resurface and escalate.

Finally, ethnic tensions and related independence claims are a nationalistic concern for the (Han) Chinese irrespective of their political stance. For secessionists, China's political system, authoritarian or not, is of little concern, and total severance from China is the ultimate goal. In that sense, political dissidents and secessionists are not natural allies because they work toward different and often conflicting goals. Likewise, those who oppose ethnic independence include groups who are supportive of and against Party rule. Those who advocate democracy over authoritarian rule may fight equally hard against ethnic independence in alliance with the Party. In other words, one is first a Han Chinese before being a democrat, and the primary nationalist identity overwhelms the secondary political identity.

[6] For a general discussion of cultural identity in Greater China region, see FCS Liu and FLK Lee, 'Country, National, and Pan-national Identification in Taiwan and Hong Kong: Standing Together as Chinese?' (2013) 53 *Asian Survey* 1112.

The political challenge of regime change – China's second security concern – is an entirely different matter. The Party monopolises political power and its closed political system necessarily invites challenges which in turn necessitates repression. To pre-empt such an eventuality, the Party, in its typical authoritarian fashion, exerts extensive ideological and organisational control over society. As in other Communist regimes, political challenges principally take the form of creating alternative political thinking, nurturing political opposition forces, and mobilising civil society to rally in support of certain legal or political changes.

For the Party, peaceful evolution or so-called 'colour revolution' is masterminded from outside China. It is foreign ideas, foreign organisation, foreign money, and above all, a foreign conspiracy, that is behind the various threats. This approach is connected to the long-standing Chinese fear of colour revolutions, traceable to the speeches of John Dulles as United States (US) Secretary of State between 1953 and 1959. At the beginning of the Cold War, Dulles provocatively called for the changing of 'Communist states through peaceful evolution towards democracy'.[7] What Dulles had in mind was to use assistance, economic or otherwise, and commerce to create conditions to 'shorten the expected life span of communism'; a speech and proposition that reportedly attracted the serious political attention of Mao himself, and may well have reinforced Mao's determination to launch the Cultural Revolution and to strengthen his resolve for continuous revolution in China.[8] Thus, from the early days of the People's Republic, hostile forces in the West, led by the US, have been identified as the main source of regime change risk. A close eye has long been kept on revolutionary movements elsewhere, especially during the collapse of communist regimes in Europe, said to be the result of 'bourgeois liberalisation'. Student-led protests in China have also been presented as an attempt to deny party leadership so that the military crackdown in response to the 1989 Tiananmen protests – the largest and longest occupation movement in contemporary Chinese history – was presented as being to frustrate a peaceful evolution attempt by enemies.[9] Yet as the Communist Party of China (CCP) has acquiesced to the development of a market economy and improved governance in China, the fear of a peaceful evolution has lingered and acute sensitivity to 'spill over' from revolutions elsewhere continues. For example, following the Arab Spring China took pre-emptive measures in 2011 to prevent an anticipated 'Jasmine Revolution'. For the first time, the Government 'disappeared' a large number of human rights lawyers who were alleged to have led and organised a colour revolution in China.[10]

[7] Cited in R Ong, *China's Security Interest in the Post-cold War Era* (London, Routledge, 2002) 117.

[8] Q Zhai, '1959: Preventing Peaceful Evolution' (2009) 18 *China Heritage Quarterly*, available at www.chinaheritagequarterly.org/features.php?searchterm=018_1959preventingpeace.inc&issue=018.

[9] J Zhang, *China's Response to the Downfall of Communism in Eastern Europe and the Soviet Union* (Stanford, Hoover Press, 1994); ME Sarotte, 'China's Fear of Contagion: Tiananmen Square and the Power of the European Example' (2012) 37 *International Security* 156.

[10] E Pils, *China's Human Rights Lawyers: Advocacy and Resistance* (London, Routledge, 2015).

China's fear of foreign forces derives from the CCP's deeply rooted belief that the West has never stopped gazing at China with hostility, which must be reconciled with the view that China must nevertheless open its doors to absorb Western ideas, concepts, and institutions – all part of Western 'soft power' to which the Party is acutely sensitive. Thus, paradoxically the Party has initiated a reform process that seems to make peaceful evolution more probable. Admittedly the reforms have energised the economy, empowered society, improved governance, and strengthened the Party, in so doing raising China to its current status. However, for the Party the process is also a risky one and if not managed well it has the potential to undermine the regime.

The most direct manifestation of this fear comes from the prosecution of human rights lawyers and defenders since 2013.[11] In convicting Xie Yang for his subversive activities, Xie allegedly confessed that he had attended training and workshops in Hong Kong that were organised by a Christian group and an organisation called the Hong Kong China Human Rights Institute.[12] In prosecuting Jiang Tianyong, the Hong Kong-based China Human Rights Law Concern Group was referred to, together with Hong Kong-based Suo Yizhi.[13] The US-based dissident Yang Jiangli was named in the case of Hu Shigen and Guo Honggou (charged with subversion) in which Hu invited Guo to attend a youth leader training camp in the US at the invitation of Yang.[14] 'Hostile news media' were also referred to in court decisions: Boxun was mentioned, for example, in Zhang Haibao's case; Falun Gong newspapers were mentioned in Liu Xiaobo's case;[15] and civil disobedience literature were also referred to in other prosecution.[16]

Foreign funding appears to be an even more sensitive issue. Li Heping was said to have been funded by unnamed foreign foundations to carry out death penalty research and advocacy.[17] Peter Dahlin, who was forced to confess on CCTV, was

[11] H Fu, 'The July 9th (709) Crackdown on Human Rights Lawyers: Legal Advocacy in an Authoritarian State' (2018) 27 *Journal of Contemporary China* 554; H Fu and H Zhu, 'After the July 9 (709) Crackdown: The Future of Human Rights Lawyering' (2018) 41 *Fordham International Law Journal* 1135.

[12] Changsha Intermediate People's Court, '谢阳案庭审直播: 法庭调查(1)' (Live television trial of Xie Yang's case: court investigation (1)) (8 May 2017), available at m.weibo.cn/1975687852/4105094889069191.

[13] Changsha Intermediate People's Court, '江天勇案一审公开开庭审理视频：控辩双方对证据进行举证质证（三）' (Video of open trial of Jiang Tianyong's case: the prosecution and defence parties provide proof and inquire about the proof (3)) (22 August 2017), available at m.weibo.cn/1975687852/4143519713680002.

[14] Tianjin No 2 Intermediate People's Court, '胡石根案一审在津公开开庭审理' (Hu Shigen's case was openly heard in Tianjin) (3 August 2016), available at m.weibo.cn/3919910570/4004374818387985; Tianjin No.2 Intermediate People's Court, '勾洪国案一审在津公开开庭审理' (Gou Hongguo's case was openly heard in Tianjin) (5 August 2016), available at m.weibo.cn/3919910570/4005103461026457.

[15] Xinjiang Uygur Autonomous Region High People's Court, '张海涛案二审裁定书' (Decision of second instance of Zhang Haitao's case) (23 November 2016), available at cmcn.org/archives/28104.

[16] Guangzhou Intermediate People's Court, '唐荆陵、袁朝阳、王清营判决书' (Verdict of Tang Jingling, Yuan Chaoyang and Wang Qingying's case) (31 January 2016), available at wqw2010.blogspot.hk/2016/01/blog-post_95.html.

[17] Xinhua Press, '人民根本利益国家法律尊严不容挑战 – – 周世锋胡石根翟岩民勾洪国颠覆国家政权犯罪案件警示录' (The fundamental interests of the people and the dignity of the state's law cannot be challenged – warnings from Zhou Shifeng, Hu Shigen, Zhai Yanmin and Gou Hongguo's case of subverting state power) (6 August 2016), available at www.xinhuanet.com/mrdx/2016-08/06/c_135569016.htm.

accused of funding human rights lawyers for their subversive activities, even though the source of Dahli's 'foreign funding' was not named.[18] Again in Jiang Tianyong's case, evidence was produced to prove that Jiang applied on behalf of his lawyer Zhang Kai for cash and a cell phone (of total value RMB 23,326) from an unnamed hostile foreign organisation for the purpose of inciting lawyer Zhang to obstruct justice.[19] In reality, since the European Union, various European governments, and the US Government are the ultimate sources of funding, the Chinese Government has so far refrained from openly naming those funding sources.

II. China's New National Security Regime

Under Xi, China has adopted a three-pronged approach to meeting the perceived security threat. The first is to securitise the Party state and to govern primarily from the perspective of national security. Upon assuming power Xi created a National Security Commission of China (NSC) to centralise leadership on matters relating to national security as broadly defined to include security in politics, the economy, society, culture and even food. The NSC is expected to exercise supreme power, provide better coordination, and enhance the protection of China's national security through powerful and comprehensive mechanisms.[20] This centralisation of national security decision-making has taken place in the wider context of an ongoing political rectification campaign that is aimed at purging corruption and dissent within Party. The anti-corruption campaign has now shifted from one against bribe-taking, embezzlement, or misuse of public funds to one that imposes political discipline and seeks to enhance loyalty so that the Party speaks with one voice and acts in synchronisation.[21] A unified Party is the best defence of Chinese national security, the argument goes.

What has been truly spectacular is not only the well-orchestrated campaigns against dissenting voices and provocative actions, but also the resort to legality to underpin this, with the creation of a new legal framework as the backdrop to securitising the Chinese state. The pace and intensity of legislative change is

[18] F Tan, '瑞典"人权活动人士"被捕真相: 捏造问题报告换取境外资助' (The truth of the arrest of the Swedish "human rights defender": taking foreign funding by fabricating reports) *Global Times*, 20 January 2016), available at world.huanqiu.com/exclusive/2016-01/8412232.html.

[19] Changsha Intermediate People's Court, '江天勇案一审公开开庭审理视频：控辩双方对证据进行举证质证（三）' (Video of open trial of Jiang Tianyong's case's first instance: the prosecution and defence parties provide proof and inquire about the proof (3)) (22 August 2017), available at m.weibo.cn/1975687852/4143519713680002.

[20] DM Lampton, 'Xi Jingping and National Security Commission: Policy Coordination and Political Power' (2015) 95 *Journal of Contemporary China* 759; J You, 'China's National Security Commission: Theory, Evolution and Operations' 98 *Journal of Contemporary China* 178.

[21] H Fu, 'Wielding the Sword: President Xi's New Anti-corruption Campaign' in S Rose-Ackerman and P Lagunes (eds), *Greed, Corruption, and the Modern State: Essays in Political Economy* (Cheltenham, Edward Elgar, 2016).

remarkable. Within a few years, a range of freshly drafted legal bills have been hastily brought on to the legislative agenda, with brief consultation and revisions where necessary, then shoe-horned through the legislative process, creating a new moment of authoritarian legality in China.[22]

First of all, there is the new National Security Law,[23] enacted in 2015, which is informally referred to as the 'Constitution' of China's national security state. The new law broadens the scope of national security matters and has effectively framed the entire sphere of political, economic and societal governance as a national security concern and as such it is placed squarely under the leadership of the NSC. The new law also for the first time brings Hong Kong and Macau into the national security framework, sending a powerful message that Hong Kong is placed on China's national security radar and owes a specific legal duty to safeguard China's national security.

Under the umbrella of the National Security, there are a number of key pillars of legislation that address China's diverse national security concerns: the 2018 Counter-Terrorism Law,[24] the 2016 Law on the Management of Domestic Activities of Overseas Non-governmental Organisations (NGOs),[25] the 2016 Internet Security Law,[26] and the 2014 Anti-Spy Law.[27] Those pieces of legislation create a new legislative framework, including statutory power for national security agencies imposing duties on citizens to inform and to cooperate. The effect of the above national security law is to provide a legal justification to authorise national security agencies to do in the open what they used to do in the dark. Without this legislation, powers were exercised in an opaque and often invisible way – something that could be done but not discussed. The enactment of those laws is not so much intended to regulate and control the exercise of power, but to crystallise it, amplify it, and legitimise its exercise. For the agencies, it is about confidence-building and morale-boosting.

The setting up of the NSC and the promulgation of empowering laws, as mentioned above, are consequential. They coincided with or have been followed by the prosecution of activists with an assumed propensity to perpetrate a colour revolution or terrorist/separatist activities: those who organise or actively participate in

[22] H Fu, 'Duality and China's Struggle for Legal Autonomy' (2019) 1 *China Perspectives* 3; T Zhang and T Ginsburg, 'Legality in Contemporary Chinese Politics' (2018) *Virginia Journal of International Law* (forthcoming), Yale Law School, Public Law Research Paper No 657 and University of Chicago, Public Law Working Paper No 689, available at ssrn.com/abstract=3250948.

[23] 中華人民共和國國家安全法 (National Security Law of the PRC), available at www.npc.gov.cn/npc/xinwen/2015-07/07/content_1941161.htm.

[24] 中華人民共和國反恐怖主義法 (Counter-Terrorism Law of the PRC), available at www.npc.gov.cn/npc/xinwen/2018-06/12/content_2055871.htm.

[25] 中華人民共和國境外非政府組織境內活動管理法 (Law on the Management of Domestic Activities of Overseas NGOs), available at www.npc.gov.cn/npc/xinwen/2017-11/28/content_2032719.htm.

[26] 中華人民共和國網絡安全法 (Internet Security Law of the PRC), available at www.npc.gov.cn/npc/xinwen/2016-11/07/content_2001605.htm.

[27] 中華人民共和國反間諜法 (Anti-Spy Law of the PRC), available at www.npc.gov.cn/npc/xinwen/2014-11/02/content_1884660.htm.

social activism, including opinion leaders, feminists, human rights lawyers, labour activists and academics. Individuals who are regarded as a political risk have been warned, punished and placed under long-term surveillance or systematic internment such as the case of Xinjiang. Their foreign supporters are punished as well on a more selective basis.

More directly among China's pre-emptive strategies, China has effectively removed what is perceived as the root cause of a colour revolution: foreign financial support for domestic activism. China will not have a so-called Twitter revolution or a Facebook revolution for the simple reason that they are banned on the Mainland. China is well-known for effective and powerful censorship that stops hostile and subversive ideas dead at its borders.[28] While foreign funding for domestic NGOs has long existed and was an indispensable part of China's growing social activism before Xi took office, with the passing of the Overseas NGO Law, China has taken effective measures to either stop foreign-funded activities or to place them under tight police control.

III. Hong Kong as a National Security Risk

Xi's speech mentioned at the beginning of the chapter is the first time a state leader has described the perceived risk that Hong Kong may pose to China in terms of infiltration and sabotage. It is a significant expansion of the traditional concern that Hong Kong may be used as a base for subverting the CCP's political and constitutional system.

Hong Kong's relationship with the mainland has always been precarious. As a British colony, Hong Kong served multiple political functions, including as a subversive base to be used by revolutionaries and dissidents of various types challenging the regime on the mainland. Sun Yat-sen is believed to have used Hong Kong for preparing his revolution in China. The Communists and Nationalists fought fiercely in Hong Kong before 1949 when the CCP won the civil war. After the establishment of the People's Republic of China (PRC), the Nationalists used Hong Kong as a bridgehead to infiltrate and sabotage mainland targets and conduct extensive psychological warfare. The political role of Hong Kong became more preeminent when Maoist policy failures on the Mainland led to waves of refugees, political or economic, flocking to Hong Kong, and forming the political backbone of Hong Kong society. Thus in Hong Kong, anti-mainland feeling is historically rooted in a unique demographic context.

The return of Hong Kong to China has not altered Hong Kong's unique position. As political and religious persecution has continued on the mainland, Hong Kong remains a crucial safe haven for the persecuted: Falun Gong finds a breathing

[28] Committee to Protect Journalists, '10 Most Censored Countries' (2015), available at cpj.org/2015/04/10-most-censored-countries.php.

space in Hong Kong for its religious survival and political resistance; political dissidents, while less active, continue to have a voice in Hong Kong and use Hong Kong to exert their influence on the mainland; more recently, rights lawyers and activists have found temporary shelter in Hong Kong. After all, Hong Kong is a place governed by the rule of law aspiring for full democracy.

All the above is thus nothing new. The mainland since the Nanjing Treaty has been authoritarian, whereas Hong Kong has offered a revolutionary, or subversive, base for those who desire regime change. This has been so, not because the colonial Government had intended to use Hong Kong to effect a subversive agenda – on the contrary, the colonial Government had harshly cracked down on activism that was deemed as unsettling or otherwise unfriendly to various Chinese governments.[29] Hong Kong has served this unique function because of its different political and legal system, which created a space that has never existed within mainland China. Resistance against the mainland system, whatever it maybe, may have been part of collective DNA of Hong Kong,[30] a fact that China knows well and has lived with, albeit with some reluctance.

The collective resistance became open since the transition because the threat of Hong Kong's system and way of life has become open and direct. The promise of universal suffrage within a region with a high degree of autonomy ruled by the people of Hong Kong is an attractive one. Generations of people have developed a strong democracy-defined identity dedicating their life to achieving that ultimate goal. This is a society with great democratic potential – free, prosperous and cosmopolitan, but unfulfilled promises can also prove fatal for Central–Special Administrative Region (SAR) relations and Hong Kong's own governance.

The tension that occurred immediately after the handover was in part just a continuation of old battles between Hong Kong and China. Where law and politics have shown themselves unable to address grievances and settle disputes, people in Hong Kong have taken to streets to exert pressure and influence policies. Public outcry, when it was effectively organised, has led successfully to policy changes and that success in turn led to further street action.[31]

What is new, and what has attracted unprecedented level of panic and anger in Beijing, is the sudden rise of a secessionist movement in Hong Kong. The resolute determination of the Central Government to rule out universal suffrage as a significant part of the social contract with Hong Kong society met with widespread criticism and an unprecedented level of socio-legal resistance. The end of the peaceful Occupy Central movement did not mean the end of resistance. On the contrary, the experiences during the months-long dispute intensified and

[29] MHK Ng and JD Wong (eds), *Civil Unrest and Governance in Hong Kong: Law and Order from Historical and Cultural Perspectives* (London, Routledge, 2017); H Fu, 'Past and Future Offences of Sedition in Hong Kong' in H Fu, C Peterson, and S Young (eds), *National Security and Fundamental Freedoms: Hong Kong's Article 23 Under Scrutiny* (Hong Kong, Hong Kong University Press, 2005).

[30] ibid.

[31] See eg the contribution of Michael C Davis in this collection.

radicalised it.[32] The court orders to clear the streets, coupled with a propaganda war to delegitimise the movement and the frustration on the part of the ordinary residents, delivered a fatal blow to the Occupy Central movement, but the resistance movement proved to be more resilient and evolved into two new forms: the resort to open and violent confrontation on the part of the young people in Hong Kong, and the emergence of secessionist advocacy.

Young activists had long been frustrated with the lack of progress in Hong Kong's democratisation and the failure on the part of the established pro-democracy political parties to achieve meaningful policy changes.[33] The new groups were more confrontational and action-oriented, adopting tactics including stalking and harassing government officials and members of the pro-government legislature, disturbing the legislative process and aggressive street action.[34] Minor frictions and confrontational tactics that had gained popularity and a degree of legitimacy during the years before Occupy gathered momentum after Occupy and peaked in the Mong Kok riot. That riot, also referred to as the Fish-ball Revolution by those with a more sympathetic view, serves as a good example of that dangerous path and Hong Kong's vulnerability.[35] Before the Chinese New Year of 2016, the government crackdown on unlicensed street vendors selling traditional Chinese food (such as curry fish balls, hence the moniker) triggered a protest from student groups on the night of 8 February 2016 and eventually a violent confrontation between students and the police that lasted into the next morning. Police used batons and pepper spray and fired two live rounds as warning shots into the air in the full glare of the media, and protesters used whatever was available to push the police back, including bricks and flowerpots. By the end of a violent night, about 90 police officers and several journalists were injured, some seriously. Arrest of those violent protesters immediately followed and to date dozens of people have been convicted of related offences.[36]

The use of force against the police was universally condemned, although supporters of students and those who are sympathetic to their cause also assigned blame to the Government and the police in particular for their provocation.

[32] FLF Lee, 'Internet Alternative Media, Movement Experience, and Radicalism: The Case of Post-Umbrella Movement Hong Kong' (2018) 27 *Social Movement Studies* 311.

[33] EW Cheng, 'Street Politics in a Hybrid Regime: The Diffusion of Political Activism in Post-Colonial Hong Kong' (2016) 226 *The China Quarterly* 383.

[34] The Central Government quickly seized the opportunity, through its propaganda machine, to attach what it referred to as 'Afghanistan-style violence': see '"Minzhu Baoli" – Baoli Shilue Xianggang' (Democratic Violence – Violence Permeating Hong Kong) *People's Daily* (overseas edn), 8 September 2011, available at paper.people.com.cn/rmrbhwb/html/2011-09/08/content_919041.htm.

[35] The official position taken by the Government in relation to the riot can be found in the answer provided by the Secretary for Security, Mr Lai Tung-kwok, to a question put forward by the Hon Mr James To, a legislative council member from the Democratic Party. See Press Release of the Hong Kong SAR Government, 'LCQ5: Mong Kok riot' (2 March 2019), available at www.info.gov.hk/gia/general/201603/02/P201603020594.htm; for a more critical view, see 'The fire-monkey stirs: Street violence and politics' *The Economist*, 11 February 2016, available at www.economist.com/china/2016/02/13/street-violence-and-politics.

[36] See eg the reports by *South China Morning Post*, available at www.scmp.com/topics/mong-kok-riot.

Regardless of one's political stance toward the unrest, the continuity and even causal relationship between the failed Occupy Central movement and the radicalisation on the part of some participants are widely recognised. Thus commentaries on the Mong Kok riot often place the use of violence in 2016 in the larger context of Hong Kong's struggle for universal suffrage and the efforts to maintain Hong Kong's way of life.

The actual use of violence in individual cases has also changed the protest discourse. Occupying Central with Peace and Love, a signature statement of the civil disobedience movement in 2014, was questioned, challenged and abandoned. In its place one finds the earlier attempt to justify and theorise the use of force or at least through escalating activism in promoting political change. Many of the ad hoc groups that have surfaced in the post-Occupy era openly endorse, if not advocate, the use of confrontation and force to achieve their political objectives, be it democratisation or the independence of Hong Kong.

A more dangerous form of resistance is the leap during the Occupy Central movement from localism,[37] a long-existing social force for maintaining Hong Kong's cultural identity, to a collective, coherent and forceful voice to assert Hong Kong's political identity leading to the open advocacy for the independence of Hong Kong.[38] Instead of fighting for genuine democracy in Hong Kong and patiently waiting for a democratic transition on the mainland, the occupiers and their supporters and sympathisers regrouped and shifted their discourse and behaviour toward Hong Kong's own political destiny without China. Localism emerged in Hong Kong at the same time as the use of violent confrontation as a resistance strategy, coinciding with the rise of young political activists on the horizon. A significant cultural change has been taking place after Occupy as Hong Kong tries to distance itself from the rest of China. All this came into focus in the 2016 LegCo election in which some of the Occupy leaders ran on a platform of extreme localism and implicit secessionism.

To the surprise of the Central Authorities, the young activists won a huge victory in the legislative election. Six young candidates from the pro-localism/independence groups won legislative seats with wide majorities, taking votes largely from the traditional pro-democratic camps rather than from the pro-government camp, indicating strongly the radicalisation of society and disappointment with the political process at large. There were initial hopes and expectations that the

[37] C Kwan, S Lam, and T Tsim, 'The rise and rise of localism among Hong Kong youth' *Hong Kong Free Press* (Hong Kong, 20 November 2016), available at www.hongkongfp.com/2016/11/20/the-rise-and-rise-of-localism-among-hong-kong-youth, accessed 20 May 2019; M Wong, H Yang, and V Tsang, 'From local identity to the pursuit of independence: The changing face of Hong Kong localism' *Hong Kong Free Press* (Hong Kong, 11 November 2016), available at www.hongkongfp.com/2016/11/11/from-local-identity-to-the-pursuit-of-independence-the-changing-face-of-hong-kong-localism, accessed 20 May 2019.

[38] S Ortmann, 'Hong Kong: Problems of Identity and Independence' in ML Weiss and E Aspinall (eds), *Student Activism in Asia: Between Protest and Powerlessness* (Minnesota, University of Minnesota Press, 2012).

young legislators, without any historical baggage on their shoulders, would be able to inject a fresh and positive force into the sterile and stagnant law-making process. Unfortunately, riding on their popularity and faithful to their belief, they made their legislative debut by appearing openly secessionist and refused to swear allegiance to China in their oath-taking ceremony, insulting a large part of the population in Hong Kong including many of their supporters, and, by doing so, inviting the Central Authorities to intervene to instigate their disqualification. Within a few months of resounding victories, the Hong Kong Government, apparently under the direct order of the Central Authorities, brought the legislators to courts with disqualification as a result.

IV. Article 23 of the Basic Law and the Chinese Constitution

The tensions manifested in Hong Kong reflect a deep structural fracture in the 'one country, two systems' design that creates a liberal sub-unit in the authoritarian whole. The SAR was created by a Constitution that is committed to its elimination; Hong Kong's rule of law is an essential part of the reform objectives of the mainland but the liberal values that sustain Hong Kong's rule of law, inherent in the Hong Kong system and universally held, also appear incompatible with the authoritarian regime that purports to promote the reform. Hong Kong's economic dynamism has played an indispensable role in supporting the Chinese reform process, but its aspirations for freedom, liberty and democratic governance challenge China's political system and are perceived to be a political liability. Hong Kong, according to a reformist vision, may be China's aspiration, but from another perspective it is a national security threat. The Party leads a securitised state and sees calls for democracy as the operation of political and cultural forces to subvert the Party state.

A legal question that has lingered in Hong Kong is the constitutionality of the Basic Law in view of its compatibility or lack thereof with the Chinese Constitution. The Chinese Constitution, notwithstanding amendments in the post-handover era, remains authoritarian to its core and has become increasingly so.[39] It entrenches the monopoly of political power by the CCP and constitutes China as a socialist state under its democratic dictatorship. Indeed, Article 6 of the Chinese Constitution aims at the elimination of the system of economic exploitation on which the success of Hong Kong was built – the capitalist system. The National People's Congress (NPC) thus creates an SAR exception ostensibly only for its ultimate elimination.

[39] Zhang and Ginsburg, 'Legality in Contemporary Chinese Politics' (2018); F Lin, 'The 2018 Constitutional Amendments: Significance and Impact on the Theories of Party-State Relationship in China' (2019) 1 *China Perspectives* 11.

The colonial Government was well-aware of that constitutional risk, which was confirmed by an expert opinion authored by Professor William Wade, who not surprisingly recommended a revision of the Chinese Constitution so as to entrench Hong Kong's alternative political system within the Chinese Constitution. Article 31 of the Constitution merely authorises the creation of an SAR without specifying its nature and as such may not be able to authorise the creation of the hostile political system that was envisaged in the Joint Declaration.

China refused to amend the Constitution on the ground that the Constitution was newly made and an amendment at an early stage of its implementation would undermine its solemnity not to say sanctity. However, to ease concerns arising from Hong Kong, the NPC made a declaration on the same day that the Basic Law was enacted, which stated that the Basic Law was authorised by and is consistent with the Constitution. The legislative history of the 1982 Constitution also makes it clear that Article 31 is made to prepare for the future unification of Taiwan and it envisages an SAR to operate in an entirely different political and economic system.

The Basic Law is not part of the Chinese Constitution. However, significantly, the exceptional authorisation by the Constitution gives the Basic Law a special constitutional status. In mainland constitutional scholarship, it is categorised as a law of constitutional nature and that quasi-constitutional status elevates the ranking of the Basic Law in the legislative hierarchy in China. The Basic Law is effective in Hong Kong. Whether it can displace and exclude the Chinese Constitution is not necessarily a question that lawyers can answer, but according to the original design, it does create a closed legal system for Hong Kong with its own values and integrity and with little reference to the system and values that prevail on the mainland.

Article 23 proves to be a controversial article in the Basic Law and has had a torturous legislative history. In essence, China insisted on having its national security, principally the socialist system under the leadership of the CCP, protected in the new SAR, but was willing to allow Hong Kong to design means suitable to its legal tradition for its protection. An earlier more liberal draft did not include the offence of subversion that is alien to Hong Kong's criminal law. Article 23 was an imposition from China in the aftermath of the 1989 bloodshed. Having observed the power of protest in Hong Kong, China was prepared for the possibility that Hong Kong may become a subversive base against China on Chinese soils.[40]

In relation to Article 23 legislation, while Hong Kong has a constitutional obligation to enact legislation to protect China's national security, Hong Kong can make law 'on its own', meaning principally that Hong Kong decides the meaning and scope of China's national security and how an act that endangers China's national security will be defined and punished. Hong Kong is entitled to enact a

[40] H Fu and R Cullen, 'National Security Law in Hong Kong: Quo Vadis: A Study of Article 23 of the Basic Law of Hong Kong' (2002) 19 *UCLA Pacific Basin Law Journal* 185. For a reflection on Art 23 debate based on the 2003 Bill, see Fu, Peterson, and Young, *National Security and Fundamental Freedoms* (2005).

national security law that takes into consideration the relevant criminal offences that already exist under Hong Kong laws and its unique legal tradition.

A constitution is a living tree that evolves and grows as circumstances change. Interestingly, China demands reinterpretation of the Basic Law to reflect a new equilibrium in power relations while Hong Kong struggles to hold the mainland to its original constitutional bargain. Because of the rebalancing of power and repositioning of Hong Kong in the Chinese order, a mainland position is now emerging that may ultimately challenge the status of the Basic Law as the territory's highest law. The new view has been much discussed on the mainland but rarely mentioned in Hong Kong. It relates to the applicability of the Chinese Constitution in Hong Kong. The question discussed is to what degree, and in what manner, the Chinese Constitution is applicable, if at all, in Hong Kong? What is the relevance of the Chinese Constitution beyond authorising the creation of the Hong Kong SAR? The debate commenced in Hong Kong when the Constitution was placed as the supreme law of Hong Kong in the official compendium.

There is no clear answer to such questions. As a unitary state, there is one constitution in China only and that Constitution applies to all parts of China, including the Hong Kong SAR. However, the enactment of the Basic Law and the implementation of the 'one country, two systems' doctrine necessitates some self-imposed constraints on sovereignty, namely for the mainland not to impose more than what is authorised by the Basic Law. The practice seems to be that those constitutional provisions which are consistent with the Basic Law can be applied in Hong Kong for the purpose of confirming and supporting the relevant Basic Law provisions. This practice may be pragmatic, but is superficial and redundant at best, and distorting of the legal order at worst, for according to this line of reasoning the application of a higher law depends on a legality test imposed by the lower law.

Mainland scholarship has tried to justify a broader and more forceful application of the Chinese Constitution in Hong Kong. There has been a tremendous amount of legal acrobatics in mainland Chinese scholarship to achieve this objective. There was, however, a consensus that the Constitution applies in principle, in spirit and in the abstract.[41] At a minimum, such application demands a necessary degree of deference and respect in Hong Kong to the constitutional order of the PRC as it is practised on the mainland.

The degree of deference varies depending on the weight one wishes to assign to the Chinese Constitution, which in turn depends on one's conceptualisation of the relations between the Basic Law and Constitution. A light-touch, weakly deferential model would conform to Jiang Zemin's 'river water–well water' analogy, according to which 'one country, two systems' means little more than

[41] X Cao, '憲法在香港特別行政區的適用：理論回顧與實踐反思' (The Application of the Constitution in the Hong Kong Special Administrative Region: Theoretical Reconnection and Practical Reflections) (2018) 1 *Politics and Law* 79; Y Wang, *論憲法在特別行政區的適用* (On the Application the Constitution in the Special Administrative Regions) (Hong Kong, Joint Publishing, 2019).

non-interference from the mainland in Hong Kong affairs and vice versa. On the contrary, a strongly deferential interpretation would be along the lines of comprehensive control involving direct rule and hands-on management from the Central Authorities in all Hong Kong affairs. With strong deference to the Chinese constitution, the Basic Law no longer prevails and the NPC or the Standing Committee of the NPC (NPCSC) can govern Hong Kong independently of the Basic Law. The issue is not so much whether Articles of the Constitution will be applied directly in Hong Kong as they probably will not. The concern is that constitutional mechanisms outside the scope of the Basic Law may be enforced in Hong Kong, such as the possibility that the NPC might try to legislate on Hong Kong affairs beyond the scope that the Basic Law permits (as in what its NPCSC has sought to do in the co-location saga[42]), or for the NPCSC to send a delegation to supervise the enforcement of the Basic Law in Hong Kong.

If a strong deference were to apply, in enacting Article 23, as Hong Kong is bound to do, Hong Kong should then defer to the Chinese test in determining what constitutes a national security offence and when the offence of treason, secession or other national security offences have been committed. With strong deference, the national security of China will be measured against a common standard with no substantive deviation from that standard permitted to safeguard the safety of the motherland, in the same way as national flag and national anthem deserve substantially equal protection in both Hong Kong and the rest of China.

The question remains as to what kind of offending act China wishes to capture through enacting Article 23 legislation. Moreover, would the law be effective in achieving the objectives that China has in mind? Part of the reason why the 2003 attempt to enact Article 23 law failed was that in 2003 there was no clear national security risk to prevent and no visible enemy on the horizon to punish, although Falun Gong was rumoured to be a target. The obvious question is therefore whether the circumstances in Hong Kong have materially changed in the subsequent years.

The pro-independence voices appeared in the aftermath of the NPCSC's Decision on 31 August 2014, which triggered the Occupy Central movement. China has been eager to kybosh emerging secessionist movements swiftly and harshly if necessary, reflecting a larger political decision to harshly repress any secessionist tendency on Chinese soil. That resolve is seen clearly in the swift legislative interpretation of Article 104 in an attempt to disqualify allegedly pro-independence members of the LegCo in a specific case before the court. A threatening message was widely spread in Hong Kong that the Central Government was determined to wipe out any independence movement in Hong Kong 'whatever it takes', and a legal method, that is disqualification through the court process, is not only preferred but the sole method can be used to eliminate this risk factor. Fix it or Hong Kong's 'one country, two systems' would be placed at risk, it was said.

[42] See also the contribution of Swati Jhaveri in this collection.

The message was clearly received and it is not hard to act on. Immediately after the Chief Executive and the Secretary of Justice brought a legal action for the disqualification of the first batch of two young legislators from assuming office for failing to taking oaths as legally required and before the court made its decision, the NPCSC hastily passed an interpretation of Article 104 of the Basic Law to lay a constitutional foundation for the disqualification. Once the court uncritically accepted the Interpretation and its rationale as givens and decided the case on a narrow legal ground, it had little choice but to disqualify the legislators who had clearly failed to take the oaths as legally required from assuming office.[43] National unity is a foundational principle in Hong Kong's constitutional order, and the court in the new political ecosystem that China has created is unwilling and also unable to save those legislators who dare to challenge it. The Interpretation has been considered retrospectively binding in Hong Kong and the court as having a duty to ensure that constitutional requirement is imposed on a member of the LegCo to validly take the oath.[44] Insisting on the particular facts of the case, and the uniqueness of the constitutional design in Hong Kong, Hong Kong courts found foreign cases unpersuasive that are sympathetic to lawmakers who failed to take their respective oaths properly and the judicial intervention into the legislative process to be justifiable and proportionate. The Appeal Committee of the Court of Final Appeal, in refusing applications for leave to appeal from the disqualified legislators, stated: 'although the questions touch upon issues of law of general and public importance, there is no reasonably arguable basis for disturbing the judgments under appeal'.[45]

While the courts have disqualified the alleged pro-independence legislators for failing to take valid oaths, the decisions have not silenced pro-independence speech or general discussion on the matter, hence the call by the Central Government for national security legislation in the aftermath of the disqualification cases. The expectation is that Article 23 legislation will perform a general deterrence function so as to root out any secessionist aspiration in Hong Kong. However, it remains to be seen whether anti-secession legislation enacted under Article 23 can be effective in stopping independence rhetoric and activities and, if it can, what the cost that Hong Kong has to pay in achieving that goal would be. Significantly, would courts in Hong Kong allow such legislation to survive a constitutional challenge even if it will inevitably infringe upon freedom of speech? Having allowed the criminalisation of desecration of the national flag, proposed to create the offence of insulting the national anthem[46] and disqualified lawmakers for their

[43] See also the contribution of PY Lo in this collection.

[44] *Chief Executive of the HKSAR v President of the Legislative Council and Leung Chung Hang Sixtus* (2017) 20 HKCFAR 390.

[45] ibid [3].

[46] At the time of writing, the Hong Kong Government's proposed National Anthem Bill is being debated in the LegCo. See eg K Carrico, 'Legal Malware: Hong Kong's National Anthem Ordinance' (Hong Kong Watch, 2019), available at static1.squarespace.com/static/58ecfa82e3df284d3a13dd41/t/5c9bfacc7817f7bd42363a98/1553726160344/hkw+report_march19+%282%29.pdf.

offensive secessionist expression, will Hong Kong continue to narrow the scope of the political dialogue in Hong Kong? It is clear that the National Security Bill as tabled in 2003 would not be able to criminalise secessionist speech and activities as they are known in Hong Kong. As provocative and offensive as they are, those speech and activities are peaceful and cannot be criminal in a liberal society like Hong Kong. At the same time, Hong Kong has stringent if not draconian public order laws that can be effectively used to selectively punish disorderly activities that any secessionist activity may cause, as the cases in the aftermath of Occupy have amply shown.[47]

An equally serious concern relates to Hong Kong's perceived role as a bastion of 'infiltration and sabotage'. 'One country, two systems' cannot be implemented through the 'the river water does not intrude on the well water' formula. Given intensive and wide-ranging social and economic interactions, mutual political influence is perhaps unavoidable. While China is trying to shape Hong Kong's political future through constitutional and extra-constitutional means, some in Hong Kong also harbour the intention to change China's authoritarian political system. Anti-communist sentiment runs deep in Hong Kong – a substantial portion of the population were refugees from Communist China for political and economic reasons. Deeply felt suspicion, if not contempt, recedes slowly if at all. The Tiananmen Square bloodshed in 1989 brought their tragic memories back and reinforced suspicion and hostility toward the regime to the North. Putting their passion to action, activist citizens created organisations with ending the one Party dictatorship written into their charters. Those organisations survived the transition and continue to thrive in Hong Kong. In addition, with the tightening of space for foreign NGOs to operate in China,[48] many of the rights-based international NGOs have relocated to Hong Kong, bringing security concerns and their minders in the security services with them. Falun Gong used to be perceived as a significant security concern for China, but now it has been replaced by various advocacy NGOs working closely with their partners on the ground.

The infiltration risk can be broadly seen as part of the democratic process in Hong Kong with an ambition to extend it to the rest of China. While Occupy was a movement geographically limited to Hong Kong protesting against a decision of the Central Government, it is also a student movement that showed similarity with that happened in Beijing in 1989. For the Central Government, Occupy was not merely a local movement that could be effectively quarantined in Hong Kong. Protest proves to be contagious and Occupy could potentially be spread across the

[47] See eg J Siu, 'Mong Kok riot: youngest of 10 defendants given heaviest sentence for "wanton use of violence that took advantage of tolerant police"' *South China Morning Post*, 1 June 2018, available at www.scmp.com/news/hong-kong/hong-kong-law-and-crime/article/2148726/mong-kok-riot-youngest-10-defendants-given.

[48] T Kellogg, 'The Foreign NGO Law and the Closing of China' in W Chen and H Fu (eds), *Authoritarian Legality in Asia: Formation, Development and Transition* (Cambridge, Cambridge University Press, 2020, forthcoming).

border. Indeed, the meaning of occupying Central itself is highly ambiguous and contentious as it can be read (in Chinese) as occupying China as well. The Central Government is eager to have it suppressed at the earliest possible stage, to have its organisers punished, and black-hands exposed.

In comparison with the cases to disqualify lawmakers, the judiciary in general and the Court of Final Appeal in particular has shown its independence and defiance and its willingness in embracing liberal values as it has done in human rights cases in the past, following precedents in the common law world and showing a strong willingness to see the similarities between Occupy and civil disobedience in liberal democracies.[49] The Central Government has been adamant in insisting on severe punishment for the organisers and Occupy leaders. Having ordered occupiers to leave the streets, effectively ending Occupy through a series of court injunctions and beefed-up bailiffs, the court, in comparison with courts in Taiwan, for example, also showed a conservative tendency in criminalising civil disobedience leaders and containing social activism through the law.[50] However, when it comes to sentencing students who organised unlawful assembly in peaceful ways, the Court of Final Appeal in stark contrast to its ruling in disqualification cases in which the courts insisted on Hong Kong's unique constitutional structure, demonstrated a more liberal legal propensity and considered the entire Occupy Central movement in the large context of the larger common law tradition in balancing rights and duties.[51] As long as the protest is non-violent, protesters and their organisers deserve sympathy and lenience. In offering a corrective to the harsh narrative of the Court of Appeal, the highest court, signalled to the larger

[49] *Secretary for Justice v Wong Chi Fung* (2018) 21 HKCFAR 35 (CFA).

[50] *Kwoon Chung Motors Co Ltd v Kwok Cheuk Kin & Ors* [2014] HKCU 2750 (CFI); *Lai Hoi Ping & Anor v Persons Occupying Portions Of Nathan Road Near To And Between Argyle Street And Dundas Street To Prevent Or Obstruct Normal Vehicular Traffic From Passing And Repassing The Occupied Areas & Ors* [2014] HKCU 2726 (CA); *Lai Hoi Ping & Anor, Chiu Luen Public Light Bus Co Ltd v Persons Unlawfully Occupying Or Remaining On The Public Highway Namely, The Westbound Carriageway Of Argyle Street Between The Junction Of Tung Choi Street And Portland Street And/Or Other Persons Hindering Or Preventing The Passing Or Repassing Of Argyle Street & Ors* [2014] HKCU 2638 (CA); *Chiu Luen Public Light Bus Co Ltd v Persons Unlawfully Occupying Or Remaining On The Public Highway Namely, The Westbound Carriageway Of Argyle Street Between The Junction Of Tung Choi Street And Portland Street And/Or Other Persons Hindering Or Preventing The Passing Or Repassing Of Argyle Street & Ors* [2014] HKCU 2569 (CFI); *Chiu Luen Public Light Bus Co Ltd v Persons Unlawfully Occupying Or Remaining On The Public Highway Namely, The Westbound Carriageway Of Argyle Street Between The Junction Of Tung Choi Street And Portland Street And/Or Other Persons Hindering Or Preventing The Passing Or Repassing Of Argyle Street* [2014] HKCU 2435 (CFI); *Goldon Investment Ltd v Persons Who Erected Or Placed Or Maintained Obstructions Or Otherwise Do Any Act To Cause Obstruction, Or To Prevent Or Hinder The Clear-Ance And Removal Of The Obstructions At The Entrances Or Exits Of Citic Tower, 1 Tim Mei Avenue, Central, Hong Kong ('Citic Tower'), And/Or The Vehicular/Pedestrian Pas-Sageway At Tim Mei Avenue And/Or Lung Wui Road Which Block Vehicular Or Pedestrian Access To Citic Tower* [2014] HKCU 2436 (CFI). For a critical analysis, see CH Ho, 'To Punish or Not to Punish: The Question of Civil Disobedience and the Umbrella Movement'; H Fu, 'Political Protest in High-income Societies: The Case of the Occupy Central Movement in Hong Kong' in BC Jones (ed), *Law and Politics of the Taiwan Sunflower and Hong Kong Umbrella Movements* (London, Routledge, 2017).

[51] *Secretary for Justice v Wong Chi Fung* (2018).

society and the Central Government that in Hong Kong, secessionists, due to their nationalist sensitivity, are the perceived 'enemies' of the Party state, who should be treated summarily and harshly, that those young activists in their wayward pursuit for democracy are at worst adversaries of the mainland system. In other words, secessionism is tantamount to political heresy and the anti-thesis of the entire 'one country, two systems' enterprise, whereas democracy is a morally and constitutionally legitimate cause to fight for.

V. Conclusion

The Central Authorities have repeatedly sounded the alarm that Hong Kong is posing a national security risk to the PRC, fearing that Hong Kong may become a 'subversive base' against the mainland political system. It has demanded Hong Kong fulfil a 'constitutional duty' to enact an Article 23 legislation. The fear breeds distrust and has, in part at least, driven the Central Authorities to take decisive measures to constrain Hong Kong's democratic impulse and pace, which in turn invited an unprecedented pushback from Hong Kong. Advocacy for Hong Kong's independence emerges, grows, and sustains in that particular context. Panicked and angered by a sudden secessionist surge, the Central Authorities were ready to mobilise all political and legal power to bring the secessionist advocacy to the effective end. With enemies at the gate what should Hong Kong do?

Hong Kong has met the Central Authorities' demands half way. The court has disqualified members of LegCo for their secessionist speeches; it has convicted those who have taken part in Mong Kok unrest and imposed lengthy prison sentences. The court, the Government and the voters in general have come to a gradual realisation that independence advocacy, because of the protest of the Central Authorities, has no place in Hong Kong. However, advocacy for Hong Kong's democratisation through civil disobedience is an entirely different matter. Hong Kong's rule of law embedded in liberal values can still hold the line against the intrusion from Beijing as long as the protest is conducted in a peaceful manner.

Would Beijing be satisfied with Hong Kong's report card? The Central Authorities seem to accept the action taken by Hong Kong Government, the decisions made by the courts and the electoral impact of the action and decisions in the disqualification cases; but seem to remain frustrated with perceived judicial lenience on the organisers of Occupy. Those risk factors associated with Hong Kong's pursuit of democracy and its likely impact on the mainland may in the eyes of Chinese security forces endanger China's state security. The Chinese security apparatus may not be restrained simply because of some legal restrictions. Their argument is a substantive one: if a national security risk exists in Hong Kong, then Hong Kong has a constitutional duty to eliminate the risk or otherwise manage it. If the Hong Kong Government has no will or capacity to address these national security concerns, the mainland will take over the matter and exert direct, hands-on control in Hong Kong. Their options remain wide open: cross-border law enforcement in violation of the Basic Law as occurred in the case of the booksellers remains on the table as an extra-legal, hard power solution;[52] China could mobilise its blunt power to impose a national security law on Hong Kong; and, in the worst case scenario, China may apply its own criminal law in Hong Kong extraterritorially on the grounds of the criminal impact of acts on Hong Kong in the mainland. Which option Hong Kong may have to face depends on how effective Hong Kong is in its dialogue with autocrats in Beijing.

[52] The Hong Kong Government has recently proposed a legislative amendment to enable Hong Kong to surrender fugitive offenders to mainland China on a case-by-case basis. For a critique of the proposed amendment, see Hong Kong Bar Association, 'Observations of the Hong Kong Bar Association ("HKBA") on the Security Bureau's Proposal to Amend the Mutual Legal Assistance in Criminal Matters Ordinance ("MLAO"), Cap 525 and the Fugitive Offenders Ordinance ("FOO"), Cap 503' (4 March 2019), available at www.hkba.org/sites/default/files/Security%20Bureau%27s%20%20Proposal%20to%20Amend%20the%20Mutual%20Legal%20Assistance%20in%20Criminal%20Matters.Fugistive.FOO%20and%20MLA%20%28Final%29%28website%29.pdf. See also the contribution of Carole Petersen, and Cora Chan and Fiona de Londras in this collection.

4

Belief in the Rule of Law and its Resilience in the Hong Kong Political Identity

WAI-MAN LAM

I. Introduction

This chapter reconstructs the popular understanding of the rule of law in Hong Kong, its resilience and related cultural concepts. It argues that the understanding of the rule of law has been disputed since colonial times, and has become even more contested in Hong Kong in recent years. The controversies surrounding the idea of the rule of law signify that the idea has been both an ideological resource and a hindrance for pro-democracy mobilisation.

Theoretically, this article argues that the idea of the rule of law is related to a basket of concepts rather than a standalone concept as it will be further explained below. This means that the reconstruction of its meanings for the people in Hong Kong and analysis of its resilience in the local culture needs to be conducted with reference to related cultural values. Using the level approach to the rule of law,[1] this chapter investigates the Hong Kong population's understanding of the purposes of law and good government as well as their view on the importance of protecting fundamental rights and democracy. Methodologically, this article analyses primary data of the Asian Barometer Surveys[2] and past survey data published by other scholars to investigate into the popular belief in the rule of law in Hong Kong.

[1] BYT Tai, 'Civil Disobedience and the Rule of Law' in MHK Ng and JD Wong (eds), *Civil Unrest and Governance in Hong Kong: Law and Order from Historical and Cultural Perspectives* (London, Routledge, 2017).

[2] The author thanks the General Research Fund (Ref: 746812 and 14614815) of the Research Grant Council of Hong Kong for the funding support of these projects.

II. The Rule of Law

The idea of the rule of law is not without controversy. The formal notion addresses the principles and manner by which the law is administered, such as 'generality; publicity; prospectivity; intelligibility; consistency; practicability; stability; and congruence'.[3] In other words, it concerns the features that any effective legal system must possess. The substantive notion takes the idea further, suggesting that it is more than the principles and procedures of the administration of the law. Instead, the scope of the rule of law should embrace the protection of individual rights (ie procedural rights, civil and political rights, and social and economic rights), justice and democracy.[4]

Despite the complexity of the principle of the rule of law, attempts have been made to combine both the formal and substantive notions and to measure the rule of law. The World Justice Project's Rule of Law Index and the United Nation's articulation of the principle are good examples. As stated by the United Nations' Secretary-General:

> [The rule of law] refers to a principle of governance in which all persons, institutions and entities, public and private, including the State itself, are accountable to laws that are publicly promulgated, equally enforced and independently adjudicated, and which are consistent with international human rights norms and standards. It requires, as well, measures to ensure adherence to the principles of supremacy of law, equality before the law, accountability to the law, fairness in the application of the law, separation of powers, participation in decision-making, legal certainty, avoidance of arbitrariness and procedural and legal transparency.[5]

Despite different interpretations of the rule of law, the 'level approach' that integrates the formal and substantive notions suggested by Benny Tai,[6] one of the initiators of the Occupy Central campaign, is relevant to the analysis here. Tai's ideas about the rule of law, social justice and civil disobedience had obviously motivated and constituted the Occupy Central campaign and the Umbrella Movement. As suggested by him, four levels of the concept can be distinguished from each other. The first level is the existence of the law, which means that major areas of activities in society are covered by laws. The second level means that government officials and citizens are bound by law and abide by the law, implying that there must be an effective mechanism to ensure the rule of law. The third level is limitation from law, which means that governmental powers are subject to legal limitation. The fourth level is justice attained through law in which fundamental

[3] J Waldron, 'The Rule of Law' in EN Zalta (ed), *The Stanford Encyclopedia of Philosophy*, Fall edn, (2016), available at plato.stanford.edu/archives/fall2016/entries/rule-of-law; L Fuller, *The Morality of Law* (New Haven, Yale University Press, 1964).

[4] PP Craig, 'Formal and Substantive Conceptions of the Rule of Law: An Analytical Framework' [1997] *Public Law* 467; Tai, 'Civil Disobedience' (2017); Waldron, 'The Rule of Law' (ibid).

[5] United Nations Secretary-General, *Report of the Secretary-General on the Rule of Law and Transitional Justice in Conflict and Post-conflict Societies* (S/2004/616, 2004) [6].

[6] Tai (n 1).

rights, such as procedural rights, civil rights, political rights, and social and economic rights, are protected. Citing Brian Tamanaha,[7] Tai has further argued that the rule of law includes a belief in legality, a law-compliant attitude, some critical attitudes, and a rights consciousness.

Under this multi-level approach, belief in the rule of law is related to a basket of ideas about law and government. Specifically these include, firstly, the presumed purposes of the law; secondly, the conceptions of good government, in other words, a government limited in power, law-abiding, just, and protecting fundamental rights and democracy; and thirdly, views on the importance of protecting freedom, rights and justice. As such, explaining the resilience of popular belief in the rule of law in Hong Kong requires an examination of popular attitudes towards all these related ideas, and if possible, these attitudes in their historical trajectories because beliefs are the products of time. In what follows, the popular belief in the rule of law in Hong Kong will be investigated based on, firstly, a reconstruction of related and available secondary data and, secondly, analysis of primary data from the Asian Barometer Survey Wave III and Wave IV (ABS3 and ABS4).

III. Political Identity, Political Values and Social Movements in Hong Kong

It is a common observation that social and political reforms started in Hong Kong after the 1966 Star Ferry riots and the 1967 riots when the colonial Government took steps to cultivate a better relationship between the Government and the people, and the popular belief took hold that Hong Kong was home, rather than a transitional place, for the Chinese in Hong Kong.[8] Various measures were taken by the colonial Government. Notably, the City District Officer scheme in 1968 introduced a three-tier participatory structure in every local district. The three-tier structure included a City District Committee that helped coordinate district affairs, an area committee with an appointed membership functioning to co-opt community leaders, and mutual aid committees formed voluntarily by residents of a building.[9] In view of the growing population and demands for social services, the colonial Government had also embarked on various campaigns and social services and welfare programmes to improve people's livelihoods since the 1970s.[10]

[7] B Tamanaha, *On the Rule of Law: History, Politics, Theory* (Cambridge, Cambridge University Press, 2004).

[8] See, eg, WM Lam, *Understanding the Political Culture of Hong Kong: The Paradox of Activism and Depoliticization* (New York, ME Sharpe, 2004).

[9] See, eg, EWY Lee, 'Civil Society Organizations and Local Governance in Hong Kong' in SWK Chiu and SL Wong (eds), *Repositioning the Hong Kong Government: Social Foundations and Political Challenges* (Hong Kong, Hong Kong University Press, 2012).

[10] See, eg, TL Lui and SWK Chiu, 'Introduction – Changing Political Opportunities and the Shaping of Collective Action: Social Movements in Hong Kong' in SWK Chiu and TL Lui (eds), *The Dynamics of Social Movements in Hong Kong* (Hong Kong, Hong Kong University Press, 2000) 5–7.

The local Hong Kong identity originated in the 1970s after the two above-mentioned riots in the 1960s. Since the 1970s, the basic identity of the Hong Kong Chinese was found to have undergone obvious changes. Previous surveys[11] found that the most popular choice of identity of the respondents was Hongkongese, but Chinese was also important.[12] Meanwhile, the political values of the people had also gradually evolved from political passivity, individualism and familism in the 1970s and 1980s to broad endorsement of universal values, such as freedom, rights, democracy and the rule of law, as their core values.[13]

Hong Kong saw the flourishing of various social and political movements with instrumental concerns and universal values during the colonial period. Notable examples included nationalist movements like the campaign for adopting Chinese as an official language and the 'defend Diaoyutai' movement, the student movement, the independent union movement, the public sector movement, and the democracy movement as the question about Hong Kong's political future grew heated.[14] These social movements aimed to fight for a better livelihood for the people, as well as improved protection of their civil, social and political rights.

Since 1997, the political system of the Hong Kong Special Administrative Region (HKSAR) has inherited the 'success formula' of colonial Hong Kong, which includes a semi-authoritarian government led by a Chief Executive elected by an election committee of only 1,200 members, and a weak legislature with only half of its legislators returned by direct elections on universal suffrage. The independence of the judiciary has been largely preserved, although the Court of Final Appeal has faced serious challenges to its final power of adjudication in the five times in which the Basic Law was reinterpreted by the Standing Committee of the Chinese National People's Congress. Moreover, both the neutrality of the judges and judicial independence have been tested by the official and unofficial claims that the judges in the HKSAR should 'love country' and 'love Hong Kong', which means that they should be patriotic.[15]

The HKSAR Government has made much effort to cultivate patriotism in the local populace, such as the use of *Putonghua* as the teaching language in primary schools and the attempted implementation of a national education curriculum. Alongside these measures, the Chinese authorities have implemented

[11] See, eg, SK Lau and HC Kuan, *The Ethos of the Hong Kong Chinese* (Hong Kong, The Chinese University Press, 1988) 2.

[12] G Mathews, EKW Ma and TL Lui, *Hong Kong, China: Learning to Belong to a Nation* (London, Routledge, 2007) 97, table 1.

[13] SK Lau, *Society and Politics in Hong Kong* (Hong Kong, Chinese University Press, 1982); Lau and Kuan, *The Ethos* (1988).

[14] Lui and Chiu, 'Introduction' (2000).

[15] Information Office of the State Council, People's Republic of China, 'The Practice of the "One Country, Two Systems" Policy in the Hong Kong Special Administrative Region' (2014), available at www.fmcoprc.gov.hk/eng/xwdt/gsxw/t1164057.htm. See also the contributions of Albert HY Chen and PY Lo in this collection.

various economic and political measures to ensure Hong Kong is better integrated into its motherland, such as the Closer Economic Partnership Arrangement, joint infrastructural projects between Hong Kong and other Chinese provinces, joint economic projects (eg the Agreement on Deepening Guangdong–Hong Kong–Macao Co-operation in the Development of the Bay Area), political co-optation and other united front works.

Despite these efforts, the HKSAR has witnessed the emergence of waves of social movements one after another since 1997. Besides the half-a-million people who protested against the national security bill in 2003, these have included the series of campaigns for preserving cultural heritages, the protest against the construction of the express rail connecting Hong Kong and China, the anti-national education curriculum campaign, the rising pro-independence sentiments and groups, the Occupy Central campaign and the Umbrella Movement, and the Mong Kok riots in 2016.[16]

The incomplete decolonisation of Hong Kong by the British and the 'mainlandisation' or recolonisation in the HKSAR in the view of some, have constituted a hybridised political identity featuring a mixture of political values.[17] Regarding the people's ethnic identity, polls have also found that their most popular choice of self-identification has been a dual Hongkongese and Chinese identity, except in the years between the political handover and the Umbrella Movement. The proportion of people who regarded themselves as Hongkongese had risen over the years, while the proportions of those who identified as only Chinese had also increased but with obvious fluctuations.[18] Recent data shows that the strength of the Hong Kong people's identification as Asians and as global citizens had reached 7.85 and 6.88 out of 10 respectively by June 2017.[19] The cosmopolitan elements of the Hong Kong identity further demonstrate its hybridity and the importance of universal values in constituting the Hong Kong population's identity, such as democracy, freedom and civil liberties, and the connection with the global world.[20]

[16] See the contribution of Michael C Davis in this collection.

[17] WM Lam, 'Political Legitimacy in Hong Kong: A Hybrid Notion' in J Chan, DC Shin and M Williams (eds), *East Asian Perspectives on Political Legitimacy: Bridging the Empirical-Normative Divide* (Cambridge, Cambridge University Press, 2016).

[18] J Downes, 'Mainland Chinese immigration in Hong Kong: Analysing anti-immigrant sentiment' in WM Lam and L Cooper (eds), *Citizenship, Identity and Social Movements in the New Hong Kong: Localism after the Umbrella Movement* (London, Routledge, 2017); N Ma, 'Changing Identity Politics: The Democracy Movement in Hong Kong' in WM Lam and L Cooper (eds), *Citizenship, Identity and Social Movements in the New Hong Kong: Localism after the Umbrella Movement* (London, Routledge, 2018); WM Lam and L Cooper (eds), *Citizenship, Identity and Social Movements in the New Hong Kong: Localism after the Umbrella Movement* (London, Routledge, 2018).

[19] Public Opinion Programme, The University of Hong Kong, 'Ethnic Identity' (2017), available at hkupop.hku.hk/chinese/popexpress/ethnic/overall/halfyr/datatables.html.

[20] See, eg, WM Lam and HC Kuan, 'Democratic Transition Frustrated: The Case of Hong Kong' in YH Chu (eds), *How East Asians View Democracy* (New York, Columbia University Press, 2008).

IV. Understandings of Law and Government in the Colonial Hong Kong

To what extent had the principle of rule of law been part of the Hong Kong identity in colonial Hong Kong? Based on past survey data, mainly from the Indicators of Social Development researches conducted by Siu-kai Lau and Hsin-chi Kuan, this section reconstructs the purposes of law as perceived by the people during colonialism, their concepts of good government and perceived importance of fundamental rights and democracy.

A. The Purposes of Law and Unjust Laws

Despite limited available data, it is obvious that popular understandings of the purposes of law in colonial Hong Kong were incoherent. For instance, in a survey conducted in 1985, 68.1 per cent of the respondents stated that the goal of law was to protect citizens' right to choose any moral criteria, whereas 17.2 per cent of them considered that the goal of law was to compel citizens to abide by society's criteria of right and wrong.[21] While the former signifies the view that law should protect and advance people's fundamental rights and attain justice, which is the highest level of understanding of the rule of law, the latter reflects a view of the law as an instrument to legally bind citizens, which is the second level of understanding of the rule of law.

Although the above findings seem to indicate the Hong Kong people's inclination to endorse a more advanced notion of the purposes of the law, there were significant internal contradictions. For instance, the above-cited 1988 survey also found that 41 per cent of the respondents chose law as the most important factor in maintaining social stability, whereas 15.8 per cent of them chose '*li*' (rituals) and 32.3 per cent of them chose 'the political system'.[22] Moreover, in another survey conducted in 1995, 37.5 per cent of the respondents considered that the purpose of law was to protect the rights of citizens to choose any moral standards, whereas 38.5 per cent thought it functioned to maintain what the majority in society regarded as right or wrong.[23] It appears that the understandings of the purposes of law had become more contentious since the 1990s.

If a law is unjust and infringes people's rights, would people still obey it? The findings from a survey conducted in 1986 again echoed the inner contradiction found above. Altogether, 47.4 per cent of respondents considered that even if a law was wrong, they should still obey it, whereas 19 per cent of them stated that

[21] Lau and Kuan (n 11) 47.

[22] Lau and Kuan (n 11) 135.

[23] SK Lau, MK Lee, PS Wan and SL Wong (eds), *Indicators of Social Development* (Hong Kong, The Chinese University Press, 1997) 173.

they should pretend to conform to it but break it in practice, and 20.6 per cent chose disobedience.[24]

B. Good Government

The level concept of the rule of law states that a good government is a government whose power is regulated. Nevertheless, in a survey conducted in 1986, 45.9 per cent of the respondents stated that they would do something if the Government proposed an unfair or harmful bill, and 46.6 per cent of them would not.[25] Similar divisions were also found in the people's perceptions of the relationship between government and people. For instance, in a 1985 survey, only 53 per cent of the respondents considered it a healthy phenomenon that more people were courageous enough to confront the Government in protests.[26] A survey conducted in 1992 nevertheless found that 88.3 per cent of the respondents agreed that a good government would not abuse its power.[27]

The highest level of the rule of law entails the belief that a good government is fair and pays attention to questions of social justice. With regard to the people's view of economic justice, in a 1985 survey, 55.3 per cent of the respondents regarded a good society as one without much difference in income, whereas 39.9 per cent of them disagreed.[28] In a 1992 survey, 65.9 per cent of the respondents agreed that a good government would not allow the rich to be too rich and the poorer to be too poor.[29]

Concerning social fairness, in a 1992 survey, 88.8 per cent of the respondents agreed that a good government should regard the public interest as most important and prevents other interests from harming the public interest. The same survey also found that 87.5 per cent of the respondents agreed that a good government treated everyone in the same way.[30]

Logically, if people endorse the importance of rights and democracy more, they also tend to agree with a more advanced level of the concept of the rule of law and like to have a government that serves these purposes. Regarding the value of freedom, in a 1985 survey, 96 per cent of the respondents agreed that everyone should have freedom of speech. Nevertheless, in the same survey, 52.9 per cent of respondents rejected the notion that government should force

[24] Lau and Kuan (n 11) 139.

[25] HC Kuan and SK Lau, 'The Civic Self in a Changing Polity in Hong Kong: The Case of Hong Kong' in K Cheek-Milby and M Mushkat (eds), *Hong Kong: The Challenge of Transformation* (Hong Kong, Centre of Asian Studies, University of Hong Kong, 1989) 109–10.

[26] Lau and Kuan (n 11) 102.

[27] SK Lau and HC Kuan, 'Public Attitudes Toward Political Authorities and Colonial Legitimacy in Hong Kong' (1995) 33 *The Journal of Commonwealth and Comparative Politics* 88.

[28] Lau and Kuan (n 11) 58.

[29] Lau and Kuan, 'Public Attitudes' (1995) 88.

[30] Lau and Kuan (n 27) 88.

people to do something against their wishes for the common interest, but 34.8 per cent agreed sometimes. More contradictorily, 62.7 per cent of the respondents agreed that government should prohibit assemblies of people who advocated something which the people were against.[31]

C. Legality or Legitimacy?

Indeed, although the concept of the rule of law and other universal values had motivated numerous social movements in Hong Kong during the colonial period, it was not uncommon to find the controversies on the purposes of law and law-abidingness running in the background of or in parallel with political mobilisations. Notable examples included the campaign for Chinese to be an official language, the movement to defend Diaoyu Island, and the Godber issue,[32] in which young activists were important participants. As protests were utterly illegal at that time, the colonial Government often resorted to arresting and charging people with illegal assembly and protest using certain repressive colonial laws and regulations, such as the Public Order Ordinance. These government actions had motivated some young activists to question why these laws deserved obedience, and to conclude that no law should command obedience simply by virtue of its status as law. They even deliberately challenged these laws by breaking them.[33]

However, not everyone agreed with the political position of the young activists. This explains why several student bodies withdrew from participating in the illegal 7 July 1971 and 13 May 1972 demonstrations in the movement to defend the Diaoyu Islands. Along with these withdrawals, the Law Students' Society also condemned the illegal 13 May demonstration, highlighting a popular view that laws, whether just or unjust, should command obedience. Among the general public, it was not uncommon to find criticisms of the young people's illegal actions. Quite often, the activists were criticised as disruptive and compared to Red Guards, followed by a claim that people in Hong Kong just wanted stability and prosperity.[34]

The above reconstruction of past survey data and analysis of relevant historical incidents thus reflect the divided understandings of the rule of law in colonial Hong Kong. There were conflicts between the different notions of the rule of law, which also signified the divided views of the roles of government and the importance of related political identities and values. Such conflicts and divisions have persisted in the HKSAR.

[31] Lau and Kuan (n 11) 47–48, 51.

[32] Peter Fitzroy Godber was a Chief Superintendent of the Royal Hong Kong Police Force. He escaped to Britain because of a bribery scandal, which led to a public outcry. Godber was extradited to Hong Kong in 1975 and convicted of corruption. The issue resulted in the establishment of the Independent Commission Against Corruption.

[33] Lam, *Understanding the Political Culture* (2004) 206–08.

[34] ibid 208.

V. Belief in the Rule of Law, the Umbrella Movement and the Mong Kok Riots

As considered above, belief in the rule of law has been important in constituting recent political episodes, notably the Umbrella Movement. Guided by the highest notion of the rule of law, the protestors believed that civil disobedience, although illegal, was a justified and useful means to advance the political rights of the Hong Kong people. The principle of the rule of law thus served as both their political ethic and ideal. For example, when the High Court extended the interim injunction against illegal and occupying areas in Mong Kok and Admiralty, its verdict stated that the rule of law demanded that both the public and the government abide by law.[35] In its press release on the verdict, the Hong Kong Federation of Students, a key initiator of the Umbrella Movement, stated that the occupiers would accept ultimate criminal liability, which was a manifestation of the spirit of the rule of law.[36]

As examined above, the understanding of the notion of the rule of law has been contested throughout Hong Kong's post-World War II history. Such contestations were also found during the movement. While the Umbrella Movement protestors upheld the highest notion of the rule of law, government officials and some pro-government sections have been relying on the Chinese Government's idea of 'law-based governance', which is a core part of Xi Jinping's governing philosophy, to counteract the influence of the discourse of the protestors. For example, on 27 September 2014, press releases of pro-government political parties such as the Democratic Alliance for the Betterment and Progress of Hong Kong, and Business and Professional Alliance in Hong Kong, all stated that the rule of law was the core value of Hong Kong and vowed support to the police to restore public order.[37] Moreover, the Alliance for Peace and Democracy, a pro-government coalition, chose to lead its signature campaign conducted from October to November 2014 with 'return the road to the people, restore order, and safeguard the rule of law' (還路於民、恢復秩序、維護法治), which reflects its attempt to highlight the importance of maintaining law and order in a different sense.

Contrary to the Government and the pro-Government camp, the more radical faction of the Umbrella Movement protestors took the movement's embedded value of the rule of law in another direction. They condemned the Hong Kong Federation of Students and Scholarism, the key initiators of the movement, as too mild. They further argued that protestors should not merely passively disobey unjust law. Instead they should learn how to defend themselves and engage in disobedience, for example, when being attacked by the police. This belief helps

[35] HKSAR Government, *Report on the Recent Community and Political Situation in Hong Kong* (2015) [2.27], [102].

[36] ibid [2.28], [102].

[37] ibid [44].

explain the subsequent emergence of divisions among the young protestors on numerous subjects, which significantly included movement tactics, such as whether protests should be *wo-lei-fei-fei* (peaceful, rational, non-violent and expletive-free resistance) or *yung mo* (confrontational), and the function of social movements in Hong Kong, that is, whether they should perform more rearguard or vanguard functions.[38]

So, while it is obvious that the Government and the pro-Government camp had used a lower version of the idea of the rule of law, which is rule by law or legality, to defend their position, the radical wing had also employed the language of the rule of law. The latter's language, nevertheless, went beyond the discourse of the rule of law and challenged the assumptions of civil disobedience. They asked, 'if we are justified in challenging unjust laws by disobeying them, then why must we challenge these laws civilly'?

How did the general public in Hong Kong echo the views of the protestors analysed above? Have the divisions on the understandings of the rule of law pervaded the psyche of the local political culture? Such questions are important in examining the resilience of the belief of the rule of law in Hong Kong's political culture and identity.

VI. Understandings of the Rule of Law and the Role of Government in the HKSAR

A. Methodology

Analysing selected survey questions and using the primary data of the questions of the Asian Barometer Survey Wave IV (ABS4) conducted in Hong Kong in 2016,[39] this section explores people's understandings of the rule of law and related cultural beliefs. As stated above, one's belief in the rule of law is related to his or her conceptions of good government and presumed purposes of the law. A dependent variable 'rule of law' comprising the following four statements from the survey was created. Tables 4.1 and 4.2 (Appendix) show the results of the factor analysis and the correlation analysis of the statements. Note that these four statements do not directly ask about the respondents' understandings of the purposes of law (unlike the earlier surveys analysed above). Rather, statements (1) and (2) tap the

[38] E Cheng, 'Street Politics in a Hybrid Regime: The Diffusion of Political Activism in Post-colonial Hong Kong' (2016) 226 *The China Quarterly* 383.

[39] The four waves of Asian Barometer surveys in Hong Kong were conducted in 2001, late 2007, late 2012, and early 2016 respectively.

respondents' acceptance of the extent of government power over society, which reflects their conceptions of good government, whereas statements (3) and (4) ask about their views of the role of judges and the law in relation to the executive, which in turn indicate their views of judicial independence and respect for the judicial system. It is assumed that the lower the support for these statements, the greater the belief in the rule of law.

(1) 'Government leaders are like the head of a family, we should all follow their decisions.'
(2) 'The Government should decide whether certain ideas should be allowed to be discussed in society.'
(3) 'When judges decide important cases, they should accept the views of the executive branch.'
(4) 'When the country is facing a difficult situation, it is ok for the Government to disregard the law in order to deal with the situation.'

Table 4.3 below shows the mean score of each of the statements of rule of law, which run from 1 to 4 with 1 indicating 'strongly agree', 2 'somewhat agree', 3 'somewhat disagree', and 4 'strongly disagree'. The respondents' mean scores for all the statements are generally high, ranging from 2.77 to 2.9 on a four-point scale.

Table 4.3 Mean scores of the statements

Statements	Mean scores
Government leaders are like the head of a family; we should all follow their decisions	2.90
The Government should decide whether certain ideas should be allowed to be discussed in society	2.85
When judges decide important cases, they should accept the view of the executive branch	2.80
When the country is facing a difficult situation, it is ok for the Government to disregard the law in order to deal with the situation	2.77

Note:
N=1188
A four-point scale: 1=strongly agree, 2=somewhat agree, 3=somewhat disagree, and 4=strongly disagree.

What are the possible factors that influence people's support for the rule of law? As argued above, the resilience of the popular belief in the rule of law is related to popular perceptions of the roles of the Government, what is good governance and some political values. In order to explore the reasons that possibly contribute to the relatively high support for rule of law and examine its resilience in Hong Kong's culture, the impacts of five sets of independent variables on rule of law are further analysed. The independent variables consist of selected survey questions on the political values related to the support for the rule of law including the following, which are not meant to be exhaustive.[40]

(1) Socio-economic variables: age, gender, educational level, economic activity status, years of residence in Hong Kong, and perceived family social status (a 10-point scale).

    These variables are included in the following analysis assuming that people with different socio-economic backgrounds would have different views on the rule of law.

(2) Views of freedom and rights (media and organisations):

    (2a) 'The Government should have the right to prevent the media from publishing things that might be politically destabilising' versus 'The media should have the right to publish news and ideas without government control'. (To choose one.)

    (2b) 'Harmony of the community will be disrupted if people organise lots of groups.' (To indicate degree of agreement on a four-point scale: 1=strongly agree, 2=somewhat agree, 3=somewhat disagree, and 4=strongly disagree.)

    These two statements are included in the analysis below because it is assumed that people's belief in the rule of law is affected by their extent of support for the protection of press freedom and right of association against government abuse of power. They also reflect views on the importance of guarding against government abuse of power.

(3) Views of democracy (the roles of government, election, and democracy as a form of government):

    (3a) 'Government leaders do what they think is best for the people' versus 'Government leaders implement what voters want.' (To choose one.)

    (3b) 'The Government is like parent, it should decide what is good for us' versus 'Government is our employee, the people should tell government what needs to be done'. (To choose one.)

    (3c) 'Political leaders are chosen on the basis on their virtue and capability even without election' versus 'Political leaders are chosen by the people through open and competitive elections'. (To choose one.)

    (3d) 'For people like me, it does not matter whether we have a democratic or a nondemocratic regime', 'Under some circumstances, an authoritarian government can be preferable to a democratic one', or 'Democracy is always preferable to any other kind of government'. (To choose one.)

[40] An interesting attempt to analyse Hong Kong people's general views of the rule of law was made by Lee and Chiu. See MYK Lee and WKS Chiu, 'Rule of Law in the Hearts of the Public? The Scoring of Hong Kong Residents of the Judicial System' *Ming Pao*, 3 December 2018, available at news.mingpao.com/pns/%e8%a7%80%e9%bb%9e/article/20181203/s00012/1543775031208.

(3e) 'Democracy may have its problems, but it is still the best form of government' (To indicate degree of agreement on a four-point scale: 1=strongly disagree, 2=somewhat disagree, 3=somewhat agree, and 4=strongly agree.)

These five statements are included in the analysis below because it is assumed that people's belief in the rule of law is affected by their extent of support for government accountability and democracy as well as rejection of elitist rule.

(4) Views of political equality and social justice

(4a) 'People with little or no education should have as much say in politics as highly educated people' (To indicate degree of agreement on a four-point scale: 1=strongly disagree, 2=somewhat disagree, 3=somewhat agree, and 4=strongly agree.)

(4b) 'It is the responsibility of the Government to reduce the differences between people with high income and those with low incomes' (To indicate degree of agreement on a four-point scale: 1=strongly disagree, 2=somewhat disagree, 3=somewhat agree, and 4=strongly agree.)

These statements are included in the following analysis because it is assumed that people's views of political and social justice constitute their views of what is good governance including the rule of law as one of the aspects.

(5) Identification with China and Hong Kong:

(5a) How proud are you to be a citizen of China? (To indicate degree of agreement on a four-point scale: 1= very proud, 2= somewhat proud, 3= not very proud, and 4= not proud at all.)

(5b) How proud are you to be a permanent resident of Hong Kong? (To indicate degree of agreement on a four-point scale: 1= very proud, 2= somewhat proud, 3= not very proud, and 4= not proud at all.)

These two statements are included in the analysis because based on previous studies, people who have stronger identification with China tends to be less supportive of democratisation in Hong Kong, while those who identify more strongly with Hong Kong hold the opposite attitude.[41]

B. Analysis

Tables 4.4 and 4.5 (Appendix) show the relationship between the demographic variables and rule of law. The socio-economic variables, including age,

[41] See, eg, SS Lin, 'Analyzing the Relationship between Identity and Democratization in Taiwan and Hong Kong in the Shadow of China' (The Asian Forum: Special Forum, 2018), available at theasanforum.org/analyzing-the-relationship-between-identity-and-democratization-in-taiwan-and-hong-kong-in-the-shadow-of-china; Ma, 'Changing Identity Politics' (2018); YH Kwong, 'The Growth of "Localism" in Hong Kong: A New Path for the Democracy Movement?' (2016) 3 *China Perspectives* 63.

educational level, perceived family social status, years of residence in Hong Kong and economic activity status are found to be significantly related to rule of law. The relationship between age and rule of law as well as that between years of residence and rule of law, is negative, which means that the older the person is, or the longer the years of his or her residence in Hong Kong (equating to being older in age), the lower is the level of rule of law.

The two statements relating to freedom and rights, including 'The Government should have the right to prevent the media from publishing things that might be politically destabilising' versus 'The media should have the right to publish news and ideas without government control', and 'Harmony of the community will be disrupted if people organise lots of groups', are significantly related to rule of law (Tables 4.6 and 4.7, Appendix). This means that the stronger the people believe that the Government should have the right to prevent the media from publishing things that might be politically destabilising and that harmony of the community will be disrupted if people organise lots of groups, the lower is the level of the rule of law.

All five views of democracy are significantly related to rule of law (Tables 4.8 and 4.9, Appendix). This means that those who consider that government leaders should implement what voters want, that government is the employee of the people, that political leaders should be chosen by the people through open and competitive elections, that democracy is always preferable to any other kind of government, and that democracy is still the best form of government although it may have problems, also tended to score a higher rule of law.

With regard to the two statements of political equality and social justice, only 'People with little or no education should have as much say in politics as highly educated people' is significantly related to rule of law. The correlation sign is negative, which means that those strongly agree with the statement tend to have a lower rule of law score (Table 4.10, Appendix).

Table 4.11 (Appendix) indicates that a person's degree of pride in being a Chinese citizen and a Hong Kong permanent resident are both significantly related to rule of law. Interestingly, the correlation coefficient is positive, which means that the less a person feels proud to be a Chinese citizen or a permanent resident of Hong Kong, the higher he or she scores in Rule of Law. Also noteworthy is the high correlation coefficient between the degree of pride in being a Chinese citizen and rule of law (r=0.348).

Table 4.12 below shows the results of a hierarchical regression analysis of five models of independent variables and rule of law. Model 1 examines the relationships between socio-economic variables and rule of law. Age, gender and perceived family social status are found to be significant. Both age and gender have a negative coefficient, which means that as age increases, rule of law decreases, and males have higher rule of law than females (1=male, 2=female). The R-square is four per cent, which means that the socio-economic variables in this model can explain only four per cent variations, out of 100 per cent, in the dependent variable 'rule of law', ie a very large extent of the probable variations in rule of law are to be explained by other factors.

Model 2 analyses the views of freedom and right controlled statistically for all the socio-economic variables. Both of the new additions of views of freedom and right contribute significantly to rule of law and account for most of the variance in predicting rule of law. With the addition of the new items, the significance of age and gender is eclipsed, and only perceived family social status remains significant in the model. Nevertheless, the addition of the new items has increased the R-square of Model 2 to 27 per cent.

Model 3 adds views of democracy to the analysis with the views of freedom and right, and controlled statistically for all the socio-economic variables. Four out of the five new views of democracy have a statistically significant impact on rule of law. The higher the values of democracy, the higher is the rule of law. The newly added items have not eclipsed the impact of the previously significant items in Model 2. They together help increase the R-square of Model 3 to 39 per cent.

Model 4 adds the items of views of political equality and social justice to the model. Only one out of the two items is significant, which is 'People with little or no education should have as much say in politics as highly educated people'. The higher the level of agreement, the lower is the Rule of Law. Again, the newly added items have not eclipsed the impact of the significant items in the previous model. The R-square of Model 4 is 42 per cent.

Lastly, Model 5 analyses all the previous factors with two additional items of identification. Only the item 'How proud are you to be a citizen of China' is significant along with the previously significant factors. Interestingly, the demographic factors, including age, have all become insignificant in this model. This shows that their predictive power on rule of law is much weaker than the political values examined in the model whose predictive power is much stronger. The young people, as commonly assumed in Hong Kong, are strong believers in the highest notion of the rule of law and civil disobedience. According to this analysis, their insistence, nevertheless, is due to their commitment to the related universal values and evaluation of China, and not so much because of their age per se.

Views of freedom and rights contribute significantly to rule of law and account for most of the variance in predicting rule of law. The first item, 'The Government should have the right to prevent the media from publishing things that might be politically destabilising' versus 'The media should have the right to publish news and ideas without government control' (β=4.074), indicates that those who believe in media freedom would have a higher rule of law. It is noteworthy that the item 'Harmony of the community will be disrupted if people organise lots of groups' is the key factor of the regression analysis with the largest coefficient (β=8.836). The four items of views of democracy have statistically significant impact on rule of law (β ranged from 2.680 to 4.050), which indicates that the higher the values of views of democracy, the higher the rule of law. The view of political justice, which is 'People with little or no education should have as much say in politics as highly educated people', is statistically significant (β=–3.653), and the higher the level of agreement, the lower the rule of law. The R-square of Model 5 is 43 per cent.

Table 4.12 Summary of hierarchical regression analysis for variables predicting rule of law (RoL)

Standardised coefficients	**Dependent variable: RoL**				
Socio-economic variables	**Model 1**	**Model 2**	**Model 3**	**Model 4**	**Model 5**
Age	−2.751**	−1.33	0.05	−0.167	0.772
Gender	−2.104*	−1.882	−2.396*	−2.144*	−1.685
Educational level	0.049	0.029	−0.089	0.605	1.004
Economic activity status	0.304	0.318	−0.617	−0.775	−0.917
Years of residence	−0.793	−0.713	−1.367	−0.888	−1.249
Perceived family social status	2.761**	2.533*	1.233	0.584	0.603
Views of freedom and rights					
The Government should have the right to prevent the media from publishing things that might be politically destabilising VS The media should have the right to publish news and ideas without government control		6.655***	4.416***	4.521***	4.074***
Harmony of the community will be disrupted if people organise lots of groups		13.612***	10.192***	9.682***	8.836***
Views of democracy					
Government leaders do what they think is best for the people VS Government leaders implement what voters want			1.14	0.678	−0.135
The Government is like parent; it should decide what is good for us VS Government is our employee, the people should tell government what needs to be done			2.86**	3.066**	2.707**

(continued)

Table 4.12 ***(Continued)***

Standardised coefficients	**Dependent variable: RoL**				
	Model 1	**Model 2**	**Model 3**	**Model 4**	**Model 5**
Political leaders are chosen on the basis on their virtue and capability even without election VS Political leaders are chosen by the people through open and competitive elections			3.384***	3.269**	2.876**
For people like me, it does not matter whether we have a democratic or a nondemocratic regime OR Under some circumstances, an authoritarian government can be preferable to a democratic one OR Democracy is always preferable to any other kind of government			4.117***	3.863***	4.05***
Democracy may have its problems, but it is still the best form of government			2.725**	3.312***	2.68**
View of political equality and social justice					
People with little or no education should have as much say in politics as highly educated people				–4.09***	–3.653***
It is the responsibility of the Government to reduce the differences between people with high income and those with low incomes				0.921	1.36

(continued)

Table 4.12 *(Continued)*

Standardised coefficients	**Dependent variable: RoL**				
	Model 1	**Model 2**	**Model 3**	**Model 4**	**Model 5**
Identification with China and HK					
How proud are you to be a citizen of China?					2.681**
How proud are you to be a permanent resident of Hong Kong?					0.311
R-square	4%	27%	39%	42%	43%
*p<.05 **p<.01 ***p<.001					

VII. Discussion and Implications for the Introduction of National Security Legislation

Overall, the above regression analysis has several important results. Firstly, it shows that the support for the more advanced notion of the rule of law, although still a contested ideal, is generally high in Hong Kong. A substantial number of people support the regulation of government power, judicial independence and the independence of law. Secondly, as argued above, investigation of the resilience of the idea of the rule of law has to be undertaken with reference to the consolidation of the related values in the political culture. The above regression analysis indicates that the views of democracy, freedom and rights, political equality and social justice are all relevant factors that have an impact on Rule of Law. A stronger conviction in these values correlates with a greater possibility of the endorsement of a higher level of the rule of law principle. Thirdly, the fact that a lower degree of pride in being a citizen of China correlates with higher Rule of Law vividly signifies the contradictions between ethnic identity and the ideal of the rule of law in Hong Kong, which deserves further research.

Another interesting question to ask is: How much did the idea of the rule of law have an impact on the general public's support for the Umbrella Movement? Tables 4.13 and 4.14 below indicate that Rule of Law is significantly correlated with the respondents' support for the Umbrella Movement. The coefficient is as high as 0.324. This implies that some likely see the Umbrella Movement as a manifestation of the principle of the rule of law.

Table 4.13 Mean scores of the support for the Umbrella Movement and rule of law (RoL)

	Mean	SD	N
Do you support or oppose the Umbrella Movement?	2.45	1.29	1089
RoL	2.83	0.48	1212

Note:
A four-point scale: 1=strongly oppose, 2=somewhat oppose, 3=support first and oppose afterwards, and 4=somewhat support, and 5=strongly support.

Table 4.14 Rule of Law (RoL) and the support for the Umbrella Movement

Statements		RoL
Do you support or oppose the Umbrella Movement?	Pearson Correlation Sig (2-tailed) N	0.324** 0.000 1086

Note:
*p<.05 **p<.01 ***p<.001.
A four-point scale: 1=strongly oppose, 2=somewhat oppose, 3=support first and oppose afterwards, and 4=somewhat support, and 5=strongly support.

Table 4.15 below further shows that the mean score of rule of law has increased from 2.7 in ABS3 (2012) to 2.83 in ABS4 (2016). The frequency and percentage distributions are shown in Table 4.16 (Appendix). It is interesting that political incidents in Hong Kong that happened up until 2016 have not decreased but rather increased the general public's endorsement of a higher-level notion of the rule of law. The finding may indicate that people in Hong Kong have acquired their higher-level understanding of the rule of law through informal learning, such as their direct or indirect experience of political participation events, and that many see such events are justified.

Overall, the strength of the Rule of Law identity in Hong Kong also reveals its strength in resisting threats to the rule of law that may come with intensifying state control measures in Hong Kong. As analysed above, the rule of law belief and the views of democracy, freedom and rights, political equality and social justice are related. Therefore, the relatively high level of support for these political values may also reveal a higher level of rule of law identity. Since those who have stronger national identity embrace a lower level of rule of law, and vice versa, Beijing's attempts to reinforce national identity (through national security legislation, and so on), if successful, will lead to more people embracing a lower level of rule of law. In that sense, there is an inevitable tension between introduction of laws that reinforce national identity and maintenance of the rule of law in Hong Kong. Lastly, given the divided understandings of the rule of law in Hong Kong, the introduction of national security legislation will likely trigger a new round of political controversy. The more the people distinguish the proposed legislation from their higher ideal of the rule of law, the more likely it is that they would rise to action. Nevertheless, this would happen only on the condition that people's conviction in democracy and so on can largely sustain, and their sense of political powerlessness does not substantially grow, making them quit politics and/or Hong Kong altogether. Further research on these areas is thus highly important.

Table 4.15 Mean scores of rule of law (RoL) in ABS3 and ABS4

	RoL				
	N	**Mean**	**SD**	**T-test**	**p-value**
ABS3	1198	2.70	0.57	−6.34	0.000
ABS4	1212	2.83	0.48		

VIII. Conclusion

This chapter reconstructs the popular understanding of the rule of law in Hong Kong and investigates the resilience of the belief and its related cultural concepts. It argues that the understanding of the rule of law has been disputed since colonial times, and has become even more contested in Hong Kong in recent years. Using the level concept of the rule of law, it shows that views of democracy, freedom and rights, and justice are all relevant factors that have an impact on the belief in the rule of law. A stronger conviction in these values highlights a greater possibility of the endorsement of a higher level of the rule of law principle. Also, it found that a lower degree of pride in being a citizen of China is related to higher support for the rule of law, which signifies the contradictions between ethnic identity and the principle in Hong Kong. Lastly, political incidents in Hong Kong that happened up until 2016 have not decreased but rather increased the general public's endorsement of a higher-level notion of the rule of law, which is a very interesting area worthy of further research.

Appendix

Table 4.1 Principal component analysis of the statements

Statements	
Government leaders are like the head of a family; we should all follow their decisions	0.759
The Government should decide whether certain ideas should be allowed to be discussed in society	0.708
When judges decide important cases, they should accept the view of the executive branch	0.717
When the country is facing a difficult situation, it is ok for the Government to disregard the law in order to deal with the situation	0.664

Table 4.2 Pearson correlation of the statements

Statements		Government leaders are like the head of a family; we should all follow their decisions (1)	The Government should decide whether certain ideas should be allowed to be discussed in society (2)	When judges decide important cases, they should accept the view of the executive branch (3)	When the country is facing a difficult situation, it is ok for the Government to disregard the law in order to deal with the situation (4)
(1)	Pearson correlation Sig (2-tailed) N	1 1207	0.415*** <.001 1200	0.392*** <.001 1200	0.314*** <.001 1200
(2)	Pearson correlation Sig (2-tailed) N		1 1203	0.318*** <.001 1197	0.291*** <.001 1197
(3)	Pearson correlation Sig (2-tailed) N			1 1205	0.332*** <.001 1196
(4)	Pearson correlation Sig (2-tailed) N				1 1203

Note:
*p<.05 **p<.01 ***p<.001.
A four-point scale: 1=strongly agree, 2=somewhat agree, 3=somewhat disagree, and 4=strongly disagree.

Table 4.4 Age, educational level, years of residence in Hong Kong, perceived family social status and rule of law (RoL)

Socio-economic variables		RoL
Age	Pearson Correlation Sig (2-tailed) N	−0.191*** <0.001 1212
Educational level	Pearson Correlation Sig (2-tailed) N	0.147*** <0.001 1212

(continued)

Table 4.4 *(Continued)*

Socio-economic variables		RoL
Perceived family social status	Pearson Correlation Sig (2-tailed) N	0.112*** <0.001 1206
Years of residence in HK	Pearson Correlation Sig (2-tailed) N	–0.133*** <0.001 1152

Note:
*p<.05 **p<.01 ***p<.001.

Table 4.5 Gender, economic activity status and rule of law (RoL)

Socio-economic variables	N	SD	T-test	p-value
Gender				
Male	525	0.50	1.77	0.077
Female	687	0.47		
Economic activity status				
Economically active	572	0.48	2.96	0.003
Economically inactive	586	0.47		

Table 4.6 Views of freedom and rights and rule of law (RoL) (the media)

Statements	N	Mean	SD	T-test	p-value
The Government should have the right to prevent the media from publishing things that might be politically destabilising (versus)	263	2.61	0.46	8.37	<.001
The media should have the right to publish news and ideas without government control	728	2.90	0.50		

Table 4.7 Views of freedom and rights and Rule of Law (RoL) (organisations)

Statement		RoL
Harmony of the community will be disrupted if people organise lots of groups	Pearson correlation Sig (2-tailed) N	0.497*** <.001 1077

Note:
*p<.05 **p<.01 ***p<.001.
A four-point scale: 1=strongly agree, 2=somewhat agree, 3=somewhat disagree, and 4=strongly disagree.

Table 4.8 Views of democracy (the role of government, election and democracy as a form of government)

Statements	N	Mean	SD	T-test	p-value
3(a)					
Government leaders do what they think is best for the people (versus)	529	2.71	0.48	7.25	<.001
Government leaders implement what voters want	468	2.93	0.50		
3(b)					
The Government is like parent; it should decide what is good for us (versus)	233	2.59	0.47	7.86	<.001
Government is our employee; the people should tell government what needs to be done	672	2.89	0.50		
3(c)					
Political leaders are chosen on the basis on their virtue and capability even without election (versus)	223	2.57	0.43	9.60	<.001
Political leaders are chosen by the people through open and competitive elections	737	2.90	0.50		
3(d)					
For people like me, it does not matter whether we have a democratic or a non-democratic regime	278	2.64	0.45	41.71	<.001
Under some circumstances, an authoritarian government can be preferable to a democratic one	165	2.68	0.49		
Democracy is always preferable to any other kind of government	547	2.94	0.50		

Table 4.9 Views of democracy (democracy as a form of government) and rule of law (RoL)

Statement		RoL
Democracy may have its problems, but it is still the best form of government	Pearson correlation Sig (2-tailed) N	0.170*** <.001 962

Note:

*p<.05 **p<.01 ***p<.001.

A four-point scale: 1=strongly disagree, 2=somewhat disagree, 3=somewhat agree, and 4=strongly agree.

Table 4.10 Views of political equality and social and justice and rule of law (RoL)

Statements		RoL
People with little or no education should have as much say in politics as highly educated people	Pearson correlation Sig (2-tailed) N	−0.185*** <.001 1124
It is the responsibility of the Government to reduce the differences between people with high income and those with low incomes	Pearson correlation Sig (2-tailed) N	−0.029 0.327 1119

Note:
*p<.05 **p<.01 ***p<.001.
A four-point scale: 1=strongly disagree, 2=somewhat disagree, 3=somewhat agree, and 4=strongly agree.

Table 4.11 Identification with China and Hong Kong and rule of law (RoL)

Statements		RoL
How proud are you to be a citizen of China?	Pearson correlation Sig (2-tailed) N	0.348*** <.001 1046
How proud are you to be a permanent resident of Hong Kong?	Pearson correlation Sig (2-tailed) N	0.072* 0.017 1121

Note:
*p<.05 **p<.01 ***p<.001.
A four-point scale: 1= very proud, 2= somewhat proud, 3= not very proud, and 4= not proud at all.

Table 4.16 Frequency distribution of rule of law (RoL) in ABS3 and ABS4

		ABS3		ABS4	
		Frequency	%	**Frequency**	%
Government leaders are like the head of a family; we should all follow their decisions	Totally agree	116	9.7%	17	1.4%
	Agree	316	26.5%	265	22.0%
	Disagree	614	51.5%	745	61.7%
	Totally disagree	147	12.3%	180	14.9%
	Total	1193	100.0%	1207	100.0%
	Chi-square = 94.048; p-value <0.001				
The Government should decide whether certain ideas should be allowed to be discussed in society	Totally agree	92	7.7%	9	.7%
	Agree	362	30.4%	337	28.0%
	Disagree	593	49.7%	678	56.4%
	Totally disagree	145	12.2%	179	14.9%
	Total	1192	100.0%	1203	100.0%

(continued)

Table 4.16 ***(Continued)***

		ABS3		ABS4	
		Frequency	**%**	**Frequency**	**%**
	Chi-square = 78.306; p-value <0.001				
When judges decide important cases, they should accept the view of the executive branch	Totally agree	85	7.1%	23	1.9%
	Agree	417	35.0%	387	32.1%
	Disagree	534	44.8%	600	49.8%
	Totally disagree	156	13.1%	195	16.2%
	Total	1192	100.0%	1205	100.0%
	Chi-square = 44.817; p-value <0.001				
When the country is facing a difficult situation, it is ok for the government to disregard the law in order to deal with the situation	Totally agree	53	4.5%	41	3.4%
	Agree	292	24.5%	330	27.4%
	Disagree	665	55.9%	698	58.0%
	Totally disagree	180	15.1%	134	11.1%
	Total	1190	100.0%	1203	100.0%
	Chi-square = 11.321; p-value <0.001				

5

Rule of Law Resilience: Comparative Perspectives from Macau[1]

PAULO CARDINAL

Drawing on experience in nearby Macau – the only other Special Administrative Region (SAR) of the People's Republic of China (PRC) – this chapter considers the future of 'one country, two systems'. As conceived and presented by Deng Xiaoping,[2] that magical formula aims to accommodate diversity within unity; to allow autonomy, fundamental rights and at least some democratic elements within the 'second' system, while insisting on the unity of both under the overarching and watchful eyes of Beijing. At this time, when many see this formula as being at risk of being abandoned or at least strongly adulterated, there is for some a feeling of the second system being under siege. In this context, and bearing in mind that much can happen and often very quickly so that any predictions are probably unwise, I will use the Macau example to try, cautiously, to forecast some possible dynamics for Hong Kong as the 'second' system.

[1] The author thanks the valuable comments and suggestions made by Cora Chan and Fiona de Londras, editors of this volume. The responsibility of any eventual mistake or insufficiency remains solely with the author.

[2] 'We have solemnly promised that our policy towards Hong Kong will remain unchanged for 50 years after 1997. Why 50 years? There is a reason for that. Not only do we need to reassure the people of Hong Kong, but we also have to take into consideration the close relation between the prosperity and stability of Hong Kong and the strategy for the development of China. … As a matter of fact, 50 years is only a vivid way of putting it. Even after 50 years our policy will not change either. That is, for the first 50 years it cannot be changed, and for the second there will be no need to change it. So this is not just idle talk', from X Deng, 'We should draw on the experience of other countries (1988) in X Deng, *Selected Works of Deng Xiaoping Volume III, 1982–1992* (Beijing, Foreign Languages Press, 1994) 262. See also 'We have also stated repeatedly that apart from stationing troops there, Beijing will not assign officials to the government of the Hong Kong Special Administrative Region. This policy too will remain unchanged. … Our policies with regard to Hong Kong will remain unchanged for 50 years, and we mean this' in X Deng, *Selected Works* (ibid) 68.

I. Macau as a Comparator

In any autonomy arrangement some tensions between the centre and the periphery are to be expected, not least because the boundary delineating what lies in the autonomous entity from that which lies within the sovereign or dominant entity may blur and shift over time. However, even then there are some core elements that are supposed to remain untouched; lines that should not be crossed if the promise of autonomy is to be fulfilled. What, then, are the basic lines that characterise the model of autonomy enjoyed by Hong Kong and Macau?

Macau and Hong Kong SARs share the same basic normative ground inasmuch as both systems stem from Joint Declarations made with former colonial or occupying powers (Portugal and the United Kingdom, respectively) and from Article 31 of the Constitution of the PRC. Both are identified as SARs of the PRC and are to be organised under the 'one country, two systems' formula. The Joint Declarations and the Basic Laws that apply to both jurisdictions are essentially the same and where differences exist,[3] they are not so weighty as to disallow Macau acting as an interesting – if not indispensable – comparator for Hong Kong as regards their relationship with China. As SARs, both Hong Kong and Macau are endowed with a rather special range of powers and a collection of guarantees that are virtually unique when considered against other constitutional arrangements. This is one of their key characteristics.

The autonomy enjoyed by both Hong Kong and Macau is rooted in an international treaty deposited at the United Nations by the contracting parties.[4] Thus, autonomy is not solely a domestic issue; rather it has been internationalised.[5] As a result, the contracting parties to these treaties –China, the United Kingdom and Portugal – are enabled to issue observations on how the Joint Declaration is or is not being respected and, in so doing, are not interfering in the internal affairs of another sovereign state but rather acting under this international treaty-based arrangement with full legitimacy. Furthermore, the Joint Declaration establishes a body of solemn and solid guarantees, embodied in a list of basic policies, that are

[3] Besides some obvious ones that derive from the particular history of Macau and of Hong Kong – Portuguese versus English as official language, reference to common law, reference to the protection of the lawful traditional rights and interests of the indigenous inhabitants of the 'New Territories' versus the interests of the residents of Portuguese descent, the different currency – there are some others such as the express provision on the Macau Basic Law to the principle of non-discrimination along with the equality one, the establishment in the Macau Basic Law that the human dignity of Macau residents shall be inviolable, in Macau the majority of the Parliament members shall be elected, whereas in Hong Kong it is stated that the Legislative Council of the Hong Kong SAR shall be constituted by election.

[4] See, for the case of Macau, United Nations Treaty Series, Vol 1498, 1-25805, stating that it was registered by China and by Portugal on 22 March 1988 – UNTS Vol 1498 (1-25804) (March 1988). As for Hong Kong, see, United Nations – Treaty Series, Vol 1399, 1-23391, stating that it was registered by China and the United Kingdom of Great Britain and Northern Ireland on 12 June 1985 – UNTS Vol 1399 (1-23391) (March 1988).

[5] See also the contribution of Carole J Petersen in this collection.

to endure and underpin the guaranteed autonomy for half a century. As well as being internationalised because of their provenance in international agreements, these basic policies are also constitutionalised because they are entrenched in the Basic Laws of both Macau and Hong Kong. In Macau (as in Hong Kong), on its face the basic policies have a status similar to especially entrenched provisions in domestic constitutions as no amendment to the Basic Law is permitted that would contravene them (Article 144 of the Macau Basic Law), and the purpose of the Basic Law itself is said to be 'to ensure the implementation of the basic policies of the People's Republic of China regarding Macau' (Preamble).

If the concept of the 'second' system enjoying a high degree of autonomy is to be meaningful, it needs to go beyond a mere guarantee of some executive, legislative and judicial power remaining with the second system to protect the essence of that system itself. In Macau (like in Hong Kong) this is reflected in the guarantee that the 'lifestyle' (as it is put in the Joint Declaration), or 'way of life' (as it appears in Article 5 of the Basic Law) is to be maintained. Arising from this broader principle, one finds guarantees of the continuation of the legal system (Article 8 of the Basic Law), of the fundamental rights *acquis* (in the Joint Declaration), of the continuation of private land recognised as such before the establishment of the SAR (Article 7 of the Basic Law), and that the interests of the residents of Portuguese descent in Macau shall be protected and their customs and cultural traditions respected (Article 42 of the Basic Law). Furthermore, there are guarantees that public servants previously serving in Macau may all remain in employment, continue service and retain their seniority with pay, allowances, benefits and conditions of service no less favourable than before (Article 98 of the Basic Law), and that the Macau Pataca shall continue to circulate as legal tender in the SAR (Article 108 of the Basic Law).[6] Taken together, these guarantees that the way of life, the legal system, fundamental rights and so on are to continue crystallise into a guarantee of the continuation of the rule of law (the *Estado de Direito*) that existed prior to 'reunification'.

All of the above paraphernalia is promised and legally guaranteed under the Joint Declarations for a period of 50 years, that is, until 2047 (for Hong Kong) and 2049 (for Macau). However, in spite of the very clear similarities between the constitutional arrangements for Hong Kong and Macau, there are several important differences in how the autonomy arrangements have operated in practice for both of them so far. It is to these differences that I now turn.

[6] There are two additional unwritten guarantees for the Macau autonomy that also apply in Hong Kong, or even more to Hong Kong. One is international monitoring, either institutionalised or by the media in general, and the other is the Taiwan question. While the latter remains unresolved, it operates as a guarantee, in the sense that the success of both Macau and Hong Kong is a card to be played in the game of reunification, an important measure of China's willingness to accommodate different systems in its attempt to attract the compatriots on the other side of the Taiwan Straits. The success will have to be not only economic but also the safeguarding of extensive autonomy in areas such as the political system and fundamental rights.

II. The Two SARs: Divergences and Convergences

As I have written elsewhere,[7] Hong Kong and Macau differ in a number of crucial aspects. First, the former is much bigger than the latter, hence attracting more attention from China. Another difference pertains to the strength of civil society. That Hong Kong civil society is much stronger and more vocal in demanding democratisation may make the PRC leadership *more anxious about Hong Kong*. Third, there are differences in the style of leadership, competence of leaders, and governing culture. Macau's top leadership has been competent and efficient, but less forthcoming in advancing democracy and protecting autonomy and freedoms of its people than the leadership of Hong Kong. Hence whilst Macau should endeavour to maintain its effective leadership, it has much to learn from Hong Kong's leaders in terms of protecting rights and advancing democracy. As I have argued elsewhere, 'provided Macau continues to manage to combine the written framework for autonomy with effective leadership, it is possible it can avoid the erosion of autonomy seen in Hong Kong as a result of poor governance'.[8]

In addition to these contextual differences, there are at least some indications that the entrenchment of the autonomy principle is occurring to different degrees in the two jurisdictions. Specifically, a number of important judicial decisions in Macau have raised doubts about whether fundamental rights have been effectively protected. For example, it has become reasonably common to deny entry to Macau for a wide variety of prospective visitors, from one-year-old children[9] to academics or Hong Kong elected politicians.[10] The criteria for exclusion seems, at least to some, to be the political orientation of prospective visitors,[11] calling into question

[7] P Cardinal, 'Macau: The internationalization of an historical autonomy' (2008) 41 *Boletín Mexicano de Derecho Comparado* 637, 688–89.

[8] ibid 688–89.

[9] For post-2014 cases involving academics, journalists, politicians, and even a case of a one-year-old child, see eg CB Soares, 'Liberdade à prova' (Plataforma Macau, 2018), available at www.plataformamacau.com/wp-content/uploads/2018/03/PM-193.pdf.

[10] ibid. Consider also the case related to the pressure to not allow the entry in Macau of writers for the Rota das Letras literary festival in 2018.

[11] D de Castro Halis, '"Post-Colonial" Legal Interpretation in Macau, China: Between European and Chinese Influences' in D de Castro Halis (ed), *East Asia's Renewed Respect for the Rule of Law in the 21st Century* (Leiden, Brill, 2015): 'Macau security officials have found ways to classify incoming visitors and block the entry of some of them into the region. They include Chinese nationals both from mainland China and Hong Kong. So far, this represents no novelty with regard to the practices adopted by many countries when controlling their borders. However, media reports have talked about a "black list" of undesirables allegedly based on their political-ideological orientation or on their political activism. Also, some of the designated "undesirables" or "dangerous visitors" (in the period from 2008 to 2013) were academics, journalists, social activists, and politicians. One of these "undesirables" was the dean of a law faculty (from Hong Kong) who came to Macau to deliver an academic seminar in a law post-graduation program of the University of Macau. In brief, they were not criminals being sought by the police and had more than sufficient means to support themselves while in Macau. Most of those visitors were not coming to protest, or threaten or inflict any "serious damage to Macau's society" and they had no connection with transnational crime. These "politically motivated denials" gained a significant amount of attention and produced unpleasant consequences: they were recorded in the formal

the continued protection of freedom of expression. This is only exacerbated by allegations of pressure being placed on academics, self-censorship in the press and allegations of irregularities by the Electoral Affairs Commission, such as demanding the removal of internet content (eg the Commission forced a newspaper to withdraw an interview published online), departing from legal criteria, and trying to impose a sort of moral criteria on election candidates and even the press.[12] Indeed, far from remaining a jurisdiction in which fundamental rights are effectively protected, one might say that Macau may be becoming a sort of modern reincarnation of what was once called a 'police state'. More policemen are being recruited, more cameras are displayed in public areas, the sense of intrusion is growing, police powers are being reinforced, the press is being warned that 'well intentioned critics' only are welcome, intrusive cyber laws are being suggested, and a new emergency civil defence service with police powers including that of detention) is being introduced.[13]

In Hong Kong, a propos the warnings and critics, one also sees now the government institutions acting in a so-called paternal way towards the citizens, advising (or threatening) them about certain behaviours or opinions, in a manner that could not be said to be typical of a sensible, mature democratic system. For instance, take this 'reminder' from the Department of Justice:

> The DoJ reminds the public to respect the rule of law and judicial independence, the latter being one of the most important facets of the rule of law .... Whilst members of the public are entitled to, within the permissible legal boundaries, to express one's opinion rationally or engage in informed discussions about the court's decision and related matters, this has to be done within the limit permitted by the law and with respect for judicial independence. Personal or scandalous attacks or insulting comments on judges or acts undermining judicial independence or in contempt of court are absolutely forbidden.[14]

reports on human/fundamental rights ... As a conclusion, one may think that rather than "dangerous visitors," this is an example of how the "legal norms can be dangerously used" to restrict freedom of ideas (including academic freedom), limit criticism of government, violate freedom of the press, formally justify official actions without truly justifying anything, and govern the "insiders" by excluding "outsiders" whose political beliefs or professions do not please the officials.'

[12] For a critique, see eg 'Instrucões, A Quem Obrigas' *Hoje Macau*, 2 May 2017, available at issuu.com/hojemacau/docs/hm-2-5-17/3. See also JP Meneses, 'Imperfect Twin: Being Basic (Law) is Good' *Macau Business*, 25 April 2018, where it was stated by the author that 'I must stress that from a technical view I am truly convinced that the Committee violated a number of legislation, including Basic Law and a number of legislation, such as the Freedom of the Press and Meetings and demonstrations ones'.

[13] See, eg, Lusa, 'Governo de Macau manifesta vontade de colaborar com os "media"' *Diário de Noticias*, 28 November 2017), available at www.dn.pt/lusa/interior/governo-de-macau-manifesta-vontade-de-colaborar-com-os-media-8949458.html; 'How will Macau's New Cybersecurity Legislation Impact Freedom of Speech?' *Global Voices*, 16 January 2018, available at advox.globalvoices.org/2018/01/16/how-will-macaus-new-cybersecurity-legislation-impact-freedom-of-speech; N Moura, 'Journalist association concerned about press freedom due to changes on civil protection law' *Macau Business*, 1 August 2018, available at www.macaubusiness.com/macau-journalist-association-concerned-about-press-freedom-due-to-changes-on-civil-protection-law.

[14] For a critique, see T Hamlett, 'Thank you Dept. of Justice, but Hongkongers will decide for themselves whether the judiciary is independent' *Hong Kong Free Press*, 19 June 2018, available at www.hongkongfp.com/2018/06/19/thank-dept-justice-hongkongers-will-decide-whether-judiciary-independent.

Also, it is with worry that one detects a trend in which some laws that were enacted to protect fundamental rights[15] and guarantee freedoms (such as the laws on personal data and freedom of demonstration), seem to have been used not to protect the citizens as the spirit and the intent of the said laws demand, but rather as tools of political repression.[16]

These kinds of developments were previously unheard of in Hong Kong, or at least were far less common there than they have been in Macau. Indeed, I could say for sure that just about a decade ago one would feel somewhat abashed or embarrassed when discussing certain features of Macau judicial activity in contrast to the Hong Kong judiciary, particularly in conferences taking place in Hong Kong. The differences were so many, so immense, and in respect of so many issues, that the preferability of the Hong Kong legal and judicial system seemed clear. At the same time as having a strong legal and judicial system, Hong Kong was the site of numerous significant political demonstrations, some of which were successful; activities that were simply not in evidence in Macau. Thus, it seemed until relatively recently that these two jurisdictions, each of which had been put on a 'one country, two systems' footing, had developed in vastly different ways since their reunification with the mainland. Now, however, one wonders whether things are changing.

In recent years, Big China has become even bigger in many domains and in many ways.[17] It has also become more visible internationally and in everyday life in the SARs of Macau and Hong Kong. At the same time, Hong Kong autonomy and differentiation in human rights has declined gradually and steadily.[18] Meanwhile, on the Macau side, one could detect some positive evolution (up to a few years ago)[19] in some prominent judicial decisions (*habeas corpus* cases,[20] freedom of

[15] JP Meneses, 'Interview: "The denial of the fundamental right of appeal means disregard of the Basic Law" Being Basic (Law) is good.' *Macau Business*, 23 April 2018, available at www.macaubusiness.com/interview-denial-fundamental-right-appeal-means-disregard-basic-law-basic-law-good.

[16] And not just as limitations on fundamental rights but further, as mechanisms of harassment as well. Consider, for example, the exaggerated and inadequate use of the disobedience crime that many peaceful demonstrators are being accused of; or the multitude of orders given by the police that in several cases are plainly illegitimate; or the many instances where the IACM or the Police try to disproportionately restrict demonstrations (in these cases the role of the Macau Court of Last Instance in putting away many of those illegal restrictions must be emphasised). See, eg, I Almeida, 'Da estranheza às suspeitas de perseguição' *Jornal Tribuna de Macau*, 15 March 2018), available at jtm.com.mo/local/da-estranheza-as-suspeitas-de-perseguicao.

[17] See eg the contribution of Hualing Fu in this collection.

[18] See eg the contribution of PY Lo in this collection.

[19] For an overview of some of recent concerns, see, eg, Meneses, 'Interview' (2018); F Master, 'In Macau, Portuguese elites feel squeezed out by Chinese influence' *Reuters*, 5 October 2018, available at www.reuters.com/article/us-macau-china-law/in-macau-portuguese-elites-feel-squeezed-out-by-chinese-influence-idUSKCN1MF0OQ; Joint Report To The European Parliament And The Council, Macao Special Administrative Region: Annual Report 2018, available at https://eeas.europa.eu/sites/eeas/files/join_2019_7_f1_report_from_commission_en_v2_p1_1019784_1.pdf.

[20] Ac TUI 20 March 2007, pr 12/2007, and Ac TUI 12 February 2008, pr 3/2008. Both were cases in which Hong Kong permanent residents were detained upon arrival in Macau at the ferry terminal. The arrests related to crimes allegedly committed in Mainland China, for which Interpol 'red notes' had

demonstration[21]), or in some signs of societal maturation. Thus, it seems that one can now detect a path of convergence between Macau and Hong Kong, albeit via two different routes: erosion of autonomy on the Hong Kong side and a slight betterment (until some time ago) on the Macau side of the estuary, even to the extent that in 2014 some 20,000 people protested against a Bill that would have greatly embellished the retirement packages of top officials, and the Government ultimately withdrew the plan[22] – a scene that would not have been imaginable in Macau a decade ago.

Recent events in Hong Kong are on a rather different trajectory. While decisions of Hong Kong's courts were previously rarely criticised, suspicion of subservience to Beijing and strong criticism of some decisions (especially in politically sensitive cases) are now evident.[23] There is a growing sense that the rule of law, which was previously used to control public powers, is beginning to be used to delineate and limit private subjects' actions, including political participation and protest. Bodies that were previously relatively invisible administrative organs, such as the Electoral Commissions of both Hong Kong and Macau, now appear to be public protagonists, intervening in sometimes remarkably transparent ways to bar candidates (in Hong Kong)[24] and appear to mis-administer elections (in Macau).[25]

These interventions by both Electoral Commissions cannot be viewed mildly or seen as benign due to their enormous impact, including on the rights and freedoms guaranteed by the Basic Law and on the integrity of the electoral process itself. In recent Macau elections many things went wrong, to put it simply, and always purporting to the same direction: more restrictions on the private sphere and on the rights of citizens, along with more interventions from public entities.[26] Increasing interventionism is also emerging in Hong Kong. Persons who pose no real threat to security and order are being denied entry, and pressure is being exerted on academics and universities, including in one instance the barring of a vocal academic from a senior management role. From a Macau perspective this all seems remarkably familiar.

been issued. The TUI (Court of Final Appeal) concluded that in the absence of specific agreements for cooperation in criminal matters between Macau and Mainland China, it was not possible to simply arrest the suspects and just hand them to the Mainland authorities.

[21] See, eg, Ac TUI 3 March 2018 pr 37/2018; Ac TUI, 11 September 2017 pr 57/2017.

[22] R Carvalho, 'Macau: The rise and fall of an empire?' *South China Morning Post*, 12 November 2015), available at multimedia.scmp.com/macau; see also J Lam, 'Thousands "surround" Macau legislature to protest retirement package bill' *South China Morning Post*, 27 May 2014, available at www.scmp.com/news/hong-kong/article/1519928/hundreds-surround-macau-legislature-protest-retirement-package-bill; 'May Protests: No Longer Silent' *Macau Daily Times*, 31 December 2014, available at macaudailytimes.com.mo/event-may-protests-no-longer-silent.html.

[23] See eg the contribution of PY Lo in this collection.

[24] See, eg, A Wong, 'Hong Kong Bars Democracy Advocate From Running for Legislature' *The New York Times*, 27 January 2018, available at www.nytimes.com/2018/01/27/world/asia/hong-kong-democracy-election.html.

[25] Meneses (n 15).

[26] 'Instrucões, A Quem Obrigas' (2017); Meneses (n 15).

So too, do the more recent interventions in the legislature. In Hong Kong, six members of the Legislative Council (LegCo), all pan-democrats elected in free and fair elections, were expelled from the legislature by judicial review unprecedentedly initiated by the Chief Executive.[27] They were disqualified on the ground that they did not properly swear their allegiance to the Hong Kong Basic Law (including Article 1, which stipulates that Hong Kong shall be an inalienable part of Hong Kong) when assuming office. The disqualification proceedings not only suggest a somewhat distorted view of the separation of powers, but also shifted the balance of power in the Hong Kong legislature. As Margaret Ng affirms in her chapter, pro-government members are now in the majority in LegCo and can change the rules of procedure to make blocking or delaying government proposals more difficult, and to prevent inquiries into government behaviours.[28]

The closest to this that we have had in Macau was the Sulu Sou suspension case and sentencing[29] but in that case the sentence was such that he was not precluded from retaking his seat. Not only was this intervention less extensive in terms of the number of legislators impacted as compared to the disqualification cases in Hong Kong, but it also resulted in a less malign outcome; something that up until a few years ago most in Hong Kong would have considered unthinkable. When seen in

[27] Two Legislative Councillors were disqualified in *Chief Executive of the HKSAR v President of the Legislative Council* (unreported, HCAL 185/2016, 15 November 2016) (CFI), [2017] 1 HKLRD 460 (CA), (2017) 20 HKCFAR 390 (leave to appeal rejected by the Court of Final Appeal). A further four were disqualified in *Chief Executive of HKSAR v President of Legislative Council* [2017] 4 HKLRD 115 (CFI), *Secretary for Justice v Leung Kwok Hung* [2019] HKCA 173 (appeal by one of the four disqualified Legislative Councillors dismissed by the Court of Appeal). Regardless of the grounds for the disqualification, the rights at stake here are the fundamental rights of the elected and of those who elected them. Although most fundamental rights are not absolute, still any restriction must be approached cautiously and vetted principles such as proportionality, adequacy, necessity, or similar methodology. A restriction or even elimination of a fundamental right should not be as approached as a mere procedural issue related to a normal right, interest, or expectation. See also the contribution of PY Lo to this collection.

[28] See the contribution of Margaret Ng to this volume.

[29] Deputy Sulu Sou, a democrat, was accused of committing crimes related to illegal demonstration and disobedience to police orders; hence the Legislative Assembly was asked to suspend him in order to allow the Court to proceed with the case. For the first time ever, and following a rather controversial procedure where several rights were curtailed, the Legislative Assembly decided to suspend the deputy. Sulu Sou was found guilty by the court but received a lenient penalty that allowed him to retain his seat. He did not appeal – otherwise he would continue to be suspended. His co-defendant decided to appeal and won. See, eg, JS Filipe, 'Suspensão de Sulu Sou | 28 deputados deixam 9123 eleitores sem representaçăo' *Hoje Macau*, 5 December 2017, available at hojemacau.com.mo/2017/12/05/suspensao-de-sulu-sou-28-deputados-deixam-9123-eleitores-sem-representacao; R Carvalho, 'Macau's youngest lawmaker Sulu Sou, suspended from office and found guilty over 2016 protest, hopes to retake his seat' *South China Morning Post*, 2 June 2018, available at www.scmp.com/news/hong-kong/politics/article/2148879/macaus-youngest-lawmaker-sulu-sou-suspended-office-and-found; 'Sulu Sou and Scott Chiang sentenced to fines and no jail time' *Macau News*, 29 May 2018, available at macaunews.mo/sulu-and-chiang-sentence-to-fines; C U, 'Sulu Sou withdraws appeal to cease suspension' *Macau Business*, 27 June 2018, available at www.macaubusiness.com/macau-breaking-news-sulu-sou-withdraws-appeal-to-cease-suspension; E Pottier, 'Scott Chiang wins appeal and could be absolved of illegal protest charges connected to 2016 Jinan University protests' *Macau Business*, 31 January 2019, available at www.macaubusiness.com/corrected-scott-chiang-wins-appeal-and-could-be-absolved-of-illegal-protest-charges-connected-to-2016-jinan-university-protests.

conjunction with the recently heavy judicial hand in respect of political protests in Hong Kong,[30] this does seem to indicate a shift in the content and use of the rule of law, bringing Hong Kong closer to a kind of stance more familiar to and in Macau, and quite beyond the pale of what most would expect of the jurisdiction.

Official political disposition is also beginning to converge in both jurisdictions. For example, now it is common for both Hong Kong and Macau authorities to respond to legitimate international reports elaborated in a technical and elevated way, with an increasing tendency to respond by way of a verbiage of gongoric and rhetorical proclamations that usually do not address the substance of criticisms made and questions raised. In both jurisdictions, subtle but important changes in language can be discerned, with phrases like 'semi autonomy' being used as if this was what has always been guaranteed, rather than an important attempt to instantiate a new normal in the SARs.

In short, and as already indicated above, Macau and Hong Kong are arguably converging around a set of regrettable developments: in Hong Kong the deterioration of the legal system, of the rule of law, of fundamental rights, of autonomy in practice, of the Basic Law and of the Joint Declaration; in Macau the continuation of semi-autonomy in practice, in spite of some tentative positive developments in recent years.

III. Convergence in Focus

In addition to the general observations already made above, there are some particular topics where comparison with the Macau experience may be instructive, especially if the convergence that I have tentatively identified is borne out. The first of these is Article 23, a significant focus of the papers in this volume. In Hong Kong, Article 23 is not only famous but infamous, and it is the centrifugal point of many tensions between Hong Kong and Beijing. As is well known, Hong Kong has not yet passed a law on national security as required by Article 23, but in Macau, where the same requirement is imposed, legislation has already been passed.

Lei nº 2/2009 is the Macau law passed to give effect to its Article 23 obligation.[31] The law has never been applied, and in terms of its content is in fact reasonable, albeit not immune to some criticism. In general, the structure and system, and the solutions are compatible with the status of Macau as the second system in a 'one country, two systems' configuration, and in line with Macau traditions of criminal law and procedure. Passed shortly after the demonstrations that scuppered an attempt to introduce an Article 23 law in Hong Kong, it may well be that

[30] See, eg, *Secretary for Justice v Wong Chi Fung & Ors* (2018) 21 HKCFAR 35.

[31] On this legislation, see J Godinho, 'The Regulation of Article 23 of the Macau Basic Law: A Commentary of the Draft Law on the Protection of State Security' (20 November 2008), available at dx.doi.org/10.2139/ssrn.1303245.

Lei nº 2/2009 was intended in part to reassure Hong Kong; to show that an Article 23 law can be introduced without sparking any particular anxieties. However, as time has passed worries have grown that the Macau law may indeed suggest Hong Kongers are right to be anxious. Prominent politicians have called for changes to the law, even though it has never been used, and there is a growing clamour for the unthinkable and unprecedented suggestion that only Chinese judges should be able to sit in any cases where the law might be invoked.[32] It is difficult to identify what is motivating these calls for change. Maybe is the law is considered too lenient? Maybe the law is too much in line with constitutional and legal principles? Maybe it needs to be vaguer? We do not know. But we do worry.[33]

The second topic in which we might consider potential learning from Macau's experience for Hong Kong is that of the courts. In both Macau and Hong Kong, courts are independent and judges do not receive orders; nor are they supposed to follow political suggestions. Needless to say, courts have an inescapable role in legal systems that adhere to the rule of law, the separation of powers, judicial independence, the protection of fundamental rights, democracy (or at least democratic traits), constitutionality, and so on. These are all characteristics of both Macau and Hong Kong as 'second systems'. Courts in Hong Kong and Macau alike have a constitutional duty to guard fundamental rights, autonomy, continuity, separation of powers and other basic constitutional principles. Although courts are supposed to be value-neutral in enforcing the law, they must be aware that the Joint Declaration and Basic Law are in fact not value-neutral. The 'basic policies' guaranteeing the autonomy, separation and continuity of systems, rights and freedoms in the second system have unequivocally placed these values at a higher rank than others. The judiciary ought therefore adopt a *pro hominem, pro libertate, friendly* approach towards fundamental rights. The constitutional and legal orders of Macau and Hong Kong are distinct from the constitutional order of mainland China, and ought to be treated as such. The legal orders of the former intersect with the legal order of the latter at times, but supposedly only in limited and expressly stated ways.

The passive approach of the Macau courts in guarding fundamental values (eg right of appeal, rights of the child, etc) has attracted many criticisms, with a damaging impact on the legitimacy of the courts. In Macau there are no specific rules concerning constitutional review and the courts do not accept that issues

[32] This was already approved by Lei nº 4/2019 by way of introducing a new art 19A in the Lei nº 9/1999 regarding the judicial system law, stating that in situations of special criminal jurisdiction regarding the crimes established by above mentioned Lei nº 2/2009, the competence to adjudicate these crimes is vested in judges that, among other requisites, are Chinese citizens. The same goes for the prosecutors.

[33] Among many others, JC Matias, 'Da proporcionalidade e do bom senso' (Plataforma Macau, 23 March 2018), available at www.plataformamacau.com/wp-content/uploads/2018/03/PM-193.pdf; Joint Report To The European Parliament And The Council, Macao Special Administrative Region: Annual Report 2018, available at https://eeas.europa.eu/sites/eeas/files/join_2019_7_f1_report_from_commission_en_v2_p1_1019784_1.pdf.

of constitutionality are raised independently from existing remedies. Although the courts are comfortable considering issues arising from the Basic Law in their rulings, they seem to prefer to decide cases without applying the Basic Law directly, relying more commonly on procedural and ordinary law instead. On the rare occasions when the Macau courts do use the Basic Law to settle cases, they have not yet ever declared an impugned law unconstitutional. This passive approach of the Macau courts is posed in stark contrast with the highly active approach of the Hong Kong courts in constitutional review.[34] Courts in Hong Kong should be wary of losing their independence, integrity and autonomy. They should be immune to political pressure, regardless of where it is coming from. The contrasting degrees of judicial autonomy that the two jurisdictions enjoy show that the building of and sustenance of judicial independence, integrity and autonomy require strong traditions, culture, supporting institutions and, most importantly, willpower and determination on the part of the judges and legal profession.[35] Judicial independence, integrity and autonomy, once compromised, will be hard to rebuild. Hong Kong courts, being endowed with a strong rule of law tradition and culture, ought to cherish and build upon this endowment.

The third topic of focus concerns the power of interpretation of the Basic Law vested in the Standing Committee of the National People's Congress (NPCSC) as stated in Article 158 of the Hong Kong Basic Law and Article 143 of that of Macau; a topic where there is significant variation between the SAR sisters. In Macau this power is virtually insignificant. So far there has only been one interpretation on the Macau Basic Law (on Annexes I and II to the Basic Law and issued in 2012). In contrast, and as considered in other contributions to this volume,[36] the power of interpretation has been used in respect of Hong Kong in ways that appear to degrade the SAR's autonomy significantly. In truth, this was always apprehended; for example, in 2011 Anthony Mason warned that the extent to which the rule of law could be maintained in Hong Kong would depend on the frequency and manner with which the NPCSC issued interpretations of the Basic Law.[37] This was, of course, also true of Macau. As I wrote more than a decade ago,[38] Article 143 of the Macau Basic Law could either threaten autonomy or create possibilities for its expansion if interpreted in that way. Given the lack of interpretations in Macau, one cannot say that Article 143 has necessarily acted as either a threat or an opportunity, but in Hong Kong it is clear that the power of interpretation has functioned as the former, in particular the NPCSC's carving out of a freestanding plenary

[34] See, eg, *W v Registrar of Marriages* (2013) 16 HKCFAR 112; *Secretary for Justice v Yau Yuk Lung* [2005] 3 HKLRD 657.

[35] See also the contribution of PY Lo in this collection.

[36] See eg the contributions of Swati Jhaveri, Michael Davis, and Cora Chan and Fiona de Londras in this collection.

[37] A Mason, 'The Rule of Law in the Shadow of the Giant: the Hong Kong Experience' (2011) 33 *Sydney Law Review* 623.

[38] P Cardinal, 'Macau: The Internationalization of an Historical Autonomy' (2008) 122 *Boletín Mexicano de Derecho Comparado* 637.

power of interpretation, quite in contrast with what the law appears to require for the interpretation power to be exercised.[39]

There have been extensive discussions on whether there should be limits on the NPCSC's powers of interpretation. I will not recap all the arguments that have been put forward by scholars. Suffice it to highlight a few points. First, as Yash Ghai has argued elsewhere, various features of the Basic Law point to its 'self-contained' character:

> But those who argue like this [ie that provisions in the PRC constitution that are inconsistent with the Basic Law ought to prevail over the latter] have not provided any criteria to distinguish constitutional provisions which prevail over the Basic Law from those which give way to it. The very fact that there is no easy way to do so is strong evidence that the Basic Law, with its detailed provisions, is intended to be self-contained.[40]

Indeed, the Basic Law limits the Chinese Government's powers in ways that are not stated in the PRC constitution. China may not apply national laws in the SARs except after consultation with the Basic Law Committee and in relation to foreign affairs, defence and other matters outside of the SARs' autonomy. China's 'basic policies' towards the SARs are even stated to be unamendable in the Basic Laws.[41] The Basic Laws should therefore not be viewed as ordinary laws in the national legal system. If there are limits even on the amendment power of the National People's Congress (NPC), one may ask why there would not be limits on the interpretation power of the NPCSC, a power that is prima facie less important and exercisable by a body lower in hierarchy than the NPC.

Moreover, there are good arguments for why courts should refuse to enforce an ultra vires interpretation by the NPCSC.[42] If an interpretation of the Basic Law amounts effectively to an amendment of the Basic Law, then the regional courts could not admit it, since that would be a violation of the special procedure for amending the Basic Law, stipulated in the Basic Law itself (Article 159 for Hong Kong and Article 144 for Macau). And if an interpretation violated China's basic policies towards the SARs, ie the substantive limitation on amendment, regional courts are again not in a position to give effect to the interpretation, as they are to follow the law including first and foremost the Basic Law. For example, if the

[39] See C Chan, 'The Legal Limits on Beijing's Powers to Interpret Hong Kong's Basic Law' (HKU Legal Scholarship Blog, November 2016), available at researchblog.law.hku.hk/2016/11/cora-chan-on-legal-limits-of-beijings.html; C Chan, 'Implementing China and Hong Kong's Preliminary Reference System: Transposability of Article 267 TFEU Principles' [2014] *Public Law* 642.

[40] Y Ghai, 'Litigating the Basic Law: Jurisdiction, Interpretation and Procedure' in J Chan, H Fu and Y Ghai (eds), *Hong Kong's Constitutional Debate, Conflict Over Interpretation* (Hong Kong, Hong Kong University Press, 2000) 45.

[41] Hong Kong Basic Law, Art 159(4); Macau Basic Law, Art 144(4).

[42] See EC Ip, 'Interpreting Interpretations: A Methodology for the Judicial Enforcement of Legislative Interpretations of the Hong Kong Basic Law' [2017] *Public Law* 552; Chan, 'The Legal Limits on Beijing's Powers' (2016).

NPCSC interprets Article 28 of the Macau Basic Law, which guarantees that Macau residents have the right to apply to the court for the issuance of a writ of *habeas corpus*, to mean that it shall not apply except in crimes related to national security and other crimes as decided by the Government, then such an interpretation should not be considered binding. Aside from being a serious erosion of a fundamental right and a guarantee that is protected by the continuity principle of fundamental rights, such an interpretation would not be an interpretation proper but rather an amendment of the Basic Law and thus unacceptable.

The fourth and final topic of focus is the rule of law. This is a key concept that distinguishes the SARs from mainland China. It is part of the way of life, the pre-handover legal systems, and the protection of fundamental rights, all guaranteed by the Joint Declaration and Basic Laws. The rule of law should be both formal and substantial.[43] It must not be empty rhetoric. And it must be resilient and not suffer a sort of transgenic mutation. The rule of law today should be no worse than that in the pre-handover era. It must not be allowed to transform into rule by law, or be functionalised into mere roles played by the law, much less regress into the rule of politics:[44]

> Certainly, a Chinese concept of 'rule of law' is the rule of something different from what westerners think the law is; it is rather a rule, and a role, akin to what is referred to, in comparative law circles, as 'socialist legality' or 'socialist rule of law.' We may also call it 'rule by law' recognizing in it the presence of what Professor Ugo Mattei calls 'the rule of politics' element. Whether 'rule by law' equates to one possible declination of 'rule of law' becomes a pure matter of taxonomy, and everyone can create their own.[45]

Even if we accept that rule by law (or what China calls 'law-based governance') suffices for 'one country,' we should not accept that it should be allowed for the 'two systems' part of the formula. The principles inherent in the rule of law are firmly guaranteed by the Joint Declaration and the Basic Laws. To accept a retrogression of the rule of law into, say, rule by law, would be depleting a part of the 'second system.' Lawyers do know that the essence and reason of the rule of law is directed primarily to public power to avert authoritarianism, abuse of power, violation of fundamental rights and so on. But a key feature of retrogression to rule by law is the above-mentioned shift in the uses of law: from using law to control public power to using it to delineate and limit private subjects. For both SARs, maintenance of the rule of law is a core part of maintaining two systems. For two systems to be maintained within one country, the rule of law must not be miniaturised to a figurine, a Pierrot, showcased in the vitrine cabinet.

[43] See eg the contribution of Wai-Man Lam in this collection.

[44] U Mattei, 'Three Patterns of Law: Taxonomy and Change in the World's Legal Systems' (1997) 45 *The American Journal of Comparative Law* 5.

[45] I Castellucci, 'Rule of Law with Chinese Characteristics' (2007) 13 *Annual Survey of International & Comparative Law* 90.

IV. Unity in Diversity: Theory and Practice

While the 'one country, two systems' governing model may be creative, in practice it has become rather different from what it apparently promises. The experiences of the two SARs confirm that to protect the rule of law, we should look for sources of resilience beyond the constitutional texts and in institutions, traditions, culture, civil society, media attention and international rapport and pressure including from the parties to the Joint Declaration. The weak ability of the Macau SAR in maintaining distinctive systems and the weakening ability of the Hong Kong SAR to do so raise doubts as to whether the model may indeed fit or appeal to Taiwan, the jurisdiction that China had in mind when formulating the 'one country, two systems' model. Indeed, China's recent reminder of their final goal of reunification with Taiwan using this model has been vehemently dismissed in Taiwan, not least because of the decline of rights in Hong Kong.[46] Whether the promise of unity in diversity held out by the 'one country, two systems' model can be realised remains to be seen. Resilience is only possible when the rule of law – dictated by the Joint Declarations, the Basic Laws and its fundamental principles such as that of continuity and autonomy – exists as an anchor. The model itself has potential but needs to be implemented adequately and in adherence to the rule of law.

[46] Compare the Chinese President Xi Jinping commemorative speech on the 40th anniversary of the so-called 'Message to Compatriots in Taiwan', proposing a Taiwan model of 'one country, two systems' for China's eventual unification and the response of the President of Taiwan, Tsai Ing-wen, stating that 'Taiwan absolutely will not accept "one country, two systems"'; see C Hsu, 'Taiwan will never accept "one country, two systems"' *The Global and Mail*, 4 January 2019, available at www.theglobeandmail.com/opinion/article-taiwan-will-never-accept-one-country-two-systems.

6

One Country, Two National Security Systems

LIN FENG[1]

In his contribution to this collection, Albert Chen writes that 'the legislative implementation of Article 23 of the Basic Law in order to protect China's national security and unity will probably be the single most controversial legal and constitutional issue in the HKSAR in the foreseeable future'. Both his and Hualing Fu's chapter have offered some reasons why it is so from different angles. This chapter intends to not only highlight their essential arguments but also to develop further the argument on the fundamental cause of the difficulty facing Article 23 legislation in the HKSAR, ie the dual systems of national security legislation in mainland China and the HKSAR respectively. In addition, this paper will also suggest the best approach to move forward on this issue by bringing in the arguments and conclusions from the other two papers in Part I of this book.

I. Duality – The Fundamental Cause of Controversy on Article 23 Legislation in the HKSAR

A. The Reasons for the Controversy

In their contributions, Chen and Fu give several reasons for the controversy over Article 23 legislation, including the overriding interpretation power of the NPCSC, evolution of the 'one country, two systems' policy, divergent views of 'one country, two systems', China's national security concerns, its new national security regime, the potential for the HKSAR as a national security risk to China, the tension between the liberal HKSAR, the authoritarian China, and so on.

[1] Professor of Law, School of Law, CityU, HKSAR; member, Law Reform Commission of the HKSAR. This paper is the output of the research project entitled 'Constitutionality of Demand for Hong Kong Independence – A Comparative and Jurisprudential Study' (GRF No 9042592).

Legally speaking, the fundamental cause behind the controversy over Article 23 legislation in the HKSAR is the duality dictated by the implementation of the principle of 'one country, two systems'. Through the Basic Law, this principle guarantees that the HKSAR's pre-existing common law system will remain after Hong Kong's change of sovereignty in 1997. Article 23 of the Basic Law authorises and requires the HKSAR to prohibit various acts endangering national security through criminal offences, which are within the scope of criminal law. Hong Kong's criminal law is within the field of the common law system under the 'two systems', meaning that it is different from the criminal law in mainland China. Two specific examples can be given to illustrate such difference. One is the difference in the definition of national security. Under Article 2 of the National Security Law of the PRC, national security refers to

> the relative absence of international or domestic threats to the state's power to govern, sovereignty, unity and territorial integrity, the welfare of the people, sustainable economic and social development, and other major national interests, and the ability to ensure a continued state of security.

In comparison, the 2003 National Security (Legislative Provisions) Bill ('the 2003 Bill[2]') defines 'national security' as 'the safeguarding of the territorial integrity and the independence of the People's Republic of China'.[3] The scope covered by the same term in mainland China is much wider than that in the HKSAR. Another example is, as discussed by Fu, that some acts covered by the crime of subversion in mainland China are not covered by the same crime proposed under the 2003 Bill because they fall within the protection of fundamental rights.

More fundamentally, such duality together with the Article 23 authorisation justifies and explains why there are and will continue to be (after Article 23 legislation) two different systems of national security legislation in mainland China and the HKSAR respectively. This is a unique and difficult question caused by the Article 23 authorisation to the HKSAR to enact its own national security legislation. A review of national security legislation around the world shows that there is only one set of national security legislation in one sovereign state, be it a federal or unitary state.[4] It also makes sense in constitutional theory that one state should have only one system of national security. But Article 23 authorisation together with the guarantee of 'one country, two systems' under both the Sino-British Joint Declaration and the Basic Law of the HKSAR has made it possible and also certain that the HKSAR's future national security legislation will be different from that in

[2] National Security (Legislative Provisions) Bill 2003, available at www.legco.gov.hk/yr02-03/english/bills/c007-e.pdf.

[3] It was defined by s 8 under Part III: Amendments to the Official Secrets Ordinance. Nowhere else was it defined. There is some uncertainty over whether that definition is a general definition or is only applicable in the context of official secrets.

[4] See 'National Security Laws around the World', available at www.basiclaw23.gov.hk/english/resources/compare/country.htm.

mainland China. It is therefore fair to say that the constitutional design under the Basic Law of the HKSAR has given rise to such duality.

B. Reasons for the Duality

The legal justification for such constitutional design is that the legal system in the mainland is markedly different from that in Hong Kong. What lies behind the legal difference is the political difference between the mainland and the HKSAR. As noted by Fu, national unity and territorial integrity are national security concerns to mainland China.[5] In a political sense, this is also one of the red lines mentioned by President Xi in his speech in Hong Kong at the ceremony to celebrate the 20th anniversary of the HKSAR. The other red lines mentioned by President Xi include: attempts to challenge the power of the Central Government or the authority of the Basic Law or to use the HKSAR to carry out infiltration and sabotage activities against the mainland.[6] A further red line not mentioned by Xi is zero tolerance of anyone advocating Hong Kong independence as an office-bearer within the HKSAR Government.

The most difficult red line for the HKSAR not to cross is for the territory to not be used to carry out infiltration and sabotage activities against the mainland, which is related to the second security concern of mainland China.[7] As Fu notes, since China adopted the Law on the Management of Domestic Activities of Overseas NGOs in 2016 many rights-based international NGOs who work closely with their partners on the ground in mainland China have relocated to the HKSAR. Some rights advocates who have been supported by those NGOs have been charged and convicted of the crime of subversion. If those NGOs continue to support and finance rights advocates in mainland China, it is foreseeable that they are likely to be regarded by mainland China as using the HKSAR to carry out infiltration and sabotage activities against the mainland. Their acts are unlikely to be caught either by the crimes of subversion or of sedition as they were defined under the 2003 Bill.

The former Chief Executive, CY Leung, has remarked that the Umbrella Movement received support from foreign states.[8] A similar view has been expressed against those that object to the Hong Kong Government's proposed amendment

[5] The other one is, as noted by professor Fu, the leadership of the Communist Party of China.

[6] See Xi's speech at the 'Meeting celebrating the 20th anniversary of Hong Kong's return to the motherland and the inaugural ceremony of the fifth term government of the HKSAR', available at www.bjreview.com/Beijing_Review_and_Kings_College_London_Joint_Translation_Project/2017/201808/t20180802_800137354.html.

[7] 'National Security Laws' (n 4).

[8] See P So, 'CY Leung Repeats Claim of "External Forces" Influencing Occupy – but Provides No Evidence' *SCMP*, 13 January 2015, available at www.scmp.com/news/hong-kong/article/1679392/cy-leung-reiterates-claim-external-forces-influencing-occupy-provides.

of the Fugitive Offenders Ordinance.[9] That is why the Central Authorities have expressed firm support for and mobilised the pro-establishment camp in the HKSAR to support the HKSAR Government's initiative to amend the Fugitive Offenders Ordinance in order to allow surrender of fugitives to mainland China and other jurisdictions on a case-by-case basis.[10]

In short, in addition to legal differences, the political and ideological differences between the HKSAR and mainland China demand a duality in national security law.

C. Problems Caused by the Duality and Possible NPCSC Interpretation

Against the backdrop of the difference in national security legislation and the existence of the red lines of the mainland discussed above, the practical issue, as observed by Fu, is whether and to what extent the HKSAR will 'defer to the Chinese test in determining what constitutes a national security offence and when the offence of treason, secession or other national security offences have been committed'. A particular example mentioned by both Professor Fu and Professor Chen is what would be done if mainland China expects that advocacy of Hong Kong independence without violence or terrorism being advocated should be prohibited under Article 23 legislation.

Indeed, this is no remote hypothetical; rather it is a situation that has almost materialised. As Hong Kong's Court of First Instance ('CFI') completed the trial on whether two newly elected legislative councillors who failed to swear their oath properly should be allowed to retake their oath, but before the court delivered its judgment, the NPCSC issued an interpretation of Article 104 of the Basic Law, the provision at stake in the case.[11] This is the NPCSC's fifth interpretation of the Basic Law since the handover. It seems that the reason for the NPCSC's move was that it did not want to risk the CFI deciding in favour of the two legislative councillors. Following that logic, it is predictable that the NPCSC would have issued an

[9] At the time of writing, the second reading of the Fugitive Offenders and Mutual Legal Assistance in Criminal Matters Legislation (Amendment) Bill 2019 is due to be resumed in the Legislative Council of Hong Kong. See Xinhua, 'Attempts to Interfere in HK Legislative Process Deplored' *China Daily*, 31 May 2019, available at www.chinadailyhk.com/articles/202/106/182/1559306952926.html. (Postscript: the Hong Kong Government announced on 15 June 2019 that the legislative proceedings on the Bill would be suspended.)

[10] See A Lum, 'Beijing Weighs in on Hong Kong Extradition Plan, Urging Doubters to Respect the Legal Process, after Law Society Calls for Alternatives' *SCMP*, 16 March 2019, available at www.scmp.com/news/hong-kong/politics/article/3001944/law-society-expresses-concerns-about-governments.

[11] See Lin Feng, 'Legal Analysis of the Fifth Interpretation of the Hong Kong Basic Law by the NPC Standing Committee' (2017) 1 *Academic Journal of One Country Two Systems* 11 (in Chinese); see also the contribution of PY Lo in this collection.

interpretation immediately had Chan Ho Tin Andy, the founder of Hong Kong National Party, applied for judicial review of the decision of the Secretary for Security to ban his party and of the Executive Council's decision to dismiss his appeal.[12] One can therefore say that a further interpretation of the NPCSC on the Basic Law has been avoided by Mr Chan's decision not to lodge a judicial review application.

However, in the future, once a red line is crossed, the NPCSC will be ready to exercise its legislative interpretation authority as has been demonstrated through its fifth interpretation of the Basic Law.[13] The lesson to be learned may be that Hong Kong people should try their best to not give the NPCSC a justification to invoke that authority, and need to know what and where the red lines are and do not cross any of them.

Because Article 23 is in the chapter entitled 'relationship between the Central Authorities and the Hong Kong Special Administrative Region' in the Basic Law, Chen has rightly noted the possibility for the NPCSC to interpret Article 23 if the local legislation in the HKSAR does not meet the expectation of the mainland on national security. But Article 23 is merely an authorisation clause and does not contain any substantive content on national security. Accordingly, it is difficult to achieve consistency on the definition of national security between mainland China and the HKSAR through a mere interpretation of Article 23 of the Basic Law. In order to achieve that objective, the interpretation has to be on some other Articles of the Basic Law in addition to Article 23. That is why an interpretation of Article 23 by the NPCSC is bound to be controversial.

D. New National Security Issue(s)

In addition to the traditional national security issues discussed above, new issues may arise in the future. For example, a question arises as to what the HKSAR can and should do in order to avoid any potential conflict between the sovereign needs of mainland China on national security on the one hand, and the local definition of national security in such new areas as technology (consider, for example, the allegations by the United States, Australia and New Zealand against the national security threat posed by China's tech giant Huawei). The issue will be relevant to the HKSAR if, say, such a Chinese tech giant is a listed company in the region.

[12] He confirmed that he would not apply for judicial review and the time limit for such an application has expired. See A Lum, 'Hong Kong National Party waives right to legally challenge ban, paving way for more government crackdowns on independence groups' *SCMP*, 22 May 2019, available at www.scmp.com/news/hong-kong/politics/article/3011266/hong-kong-national-party-waives-right-legally-challenge-ban.

[13] See 'Interpretation of Article 104 of the Basic Law of the Hong Kong Special Administrative Region of the People's Republic of China by the Standing Committee of the National People's Congress', available at www.basiclaw.gov.hk/en/basiclawtext/images/basiclawtext_doc25.pdf.

II. The Way Forward

In order to avoid an NPCSC interpretation of Article 23 and the application of Chinese National Security Law to the HKSAR, a proactive approach to enact a local Article 23 legislation is preferable to a resistance approach.

A. Macau Experience

In his contribution, Cardinal makes an interesting comparison between the HKSAR and Macau SAR. Macau fulfilled its constitutional duty to enact local Article 23 legislation in 2009. As has been noted, it was considered better to enact one which Macau deems desirable than applying mainland Chinese national security legislation to Macau.

In the case of Macau, Cardinal observes that

> the law has never been applied, and in terms of its content is in fact reasonable. In general, the structure and system, and the solutions are compatible with the status of Macau as the second system in a 'one country, two systems' configuration, and in line with Macau traditions of criminal law and procedure.

Since the enactment of Macau Article 23 legislation was shortly after the HKSAR's failure to enact a similar law, he opines that the intention behind Macau's legislation might have been to reassure and demonstrate to the HKSAR that such a law can be introduced without causing too much anxiety. Cardinal, however, suggests that it might be justifiable for Hong Kong people to be anxious even though the law has never been used in Macau.

In contrast, this author suggests that while it is reasonable to be cautious, the fact that the Macau National Security Law has never been used for more than a decade is good evidence to support the argument that the legislative intent behind Article 23 legislation is to protect national security rather than to restrict civil liberties of ordinary residents in the SARs.[14]

B. Voluntary Legislation and the Importance of Mutual Trust

The pan-democratic camp is now strongly against Article 23 legislation in the HKSAR. Its strong opposition to the Hong Kong Government's proposed revisions to the extradition law is a good indicator of its level of resentment of any attempt to reintroduce Article 23 Legislation.[15] Back in 2003, much criticism

[14] Although one may argue that Macau did not need to rely on Art 23 legislation because it has other ways of controlling dissent.

[15] See T Cheung, 'One Extradition Bill, Hundreds of Thousands of Protesters: Why is the Hong Kong Government Sticking to its Guns and Will the Opposition Relent?' *SCMP*, 11 June 2019, available at www.scmp.com/news/hong-kong/politics/article/3013929/one-extradition-bill-hundreds-thousands-protesters-why-hong.

was directed against the HKSAR Government's refusal to issue a White Paper for further consultation. The final Bill incorporating the concessions made by the Hong Kong Government after the demonstration on 1 July 2003 was in fact acceptable to some quarters of the pan-democrats. However, at the 2017 conference that led to this publication, the idea to start the legislative progress again by relying on the 2003 Bill was categorically rejected by some participants from the pan-democratic camp.[16]

Chen suggests that if the HKSAR Government fails to fulfil its constitutional duty to enact Article 23 legislation for too long, it will 'give rise to a remedy that can be pursued by the Central Authorities under Article 18 of the Basic Law', ie to apply the relevant laws in the mainland to the HKSAR, especially its National Security Law. This argument is not far-fetched at all if the HKSAR could not prove that the mainland's concerns over national security can be dealt with successfully by Hong Kong's existing laws.

This author argues that it is strategically unwise to oppose Article 23 legislation with all efforts in the HKSAR. Doing so will not best protect the fundamental rights of Hong Kong people. On the contrary, undue delay in fulfilling the HKSAR's constitutional duty to enact national security legislation will give the Central Authorities justification to apply Chinese National Security Law to the HKSAR. A better approach is to start the consultation process of Article 23 legislation as soon as possible, relying on the 2003 Bill. Since proper procedure is as important as the substance of the legislation, the HKSAR Government should use the 2003 Bill as the blueprint to produce a White Paper for consultation.

Another advantage of starting the legislative process as soon as possible is to show the Central Authorities that the HKSAR has a genuine intention to fulfil its constitutional duty and is doing that already. Such goodwill will be conducive to the establishment of mutual trust, which is essential for the proper operation of the principle of 'one country, two systems'.

On the other hand, as I have argued elsewhere,[17] the establishment of mutual trust requires effort from both sides, especially the party that enjoys greater bargaining power, ie the Central Authorities. Over the years, neither the Central Authorities nor the HKSAR Government has really made good efforts to win the trust of Hong Kong people. Instead, both have been heavy-handed. For example, with hindsight, if the HKSAR Government had been willing to introduce a White Paper on national security legislation in 2003, the situation might be quite different and the constitutional duty might have already been fulfilled.

The same is true with regard to the current dispute over the above-mentioned proposed amendments to the Fugitive Offenders Ordinance. What the HKSAR Government intended to do with this reform is to allow surrender of fugitives on a case-by-case basis to those jurisdictions the HKSAR has not entered into

[16] This book is very much the result of that conference.

[17] See Lin Feng, 'Constitutionality of the Co-location Arrangement at the West Kowloon High-Speed Rail Terminus' (2017) 47 *Hong Kong Law Journal* 699, 723–24.

extradition agreements with, including mainland China. Since such extradition is by nature ad hoc, it will be justifiable to limit its application to a narrow range of more serious offences than under a normal extradition agreement. The concerns of Hong Kong people and international communities,[18] and the complexity of the issue, justify an extended consultation time, but the Government has had only a 20-day consultation. There also seems to be possible alternatives to deal with the need to extradite a murder suspect to Taiwan, which the Government suggests is a key reason why the proposed Bill has to be passed as soon as possible. At the time of writing, in the face of mounting pressure from not only pan-democratic camp but also foreign countries and even some members of the pro-establishment camp, the HKSAR Government has agreed to incorporate some reasonable suggestions into its amendment Bill.[19] This is of course to be welcomed, but the process by which all of this has proceeded (eg refusing to extend the consultation period) is not conducive to building mutual trust. On the contrary, it destroys trust even further.

The author submits that it is necessary for both sides to make efforts to build mutual trust, but it has to start somewhere. Although it is better for the more powerful side to start, it is not impossible and unimaginable for the weaker side to take the initiative. Indeed, in reality this is often what happens.[20]

C. Value of the Rule of Law and Civil Liberties

Chen writes that national security legislation 'stands at the core of the tension and contradiction between the "two systems" in "one country"'. To put it in another way, what is in conflict is the national security concern of mainland China on the one hand and the civil liberties of residents in the HKSAR on the other. The concerns are mainly over the protection of civil liberties.

A very interesting finding of Lam's paper is that 'political incidents in Hong Kong that happened up until 2016 have not decreased but rather increased the general public's endorsement of a higher-level notion of the rule of law, which is a very interesting area worthy of further research'. From a doctrinal perspective, this

[18] See Cheung, 'One Extradition Bill' (2019); S Xinqi, and S Lok-kei, 'Top Foreign Diplomats Express Serious Concerns about Hong Kong Government's Extradition Proposal at Legislative Council' *SCMP*, 27 May 2019, available at www.scmp.com/news/hong-kong/politics/article/3011931/hong-kong-extradition-row-rages-diplomats-and-lawmakers.

[19] See A Lum, S Lok-kei and J Lam, 'Hong Kong Extradition Bill: Security Chief Announces Safeguards to Win Support of Major Business Groups and Political Allies' *SCMP*, 30 May 2019, available at www.scmp.com/news/hong-kong/politics/article/3012498/hong-kong-security-chief-john-lee-rolls-out-new-measures.

[20] It has been demonstrated not only domestically in the dispute over the allocation of interpretation authority over the Basic Law between Hong Kong courts and the NPCSC, but also internationally in the current trade dispute between China and the US. The one with the weaker bargaining power may have to compromise first.

is not too difficult to explain. One possibility is that through those political incidents, Hong Kong people have developed a better understanding of the difference between the mainland's system, which is at most at the 'rule by law' stage, and the HKSAR's system, which is at least already at the 'thin rule of law' stage (and many would consider it as having reached the 'rule of law' stage). Such an understanding makes Hong Kong people treasure their system more, particularly its ability to protect the civil liberties of Hong Kong people.

Given that Article 39 of the Basic Law provides that the ICCPR will continue to apply in the HKSAR, and Chapter 3 of the Basic Law also contains most of the rights in the ICCPR, there exists a sound constitutional foundation to include necessary provisions for the protection of civil liberties in any local national security legislation. If all sectors in the HKSAR including the Hong Kong Government agree to start the legislative process as soon as possible, they can include the necessary safeguards for civil liberties in the draft Bill for consultation. In fact, the 2003 Bill proposed to include such provisions into various local ordinances. For example, with regard to the amendments to the crimes contained in the Crimes Ordinance, the following new section was proposed to be included: 'The provisions of Parts I and II and this Part are to be interpreted, applied and enforced in a manner that is consistent with Chapter III of the Basic Law'.

If Hong Kong residents are of the view that the safeguards in the 2003 Bill are not enough, more could be suggested. For example, the inclusion of Johannesburg Principles could be considered.

D. New National Security Issues and Referral Mechanism

With regard to new national security issues which may arise in the future, the author submits that the referral mechanism created under Article 158(3) of the Basic Law should be applied. This mechanism requires Hong Kong's Court of Final Appeal to seek an interpretation from the NPCSC, if it needs to interpret a provision concerning the responsibilities of the Central People's Government or the relationship between HKSAR and Central Authorities in order to resolve a case. This will be the best mechanism to resolve any potential conflict in the interpretation of national security between the HKSAR and the mainland. However, smooth operation of this referral mechanism needs mutual trust.

III. Conclusion

One common theme coming out of all four chapters in Part I of this collection is the importance of protection of civil liberties in the HKSAR and Hong Kong people's concern over whether Article 23 legislation will unduly restrict the civil liberties they enjoy. These concerns are legitimate. What the HKSAR Government needs to do is to be an effective bridge between Hong Kong people and the Central Authorities. On the one hand, it should fully explain to the Central Authorities the precise concerns of Hong Kong people and the reasons why they have those concerns. On the other hand, it should convince Hong Kong people of the genuine national security concerns of the Central Authorities and of the advantages to the HKSAR taking the initiative to start the legislative process for national security legislation as soon as possible.

Since proper protection of civil liberties under any future Article 23 legislation is the core issue, the HKSAR Government can make it clear that any such legislation it will propose will give Hong Kong people confidence in this aspect and will also go through thorough consultation in the form of a White Paper. More than two decades have passed without such legislation. The Government ought not mind spending another year on consultation. The key is to commence the process as soon as possible.

If the pan-democratic camp and their representatives in the Legislative Council continue to try their best to prevent the enactment of Article 23 legislation, and if the HKSAR Government, especially the Chief Executive, continues to say that the social environment in the HKSAR is not ready for Article 23 legislation, it is likely that sooner or later the Central Authorities will take action either by applying the mainland National Security Law to the HKSAR or by issuing an interpretation of the relevant provisions in the Basic Law. The day on which this happens – should it happen – would be the day when 'one country' would replace the principle of 'one country, two systems'. Since the stake is too high for the HKSAR, the author suggests that the HKSAR Government and those in the pan-democratic camp take this issue seriously and change their strategies accordingly.

PART II

Sources of Resilience in Hong Kong's Politico-Legal Culture

7

Administrative Law as a Modest Guardian of the Rule of Law

SWATI JHAVERI

Article 23 of the Basic Law of Hong Kong mandates the enactment of national security legislation to prohibit, among other things, treason, secession, sedition and subversion against the Central People's Government. Earlier attempts to introduce this legislation were highly unpopular, leading to the shelving of the Government's proposals.[1] However, the enactment of such legislation is inevitable.[2] Indeed, the issue has recently become a live one, with the local Government coming under increasing pressure to enact national security legislation.[3] This paper considers specifically the role of administrative law in safeguarding the rule of law once this is done.

The need to balance the Government's interest in protecting national security against broader rule of law concerns is one faced by most common law jurisdictions. Most systems accept a role for the courts in striking this balance. The scope of the courts' role depends on reconciling a familiar set of concerns: the democratic credentials, institutional expertise and legitimacy of the courts, on the one hand, and legitimacy and accountability concerns with the political branches of government and the importance of fundamental rights and the rule of law, on the other.[4] Any discussion of these issues in Hong Kong needs to factor in three further unique and major caveats that are specific to the local context in determining a role for the courts.

[1] See, eg, H Fu, CJ Petersen and SNM Young, *National Security and Fundamental Freedoms: Hong Kong's Article 23 Under Scrutiny* (Hong Kong, Hong Kong University Press, 2005), and the contribution of Michael C Davis in this collection.

[2] See the contribution of Albert HY Chen in this collection.

[3] See, eg, 'National security law looms over Hong Kong freedoms' *South China Morning Pos*, 27 September 2018.

[4] See, eg, M Kirby, 'National Security: Proportionality, Restraint and Commonsense' (2005) *Privacy Law and Policy Reporter* 151, and the contribution of Albert HY Chen in this collection.

First, there is a lack of clarity on the role of the Central Government in the local governance of Hong Kong under the 'one country, two systems' framework set out in the Basic Law.[5] The precise degree of autonomy to be accorded to Hong Kong has been a particular site of contention.[6] This manifests in particularly problematic ways in respect of the question of the power to interpret the provisions of the Basic Law. As considered elsewhere in this collection, both the judiciary in Hong Kong and the legislative body in China – the Standing Committee of the National People's Congress (NPCSC) – have powers to interpret the Basic Law.[7] Both institutions are likely to assert interpretive power over Article 23 of the Basic Law in any cases involving national security legislation, raising territorial questions.

Secondly, Article 23 is unique in imposing a constitutional *duty* on the executive in Hong Kong to implement some form of national security law. Other jurisdictions typically empower or permit the Government and legislature to act in furtherance of national security.[8] *Mandating* legislation in the Hong Kong context,

[5] Ch II of the Basic Law of Hong Kong (Relationship between the Central Authorities and the HongKong Special Administrative Region) purports to divide governance issues between the central and local government. The former are responsible for foreign affairs, defence and appointment of key officials, including the Chief Executive of Hong Kong. Article 16 then states that 'The Hong Kong Special Administrative Region shall be vested with executive power. It shall, on its own, conduct the administrative affairs of the Region in accordance with the relevant provisions of this Law'. See W Xiao, 'A Study of the Political System of the Hong Kong Special Administrative Region under the Basic Law' (1988) 2 *Journal of Chinese Law* 95 on the principles governing the 'one country, two systems' model of governance in Hong Kong. There is a considerable uncertainty on the boundaries of these various provisions. See also the contributions of Michael C Davis and Albert HY Chen in this collection.

[6] Here, the Central Government of China takes the view that Hong Kong only has as much authority as may be determined by it from time to time. For example, in 2007, Wu Bangguo, the head of the National People's Congress stated that Hong Kong only has as much autonomy as Beijing authorises. The Basic Law, while referenced in this statement, was seen as capable of being recalibrated by new rulings from the Beijing Central Government. See 'Wu Bangguo: Hong Kong's autonomy laid down by Beijing' *AsiaNews*, 6 July 2007, available at www.asianews.it/news-en/Wu-Bangguo:-Hong-Kong%E2%80%99s-autonomy-laid-down-by-Beijing-9487.html. More recently, President Xi Jinping reiterated China's 'comprehensive jurisdiction' over Hong Kong in his speech at the 19th Communist Party National Congress. This meant that Hong Kong's autonomy would always be subject to the Central Government's supervision and, presumably, revision. See J Xi, 'Secure a Decisive Victory in Building a Moderately Prosperous Society in All Respects and Strive for the Great Success of Socialism with Chinese Characteristics for a New Era' (Report at the 19th National Congress of the Communist Party of China, 18 October 2017), available at news.xinhuanet.com/english/special/2017-11/03/c_136725942.htm. This echoes earlier statements made by the State Council in a White Paper on 'The Practice of the "One Country, Two Systems" Policy in the Hong Kong Special Administrative Region', available at www.scmp.com/news/hong-kong/article/1529167/full-text-practice-one-country-two-systems-policy-hong-kong-special. See also the contribution of Albert HY Chen in this collection.

[7] Basic Law, Art 158: see JMM Chan, HL Fu and Y Ghai (eds), *Hong Kong's Constitutional Debate: Conflict Over Interpretation* (Hong Kong, Hong Kong University Press, 2000). See also the Introduction of this collection.

[8] For example, through provisos to fundamental rights provisions – see eg Human Rights Act 1998, Sch 1.

therefore, provides a sense of the pro-security approach to national security as a matter of constitutional design.

Thirdly, the definition of the various offences in the enacted legislation will be a uniquely complex task. Article 23 envisages enacting laws that relate mostly to the sedition family of offences (as opposed to terrorism, for example) and, more importantly, laws that protect the Central People's Government of the People's Republic of China (PRC). The features of these various offences – the *actus reus* and *mens rea* – are likely to draw on both common law and Chinese law reference points, given they will be offences enacted in legislation in Hong Kong but with the protection of the Central Government in mind.

The role for the local courts in striking a balance between national security and rule of law concerns is, therefore, a constitutionally and politically difficult one. The courts will need to strategically chart and concretise a position for themselves in this environment. This paper considers two facets of the courts' role in this respect that merit particular attention: first, in the interpretation of Article 23; and secondly, in adjudicating cases brought by applicants seeking to challenge decisions made under any national security legislation.

On the first, the discussion in Part I will demonstrate how the judicial role in interpreting Article 23 is important but ultimately precarious. Part II, therefore, proposes that it will be equally important for the courts to focus on the second aspect of its role by cultivating alternative sites where they can have a common law influence in the realm of national security. Part III of this paper proposes that an optimal tool for this is the use of administrative law principles to adjudicate on the legality of executive action taken under national security legislation. The avoidance of constitutional adjudication may be necessary for the courts to preserve their role in the arena of national security.[9]

Ultimately, controlling the scope and operation of national security legislation will need to be a multi-event and multi-actor effort. This will include upstream efforts during legislative debates on the proposed legislation and associated civil society movements to, for example, lobby members of the Legislative Council (LegCo) to raise questions during debate.[10] There will also need to be a concerted effort on the part of administrative watchdogs (like the Ombudsman and Independent Police Complaints Commission) to check the integrity of law enforcement bodies involved in operationalising national security legislation. Administrative law and the courts will ultimately be a modest guardian of the rule of law.

[9] Arguments in favour of constitutional avoidance have been made in other contexts (all in the furtherance of the rule of law): see, eg, PJ Yap, *Constitutional Dialogue in Common Law Asia* (Oxford, Oxford University Press, 2015) ch 5; F Ahmed and T Khaitan, 'Constitutional Avoidance in Social Rights Adjudication' (2015) 35 *Oxford Journal of Legal Studies* 607. The author has argued elsewhere that a constitutional plane for adjudication may be appropriate, however, on the issue of political reform and democratisation in Hong Kong: S Jhaveri, 'Reconstitutionalising Politics in the Hong Kong SAR' (2017) *Asian Journal of Comparative Law* 1.

[10] See the contribution of Margaret Ng in this collection.

I. Power-Sharing in the Interpretation of Article 23: Retaining a Foothold for Courts

An interpretation of Article 23 grounded in the common law is likely to be more sensitive to the need to balance rule of law and national security concerns than a political interpretation by the NPCSC. The Hong Kong courts will, therefore, need to clarify uncertainties in the division of interpretive powers under Article 158. While this has been a long-standing issue, it is manifesting in new and distinct ways. The latter part of this section of the chapter looks at the recent manifestation of the NPCSC's powers of interpretation to demonstrate the challenges the local courts face on questions of interpretation, but first I consider the need for the local courts to maintain a foothold in the interpretation of Article 23.

A. The Necessity of Maintaining a Foothold: A Common Law Sense of Balance on National Security Issues

The NPCSC as a political legislative body will be informed by conceptions of national security from the Chinese legal tradition.[11] An examination of such concepts highlights the difference between Chinese and common law approaches to national security. Article 7 of the National Security Law of the PRC states:

> National security shall be maintained in accordance with the Constitution and laws and the principle of socialist rule of law by respecting and safeguarding human rights and protecting citizens' rights and freedom in accordance with the law.

Provisions like Article 7 seek to balance the implementation of the law in the interests of national security with respect for the rule of law and human rights. However, Article 7 needs to be contextualised against a vast number of other provisions that refer to the responsibility of citizens and public bodies to preserve national security (eg Article 11). This pro-security slant is reinforced by the promulgation of numerous laws that operationalise this including, most recently, the Cybersecurity Law. This gives the state vast powers to ask for cyber data held by private companies, to identify threats to national security (broadly construed under the National Security Law).[12]

This is significantly different from the relatively more balanced approach taken to public order and security issues in the common law tradition in Hong Kong.

[11] See Z Wang, 'From the Judicial Committee of the British Privy Council to the Standing Committee of the Chinese National People's Congress – An Evaluation of the Legal Interpretive System After the Handover' (2007) 37 *Hong Kong Law Journal* 605, 618; L Bing, 'Subject Matter Limitation on the NPCSC's Power to Interpret the Basic Law' 27 *Hong Kong Law Journal* 619, 646.

[12] See Cybersecurity Law, ch 1, available at www.lawinfochina.com/display.aspx?id=22826&lib=law; National Security Law, available at eng.mod.gov.cn/publications/2017-03/03/content_4774229.htm.

The courts have on multiple occasions confirmed that, while public order and security are important concerns for the political arms of government, these imperatives must be balanced against the protection of rights and the rule of law (the latter imports the need for certainty and transparency in decision-making that purports to restrict rights).[13] In striking the balance, the courts have also made clear that they will adopt a generous interpretation of any affected rights and a narrow interpretation of any restrictions on those rights to give the full measure of protection afforded by the rights.[14] The courts will, therefore, carefully scrutinise any provisions that seek to encroach on rights and any ambiguity in language is resolved in favour of the enforcement of rights.[15] In addition, the Hong Kong courts have indicated that certain rights are more fundamental in nature and will prompt a stronger degree of judicial scrutiny of restrictions.[16] These approaches to national security in the Hong Kong legal system could be an important defence against the advance of Chinese law-based conceptions. This is the prompt for clarifying the role of the Hong Kong courts in the interpretation of Article 23.

This will be important in cases where the courts are called upon to review the constitutionality of Article 23 legislation or executive action taken thereunder against fundamental rights provisions. In such cases, the courts will need to consider whether the rights provision trumps the imperatives of Article 23 (as they interpret them) and how to balance the two. The courts can constrain the scope of Article 23 through interpretation.[17] There are two main avenues for this.

First, phrases like 'treason', 'secession', 'sedition' and 'subversion' are offences found across most common law jurisdictions. There are variants across the jurisdictions in the scope and content of these offences and in the way they balance restrictions on rights against the political ends of these offences. This is not the forum for discussing and comparing the various interpretations across different jurisdictions. However, the comparative common law jurisprudence on the

[13] *Leung Kwok Hung & Ors v HKSAR* [2005] 3 HKLRD 164, 192C–195A, which can be contrasted with *HKSAR v Ng Kung Siu & Another* [1999] 3 HKLRD 907, 923, where the courts took a more public order-balanced approach to restrictions. There are variations but always with a view to striking a balance rather than giving one side of the equation a presumptively more important position as may be the case on one reading of the Chinese National Security Law.

[14] *Leung Kwok Hung v HKSAR* [2005] 3 HKLRD 164, 175F–176B, 178G – J; *Ng Ka Ling & Ors v Director of Immigration* [1999] 1 HKLRD 315, 340G.

[15] *Ng Ka Ling & Ors v Director of Immigration* [1999] 1 HKLRD 315, 339I–340J; *HKSAR v Ng Kung Siu v Another* [1999] 3 HKLRD 907, 922C.

[16] Most notably, liberty and political rights like the freedom of expression: *HKSAR v Ng Kung Siu & Anor* [1999] 3 HKLRD 907, 921I–922B. These political rights are the ones most impacted by national security legislation.

[17] PJ Yap, *Courts and Democracies in Asia* (Cambridge, Cambridge University Press, 2017) ch 12 (discussing *Director of Immigration v Chong Fung Yuen* (2001) 4 HKCFAR 211, 222G – H (Li CJ)); S Marsden, 'Constitutional Interpretation in Hong Kong: Do Common Law Approaches Apply When the National People's Congress Standing Committee Interprets the Basic Law?' (2006) *LAWASIA Journal* 99.

meaning of these phrases is a useful interpretative tool for such text.[18] More importantly, the experience of other common law jurisdictions shows a general reluctance by courts against the expansion of the scope of these offences.[19] This, therefore, allows access to existential debates about the nature of these offences: that they should be narrowly construed to be rights-compliant.[20]

Secondly, the courts can constrain the reach of national security legislation through their interpretation of open-ended phrases like: 'to prohibit foreign political organizations or bodies from *conducting political activities in the Region*' (emphasis added) in Article 23. While it may be readily ascertainable whether an association is a 'foreign political organization or body', what constitutes 'conducting political activities' is less clear, and the NPCSC and Hong Kong courts may take vastly different approaches to it. Thus, the task of clarifying the respective roles of the NPCSC and the local courts in interpreting Article 23 is critical, but it has become an increasingly complex one. How the powers of interpretation are divided between the Hong Kong courts and the NPCSC has significant consequences on the way in which the Basic Law is interpreted. When viewed from the perspective of Chinese law, the Basic Law is merely legislative, rather than constitutional in nature. 'Interpretation' of statutes in the Chinese legal system can include the amendment of text.[21] However, locally, the Basic Law is viewed as a constitutional document. This imbues the Basic Law with supremacy over local legislation: it is treated as establishing a meta-structure and value system that is protective of rights and the rule of law.[22] Therefore, Article 158 provides a conduit

[18] Article 84 of the Basic Law, in fact, envisages a common law comparative base for adjudicating cases: 'The courts of the Hong Kong Special Administrative Region shall adjudicate cases in accordance with the laws applicable in the Region as prescribed in Article 18 of this Law and may refer to precedents of other common law jurisdictions'. Indeed, the system of appointing non-permanent judges (judges from the highest appellate courts of other common law jurisdictions) to the Court of Final Appeal is part of the design features of the Basic Law that seeks to sustain the presence of common law principles in jurisprudence.

[19] This is not only for pro-free speech or pro-liberty reasons, but also because these offences are seen as out-dated and draconian modes of dealing with national security concerns: K Roach, 'Old and New Visions of Security: Article 23 Compared to Post-September 11 Security Laws' in Fu, Peterson and Young, *National Security and Fundamental Freedoms* (2005) 119.

[20] See HP Gupta and PK Sarkar, *Law Relating to Press and Sedition in India*, 1st edn (New Delhi, Orient Publishing Company, 2002); LW Maher, 'The Use and Abuse of Sedition' (1992) 14 *Sydney Law Review* 287; HL Packer, 'Offenses against the State' (1962) 339 *The Annals of the American Academy of Political and Social Science* 77; K Gelber, 'Critique and Comment: The False Analogy between Vilification and Sedition' (2009) 33 *Melbourne University Law Review* 270; J Neo, 'Seditious in Singapore! Free Speech and The Offence of Promoting Ill-Will and Hostility Between Different Racial Groups' [2011] *Singapore Journal of Legal Studies* 351.

[21] Interpretations of the Basic Law by the NPCSC are issued pursuant to Art 67(4) of the Chinese Constitution which gives the NPCSC the power 'to interpret *statutes*'. See S Marsden, 'Constitutional Interpretation in Hong Kong' (2006) on the blurred lines between interpretation and amendment of legislation under Chinese law.

[22] The constitutional nature of the document and its implications for rights-friendly interpretation was confirmed by the Hong Kong courts early on in the founding of the special administrative region: see *Ng Ka Ling & Ors v Director of Immigration* [1999] 1 HKLRD 315 [10], [73]–[79] (Li CJ), as borne out by Arts 4 and 11 of the Basic Law. See S Jhaveri, 'The Role of Courts in Advancing Constitutional

for the NPCSC to substitute its political perspective on the Basic Law for the judicial perspective of the Hong Kong judiciary. These different understandings of the nature of the Basic Law are likely to manifest in the interpretation of Article 23. Such interpretations by the NPCSC will also be one of the main vehicles for the import of Chinese concepts of security into Hong Kong's legal system. The local courts will, thus, need to retain a foothold in Article 23 to combat these interpretations with common law concepts of national security.

B. Division of Interpretive Powers under Article 158: A Moving Target

Article 158 of the Basic Law vests the plenary power of interpretation with the NPCSC. Article 158(1) then authorises the Hong Kong courts 'To interpret on their own, in adjudicating cases, the provisions of [the Basic Law] which are *within the limits of the autonomy of [Hong Kong]*' (emphasis added). It also mandates the courts in Hong Kong to refer particular matters of interpretation to the NPCSC (those concerning affairs which are the responsibility of the Central People's Government and those concerning the relationship between the Central Authorities and the region). Especially if given a broad interpretation, Article 158 could thus be seen as considerably reducing the Hong Kong courts' power of interpretation. The courts have, however, not assumed an automatically deferential posture on questions of interpretation. The question of the precise limits on its autonomy has been the subject of extensive litigation and academic discussion.[23] The NPCSC now issues interpretations in a myriad of ways and the courts' response will need to vary to maintain their jurisdiction. This section considers each of the possible causal events for an interpretation by the NPCSC and how the local courts can and should respond to maintain the necessary foothold.

To understand the NPCSC's current role in the interpretation of the Basic Law, it is important to look at their approach to the interpretation of a group of provisions in the Basic Law that are aimed at the realisation of governance by universal suffrage of Hong Kong through locally held elections. The development of a system of direct elections was a significant focus during the Sino–British negotiations

Moments: Constitutionalising the Constitution' in R Albert, M Guruswamy and N Basnyat (eds), *Founding Moments in Constitutionalism* (Hart Publishing, 2019), 33–51; E Ip, 'The Politics of Constitutional Common Law in Hong Kong Under Chinese Sovereignty' (2016) 25 *Washington International Law Journal* 565.

[23] *HKSAR v Ma Wai Kwan David* [1997] 1 HKLRD 761 (CA); *Ng Ka Ling v Director of Immigration* (1999) 2 HKCFAR 4 (CFA); *Ng Ka Ling v Director of Immigration (No 2)* (1999) 2 HKCFAR 141 (CFA); JMM Chan et al (eds), *Hong Kong's Constitutional Debate: Conflict Over Interpretation* (Hong Kong, Hong Kong University Press, 2000). Such confrontations were foreshadowed by commentators during the drafting of the Basic Law of Hong Kong. See M Davis, *Constitutional Confrontation in Hong Kong: Issues and Implications of the Basic Law* (New York, St Martin's Press, 1990).

prior to Hong Kong's handover to China.[24] The provisions of the Basic Law set out the parameters for reforming the mode of electing the Chief Executive and the members of LegCo respectively. The process for reform (in terms of the requisite majority in LegCo, the consent of the Chief Executive and the role of the legislative body of the PRC (NPCSC)) is also set out in the text. Annexes I and II to the Basic Law state that any changes should 'be reported to the [NPCSC] for the record' (in the case of the election of members of LegCo) or 'for approval' (in the case of the election of the Chief Executive).[25] While Annexes I and II make clear that the NPCSC has a role to play in political reform, this is only at the end of the reform process once any reform package has been voted on by LegCo and approved by the Chief Executive: paragraph 7 of Annex I states that any amendments to the method for selecting the Chief Executive 'shall be reported to the [NPCSC] *for approval*' (emphasis added). Paragraph (III) of Annex II states that any amendments to the method for selecting LegCo 'shall be reported to the [NPCSC] *for the record*' (emphasis added). The political reform process was therefore envisaged as a process that would be primarily locally initiated, driven and led. However, through various interpretations and decisions relating to the relevant provisions of the Basic Law, the NPCSC has created a new role for itself at the *inception* of the reform exercise and has then exercised this role in numerous ways.[26] The distinction between a 'decision' and an 'interpretation' by the NPCSC is unclear. The NPCSC has provided no indicators or guidance on when it will issue one over the other on a particular issue, but the purported effect of both instruments appears to be the same from the text of the instruments: they are promulgated as authoritative positions on the meaning of a particular provision of the Basic Law. These various 'interpretations' and 'decisions' on the meaning and implementation of these provisions of the Basic Law arguably augment and amend the provisions outside the proper constitutional amendment procedures set out in the Basic Law. This reality is augmented by the recent decision of the High Court of Hong Kong on the application of Chinese law and jurisdiction in Hong Kong. The case concerned the development of a cross-border rail link and, in particular, the co-location of immigration and customs clearance facilities for both Hong Kong and mainland China on the Hong Kong side of the rail link. Multiple applications for judicial review were lodged to challenge the validity of the co-location agreement on the basis that it violated the 'one country, two systems' rubric of the Basic Law and, in particular the fact that Chinese laws should not apply in Hong Kong unless expressly listed in Annex III. These laws generally tend to be restricted to those matters that China does have authority over with respect to Hong Kong (namely, defence and foreign affairs). In rejecting the applications for judicial review, the Court was swayed

[24] See Davis, *Constitutional Confrontation in Hong Kong* (ibid) esp 27–29. See also, S Jhaveri, 'Reconsitutionalizing Politics in the Hong Kong Special Administrative Region' (2018) 13 *Asian Journal of Comparative Law* 27.

[25] Basic Law, Annex II, Part III and Annex I, para 7.

[26] See also the contribution of Michael C Davis in this collection.

by, inter alia, a decision of the NPCSC approving the co-location agreement and confirming that it was consistent with the Chinese Constitution, the Basic Law and the principle of 'one country two systems'.[27] This was despite the fact that this decision had no specific basis in the Basic Law.[28] This raises the general spectre of increasing input from the NPCSC in Hong Kong affairs.[29]

In this environment there is a case for a stronger role for the local courts in dealing with these issues and retaining a foothold in the interpretation of the Basic Law. This involves resolving some problematic issues relating to the nature of and approach to the interpretation of the Basic Law. Under Article 158(1) of the Basic Law, plenary powers of interpretation are vested in the NPCSC. Under Article 158(2), the NPCSC authorises the Hong Kong courts to interpret 'on their own … thc provisions of the Basic Law' in adjudicating cases. However, in respect of certain provisions (described in Article 158(3)), where the courts are unclear about the meaning of those provisions, they must consult the NPCSC for an interpretation before making a decision, and then must do so in accordance with the interpretation so provided. Importantly, the role of the Hong Kong courts is in no way *automatically* abridged by the plenary interpretation powers of the NPCSC under Article 158, either as a matter of design or in the way the powers have been utilised to date. The lack of clarity in the constitutional set-up should, therefore, not be utilised to automatically weaken the role of the courts. The Hong Kong courts have discretion on whether or not they should refer something for interpretation to the NPCSC.[30] It is not suggested that the courts challenge the authority of or any legitimate input by the NPCSC on Article 23 issues, or reverse the established jurisprudence on the scope of Article 158(3). Instead, it is argued that the courts should not *automatically* assume a deferential and self-excluding role for itself. Instead they should deal with the issue on a case-by-case basis.

Where the NPCSC issues interpretations outside of any judicial request, the courts can respond to such interpretations in one of four possible ways (in order of decreasing deference). First, the court might consider the extent to which it is bound by such interpretations.[31] Second, the court could (and, I would argue, should) apply common law interpretive techniques to any such NPCSC interpretations rather than accept them at 'face value'. Such common law interpretive

[27] *Leung Chung Hang Sixtus & Ors v President Of Legislative Council & Ors* [2018] HKCFI 2657.

[28] 'Decision of the Standing Committee of the National People's Congress on Approving the Co-Operation Agreement between the Mainland and the Hong Kong Special Administrative Region on the Establishment of the Port at the West Kowloon Station of the Guangzhou-Shenzhen-Hong Kong Express Rail Link for Implementing Co-Location Arrangement' (27 December 2017), available at www.thb.gov.hk/eng/policy/transport/policy/colocation/EN%20Decision%20(2%20Jan).pdf.

[29] See also the contribution of Albert HY Chen in this collection.

[30] C Chan, 'State Immunity: Reassessing the Boundaries of Judicial Autonomy in Hong Kong' [2012] *Public Law* 601; C Chan, 'Reconceptualising the Relationship Between the Mainland Chinese Legal System and the Hong Kong Legal System' (2011) 6 *Asian Journal of Comparative Law* 1.

[31] PJ Yap, *Courts and Democracies in Asia* (Cambridge University Press, 2017) ch 12 (relying on *Director of Immigration v Chong Fung Yuen* (2001) 4 HKCFAR 211, 222G – H (Li CJ)).

techniques include, most importantly, the purposive approach to interpretation.[32] Here the courts could have a role to play in adopting a more Basic Law-consonant and -compliant interpretation of an NPCSC interpretation. The text of the NPCSC's interpretation would be construed in the light of its text, context and purpose. With respect to context, this would include construing the text of the NPCSC interpretation in a way that complies with other relevant provisions of the Basic Law.[33] Third, the court could evaluate the validity of such 'interpretations' and 'strike them down' should they amount to, for example, 'amendments' via the back door outside the prescribed Article 159 amendment procedure.[34] A fourth possibility, which has been under-explored in the literature or cases in Hong Kong, is the utilisation of some form of a basic structure or basic features doctrine to evaluate the legitimacy of such interpretations that amount to 'unconstitutional' or 'questionable' 'amendments through interpretation' by the NPCSC. Courts in various common law jurisdictions have sought to identify 'basic features' or the 'basic structure' of the Constitution to varying ends. The Supreme Court of India, for example, has stated on multiple occasions that such basic features are beyond amendment by Parliament and the courts will strike down any amendments that seek to limit or constrain or violate such features.[35] This idea of the basic structure or features of a constitution makes particular sense in the Hong Kong context. It could serve as a constitutional hurdle for any decisions or interpretations by the NPCSC that have to comply with certain constitutional fundamentals of the Basic Law, including the idea of autonomy and the division of power built into the Basic Law. Article 159(4) states that: 'No amendment to this Law shall contravene the established basic policies of the People's Republic of China regarding Hong Kong'. The interpretive division of powers is a key aspect

[32] See PW Hogg, 'Canada: From Privy Council to Supreme Court' in J Goldsworthy (ed), *Interpreting Constitutions: A Comparative Study* (Oxford, Oxford University Press, 2006) 82 for a summary of the main approaches to constitutional interpretation.

[33] See C Chan, 'How Hong Kong's Courts Interpret Beijing's Interpretation of the Basic Law May Yet Surprise' *South China Morning Post*, 10 November 2016, available at www.scmp.com/comment/insight-opinion/article/2044385/how-hong-kongs-courts-interpret-beijings-interpretation. See also, C Chan, 'Thirty Years from Tiananmem: China, Hong Kong, and the Ongoing Experiment to Preserve Liberal Values in an Authoritarian State' *International Journal of Constitutional Law* 17(2) April 2019 439–452.

[34] Following *Ng Ka Ling v Director of Immigration* [1999] 1 HKLRD 315, the Court of Final Appeal asserted such a role for itself. This has not been directly challenged or undermined, and some academics argue is still a possible role for the Hong Kong courts: see C Chan, 'The Legal Limits on Beijing's Power to Interpret Hong Kong's Basic Law' (HKU Legal Scholarship blog, 3 November 2016), available at researchblog.law.hku.hk/2016/11/cora-chan-on-legal-limits-of-beijings.html.

[35] *Kesavananda Bharati v State Of Kerala* [1973] AIR SC 1461 (Supreme Court of India); *Minerva Mills v Union Of India* [1980] AIR SC 1789 (Supreme Court of India). Singapore has a more muted version of the doctrine: *Yong Vui Kong v Public Prosecutor* [2015] 2 SLR 1158; AJ Harding, 'Does the "Basic Structure Doctrine" Apply in Singapore's Constitution? An Inquiry into Some Fundamental Constitutional Premises' in JL Neo (ed), *Constitutional Interpretation in Singapore: Theory and Practice* (London, Routledge, 2016). See also S Jhaveri, 'Recent Judicial Comments on the Basic Structure of the Constitution' (Singapore Public Law blog, 20 April 2016), available at singaporepubliclaw.com/2016/04/20/recent-judicial-comments-on-the-basic-structure-of-the-constitution.

of these 'basic policies' and one that can be the subject of review by the courts in Hong Kong on the basis of a 'basic features doctrine'-style approach to interpreting NPCSC interpretations and decisions.[36]

The above discussion has proposed a range of strategies the courts might use to maintain a role in the interpretation of Article 23. However, it has to be recognised that the court's position may ultimately be precarious. As a matter of political reality, the NPCSC and the Central People's Government are unlikely to be invisible in the interpretation of the Basic Law. This is not the direction in which local–Central Government relations are going, with ever increasing central involvement in the political governance and autonomy of Hong Kong.[37] If the courts took a stronger role in pushing back against or reinterpreting NPCSC interpretations, they might lose their perceived legitimacy and influence once they are viewed as being more active in constitutional adjudication in this area. This could lead to push back from the NPCSC, which may issue retaliatory interpretations of the Basic Law. Worse still, the NPCSC may issue a 'clarifying' and perhaps contrary interpretation of Article 158 on the conditions for an interpretation by the NPCSC. This could ultimately lead to the diminishment of the judicial role, as the courts would become bound by more interpretations of the Basic Law from the NPCSC in future cases. This could be an irreversible position in the absence of any democratic or constitutional mechanisms to combat any unilateral constitutional usurpation by the NPCSC.[38]

This paper, therefore, proposes a bifurcated approach for the courts. While retaining a role in the interpretation of Article 23, cases should also be diverted to administrative law.[39] The latter is primarily concerned with enforcing *statutory* boundaries to the exercise of executive power. This minimises engagement with Article 23 of the Basic Law. It takes the court's jurisdiction to the constitutionally subcutaneous realm of the common law (which is entrenched and protected under Article 8). This diversion from constitutional to common law administrative law will be critical should there be further shifts in power to the NPCSC in the interpretation of the Basic Law.

[36] S Jhaveri, 'Reconsitutionalizing Politics in the Hong Kong Special Administrative Region' (2018) 13 *Asian Journal of Comparative Law* 27 for an analysis of recent cases that may indicate the court's likely approach.

[37] See, eg, the State Council's White Paper (n 6). More recently, President Xi Jinping reiterated China's 'comprehensive jurisdiction' over Hong Kong in his speech at the 19th Communist Party National Congress: see J Xi, 'Secure a Decisive Victory' (2017). This meant that Hong Kong's autonomy would always be subject to the Central Government's supervision and, presumably, revision. See also the contributions of Michael C Davis and Albert HY Chen in this collection.

[38] The concern being that there could be retaliation against strong judicial review. See Yap, *Constitutional Dialogue* (2015) chs 1 and 12; S Issacharoff, *Fragile Democracies: Contested Power in the Era of Constitutional Courts* (Cambridge, Cambridge University Press, 2017) ch 11; S Gardbaum, 'Are Strong Constitutional Courts Always a Good Thing for New Democracies?' (2015) 53 *Columbia Journal of Transnational Law* 285, 289.

[39] It is, of course, possible for common law principles to be effectively eclipsed by subsequent legislative enactments. However, there is an inertia argument in their favour: they remain effective until and unless this happens, leaving space for the courts to continue to develop and augment such principles.

II. Mainstreaming Administrative Law

This section highlights the administrative law tools that might be utilised by applicants seeking to challenge executive action taken under the national security legislation that will inevitably be introduced to comply with the Article 23 duty.[40] It maps out three possible scenarios to exemplify possible uses for the administrative law grounds of review. The discussion in this section is based on content from the 2003 draft National Security (Legislative Provisions) Ordinance – it is, of course, not clear that the executive will use that as a foundation (it would be politically unpopular to do so). However, the 2003 Draft Bill is used to generally identify possible flash points in the legislation that will be likely sites for administrative law challenges.[41]

A. Challenging the Secretary of Justice's Prosecutorial Discretion

The extent to which the courts will engage in the substantive review of decisions to prosecute someone under national security legislation is topical in recent history with the prosecution of student activists involved in the Occupy Central movement.[42] Article 63 of the Basic Law provides that: 'The Department of Justice of the Hong Kong Special Administrative Region shall control criminal prosecutions, free from any interference'. The Secretary of Justice exercises a range of discretionary powers pursuant to this constitutional provision, including the choice whether to prosecute suspects, to grant a stay or withdrawal of criminal proceedings, to make decisions on plea bargaining and to prepare charges before the court. Section 18C of the 2003 Draft Bill stated that prosecution for any offence was to be done with the written consent of the Secretary for Justice. Should such a provision reappear in the Article 23 law that is finally passed, such decisions are likely to be the subject of challenge.

The courts have expressed some reservations about the review of prosecutorial discretion. It is firmly established that prosecutorial independence is a 'linchpin of the rule of law'.[43] The decision as to whether an individual should be prosecuted is a matter for the prosecuting authorities to decide without

[40] Applicants will need to exhaust all appeals and alternative remedies before they commence administrative law proceedings: the national security legislation is likely to set up an internal appeals process.

[41] The 2003 Draft Bill is available at www.basiclaw23.gov.hk/english/download/CSA-markup-e3.pdf.

[42] Including applications to review sentences by the Department of Justice. See R Yuen, 'Joshua Wong, Nathan Law and Alex Chow are in jail because Hong Kong law demands it' *South China Morning Post*, 23 August 2017, available at www.scmp.com/comment/insight-opinion/article/2107959/joshua-wong-nathan-law-and-alex-chow-are-jail-because-hong.

[43] *RV v Director of Immigration* [2008] 4 HKLRD 529 (CFI) [74] (Hartmann J).

'any practice savouring of political pressure either by the executive or Parliament, being brought to bear upon the law officers when engaged in reaching a decision in any particular case …'.[44] The courts have held that this fundamental principle is preserved by Article 63 of the Basic Law and is underpinned by Sections 14 and 15 of the Criminal Procedure Ordinance (Cap 221).[45] The courts accept arguments that they may not be suited – they lack political legitimacy and competency – to make assessments about the 'public interest' embodied in prosecutorial decisions.[46]

However, a number of arguments can be made that prosecutorial discretion should be subject to judicial review in appropriate circumstances, especially in the area of national security. It is necessary for the prosecutor to be accountable to those affected by prosecutorial decisions and also the public at large. This is especially in the context of national security legislation, which is likely to be skewed in favour of crime control over due process. The political nature of the national security offences also points towards the need for some judicial oversight. In addition, the deferential approach to judicial review of prosecutorial decisions adopted in other jurisdictions is justified on the basis that there exist appropriate political safeguards to protect against any abuses of power. In Hong Kong it could be argued that there is a lack of effective political channels to ensure close oversight. Indeed, legislative supervision is seemingly only effective over general prosecutorial policies or those decisions that are well publicised.[47]

This was recognised by the courts in *RV v Director of Immigration*[48] where the courts sought to revisit its earlier deferential position taken in *Keung Siu Wah v Attorney-General*.[49] In the latter case, Fuad V-P of the Court of Appeal had observed that 'Few subjects [are] less adapted to the judicial review procedure … than the exercise of the Attorney-General's discretion in deciding whether to institute criminal proceedings and what charge should be preferred'.[50] In *RV*, Hartmann J observed that 'since the Basic Law came into effect, this court has the power to determine whether the Secretary for Justice, in his control of criminal prosecutions, has, or has not, acted within the limits of his constitutional power'. In that fundamental respect, 'the source and nature of the power must be different from

[44] J Li and J Edwards, *The Law Officers of the Crown* (London, Sweet and Maxwell, 1964) 224–25; *Sharma v Brown-Antoine* [2007] 1 WLR 780 [788]. For further commentary, see WS Clark, *Judicial Review of The Discretionary Powers of the Attorney-General of Hong Kong in the Conduct of Criminal Proceedings* (1983) 13 *Hong Kong Law Journal* 133; M Thomas, *Prosecution of Corruption Cases in Hong Kong* (1988) 10 *Asian Journal of Public Administration* 99.

[45] *Re C (A Bankrupt)* [2006] 4 HKC 582.

[46] G Cross, *Judicial Review: Prosecution Decisions and Criminal Trials, Conference Presentation at Effective Judicial Review: A Cornerstone of Good Governance*, available at www.doj.gov.hk/eng/public/pdf/2008/dpp20081212e.pdf.

[47] See, eg, M McConville, *Politicians and Prosecutorial Accountability in Hong Kong* (2007) *Common Law World Review* 355, 364 and K Amirthalingam, 'The Public Prosecutor and Sentencing: Drug Trafficking and the Death Penalty in Singapore' (2018) 18 Oxford University Commonwealth Law Journal 46–72.

[48] [2008] 4 HKLRD 529.

[49] [1989] HKCFI 269 (CFI); [1990] 2 HKLR 238 (CA).

[50] ibid 253.

the source and nature of the power as it was exercised when the Court of Appeal gave its judgment in *Keung Siu Wah v Attorney General*'.[51] In *RV*, Hartmann J considered that there are circumstances where judicial review would lie against prosecutorial decisions. These circumstances 'must demonstrate that the Secretary has acted outside of his very broad powers', in particular where bad faith or rigid fettering of discretion is evident. Added to that a prosecution decision can be reviewed where it amounts to an abuse of process. This may be an important ground of judicial review in the context of the national security legislation in order to ensure that prosecutions are not politically motivated. Indeed, Hartmann J has also suggested elsewhere that judicial review would lie where the 'Department of Justice came to a plainly wrong decision not to prosecute; that is, a decision which is unreasonable in law'.[52] This would seem to suggest reviewability on the grounds of irrationality, bad faith, abuse of process or if the prosecutor unduly fetters their discretion in making prosecutorial decisions.[53] The continued opening up of judicial review on administrative law grounds of prosecutorial discretion will be important going forward.[54]

B. Decisions under the Societies Ordinance

Another likely challenge in this area is going to be restrictions on the creation or continuance of political parties or societies. This is topical with the recent establishment of parties advocating, in some form, the idea of the complete independence of Hong Kong from China. There are concerns that such pro-independence movements undermine sovereignty arrangements established by the Basic Law.[55]

[51] This approach to the court may be necessary given the recent unsuccessful attempts to hold the Secretary of Justice to account via the LegCo: L Sum, 'Lawmaker loses bid to summon Hong Kong justice minister Teresa Cheng to discuss CY Leung decision with Legislative Council' *South China Morning Post*, 24 January 2019, available at www.scmp.com/news/hong-kong/politics/article/2183445/lawmaker-loses-bid-summon-hong-kong-justice-minister-discus.

[52] *Kwan Pearl Sun Chu v Department of Justice* [2007] HKCU 8 [10].

[53] See also S Jhaveri, M Ramsden, and A Scully-Hill, *Administrative Law in Hong Kong*, 3rd edn (Hong Kong, LexisNexis, 2013) chs 6 and 9.

[54] For example, there is a pending application for judicial review of the Secretary of Justice's decision not to prosecute the former Chief Executive of Hong Kong, Leung Chun-ying, on corruption charges: see C Lau, 'Activist applies for judicial review of Hong Kong justice minister's decision not to prosecute CY Leung' *South China Morning Post*, 12 March 2019.

[55] Article 1 of the Basic Law states that 'The Hong Kong Special Administrative Region is an inalienable part of the People's Republic of China'. A number of members from these political parties were barred from running in the most recent general elections for seats in LegCo in September 2016. They have issued election petitions to challenge this, and the proceedings are ongoing. See also T Cheung, 'Explain this: why all the fuss about Hong Kong independence?' *South China Morning Post*, 7 September 2017, available at www.scmp.com/news/hong-kong/politics/article/2110059/explain-why-all-fuss-about-hong-kong-independence. See also recent events surrounding public advocacy (mostly by students) of pro-independence ideas: T Tam, 'Hong Kong independence banners present a real test of Carrie Lam's political wisdom' *South China Morning Post*, 10 September 2017, available at www.scmp.com/news/hong-kong/article/2110528/hong-kong-independence-banners-present-real-test-carrie-lams.

Most recently, a party was banned for the first time under the Societies Ordinance for its advocacy of independence from the rest of China, which posed a threat to national security and public safety.[56] This in turn could come within the scope of the proposed offences that existed within the 2003 Draft Bill and may well be present in the Article 23 law that is finally introduced. For example, the 2003 Draft Bill proposed a new offence of subversion where any person 'disestablishes the basic system of the People's Republic of China as established by the Constitution of the People's Republic of China … by using force or serious criminal means'. 'Serious criminal means' could include 'any act which … seriously endangers the health or safety of the public or a section of the public'.[57] Section 15 of the 2003 Draft Bill amended the Societies Ordinance to allow the Secretary for Security to proscribe any local organisation 'if he reasonably believes that the proscription is necessary in the interests of national security and is proportionate for such purpose'.[58] This could include where the organisation had committed or was attempting to commit any of the offences, including subversion. Therefore, the Secretary for Security could argue that an organisation that was advocating the independence of Hong Kong (which is not in line with the basic system of governance established under the Chinese Constitution) through mass movement comes within the scope of a proscription of this kind.

It is possible, therefore, for administrative law challenges of the application of such restrictions on new political parties.[59] The courts have routinely sought to determine the legality of a decision by the executive by construing the statutory provisions that confer power on the decision-maker. This exercise of statutory interpretation is designed to identify the scope or extent of the power-conferring clause. If the decision-maker has acted beyond that scope, then his decision is illegal or ultra vires. This is even the case where a statutory provision is framed in subjective language, granting what appears to be unfettered or unlimited discretion to the decision-maker to act as he thinks fit. This could be the case under a provision such as Section 15 of the 2003 Draft Bill which proposed to empower the Secretary for Security to proscribe an organisation 'if he reasonably believes' it is in the interests of national security.

The courts have had to consider whether a statutory provision, read alone, confers complete discretion on the decision-maker to decide as he wishes or

[56] The ban is currently being reviewed by a three-member panel of the Executive Council (the Cabinet of Hong Kong): A Lum, 'Leaders of banned Hong Kong National Party to face three-man Exco panel for appeal' *South China Morning Post*, 12 December 2018, available at www.scmp.com/news/hong-kong/politics/article/2177525/leaders-banned-hong-kong-national-party-face-three-man-exco.

[57] 2003 Draft Bill, cl 4.

[58] See also the contribution of Simon NM Young in this collection.

[59] The analysis here can apply to other executive / administrative decisions under the national security legislative framework: eg, s 15(1)(a)(iii) of the Pensions Ordinance (Cap 89) which allows for the cancellation of pensions for government officers if convicted of any of the offences, or s 31(1)(a) of the Education Ordinance (Cap 279) which allows for the cancellation of the registration of a manager of a school convicted of any offences.

whether the statutory discretion must be read, notwithstanding the subjective language in which it is drafted, within the meaning of the legislative framework as a whole. That is, a public body may exercise such decision-making power as is granted to it by law but it must not act outside the scope of that power. In order to remain intra vires, the decision maker must know the limits of the power granted to him and he must limit himself to a consideration only of relevant factors when exercising that power. The courts have consistently held that such language does not displace judicial review. The court will review it on traditional administrative law grounds.[60]

Obviating the effect of subjectively couched discretion in Article 23 legislation will be an important component of judicial review, especially to consider arguments that the Secretary of Security's decision was based on an irrelevant consideration or an improper purpose. Interestingly, the wording of Section 15 also provided the courts with the opportunity to revisit whether the proscription was indeed 'necessary in the interests of national security and is proportionate for such purpose'. The courts in Hong Kong have, on occasion, shown a willingness to make this assessment in public order situations.[61] However, more recently, there are indications of a shift in the court's approach. For example, the Court of First Instance has held that *ordre public* – broadly interpreted – is a legitimate aim for requiring candidates seeking a LegCo seat to declare that they will uphold the Basic Law and pledge allegiance to the Hong Kong Special Administrative Region.[62] The proportionality analysis that followed from this conclusion was cursory and brief. There is thus a growing concern that the courts are becoming increasingly cautious about review where the case raises such politically sensitive questions.[63]

This is a further indicator that there is a growing need for the courts to move outside the specific context of the rights set out in the Basic Law in adjudicating cases. As the discussion in Part 2(c) demonstrates, applicants have fared better when they redirect their claim to common law rights and standards of administrative law than when they have relied on rights in the Basic Law. This section has focused on the use of the latter: the following focuses on the former.

[60] *Padfield v Minister for Agriculture, Fisheries and Food* [1968] AC 997 applied in *Li Yiu Kee v Chinese University of Hong Kong* [2009] HKEC 184. See also [2010] HKEC 1159 (CA) and *Fok Chun Wa v Hospital Authority* [2012] HKEC 471; *Re Tran Quoc Cuong v Khuc The Loc* [1991] 2 HKLR 312; *Capital Rich Development & Anor v Town Planning Board* [2007] 2 HKC 542; *Roberts v Hopwood* [1925] AC 578 applied in *Chan Noi Heung* [2007] HKEC 885.

[61] *Leung Kwok Hung & Ors v HKSAR* [2005] 3 HKLRD 164.

[62] *Chan Ho Tin v Lo Ying Ki Alan* [2018] 2 HKLRD 7 [180]–[183]. This builds on an earlier decision of the Court of Final Appeal in *HKSAR v Ng Kung Siu* where the then Chief Justice Li held *Ng Kung Siu*, the Court of Final Appeal held that: (a) the boundary of the concept cannot be precisely defined; (b) the concept includes what is necessary for the protection of the general welfare or for the interests of the collectivity as a whole; and (c) the concept must remain a function of time, place, and circumstances (459I–460E). See also the contribution of Simon NM Young in this collection.

[63] See C Petersen, 'Prohibiting the Hong Kong National Party: Has Hong Kong Violated the International Covenant on Civil and Political Rights' [2018] 3 *Hong Kong Law Journal* 789 for a critique of the courts' proportionality analysis.

C. Procedural Fairness of Any Investigatory or Criminal Process

Various provisions of the 2003 Draft Bill recognised the need for procedural integrity in the making of decisions. The courts in Hong Kong have long recognised a general duty to act fairly.[64] Even if the national security legislation implements its own procedural scheme for making decisions of arrest, detention and decisions to deregister societies under the Societies Ordinance, the courts will consider whether they need to be supplemented by the common law. Where a statutory scheme is 'insufficient to achieve justice and fairness' the courts will find that the common law can supplement the statutory scheme.[65]

The content of the common law duty to act fairly (for example, whether it includes a right to legal representation, oral hearing, right to reasons, etc) has been the subject of detailed judicial analysis. For present purposes, the most important strand of discussion of the courts' analysis relates to how potential impacts on fundamental rights impact on standards of procedural fairness. This is important for the strategy proposed in this paper. The argument is that the courts should divert cases from the Basic Law to utilise administrative law. In this regard, courts do get inspiration from the rights context to augment its scrutiny and heightens the standard of fairness expected of the executive in decision-making. In *Secretary for Security v Sakthevel Prabakar*,[66] the courts had to consider the extent to which Hong Kong is under a duty not to return (*non-refoulement*) individuals to a place where they are at risk of persecution or human rights abuse. The issue that came before the Court of Final Appeal was whether the Government was under a duty to screen *non-refoulement* claims made under the Convention against Torture and, if so, what degree of procedural protection was to be observed. In *Prabakar* the Court of Final Appeal recognised that a higher standard of procedural fairness is called for where fundamental rights of 'momentous' importance are at stake, in this case the risk that *refoulement* could infringe the right to be free from torture. In turn, the Government had to undertake a procedurally fair investigation in three major respects. Firstly, it was necessary to provide the claimant with every reasonable opportunity to establish the claim. Secondly, the Government had to properly assess the claim, taking into account: (i) country of origin information; (ii) evidence of torture; (iii) the claimant's involvement in activities that makes them vulnerable to torture if returned; and (iv) the claimant's credibility.[67] Thirdly, where a claim was rejected, the Government should furnish reasons which

[64] *In re HK* [1967] 1 All ER 226, applied in multiple cases in Hong Kong (see, eg, *Wong Chi Sung v Chinese Medicine Practitioners Board of the Chinese Medical Council of Hong Kong* (unreported, HCAL 33/2003, 20 February 2004)).

[65] *Lau Tak-pui v Immigration Tribunal* [1992] 1 HKLR 374, 384 (Clough JA).

[66] *Secretary for Security v Sakthevel Prabakar* (unreported, FACV 16/2033, 8 June 2004).

[67] See M Ramsden, 'Hong Kong's High Standard of Fairness and New Statutory Torture Screening Mechanism' [2013] *Public Law* 232.

were sufficient to enable the claimant to consider the possibilities of administrative and judicial review. Accordingly, in relying on the bare conclusions of the United Nations High Commissioner for Refugees (UNHCR), the Hong Kong authorities would be unable to give cogent reasons for their decision to remove a torture claimant from the territory. This meant that the Government could not simply delegate the investigation of claims made under the Torture Convention to the UNHCR.

Following *Prabakar*, the Government established a torture screening mechanism that in broad terms followed the same procedure that was used by the UNHCR in investigating claims. This screening mechanism was successfully challenged in the Court of First Instance in *FB v Director of Immigration*.[68] The court held that the government's refusal to allow torture claimants to have legal representation violated a 'high standard of fairness'. Legal representation at every stage of the screening process was necessary because of the 'seriousness and complexity' of the issues. Moreover, given that most claimants would not have the financial means to pay for lawyers, and given that the right to legal representation would be illusory without the provision of financial support, the government was under a duty to provide legal aid. Similarly, a number of components of the screening mechanism did not meet a high standard of fairness. In particular, the officer responsible for interviewing the torture claimant was not the same person who made the decision as to whether the claim was substantiated. This division of roles was deemed to be inherently unfair given that it prevented a proper assessment of credibility where the decision-maker has not interviewed the claimant in person.[69]

Taken together the *Prabakar* and *FB* decisions provide a good illustration of how the importance of the legal interest at stake impacts on the nature of government decision-making processes. Where the court finds a legal interest to be of particular importance (such as the right to be free from torture), this in turn will justify closer judicial scrutiny of the Government's procedure and also a greater willingness from the courts to declare that such procedures are unlawful. This newly developed ground of fairness is significantly more far-reaching than 'procedural fairness' and other existing uses of fairness in judicial review. Key innovations include: (a) the courts' review of systemic problems with decision-making processes; (b) the extension of the courts' review of the fairness of such processes beyond the traditional focus on, for example, the right to a hearing; and (c) the introduction of a sliding scale of review with stronger or 'anxious' scrutiny

[68] *FB v Director of Immigration* [2009] 2 HKLRD 346.

[69] Since then the legislature has established a statutory torture screening mechanism, for a critique see: CS Kochhar-George, 'Recent Developments in Hong Kong's Torture Screening Process' (2012) 42 *Hong Kong Law Journal* 385. See also K Loper, 'Towards Comprehensive Refugee Legislation in Hong Kong? Reflections of the "Torture Screening" Procedures' (2009) 39 *Hong Kong Law Journal* 253.

of decision-making processes.[70] This will be an important background consideration for the courts in augmenting procedural fairness in decision-making under national security legislation which has similar implications for the liberty and rights of an individual. It will only indirectly utilise Basic Law and Bill of Rights Ordinance rights to augment procedural protections of individuals affected by the application of the legislation.

III. Conclusion

The paper looks at two major roles for the courts and the common law: first, an interpretive role under Article 23 and the Basic Law; and secondly an administrative law role. However, this proposal needs to be contextualised. Courts will always be a final defence: they generally act ex post and in response to specific controversies. The political reality is that the courts cannot have a dominant voice on these issues and be effective tools for systemic change.[71] Their work will need to be reinforced by co-operation and commitment from the other branches to strike an optimal balance between national security and the rule of law. A culture of constitutional polyphony will be critical.[72] The executive will need to be mindful of the need to strike a balance when considering questions of institutional design of law enforcement agencies under Article 23 legislation.[73] Secondly, legislative debates during the passing of Article 23 legislation must be robust. This is especially so as, as discussed above, there is the possibility of the NPCSC issuing interpretations under Article 23 *during* legislative drafting and debates. Should that happen, there will need to be sufficient push-back on these interpretations built into legislative debates.[74] Thoughtful and considered interventions during legislative debates upstream can have important secondary outcomes further downstream in setting out what the courts can then rely on to clarify grey areas in the course of constitutional interpretation; what the executive can utilise to operationalise new provisions in new contexts; and indeed how the electorate debate and discuss issues of constitutional importance.

[70] See further S Jhaveri, 'Transforming "fairness" as a ground of judicial review in Hong Kong' (2013) 11 *International Journal of Constitutional Law* 358.

[71] See F de Londras and F Davis, 'Controlling the Executive in Times of Terrorism: Competing Perspectives on Effective Oversight' (2010) 30 *Oxford Journal of Legal Studies* 19.

[72] See FAR Bennion, *Bennion on Statutory Interpretation: A Code*, 5th edn (London, LexisNexis, 2008) 26–36: proposing that there are four types of 'interpreter', namely, the legislator, courts and other enforcement agencies, the jurist or text writer, and the subject who is bound by legislation. See also D Kyritsis, *Where Our Protection Lies: Separation of Powers and Constitutional Review* (Oxford, Oxford University Press, 2017) ch 2.

[73] See the contributions by Johannes Chan, PY Lo and Fiona de Londras and Cora Chan in this collection.

[74] See also the contribution of Margaret Ng in this collection.

Third, there is a need to have a considered and strategic approach to civil society movements surrounding Article 23 matters.[75] There are many lessons to be learnt from recent significant movements: Occupy Central and the more recent protests of 2019. Fourthly, the efforts to push political reform and democratisation under Articles 45 and 68 of the Basic Law need to continue with the ultimate aim of politically empowering local citizens to speak up and be represented on issues of local governance.[76] This will necessarily need to be a multi-actor project.

[75] See the contribution of Michael C Davis in this collection; Fu, Peterson, and Young (n 1); AHY Chen, 'The Law and Politics of the Struggle for Universal Suffrage in Hong Kong 2013–15' (2016) 3 *Asian Journal of Law and Society* 189; MC Davis, 'Promises to Keep: The Basic Law, the "Umbrella Movement," and Democratic Reform in Hong Kong' in M Monshipouri (ed), *Information Politics, Protests, and Human Rights in the Digital Age* (New York, Cambridge University Press, 2016) 239. These provide an indicator of lessons to be learned from previous movements.

[76] S Jhaveri, 'Reconstitutionalising Politics in the Hong Kong SAR' (2017) *Asian Journal of Comparative Law* 1.

8

Twilight of the Idolised: Backsliding in Hong Kong's Legal and Judicial Cultures

PUI-YIN LO[1]

A key strength and core value of Hong Kong that has endured beyond Chinese resumption of exercise of sovereignty in 1997 is the adherence to the Rule of Law under a common law-based system developed during British colonial rule.[2] Both the Government of the Hong Kong Special Administrative Region (HKSAR) and Hong Kong civil society have lauded this particularity of the HKSAR's systems, albeit for different purposes.

The Government highlights it to promote not only the distinctiveness of Hong Kong as a Special Administrative Region (SAR) of the People's Republic of China (PRC) but also the attractiveness of Hong Kong as a place for investment and for headquartering and obtaining legal services (particularly to address dispute resolution risks with Chinese counterparts),[3] as well as to prove that the

[1] LLB (Lond), PhD (HKU), Barrister-at-law (England and Wales, Hong Kong), Visiting Fellow, Centre for Comparative and Public Law, The University of Hong Kong (2018–19).

[2] A recently published study suggests that the British colonial administration built up the institutions for the independent and impartial administration of justice and the Rule of Law, including the creation of a single Judicial Department, the creation of a single Legal Department encompassing prosecutions and government-related legal services, and the establishment of the Legal Aid Department and the Department of Law of the University of Hong Kong, to cater for the challenges of the geopolitical situation of East Asia post-World War II and post-Chinese civil war; see N Lee and S Choi, 'The Legalisation of Politics' *Ming Pao*, 30 September 2018, 7 October 2018 and 14 October 2018, available at news.mingpao.com/pns/%e5%89%af%e5%88%8a/article/20180930/s00005/1538244808444, news.mingpao.com/pns/%e5%89%af%e5%88%8a/article/20181007/s00005/1538849258360 and news.mingpao.com/pns/%e5%89%af%e5%88%8a/article/20181014/s00005/1539453986591 respectively; S Choi and N Lee, 'Legalization of Politics: The Geopolitical Situations of Hong Kong and the Consolidation of its Rule of Law in the Cold War' (2017) 55 *Thoughts and Words: Journal of the Humanities and Social Sciences* 187 (which discussed the strengthening of Hong Kong's legal system in the period between 1949 and 1967).

[3] Successive Secretaries for Justice have promoted Hong Kong as a 'legal service hub' based on the common law outside Hong Kong, referring to the top or near-top position Hong Kong has consistently scored in global league tables on rule of law or Independence of the Judiciary;

international media had erred in predicting 'the death of Hong Kong' at the time of the handover and recently, to allay or defend against international concerns and criticisms over controversial legislative proposals.[4] Meanwhile, civil society has been portraying Hong Kong's judges and lawyers as guardians and champions of Hong Kong residents' rights and other fundamental values against encroachments by the Chinese Central Authorities and the Government of the HKSAR.[5] At the same time, Hong Kong civil society has developed 'cause lawyering' strategies: using lawsuits to extend the protection afforded by the HKSAR's constitutional instrument, the Basic Law, thereby achieving breakthroughs on neglected or intractable social issues.[6]

Civil society's positive perception of judges and lawyers in Hong Kong was formed over time. Notable post-handover cases that reinforced this positive image include: the right of abode cases between 1997 and 2001, which involved lawyers taking on numerous cases at the request of civil or community organisations often at short notice and at first at no fee;[7] judges advancing constitutional review and

see, eg, T Cheng, 'Speech by SJ at ASIFMA Compliance and Legal Conference' (29 May 2019), available at www.info.gov.hk/gia/general/201905/29/P2019052900638.htm; R Yuen, 'Speech at the Asia House' (24 May 2017), available at www.doj.gov.hk/eng/public/pdf/2017/sj20170525e2.pdf; YL Wong, 'Role of Hong Kong as East Asia Rises – A Legal Perspective' (Seoul, 8 December 2011), available at www.doj.gov.hk/eng/public/pdf/2011/pr20111208e2.pdf; E Leung, 'Hong Kong as Your Fast Track to China and Asia-Pacific: A Legal Perspective' (Vancouver, 20 November 2003), available at www.doj.gov.hk/eng/archive/pdf/sj211103e.pdf.

[4] See CH Tung, 'Hong Kong: Change in the Air?' *The Diplomat*, 20 June 2017, available at thediplomat.com/2017/06/hong-kong-change-in-the-air (which referred to the World Bank Worldwide Governance Indicators 2016); N Lung and S Kwan, 'Hong Kong's Lost Decade, as Shown by These 12 Global Surveys' *Bloomberg*, 22 December 2018, available at www.bloomberg.com/news/articles/2018-12-21/hong-kong-s-lost-decade-as-shown-by-these-12-global-surveys (which accepted that Hong Kong's ranking on 'rule of law' has improved between 2008 and 2017 in surveys of economies worldwide); M Cheung, 'Transcript of remarks by CS and S for S', Press Release of the Government of the Hong Kong Special Administrative Region, 25 May 2019, available at www.info.gov.hk/gia/general/201905/25/P2019052500474.htm (where the Chief Secretary for Administration relied on the 'very effective judicial review mechanism in the Court of Final Appeal' to persuade chambers of commerce to accept proposed amendments to fugitive offender and mutual legal assistance in criminal matters legislation that would enable, inter alia, ad hoc rendition of persons in Hong Kong to mainland China for trial of a criminal charge or serving of the sentence for a criminal conviction).

[5] See KMY Lee, 'Lawyers as an interest group in Hong Kong's democracy movement' in SS Lo (ed), *Interest Groups and the New Democracy Movement in Hong Kong*, 1st edn (London, Routledge, 2018) 34–61; KMY Lee, 'Beyond the "Professional Project": The Political Positioning of Hong Kong Lawyers' (2017) 50 *International Journal of Law, Crime and Justice* 1.

[6] See, generally, W Tam, *Legal Mobilization under Authoritarianism: The Case of Post-Colonial Hong Kong* (Cambridge, Cambridge University Press, 2013); PY Lo, *The Judicial Construction of Hong Kong's Basic Law: Courts, Politics and Society after 1997* (Hong Kong, Hong Kong University Press, 2014) 328–37. A recent success was the judgment of the Court of Final Appeal dated 6 June 2019 holding that the Government had failed to justify the different treatment between a person who is a party to marriage as understood in and under the laws of Hong Kong and a person who is a party to a same-sex marriage entered into outside Hong Kong according to the place in which it was entered, for the purpose of conferral of spousal benefits under the regulations of the Hong Kong civil service and for eligibility for joint assessment of salaries tax: *Leung Chun Kwong v Secretary for the Civil Service & Anor* [2019] HKCFA 19.

[7] See *Ng Ka Ling v Director of Immigration* (1999) 2 HKCFAR 4; *Director of Immigration v Chong Fung Yuen* (2001) 4 HKCFAR 221; *Ng Siu Tung v Director of Immigration* (2002) 5 HKCFAR 1.

important interpretative principles on the Basic Law (in light of submissions by the legal teams involved);[8] and between 2002 and 2003, as Carole Petersen has chronicled, many members of the legal profession and academia,[9] the Hong Kong Bar Association (HKBA) and the Law Society of Hong Kong (LSHK)[10] contributed copiously to the debate regarding the HKSAR Government's proposed introduction of national security legislation to fulfil Article 23 of the Basic Law. The last-mentioned involvement fuelled up a popular opposition movement that managed to force the Government to ultimately shelf the bill.[11]

After 2003, members of the legal profession, the HKBA, and the LSHK have continued to voice concerns over acts of the HKSAR Government and even the Central Authorities that might have an impact on the rule of law.[12] One senior judge warned of a 'storm of unprecedented ferocity' over the rule of law in Hong Kong when he retired in 2013.[13] Hundreds of lawyers have joined five 'silent marches' to express their belief that certain Chinese acts or Hong Kong legislative proposals might undermine the integrity of the HKSAR's legal system and judicial

[8] Significant acts of the judges in the period between 1997 and 2001 included assertion of jurisdiction to review acts of the Central Authorities affecting Hong Kong on consistency with the Basic Law (*Ng Ka Ling* (ibid)), a discriminating approach narrowing the ambit of an NPCSC interpretation of the Basic Law adopted in 1999 (*Chong Fung Yuen* (ibid)), and the construction of a framework to protecting fundamental rights that requires the Government to justify restrictions thereon (see *HKSAR v Ng Kung Siu* (1999) 2 HKCFAR 442).

[9] Of particular note is the Article 23 Concern Group formed by, among others, three former Chairmen of the HKBA.

[10] Hong Kong's legal profession is a divided profession consisting of barristers and solicitors in the English tradition. Barristers are advocates specialising in litigation; they have general rights of audience before all HKSAR courts. Solicitors are qualified to provide legal advice and legal services to clients, including representation in litigation, but their rights of audience before the courts are limited, though some experienced solicitors are granted 'higher rights of audience' to appear before all HKSAR courts after assessment. Barristers are members of the HKBA. Solicitors are members of the LSHK. The HKBA and the LSHK together constitute the mainstream voice of the legal profession.

[11] C Petersen, 'Hong Kong's Spring of Discontent: The Rise and Fall of the National Security Bill in 2003' in H Fu, C Petersen and SNM Young (eds), *National Security and Fundamental Freedoms* (Hong Kong, Hong Kong University Press, 2005) (including references to comments and statements of the HKBA and LSHK in 2002, the formation and activities of the Article 23 Concern Group of prominent lawyers, and the two-day conference on the draft national security legislation co-organised by the Faculty of Law of the University of Hong Kong, the School of Law of City University of Hong Kong, and the HKBA in June 2013). For the conference, see also the University of Hong Kong's website, available at www.law.hku.hk/hrportal/basic-law/conference-14-15-june-2003. See also the contributions of Michael C Davis and Margaret Ng in this collection.

[12] Published statements of the HKBA are found at hkba.org/events-publication/press-releases-coverage. Among them are statements critical of the words of Vice-President Xi Jinping in July 2008 urging 'mutual understanding and support' and 'cooperation and coordination' among the executive, the legislature and the judiciary of the HKSAR and the White Paper on the practice of the 'one country, two systems' policy in the HKSAR which suggested that members of the executive, legislature, and the judiciary should all be 'patriots'. The HKBA and the LSHK have also issued joint statements condemning personal attacks on judges and judicial officers and responding to inappropriate open questioning of judicial independence and the due administration of justice in Hong Kong.

[13] *Farewell Sitting for the Honourable Mr Justice Bokhary PJ* (2012) 15 HKCFAR 861, 866.

autonomy of the HKSAR.[14] In 2015, the *Financial Times* quoted Hong Kong legal practitioners expressing that the continued practice in Hong Kong of wearing wigs and gowns in courts and ceremonies could be regarded as 'symbolic' of the wishes of the Hong Kong society 'to see the rule of law and judicial independence being entrenched on a permanent basis'. They also indicated that the inability to resolve contentious issues in the political arena in Hong Kong had forced people to go to the streets *and* the courts, and that the people in Hong Kong 'will rely, more than ever, on Hong Kong's judges, steeped in their tradition of independence and neutrality, to provide the stability necessary for their continued prosperity'.[15]

These and other actions and expressions have generated an ardent expectation on the part of the press, civil society and some politicians that lawyers and judges will be a source of resilience against Chinese encroachments of Basic Law rights and other values that define or distinguish Hong Kong's systems and way of life – encroachments that come under the guise of safeguarding the nation's 'sovereignty, security and development interests'.[16]

[14] The five silent marches were organised in 1999 (in respect of the interpretation of the NPCSC to nullify the interpretation of the provisions of the Basic Law of the HKSAR in the right of abode cases), in 2005 (in respect of the NPCSC's interpretation on the term of office of the Chief Executive of the HKSAR elected to fill the casual vacancy of the office arising before completion of the term of his predecessor), in 2014 (in respect of the State Council Information Office's White Paper on the practice of 'one country, two systems' policy in the HKSAR), in 2016 (in respect of the NPCSC's interpretation of Art 104 of the Basic Law that pre-empted the ruling of the HKSAR courts on the validity of oaths of office purportedly taken by two newly elected members of the HKSAR's legislature) and in 2019 (for the purpose of warning and urging the Government to withdraw a controversial set of legislative amendments that would enable the surrender of fugitives and mutual legal assistance in criminal matters by 'special arrangement' on a *per case* basis with *any* jurisdiction, including mainland China). See M Landler, 'After 2 Years, Hong Kong Looks More Like China' *The New York Times*, 1 July 1999, available at www.nytimes.com/1999/07/01/world/after-2-years-hong-kong-looks-more-like-china.html; K Lee, 'Lawyers speak volumes in silent rally' *South China Morning Post*, 20 April 2005, available at www.scmp.com/article/497381/lawyers-speak-volumes-silent-rally; S Lau, A Chu, and B Yap, 'Hong Kong lawyers march to defend judiciary in wake of Beijing's white paper' *South China Morning Post*, 27 June 2014, available at www.scmp.com/news/hong-kong/article/1541814/hong-kong-lawyers-stage-silent-march-oppose-beijings-white-paper; J Ng and R Yeung, 'Hundreds of Hong Kong lawyers in silent march against Beijing oath ruling' *South China Morning Post*, 8 November 2016, available at www.scmp.com/news/hong-kong/politics/article/2044122/hundreds-hong-kong-lawyers-silent-march-against-beijing-oath; L Sum and A Lum, 'Hong Kong extradition bill: lawyers announce rare silent protest as city's leader Carrie Lam survives no confidence vote' *South China Morning Post*, 29 May 2019, available at www.scmp.com/news/hong-kong/politics/article/3012330/hong-kong-extradition-bill-lawyers-announce-rare-silent and A Lum and L Sum, '"Record 3,000" Hong Kong lawyers in silent march against controversial extradition bill' *South China Morning Post*, 6 June 2019, available at www.scmp.com/news/hong-kong/politics/article/3013461/thousands-hong-kong-lawyers-launch-silent-march-against.

[15] M Skapinker, 'Hong Kong law: A trial for wig and gown' *Financial Times*, 23 July 2015, available at www.ft.com/content/df201112-23c3-11e5-9c4e-a775d2b173ca.

[16] President Xi Jinping gave instructions to the Fifth Term Government of the HKSAR in this regard on 1 July 2017; see J Xi, 'Speech at the Meeting Celebrating the 20th Anniversary of Hong Kong's Return to the Motherland and the Inaugural Ceremony of the Fifth Term Government of the Hong Kong Special Administrative Region' (1 July 2017), available at www.chinadaily.com.cn/china/hk20threturn/2017-07/01/content_29959860.htm.

This chapter examines whether this expectation is justified. It does so by two approaches. Firstly, it looks into relevant events and developments in judicial and legal circles, and their interactions with the general civil and communicative communities both inside and outside Hong Kong between 2003 and 2019. Secondly, it considers the organisational features of both the judicial corps and the legal profession in Hong Kong in order to identify institutional, economic, social and cultural characteristics that inform the question. When the essential observations from these two approaches are combined, some trends are spotted. From these trends, it is possible to identify pointers of backsliding of elements that are needed to maintain the rule of law. In the light of what judges and lawyers in Hong Kong have done recently, *it is clear that such backsliding can happen here.*

I. The Judges

The courts of the HKSAR are vested with independent judicial power (including that of final adjudication) of the HKSAR. The apex court, the Court of Final Appeal (CFA), exercises the power of final adjudication in the HKSAR. All these are established pursuant to the Basic Law.[17] The qualifications, tenure, immunities and financial security of judges are guaranteed under the Basic Law, as well as by local legislation[18] and an established system for determining judicial remuneration.

The Basic Law provides that judges and judicial officers are appointed by the Chief Executive upon the recommendation of a Judicial Officers Recommendation Commission (JORC).[19] The Basic Law further provides that the most senior judicial appointments, namely the Chief Justice of the CFA, the judges of the CFA and the Chief Judge of the High Court, must be endorsed by the Legislative Council (LegCo) and reported to the Standing Committee of the National People's Congress (NPCSC) for the record; and that the Chief Justice and the Chief Judge must be Chinese nationals with no right of abode in any foreign country.[20] The Basic Law provides that when assuming office, judges and other members

[17] See Basic Law, Arts 2, 19, 80, 81, 82 and 85. For discussions of the HKSAR courts, see PY Lo 'Hong Kong: Common Law Courts in China' in JR Yeh and WC Chang (eds), *Asian Courts in Context* (Cambridge, Cambridge University Press, 2014) 183–227; AHY Chen and PY Lo, 'Hong Kong's Judiciary under "One Country, Two Systems"' in HP Lee and M Pittard (eds), *Asia-Pacific Judiciaries: Independence, Impartiality and Integrity* (Cambridge, Cambridge University Press, 2018) 131–68.

[18] See, principally, the Hong Kong Court of Final Appeal Ordinance (Cap 484), the High Court Ordinance (Cap 4), the District Court Ordinance (Cap 336), the Magistrates Ordinance (Cap 227), the Judicial Officers (Tenure of Office) Ordinance (Cap 433), and the Pension Benefits (Judicial Officers) Ordinance (Cap 401).

[19] Basic Law, Art 88. The JORC is governed by the Judicial Officers Recommendation Commission Ordinance (Cap 92). The predecessor of the JORC was the Judicial Service Commission established in 1976. For a list of judicial offices appointed by the Chief Executive upon the recommendation of the JORC, see Sch 1 to the Ordinance. For the annual reports of the JORC, see www.judiciary.hk/en/about_us/judicial_officers_reports.html.

[20] Basic Law, Art 90.

of the judiciary in the HKSAR shall, in accordance with law, swear to uphold the Basic Law and swear allegiance to the HKSAR of the PRC.[21]

Judges and judicial officers shall be chosen for their judicial and professional qualities. Recruitment of judges and judicial officers from other common law jurisdictions is allowed.[22] The Judiciary is staffed by both Chinese-speaking and non-Chinese speaking expatriate judges and judicial officers at various levels of courts. The number of non-Chinese speaking expatriate judges has been decreasing since 1997 due to retirement.[23] While there have been temporary appointments of retired English judges to the High Court,[24] nowadays most of the newly recruited members of the Judiciary in the permanent establishment are Chinese HKSAR permanent residents who often received their legal education in Hong Kong.

On the other hand, a particular and distinctive feature of the CFA is the panel of Non-Permanent Judges (NPJs) from common law jurisdictions outside Hong Kong.[25] This panel has continued to be an illustrious list of current and retired judges of the supreme courts of the United Kingdom, Australia, New Zealand and Canada.[26] It has been a practice of the CFA to invite one such 'foreign judge' from this panel to join the five-judge bench hearing final appeals, including appeals that involve the interpretation of the Basic Law.[27] This practice has, to some extent, ensured that the CFA's jurisprudence adheres to the generally accepted standards of the common law[28] and furthered the reputation of the CFA as a source of reliable and sometimes innovative jurisprudence among common law jurisdictions.[29]

The CFA has been lauded for pioneering judgments in establishing and expanding the constitutional jurisdiction of the HKSAR, particularly in respect of

[21] Basic Law, Art 104. It is expected that HKSAR legislation will be enacted to require the playing of the national anthem on the swearing in occasion of judges and judicial officers, in implementation of the National Anthem Law of the PRC, which has been made applicable to the HKSAR by the NPCSC in 2017.

[22] Basic Law, Art 92.

[23] At the end of 2018, three of the 12 members of the Court of Appeal were expatriate judges, two out of 26 judges of the CFI were expatriates, four out of 43 judges of the District Court were expatriates, and one out of 68 magistrates was non-Chinese speaking.

[24] These retired English judges included Sir Brian Keith (who was a Justice of Appeal of the HKSAR before he was appointed a judge of the Queen's Bench Division of the High Court of England and Wales), Sir William Blair, and Sir Richard Field.

[25] Basic Law, Art 82.

[26] The panel of NPJs from a common law jurisdiction outside Hong Kong stood at 14 at the end of 2018 and included two current serving members of the United Kingdom Supreme Court (including its President and Deputy President), two former Presidents of the United Kingdom Supreme Court, two former Chief Justices of Australia, and one former Chief Justice of Canada.

[27] Sir Anthony Mason NPJ, formerly Chief Justice of Australia, had sat in all the major Basic Law cases of the CFA between 1999 and 2014; see A Mason, 'The Rule of Law in the Shadow of the Giant: The Hong Kong Experience' (2011) 33 *Sydney Law Review* 623.

[28] See *Chen Li Hong v Ting Lei Miao* (2000) 3 HKCFAR 9, 23B–C (Lord Cooke of Thorndon NPJ).

[29] See PY Lo, 'Impact of Jurisprudence beyond Hong Kong' in SNM Young and Y Ghai (eds), *Hong Kong's Court of Final Appeal: The Development of the Law in China's Hong Kong* (Cambridge, Cambridge University Press, 2014).

realising the guarantees of fundamental rights and freedoms in the Basic Law and the Hong Kong Bill of Rights.[30] The CFA has adopted a cosmopolitan approach in the use of comparative human rights jurisprudence, resulting in, for example, the adoption of the four-step proportionality analysis as the test for determining the validity of legislative or executive actions that impinge on constitutional rights, on a par with international human rights jurisprudence.[31] Judgments of the CFA have been widely cited and accepted as stating what the law is or as contributing to the development of the law in major common law jurisdictions, including England and Wales.[32] The HKSAR's judicial system is self-contained when administering the HKSAR's laws (including the Basic Law) purely in the common law tradition. Judgments of the HKSAR courts, including those of the CFA, are not subject to appeal or review by another court or body of the PRC. HKSAR courts' interpretations of the Basic Law may be superseded only by the NPCSC, which is vested with the power of interpreting the Basic Law under Article 158 of the same. Thus it has been said that judicial power has been 'thoroughly devolved' to the HKSAR and its courts.[33]

These features have to be read together with undercurrents concerning sustainability. The first generation of senior judges of the CFA have all retired,[34] albeit that two of them have continued as Hong Kong NPJs.[35] The second generation of senior judges of the CFA are approaching retirement.[36] As experiences elsewhere have shown, appointments at the apex level can be politicised. Three features regarding the composition of the JORC[37] and the voting arrangement for

[30] See J Chan and CL Lim (eds), *Law of the Hong Kong Constitution*, 2nd edn (Hong Kong, Sweet & Maxwell, 2015); AHY Chen and PY Lo, 'The Basic Law Jurisprudence of the Court of Final Appeal' in Young and Ghai, *Hong Kong's Court of Final Appeal* (n 29) 352–90; SNM Young, 'Constitutional Rights in Hong Kong's Court of Final Appeal' (2011) 27 *Chinese (Taiwan) Yearbook of International Law and Affairs* 67.

[31] See *Hysan Development Co Ltd v Town Planning Board* (2016) 19 HKCFAR 372 (on the protection of property rights); *HKSAR v Fong Kwok Shan Christine* (2017) 20 HKCFAR 425 (on the permissible restriction of the freedoms of expression and peaceful assembly); *HKSAR v Choi Wai Lun* (2018) 21 HKCFAR 167 (on the presumption of innocence and the reverse onus of proof of a criminal offence); *Director of Immigration v QT* [2018] 4 HKC 403 (on the application of the principle of equality to the proper administration of an immigration policy).

[32] See PY Lo 'Impact of Jurisprudence beyond Hong Kong' (n 29). For a recent example, see *Quan v Bray & Ors* [2018] EWHC 3558, citing in agreement *KEWS v NCHC* (2013) 16 HKCFAR 1, [53] (Ma CJ).

[33] See J Cheng, 'The Story of A New Policy in Hong Kong Journal' (July 2009), available at www.hkbasiclaw.com/Hong%20Kong%20Journal/Cheng%20Jie%20article.htm. Associate Professor Cheng is of the School of Law, Tsinghua University, PRC.

[34] Namely, Chief Justice Li and Permanent Judges Litton and Ching.

[35] Namely, NPJs Chan and Bokhary.

[36] Permanent Judge Tang retired in 2018 but has continued to serve as a Hong Kong NPJ. On the other hand, the Judicial Officers (Extension of Retirement Age) (Amendment) Bill 2019, which is expected to become law in 2019, will postpone retirement of the second generation of CFA judges for five years.

[37] The JORC is chaired by the Chief Justice of the CFA and has the following members: the Secretary for Justice (*ex officio*), and seven members appointed by the Chief Executive, two of whom shall be judges, one of whom shall be a barrister, one of whom shall be a solicitor and the remainder three shall be persons not connected in any way with the practice of law. The Chief Executive is obliged to consult

adoption of appointments[38] are worth highlighting.[39] The first is that the judges and the legally qualified members, including the Secretary for Justice, dominate the JORC. The second is that while the judges and the two members from the legal profession together can constitute a simple majority of five, a recommendation of a judicial appointment will usually be approved only with the blessing of the Secretary for Justice[40] and the non-legal personalities appointed by the Chief Executive. The third is that the Chief Executive can decline or 'return' a recommendation.[41] The next step for CFA appointments is the endorsement of the LegCo. Although the Judiciary has secured with the legislature an established procedure that does not involve attendance by the proposed appointee of a hearing of a committee of legislators – and this reduces the potential for politicisation[42] – in the 2018 round of endorsements, several members of the LegCo expressed concerns over the appointments of Lady Hale, the then President of the United Kingdom Supreme Court, and Beverley McLachlin, the recently retired Chief Justice of Canada, over their liberal judicial records in adjudicating equality cases, particularly those relating to same-sex marriage. Two members also made remarks about the suitability of an NPJ from a common law jurisdiction outside Hong Kong participating in the determination of a final appeal with a 'national interest' dimension.[43] Should such expressions become more frequent and transform into votes this would be a matter of concern, since it has been said that eminent judicial figures of the common law world would not have accepted or continued appointments had Hong Kong's judicial system become less institutionally independent and its judges less personally impartial than in their home jurisdictions.[44] It would be catastrophic to Hong Kong's reputation and credibility as a liberal common law jurisdiction for

the HKBA and the LSHK before appointing the barrister member and the solicitor member. The Chief Executive has so far accepted the recommendations of the HKBA and the LSHK.

[38] The voting arrangement ensures that a more than simple majority is required for a resolution to be effective; see Judicial Officers Recommendation Commission Ordinance, s 3(3A).

[39] See also the contribution of Johannes Chan in this collection.

[40] This has given rise to some concerns on the ground that the Secretary for Justice is not only the head of the Department of Justice, a most frequent user of court services, but also the chief legal advisor to the Government and one of the most senior principal officials of the HKSAR Government, the executive authorities of the HKSAR, appointed by the Central People's Government on the recommendation of the Chief Executive.

[41] The Chief Executive's substantive appointment power and its potential utilisation have been raised both in mainland China and Hong Kong; see J Cheng, 'Hong Kong's Constitutional Development and the Executive-led System' (2009) 1 *Legal Science* 45 (in Chinese); G Torode and J Pomfret 'Hong Kong's judges voice fears over China influence in judiciary' *Reuters* (15 March 2018), available at uk.reuters.com/article/uk-hongkong-law-insight/hong-kongs-judges-voice-fears-over-china-influence-in-judiciary-idUKKCN1GR0LN.

[42] See, eg, *Farewell Sitting for the Honourable Mr Justice Chan PJ* (2013) 16 HKCFAR 1012, 1019.

[43] See K Chung, 'Baroness Hale and Beverley McLachlin become first female judges to join Hong Kong's Court of Final Appeal despite "national interest" concerns' *South China Morning Post*, 30 May 2018, available at www.scmp.com/news/hong-kong/politics/article/2148521/resounding-show-support-lawmakers-baroness-hale-and-beverly.

[44] See D Neuberger, 'Judges, Access to Justice, the Rule of Law and the Court of Final Appeal under "One Country, Two Systems"' (2017) 47 *Hong Kong Law Journal* 899.

such eminent judges to be deterred from coming by a sidewind of distrust from legislators seeking to promote their 'family values' and 'nationalist' credentials.

Locally, judges have also been criticised by legislators, some quarters of the press and vocal members of the public for their judgments and sentences.[45] These criticisms began to emerge around the time of the Occupy Central sit-in in 2014, as prosecutions arising from clashes between protestors and the police came before the courts. Some judges and magistrates have been accused of political partiality in light of apparently lenient sentences being handed down to the convicted protestors and apparently harsh sentences to police officers who had been adjudged to have used unlawful force. One District Judge who convicted seven police officers for beating up an arrested protestor was vilified because of his British expatriate status.[46] More recently and worryingly, judges and magistrates have been 'trolled' by legislators, individuals and groups of differing political affiliations for passing judgment or imposing sentences on politically active defendants that these individuals and groups support or detest.[47] Chief Justice Ma has devoted much time in recent public speeches to informing the public of 'the fundamental point that courts deal only with the law'.[48] How these increasingly frequent personal attacks

[45] See also the contribution of Johannes Chan in this collection.

[46] See J Siu and E Lee, 'Outrage at two-year prison terms for Hong Kong policemen who beat up political activist' *South China Morning Post*, 17 February 2017, available at www.scmp.com/news/hong-kong/law-crime/article/2071703/two-years-jail-seven-policemen-who-beat-occupy-activist-ken; C Leung and T Cheung, 'Hong Kong lawmaker brands British judge a "yellow heart" after seven policemen are jailed' *South China Morning Post*, 17 February 2017, available at www.scmp.com/news/hong-kong/law-crime/article/2071853/hong-kong-lawmaker-brands-british-judge-yellow-heart-after; J Lam, 'Son of PLA general under fire over reward to beat up Hong Kong judge' *South China Morning Post*, 19 February 2017, available at www.scmp.com/news/hong-kong/law-crime/article/2072174/son-late-mainland-commander-may-face-contempt-court-over; N Fraser and D Mok, '33,000 gather in support of Hong Kong officers jailed for beating up Occupy protester Ken Tsang' *South China Morning Post*, 22 February 2017, available at www.scmp.com/news/hong-kong/article/2073069/mass-meeting-police-support-hong-kong-officers-jailed-beating-occupy.

[47] A judge of the CFI who sentenced a former candidate in the LegCo elections with a 'localist' agenda was subjected to insults and personal attacks online; see A Lum, 'Hong Kong Bar Association, Law Society condemns online trolls targeting judge who sentenced Edward Leung for Mong Kok riot' *South China Morning Post*, 4 July 2018, available at www.scmp.com/news/hong-kong/hong-kong-law-and-crime/article/2153783/hong-kong-bar-association-law-society-condemn. Another judge of the CFI who allowed the appeal of a former Member of the LegCo against conviction for assaulting the Chief Executive during a question session by allegedly throwing a glass at him had her judgment openly criticised by legislators as 'anti-intellect'; see *Ming Pao*, 30 September 2018, available at news.mingpao.com/ins/%e6%b8%af%e8%81%9e/article/20180930/s00001/1538283275189. A further judge of the CFI who dismissed the magistracy appeal of four persons convicted of unlawful assembly and assault at the Hong Kong International Airport over their violent acts against a former student leader and 'localist' politician became the subject of verbal abuse by members of the public in court who claimed themselves to be supporters of the Communist Party of China; see C Lau, 'Public gallery erupts as four pro-establishment supporters sent to jail after losing appeal over Hong Kong airport protest where activist Nathan Law was attacked' *South China Morning Post*, 21 December 2018, available at www.scmp.com/news/hong-kong/law-and-crime/article/2179118/public-gallery-erupts-four-pro-establishment-supporters.

[48] G Ma, 'CJ's address at the Ceremony for the Admission of the New Senior Counsel' (9 June 2018), available at www.info.gov.hk/gia/general/201806/09/P2018060800495.htm; G Ma, 'CJ's speech at the Ceremonial Opening of the Legal Year 2018' (8 January 2018), available at www.info.gov.hk/gia/general/201801/08/P2018010800491.htm.

on judges and magistrates will affect recruitment of the most qualified legal practitioners to the local Bench requires careful observation, bearing in mind that the Chief Justice had indicated for some time already a difficulty in attracting such candidates to the Court of First Instance (CFI) (although this might have more to do with terms and conditions of service).[49] Meanwhile, Philip Dykes SC, the chairman of the HKBA, acknowledged not only that the respect that society traditionally accorded to judges has eroded but also that the Judiciary 'does not have a Facebook mentality', judges 'cannot engage proactively with their critics', and unwarranted attacks do have 'a corrosive effect' on the morale of judges and the likelihood of the best qualified legal practitioners, who value both their reputation and their privacy, to accept judicial office. He quoted Lord Bingham on the risks involved:

> If the bench were to become the refuge of the mediocre, the unambitious, the timid and the unsuccessful or if the appointment of judges were to be blighted by a search for the safe, the conformist and the representative I have no doubt the quality of justice would suffer and respect for the law decline.[50]

Controversially, judges and the judicial system have been heaped with praise from the Government of the HKSAR when it sought to introduce legislative amendments in 2019 that would enable (on the authority to proceed by the Chief Executive), inter alia, extradition or rendition of Hong Kong residents or foreign visitors of Hong Kong to countries and territories that have not concluded a surrender of fugitive offenders arrangement with the HKSAR, including mainland China. The rendition could be for prosecution and trial or serving a sentence and would be approved on a case-by-case basis by 'special arrangement'. Legislators supporting the proposal promoted the statutory role of judges and magistrates. However, none of them bothered to explain that the courts have a limited role in examining the documentary request – to check whether the relevant statutory requirement of the ad hoc request are met before the final decision of the Chief Executive to order surrender. Legislators opposing the proposal had been chided by the Chief Executive for defaming the judicial system and suggesting that there is no judicial independence in Hong Kong.[51] The Government and its supporters

[49] G Ma, 'CJ's speech at Ceremonial Opening of the Legal Year 2017' (9 January 2017), available at www.info.gov.hk/gia/general/201701/09/P2017010900457.htm. See also the contribution of Johannes Chan in this collection.

[50] P Dykes, 'Who defends the Judges?' *Next Media*, 24 June 2018, available at s.nextmedia.com/realtime/a.php?i=20180624&s=11272286&a=58346685.

[51] See LK Sum, 'Hong Kong will look into real reasons for extradition requests before moving fugitives, justice minister Teresa Cheng says' *South China Morning Post*, 3 April 2019, available at www.scmp.com/news/hong-kong/politics/article/3004462/hong-kong-will-look-real-reasons-extradition-requests; R Tong, 'Hong Kong should trust its own judiciary on all extradition requests – whether or not they come from Mainland China' *South China Morning Post*, 3 April 2019, available at www.scmp.com/comment/insight-opinion/article/3004273/hong-kong-should-trust-its-own-judiciary-all-extradition; H Chan, 'Hong Kong's justice chief dismisses alternatives for extradition law proposed by scholars

have been 'cashing in' the credit of the good name of the Judiciary for their objective. They, however, have been met with critical comments against the proposal from three anonymous senior judges, one High Court judge, 12 former chairmen of the HKBA, the HKBA, the HKLS, legal academics in and outside Hong Kong and other critics. One of the three senior judges stated that the proposed amendments 'ignore the importance of [the core trust underlying extraditions of the receiving country being one that will afford the fugitive both fair trial and humane punishment] – and in the case of [mainland China], it simply doesn't exist'.[52]

and lawmakers' *Hong Kong Free Press*, 8 May 2019, available at www.hongkongfp.com/2019/05/08/hong-kongs-justice-chief-dismisses-alternatives-extradition-law-proposed-scholars-lawmakers; J Lam, 'Hong Kong extradition bill: how murder of a pregnant woman, the US-China trade war and a determined leader have cranked up the heat in city's political arena' *South China Morning Post*, 17 May 2019, available at www.scmp.com/news/hong-kong/politics/article/3010570/hong-kong-extradition-bill-how-murder-pregnant-woman-us; A Lum, 'Hong Kong leader Carrie Lam hits back at EU officials who protested against controversial extradition bill, saying they did not pinpoint concerns' *South China Morning Post*, 25 May 2019, available at www.scmp.com/news/hong-kong/politics/article/3011783/hong-kong-leader-carrie-lam-hits-back-protest-eu-officials; D Mok, 'Hong Kong government releases long defence of contentious extradition bill against American Chamber of Commerce criticism' *South China Morning Post*, 4 June 2019, available at: https://www.scmp.com/news/hong-kong/politics/article/3012973/hong-kong-government-releases-long-defence-contentious; and the Security Bureau of the Government of the Hong Kong Special Administrative Region's website of promotional materials at www.sb.gov.hk/eng/special/cooperation/index.htm.

[52] See G Torode and J Pomfret, 'Exclusive: Hong Kong judges sees risks in proposed extradiction changes' *Reuters* (29 May 2019), available at: uk.reuters.com/article/uk-hongkong-politics-extradition-judges/exclusive-hong-kong-judges-see-risks-in-proposed-extradition-changes-idUKKCN1SZ09S; A Lum, 'High Court judge gets warning from Hong Kong's chief justice after name appears on petition against extradition bill' *South China Morning Post*, 8 June 2019, available at www.scmp.com/news/hong-kong/politics/article/3013697/high-court-judge-gets-warning-hong-kongs-chief-justice; JA Cohen, 'If Beijing wants an extradition law with Hong Kong – and elsewhere – it should reform its judicial process' *South China Morning Post*, 23 May 2019, available at www.scmp.com/comment/insight-opinion/article/3011117/if-beijing-wants-extradition-law-hong-kong-and-elsewhere-it; 'Top barristers "dismayed" by extradition law plans' *RTHK*, 15 May 2019, available at news.rthk.hk/rthk/en/component/k2/1457691-20190515.htm; International Chamber of Commerce-Hong Kong, 'Fugitive Offenders and Mutual Legal Assistance in Criminal Matters Legislation (Amendment) Bill 2019' (8 May 2019), available at www.icchkcbc.org/download/ICC-HK%20letter%20to%20LegCo.pdf; AHY Chen, 'A Commentary on the Fugitive Offenders and Mutual Legal Assistance in Criminal Matters Legislation (Amendment) Bill 2019' (3 May 2019), available at researchblog.law.hku.hk/2019/05/albert-chens-commentary-on-proposed.html; HKBA, 'Additional Observations of the HKBA on the HKSAR Government's proposed further changes to the Fugitive Offenders and Mutual Legal Assistance in Criminal Matters Legislation (Amendment) Bill 2019' (6 June 2019), available at https://www.hkba.org/sites/default/files/Additional%20Observations%20of%20the%20Hong%20Kong%20Bar%20Association%20%28"HKBA"%29%20on%20the%20HKSAR%20Government%27s%20proposed%20further%20changes%20to%20the%20Fugitive%20Offenders%20and%20Mutual%20Legal%20Assistance%20in%20Criminal%20Matters.pdf; HKBA, 'Observations of the Hong Kong Bar Association on the Fugitive Offenders and Mutual Legal Assistance in Criminal Matters Legislation (Amendment) Bill 2019' (2 April 2019), available at www.hkba.org/sites/default/files/HKBA%20Observations%20on%20FOMLACM%20Bill%202019%20%28Final%29.pdf; LSHK, 'Fugitive Offenders and Mutual Legal Assistance in Criminal Matters Legislation (Amendment) Bill 2019: Submission' (5 June 2019), available at http://www.hklawsoc.org.hk/pub_e/news/submissions/20190605.pdf; C Buddle, 'Carrie Lam may win the battle to pass Hong Kong's extradition law. But at what costs?' *South China Morning Post*, 7 June 2019, available at: www.scmp.com/comment/opinion/article/3013351/carrie-lam-may-win-battle-pass-hong-kongs-extradition-law-what-cost; A Ramzy, 'Hong Kong Protest Against Proposed Extradition Law Draws Hundreds of Thousands' *The New York Times*, 9 June 2019, available at www.nytimes.com/2019/06/09/world/asia/hong-kong-extradition-protest.html.

The Government brushed aside these critics, and the voice of hundreds of thousands of Hong Kong residents who marched through the streets of Hong Kong Island on 9 June 2019, and only announced the suspension of the amendment exercise on 15 June 2019, after a violent confrontation between protestors and the police occurred on the streets outside the LegCo Complex building on 12 June 2019.

Any discussion of the state of Hong Kong's Judiciary is not complete without having regard to the elephant in the room, namely the Central Authorities. A news report from March 2018 cited anonymous judicial sources stating that Hong Kong judges are losing sleep over the influence that the Central Authorities is able to exert on adjudication in Hong Kong through its power of interpreting the Basic Law. Such interpretations can effectively tell judges 'what to do, limiting their authority on key political and security issues'. One judge was rather explicit: '[If the NPCSC] interprets too frequently, the risk is they will leave us nothing left on which to rule'.[53] In other words, judges in the HKSAR might become 'mere' administrators of the law handed down by the NPCSC.[54] These concerns were expressed in light of an interpretation of Article 104 of the Basic Law adopted by the NPCSC on 7 November 2016 when adjudication on the legal validity of oaths taken by two elected legislators (who were known to be in the pro-self-determination camp) to assume office was already underway. This interpretation was initiated by the NPCSC on its own in the absence of a request from the CFA. The relevant Basic Law provision confines such requests to final adjudication that necessarily involves the interpretation of a Basic Law provision concerning a matter that is the responsibility of the Central People's Government or concerning the relationship between the Central Authorities and the HKSAR.[55] The timing of the adoption of this interpretation also pre-empted the first instance judgment by an HKSAR court on the same and related questions. Johannes Chan has called this 2016 NPCSC Interpretation a 'blatant interference with judicial independence'.[56]

The breadth of the 2016 NPCSC Interpretation should also be appreciated. As Chan has noted, this interpretation went beyond the scope of Article 104 of

[53] See Torode and Pomfret, 'Hong Kong's judges voice fears' (2018).

[54] 'Administrators' was an expression used in a White Paper issued by the Central Authorities on the practice of 'one country, two systems' in Hong Kong in 2014 to refer to all those who 'administrate Hong Kong', including the judges at all levels, who 'have on their shoulders the responsibility of correctly understanding and implementing the Basic Law, of safeguarding the country's sovereignty, security and development interests, and of ensuring the long-term prosperity and stability of Hong Kong. In a word, loving the country, is the basic political requirement for Hong Kong's administrators'; see State Council Information Office, 'The Practice of the "One Country, Two Systems" Policy in the Hong Kong Special Administrative Region' (10 June 2014), available at www.scio.gov.cn/zfbps/ndhf/2014/Document/1373163/1373163.htm.

[55] Basic Law, Art 158(3).

[56] J Chan, 'A storm of unprecedented ferocity: The shrinking space of the right of political participation, peaceful demonstration and judicial independence in Hong Kong' (2018) 16 *International Journal of Constitutional Law* 373.

the Basic Law in at least three ways: it was adopted to address incidents that had already taken place and which have become the subject of litigation; it sought to introduce a code on the manner of taking an oath, a matter that Article 104 left to the local legislature; and it laid down that upholding the Basic Law and paying allegiance to the HKSAR were prerequisites for standing in elections in the HKSAR. It was down to the judges adjudicating the cases on the 2016 NPCSC Interpretation to construe its effect, and (perhaps unsurprisingly) without question, the courts held that the entire interpretation was binding on them, proceeded to administer them to disqualify six members of the legislature and rejected the election petition of a candidate.[57] Analyses of these judgments have shown that the courts, in choosing to implement the 2016 NPCSC Interpretation to the last letter, have failed to apply the common law presumption against retrospective legislation and common law approaches that would require courts to construe the 2016 NPCSC Interpretation as provisions of the Basic Law, to be read together and in accordance with the purposes and principles underlying the Basic Law, including its emphasis on protection of fundamental rights.[58] Worse, the justification the Court of Appeal offered for rejecting the claim that the 2016 NPCSC Interpretation was impermissible supplementation, ie that the interpretation 'stated what the Hong Kong has always been', focused on the wrong issue; the real issue was whether the NPCSC's interpretation supplemented Article 104, the provision of the Basic Law that was supposed to be interpreted.[59]

The same judges, who are all Chinese and mostly educated locally, and of the right age and qualifications to be elevated to the CFA in due course,[60] also expressed the view that generally,

> the court is neither constitutionally nor institutionally equipped to deal with a political issue, that is, an issue essentially involving political rather than legal judgment, or for that matter, a complicated polycentric, socio-economic issue raising sensitive questions of resource allocation

and as regards 'political issues', the court 'should accord a broad margin of appreciation to the legislature … and will not lightly interfere with their

[57] *Chief Executive of the HKSAR v President of the Legislative Council* [2017] 2 HKLRD 53; *Chief Executive of the HKSAR v President of the Legislative Council* [2017] 1 HKLRD 460; *Chief Executive of the HKSAR v President of the Legislative Council* [2017] 4 HKLRD 115; *Chan Ho Tin v Lo Ying Ki Alan* [2018] 2 HKLRD 7; and *Secretary for Justice v Leung Kwok Hung* [2019] 2 HKC 244.

[58] For a consideration of the litigation, see PY Lo, 'Enforcing an Unfortunate, Unnecessary and "Unquestionably Binding" NPCSC Interpretation: The Hong Kong Judiciary's Deconstruction of Its Constitution of the Basic Law' (2018) 48 *Hong Kong Law Journal* 399. For techniques to deal with NPCSC interpretations, see E Ip, 'Interpreting interpretations: a methodology for the judicial enforcement of legislative interpretations of the Hong Kong Basic Law' [2017] *Public Law* 552; F Lin, 'The Duty of Hong Kong Courts to Follow the NPCSC's Interpretation of the Basic Law: Are There Any Limits?' (2018) 48 *Hong Kong Law Journal* 167.

[59] See *Secretary for Justice v Leung Kwok Hung* [2019] 2 HKC 244, [50].

[60] One of them, Cheung CJHC, was appointed a permanent judge of the CFA and assumed office in October 2018.

political judgment'.[61] In fact, judicial deference has become a core doctrine in Hong Kong.[62] Another of them had indicated, formalistically, that in Hong Kong, a principle of 'reciprocity' applies in that the Hong Kong resident

> cannot ignore their obligation to obey the law in the name of exercising their rights. … [The] Basic Law has expressly provided that when Hong Kong residents exercise their rights guaranteed by law, they must also obey the law. They can only exercise their rights in accordance with law.[63]

Coincidentally, the same judges had upheld the strict immigration control of Hong Kong against foreigners seeking to remain in Hong Kong with spouses or family members who were HKSAR permanent residents;[64] and adopted a particular approach to 'ring fence the institution and status of marriage, that is, heterosexual marriage, in Hong Kong' for full protection under the law on the basis that 'what society regards as constituting a marriage relationship and is prepared to accord the status of marriage to … is rooted in its traditional, historical, social, moral or religious background and values', at the expense of a claim for spousal benefits under HKSAR law and HKSAR Government policy by a party to a same-sex marriage entered outside Hong Kong.[65]

Separately, a judge of the CFI ruled in 2018 that local legislation implementing an agreement between the HKSAR and its neighbouring Guangdong Province

[61] See *Kwok Cheuk Kin v Secretary for Constitutional and Mainland Affairs* [2015] 5 HKLRD 881. The Court of Appeal judgment was upheld by the CFA ((2017) 20 HKCFAR 353) and thereafter was criticised in *Public Law* for its 'light touch' approach to proportionality, notwithstanding the fact that the questions presented raised profound questions on the constitutional arrangements of the HKSAR; see R Clayton, 'Keeping a sense of proportion: political protest and the Hong Kong courts' [2018] *Public Law* 375.

[62] Deference (or the margin of appreciation) has become firmly established since *Fok Chun Wa v Hospital Authority* (2012) 15 HKCFAR 409. The CFA used it to calibrate the level of scrutiny in the proportionality analysis in human rights cases, particularly where they thought that the legislature or the executive is 'better placed' than the courts to decide on matters of 'socio-economic policy' or involving resource allocation. The restatement of the proportionality analysis in *Hysan Development Co Ltd v Town Planning Board* (2016) 19 HKCFAR 372, which introduced the fourth step of 'fair balance', had not changed the role or importance of judicial deference; the CFA indicated that courts should afford a wide margin of discretion reflected by the use of a 'manifestly without reasonable foundation' standard in certain circumstances, including where national security matters are involved ([117]). For an account from the Judiciary on the use of 'margin of appreciation', see G Ma, 'Limits and Limitations: How effective are the Courts in the Protection of Human Rights' (speech at the University of Zurich, 14 March 2019), available at www.hkcfa.hk/filemanager/speech/en/upload/2225/2019.03.14%20-%20 University%20of%20Zurich%20(Zurich,%20Switzerland).pdf. For a systematic and empirical study of the application of deference or 'margin of appreciation' by the HKSAR courts, see C Chan, 'Rights, Proportionality, and Deference: A Study of Post-Handover Judgments in Hong Kong' (2018) 48 *Hong Kong Law Journal* 51.

[63] See *Secretary for Justice v Leung Hiu Yeung & Ors* [2018] 1 HKLRD 702, [89] (Poon JA, who will assume the office of Chief Judge of the High Court in 2019 after his appointment receives endorsement of LegCo).

[64] See *BI v Director of Immigration* [2016] 2 HKLRD 520; *Comilang v Director of Immigration* [2018] 2 HKLRD 534 (affirmed on final appeal in *Comilang v Director of Immigration* [2019] HKCFA 10).

[65] See *Leung Chun Kwong v Secretary for the Civil Service & Anor* [2018] 3 HKLRD 84 (reversed on appeal, see n 6).

to implement the 'co-location' arrangement: co-location of immigration, customs, and quarantine checkpoints at the West Kowloon Station of the Express Rail Link between Hong Kong, Shenzhen and Guangzhou. This agreement was backed by a decision of the NPCSC indicating that the arrangement was 'consistent' with the Basic Law. This was notwithstanding the fact that that piece of legislation designates one part of the HKSAR as an area lying outside the HKSAR but within mainland China for the purposes of the application of mainland Chinese laws in that area and the delineation of jurisdiction (including jurisdiction of the courts) over that area.[66] This purports to designate that part of the HKSAR as the *only* part of the PRC that is not subject to the Basic Law and apparently violates several provisions of the Basic Law, including Article 18, which states that national laws are not applicable in Hong Kong unless they are listed in Annex III of the Basic Law. Despite forceful submissions from counsel, the judge did not subject these alleged violations to rigorous legal scrutiny, as a common law judge is expected to do. Rather, the judge reasoned that from a 'macro' perspective of the Basic Law 'establishing a broad framework for the exercise of a high degree of autonomy of Hong Kong', the co-location arrangement was not inconsistent with the purpose of the Basic Law, that the co-location arrangement was to advance the overall best interests of Hong Kong, that the Basic Law should be capable of growth and development to meet new 'realities', and that the establishment of the co-location arrangement itself was an exercise of a high degree of autonomy by the HKSAR. The court was also ready to accept the NPCSC decision endorsing the arrangement as a post-enactment material for construing the Basic Law, regarding the decision as possessing 'high persuasive value in the particular circumstances of the case' despite the apparent lack of legal basis in the Basic Law for the NPCSC to issue the decision. The judge reasoned, inter alia, that since the NPCSC had the ultimate power of interpretation of the Basic Law, 'it would be acting contrary to common sense not to accord the NPCSC decision with weight and respect'.[67] These lines of reasoning suggest a departure from the courts' earlier jurisprudence on constitutional jurisdiction, on the adoption of a language-based deductive approach in the interpretation of the Basic Law, and on receiving NPCSC acts cautiously and restrictively and only those that are exercised pursuant to procedures laid down in the Basic Law, in preference for a centralist, state policy-oriented, and consequentialist approach that subordinates Hong Kong's legal system to the national socialist system of the 'one country'.[68] In short, some might perceive that the court is a willing 'enabler' in advancing the State's 'sovereignty, security and development interests'.

Tang PJ, in a speech delivered at his farewell sitting in October 2018, stated the obvious: 'The independence of the judiciary and maintenance of the rule of law

[66] *Leung Chung Hang Sixtus & Ors v President of the Legislative Council* [2019] 1 HKLRD 292.

[67] *Leung Chung Hang Sixtus & Ors v President of the Legislative Council* (ibid) [69]–[74].

[68] See W Partlett and E Ip, 'Is Socialist Law Really Dead?' (2016) 48 *New York University Journal of International Law and Politics* 463, 508.

must depend on the local judges. *The buck must stop at us*' (emphasis added).[69] Only time can tell how the senior judges of the next generation go about safeguarding Basic Law rights against national security legislation and acts. However, the above-discussed risks on politicisation of the judiciary, problems in recruiting judges, and trends of judicial subservience, deference and even apparently 'enabling' on matters that touch on Beijing's core interests, do raise doubts on the Judiciary's ability to guard rights against security imperatives from China. There is moreover a paradox that each member of the Judiciary must resolve by him or herself. The judicial oath requires HKSAR judges to

> uphold the Basic Law of the Hong Kong Special Administrative Region of the People's Republic of China, serve the Hong Kong Special Administrative Region conscientiously, dutifully, in full accordance with the law, honestly and with integrity, safeguard the law and administer justice without fear or favour, self-interest or deceit.[70]

This gives rise to an inherent conflict between, on the one hand, safeguarding the *law* prescribed by the state (say, by an NPCSC interpretation or decision) and the national sovereignty, security and development interests underlying it, and on the other, administering *justice* commensurate with the protection of the fundamental rights guaranteed to Hong Kong residents. The answer of the courts to this paradox awaits.

II. The Legal Profession

The legal profession in Hong Kong may be analysed in two dimensions: the professional bodies serving as the voices of the profession; and the individual practitioners themselves.

The HKBA and the LSHK are the professional bodies and voices of the legal profession in Hong Kong. They have joined hands to defend the Judiciary from unwarranted attacks, whether or not such attacks had also been condemned by the HKSAR Government. Generally, on legal issues involving the public interest, the HKBA has been more robust and forthcoming in expressing its views. Indeed, the elections to the offices of the HKBA in 2018 were contested, in part, in relation to this 'function' of the HKBA: some members of the HKBA (who were also members of the Election Committee that returns the Chief Executive and who also happened to have acted as counsel for the pan-democrats in political cases) ran, with success, against the incumbent team. The winning team's platform included a claim that the incumbent team had not been sufficiently robust on the 'co-location' issue.[71]

[69] *Farewell Sitting for the Honourable Mr Justice Tang PJ* (2018) 21 HKCFAR 530, 535.

[70] Oaths and Declarations Ordinance (Cap 11), Sch 2, Pt V.

[71] See J Lam, 'Philip Dykes elected new head of Hong Kong Bar Association in upset win' *South China Morning Post*, 19 January 2018, available at www.scmp.com/news/hong-kong/law-crime/article/2129589/philip-dykes-elected-new-head-hong-kong-bar-association.

The LSHK is generally less vocal than the HKBA, but it has also been robust at times. For example, its membership had adopted a motion of no-confidence against its President in 2014, primarily because he commented positively on the State Council's White Paper on the practice of the 'one country, two systems' policy in Hong Kong, a highly controversial document that considered judges 'administrators' of Hong Kong who must be 'patriots'.[72] The vote led to his resignation.[73] Another, and more recent, example was the LSHK's submission urging the Government not to rush through its proposed legislative amendments to fugitive offenders and mutual legal assistance legislation.

Some Hong Kong lawyers have followed the usual path in fledgling democracies to enter politics. The four former Chairmen of the HKBA who led the opposition against Article 23 legislation in 2003, changed gear in 2004 to call for greater democracy for the HKSAR pursuant to Article 45 of the Basic Law, and then banded themselves with others to form the Civic Party in 2006. Yet this political party has not been as successful as expected since it suffered from an identity crisis between an elitist/professional outlook and the need to develop an agenda on social issues for the grassroots. Its popularity with the public also suffered when it became known that its members were involved in a successful judicial review application, funded through legal aid (hence tapping on the public purse), against a major infrastructure project;[74] and when it was accused of supporting foreign domestic helpers in their strive to gain permanent residency in the HKSAR.[75] These cases generated fears that important infrastructure projects in Hong Kong would be much delayed and become more costly, and that the strict immigration policy hitherto applied to foreign domestic helpers (who are mostly from South-East Asia) would be undermined, leading to stress on social resources.[76] On the matter of democratic development in Hong Kong, the Civic Party backed an initiative to engineer a de facto referendum of the Hong Kong electorate through the resignation of all or some pro-democracy legislators, attracting a strong response from the Central Authorities, who denounced this move as a violation of the Basic Law.[77] The Civic Party's lawyers have had their political futures stymied by their local political opponents, the HKSAR Government and the Central Authorities.

[72] See T Cheung and P Siu, 'Law Society defends white paper on Hong Kong after harsh words from Bar Association' *South China Morning Post*, 16 June 2014, available at www.scmp.com/news/hong-kong/article/1534091/law-society-defends-white-paper-hong-kong-after-harsh-words-bar.

[73] See J Ng, 'Law Society president Ambrose Lam resigns after historic no-confidence vote' *South China Morning Post*, 19 August 2014, available at www.scmp.com/news/hong-kong/article/1576791/law-society-president-ambrose-lam-resigns-following-historic-no.

[74] See Press Release of the HKSAR Government, 'LCQ6: Regarding the judicial review of Hong Kong-Zhuhai-Macao Bridge' (8 June 2011), available at www.info.gov.hk/gia/general/201106/08/P201106080155.htm.

[75] See Civic Party, 'Recent Judicial Review on the Right of Abode of Foreign Domestic Helpers' (9 August 2011), available at www.civicparty.hk/?q=en/node/2744.

[76] See Press Release of the HKSAR Government, 'LCQ15: Judicial review cases involving the Government' (23 May 2012), available at www.info.gov.hk/gia/general/201205/23/P201205230300.htm.

[77] See N Ma, 'Hong Kong's Democrats Divide' (2011) 22 *Journal of Democracy* 54.

Hong Kong's legal talent is needed by all involved in Hong Kong affairs, including the Liaison Office, which has a department of officers dedicated to legal affairs. Many Hong Kong lawyers have been appointed in various Hong Kong Government boards and committees and public authorities for their legal knowledge and skills. Some were given appointments in the political consultation system of the PRC.[78] Many have been approached to express views or adopt legal analysis sympathetic or opposed to Beijing's position in public debates over political or socio-legal issue. This last matter had prompted Paul Shieh SC, then Chairman of the HKBA, to address openly the question of 'whose side is the Bar on' in January 2015, emphasising that the HKBA owes

> no affiliation to any side. We are independent, not only from the Establishment but also from party political forces irrespective of their leadership or pedigree. Our independence makes our views on Rule of Law all the more valuable and balanced. We are not the 'Reserve Team' of political parties who have – for many years – wrongly assumed that they could call upon the Bar to readily rally for their political acts from a 'Rule of Law angle'.[79]

The next Chairman of HKBA, Winnie Tam SC, expressed in a speech in 2017 the need for meaningful exchanges between Hong Kong and mainland China on legal issues in order to maintain the HKBA's influence over the Central Authorities and the mainland Chinese legal profession and to contribute to the development of the rule of law and legal professionalism on both sides.[80]

The change in leadership of the HKBA in 2018 led to difficulties in maintaining and furthering these positions expressed by the previous Chairmen. Whether independent and apolitical channels of communication between the two systems can be maintained is an open question following the ascension of politically/civically active members to the HKBA's leadership. The professionalism of the HKBA's statements on controversial legal issues has been doubted by some political figures.[81] Another area of deep concern is the suspension of official contacts and exchanges between the Central Authorities and the HKBA, including the remarkable incident in 2018 of the suspension of the HKBA's co-operation with Peking

[78] Rimsky Yuen SC, who accepted such a position at the Guangdong Province level in 2007, while he was Chairman of the HKBA, was later appointed Secretary for Justice and served in the HKSAR Government between 2012 and 2018.

[79] See P Shieh, 'Speech of Mr Paul Shieh SC, Chairman of the Hong Kong Bar Association at the Opening of the Legal Year 2015' (12 January 2015), available at www.hkba.org/sites/default/files/OLY%20Speech%202015%20%28E%29%20web.pdf.

[80] See W Tam, 'Speech of Ms Winnie Tam SC, Chairman of the Hong Kong Bar Association at the Opening of the Legal Year 2017' (9 January 2017), available at www.hkba.org/sites/default/files/OLY%202017%20Speech%20E%20Final%20%28for%20publication%29%20PERFECTED%20-%20Webpage_0.pdf.

[81] See 'Bar Association should stay out of politics' *RTHK*, 3 April 2019), available at news.rthk.hk/rthk/en/component/k2/1451118-20190403.htm; 'Tsang Yok-sing: Lack of Rational Discussion on Amendments to the Fugitive Offenders Ordinance is Disturbing' *RTHK*, 7 April 2019 (in Chinese), available at news.rthk.hk/rthk/ch/component/k2/1451677-20190407.htm.

University in the teaching of a course on the common law system.[82] While this might not matter to the Central Authorities or its Liaison Office in Hong Kong, given the variety of legal groups of different persuasion (including the Progressive Lawyers Group, Law Daydream, the Small and Medium Law Firms Association of Hong Kong, the Hong Kong Legal Exchange Foundation, the Hong Kong and Mainland Legal Profession Association, the Hong Kong Basic Law Education Association, Global Chinese Speaking Lawyers' Association Limited, the Basic Law Foundation, the Hong Kong Legal Professional Employees Association, the International Youth Legal Exchange Federation, and the International Dispute Resolution & Risk Management Institute, which have emerged since 2014), the resurgence of a negative perception of the HKBA and the official sidelining of the HKBA are likely to be detrimental to both sides. The Central Authorities and the HKSAR Government would miss opportunities of accessing quality legal opinions and conducting uninhibited and discrete discussions on topics of importance to Hong Kong's present and future. The HKBA would have to regain the mutual respect and re-establish regular contacts with the Central Authorities, a task that is already difficult after 2014, but this would be even more difficult given the political profiles of the HKBA's leadership.[83]

A thorough discussion of Hong Kong's legal profession should also cover the usually undiscussed matter of earnings and sources of earnings. Regarding earnings, it is clear that the expansion of legal education in Hong Kong has not been proportionately met by the expansion of the local legal services market. New members of the legal profession endure lower monthly income, higher overheads and greater job insecurity. And they face competition not only amongst themselves but also from foreign lawyers hired by law firms. All these will have an attrition effect on both barristers and solicitors, with perhaps a greater concern for barristers since their mode of working has remained that of sole proprietorship.

Regarding sources of earnings, one growing factor has been the maturing of the mainland Chinese legal services market and the access that Hong Kong legal professionals can have to it through the Closer Economic Partnership Arrangement between Mainland China and the HKSAR. This is in addition to the grant of the status of China Attesting Officers to certain qualified solicitors to perform

[82] See P Dykes, 'Hong Kong Bar Association happy to revive Peking University course, but only if last-minute changes are off the table' *South China Morning Post*, 10 September 2018, available at www.scmp.com/comment/letters/article/2163202/hong-kong-bar-association-happy-revive-peking-university-course-only.

[83] For example, the members of the legal subsector of the Chief Executive Election Committee issued on 8 April 2019 a statement calling for the HKSAR Government to withdraw a bill to amend the Fugitive Offenders Ordinance (Cap 503) and the Mutual Legal Assistance in Criminal Matters Ordinance (Cap 525) to allow for extradition between mainland China and Hong Kong; see 'Legal sector warns fugitive plan must be dropped' *RTHK*, 8 April 2019, available at news.rthk.hk/rthk/en/component/k2/1451808-20190408.htm. They also called upon the public to sign on a petition prepared by them advocating withdrawal of the bill, available at www.change.org/p/全體法律界選委-撤回逃犯條例草案-withdraw-the-fugitive-offenders-bill. Members of this subsector included the current Chairman and two members of the council of the HKBA.

services similar to notaries for mainland Chinese-related legal transactions, and the arrangement for Hong Kong individuals to take the State Judicial Examination to qualify as mainland Chinese lawyers. From 2004 onwards, Hong Kong firms have been able not only to establish a representative office in mainland China but also to enter into association with a mainland Chinese law firm involving either partnership or non-partnership. Hong Kong legal practitioners, including barristers, can also be employed by mainland law firms as legal consultants on matters relating to Hong Kong, Macao and countries other than the PRC, and they are permitted to handle such matters in their legal practice.[84] The HKBA has also promoted the services that Hong Kong barristers can perform for and in collaboration with mainland Chinese legal professionals on an ad hoc basis, including those in arbitration and litigation.[85] The relevant legal services market is likely to expand with the ongoing development of the PRC's initiative of the Greater Bay Area for further integration of Hong Kong's economy with those of its immediate neighbouring regions, with a particular emphasis on the service and innovation sectors.[86]

Overall it can be said with some confidence that the resilience of the Hong Kong legal profession is not a truth that can be taken for granted. Attrition in early practice can leave the profession made up of only survivors who are keener on economic gain than public altruistic contribution. But more critically, the hold of the mainland legal services market on the income of Hong Kong lawyers can have the subtle effect of imposing a certain discipline in personal and professional conduct. And here one has yet to mention the party leadership and discipline that the Communist Party of China has imposed on all law firms in mainland China under the banner of 'Party building work', including the establishment of Party branches in law firms.[87] One could imagine that there have been Party efforts on mainland Chinese law firms which Hong Kong law firms have engaged with as well as those employing Hong Kong lawyers. All of these gives rise to a possible perception that Hong Kong lawyers with Mainland Chinese business relations are compromised, including in their robustness to publicly confront rule of law issues in Hong Kong.[88]

[84] For information, see Trade and Industry Department, 'Mainland and Hong Kong Closer Economic Partnership Arrangement (CEPA): Legal Services', available at www.tid.gov.hk/english/cepa/tradeservices/leg_relevant.html.

[85] For information, see HKBA, 'Cross-Border Legal Services', available at www.hkba.org/gca/cross-borderservices.

[86] See B Bland, 'Greater Bay Area: Xi Jinping's other grand plan' *Financial Times*, 3 September 2018, available at www.ft.com/content/fe5976d8-ab81-11e8-94bd-cba20d67390c; 'Outline Development Plan for the Guangdong-Hong Kong-Macao Greater Bay Area' (English translation), available at www.bayarea.gov.hk/filemanager/en/share/pdf/Outline_Development_Plan.pdf.

[87] See 'CPC national committee set up for lawyers' *China Daily*, 1 November 2017, available at www.chinadaily.com.cn/china/2017-11/01/content_33984490.htm; 'Chinese justice minister stresses CPC leadership of lawyers' *Xinhuanet*, 19 January 2018, available at www.xinhuanet.com/english/2018-01/19/c_136908219.htm.

[88] An example is in the recent column entry of the librettist Lin Xi, who questioned on 30 December 2018 whether Hong Kong lawyers with mainland Chinese business would give legal

III. Rule of Law Backsliding in Hong Kong

Professor Jerome A Cohen stated, in an interview with the *National Review* in April 2018, that 'Hong Kong is right now the battleground between the Chinese Communist dictatorship and Western liberal values and political institutions'. He described it as a 'daily struggle' that the 'liberal side is losing'.[89]

Courts and the legal profession in Hong Kong are at the heart of this 'struggle'. The previous two sections of this chapter have sought to show what the weaknesses and vulnerabilities of these institutions are since 2003. What makes this uneasy reading is that they rather readily fit into a script of 'backsliding' that political scientists have found across the world.

Laurent Pech and Kim Lane Scheppele have maintained a continuous study of the decay of liberal democracy in Europe, particularly in Hungary and Poland. This decay has been due not just to the rise of populist politicians projecting impressions of tradition, religion and strength, but also to the capture or decline of institutions to safeguard foundational values. This they consider to be 'rule of law backsliding' and involves a process

> through which elected public authorities deliberately implement governmental blueprints which aim to systematically weaken, annihilate, or capture internal checks on power with the view of dismantling the liberal democratic state and entrenching the long-term rule of the dominant party. It enables the establishment of electoral autocracies and the solidification of one-party states in which elected officials of the ruling party claim exclusive authority to act on behalf of 'the people'.[90]

Jan-Werner Müller has also spoken of 'constitutional capture' in terms of the systematic weakening of 'checks and balances and, in the extreme case, making genuine changes in power exceedingly difficult'.[91]

It is regrettable to say that this *might* happen in Hong Kong. Inherently, Hong Kong is not a liberal democracy but an SAR of the PRC with very limited democratic institutions.[92] There is no effective supra-national mechanism like the regime under Article 7 of the Treaty of the European Union that Hong Kong can rely on to restrain the undermining of the rule of law and other fundamental values.

advice unfavourable to a former Chief Executive and present State Leader, available at s.nextmedia.com/apple_sub/a.php?i=20181230&sec_id=12187389&s=12187389&a=20579646.

[89] J Nordlinger, 'Cohen of China' *National Review* (30 April 2018), available at www.nationalreview.com/2018/04/jerome-a-cohen-venerable-china-scholar-democracy-advocate.

[90] L Pech and KL Scheppele, 'Illiberalism Within: Rule of Law Backsliding in the EU' (2017) 19 *Cambridge Yearbook of European Legal Studies* 3, 10.

[91] JW Müller, 'Rising to the challenge of constitutional capture' *Eurozine*, 21 March 2014, available at www.eurozine.com/rising-to-the-challenge-of-constitutional-capture. See also JW Müller, 'Populism and the People' 41 *London Review of Books* 35.

[92] Hong Kong's Chief Executive (head of the HKSAR and head of HKSAR Government) is elected by an election committee of 1,200 members from sectors of the community with a preferential emphasis on the commercial, industrial, and finance sectors, and the professions. Half of Hong Kong's legislature is returned by geographical constituency-based elections and the other half by functional constituency-based elections.

Any talk of the Sino–British Joint Declaration 1984 providing international redress is hollow since the PRC, a party to the treaty and the sovereign of Hong Kong, made it known in 2017 that it regards the treaty as 'spent'.[93] Any suggestion or attempt by Britain, the only other party to the treaty, to hold the PRC to the treaty,[94] would be denounced as intervention of Chinese sovereignty and ignored.[95]

Can one rely on Hong Kong's legal institutions to prevent 'backsliding' from happening? The answer, having considered the above, no longer seems to be a confident 'yes'. The court leaders of the succeeding generations are disposed towards disavowing liberal notions of multiculturalism/cosmopolitanism, immigrant rights, and adaptable family models, thereby potentially gifting the Executive and the Legislature of the HKSAR a 'free hand' or 'ample room of manoeuvre' to establish or maintain primacy of Chinese culture, strict immigration control, and a family model based on the civil equivalent of the Christian marriage of one man and one woman.[96] In short, they have adopted the kind of populist agenda favoured by some Central and Eastern European political parties. In addition, their 'principle of reciprocity' between the exercise of rights and compliance with the law dovetails neatly with the 'law based governance' of the 'system of socialist rule of law with Chinese characteristics' maintained under the banner of 'Xi Jinping thought on socialism with Chinese characteristics for a new era', which, as Professor Cohen has recently noted, is a reinforcement of 'the Stalinist model of using law as an instrument of authoritarian modernization and control'.[97] These inclinations, joined by the adoption of the margin of appreciation for 'political judgments' and 'national security claims', and the dual duties of fidelity in the judicial oath to the law (inclusive of the law prescribed on the HKSAR by the NPCSC) and to justice, all described above, present a bleak picture of judicial reticence in addressing and redressing attempts to undermine the rule of law by the Central Authorities and the HKSAR Government using powers that they claim they

[93] See J Ng, 'Sino-British Joint Declaration on Hong Kong "no longer has any realistic meaning", Chinese Foreign Ministry says' *South China Morning Post*, 30 June 2017, available at www.scmp.com/news/hong-kong/politics/article/2100779/sino-british-joint-declaration-hong-kong-no-longer-has-any.

[94] See House of Commons Foreign Affairs Committee, 'China and the Rules-Based International System' (4 April 2019) ch 5, available at publications.parliament.uk/pa/cm201719/cmselect/cmfaff/612/61202.htm; 'UK formally raises concerns over extradition law' *RTHK*, 8 April 2019, available at news.rthk.hk/rthk/en/component/k2/1451788-20190408.htm.

[95] See, eg, the response of the PRC's Foreign Ministry Spokesperson on the British Government's biannual report on Hong Kong on 27 March 2019, available at www.chinese-embassy.org.uk/eng/zywl/t1649722.htm (stating that since 1 July 1997, 'Hong Kong affairs have become China's internal affairs. The British side has no right to point fingers and shall not interfere in Hong Kong affairs under whatever pretexts').

[96] Coincidentally, these social and policy themes have been proudly proclaimed as 'illiberal' in Central Europe. See V Orbán, 'Speech at the 29th Bálványos Summer Open University and Student Camp' (Prime Minister's Office, Hungary, 28 July 2018), available at www.kormany.hu/en/the-prime-minister/the-prime-minister-s-speeches/prime-minister-viktor-orban-s-speech-at-the-29th-balvanyos-summer-open-university-and-student-camp.

[97] See JA Cohen, 'Foreword' in AHY Chen, *An Introduction to the Legal System of the People's Republic of China*, 5th edn (Hong Kong, LexisNexis, 2019) v–vi.

possess 'constitutionally'. Coupled with the institutional and other vulnerabilities the Judiciary faces, such as the shortage of judges, the potential for Executive influence in appointments and the politicisation of judging by the community, also discussed above, backsliding by the Judiciary is not unthinkable.

Perhaps one ought not to expect the legal profession to be able to resist any such slide either. The ecology of legal practice, including the symbiotic relationship with the judiciary, the increasing interaction and co-operation with mainland Chinese counterparties, the hardening of the popular attitude against 'cause lawyering', and the decline of respect for the considered views of the legal profession, all discussed above, mean that the informed opinions of the legal profession may well be more bark than bite.

In his farewell sitting speech, Tang PJ also noted that 'faith in the judiciary once lost, can never be regained'.[98] He drew attention to the 'protean power' of the common law, which, 'unless adequately controlled by the proper application of human rights law, can be misused' and called on the community to support the judges through 'endeavour to nurture an atmosphere friendly to the rule of law'. He said:

> We have a free press and free elections in Hong Kong. Make your voice heard and your vote count. Believe me, the price of freedom is indeed eternal vigilance. Above all else, do not give up or underestimate your strength. If we as a community insist on the rule of law, it cannot be taken from us easily. *Do not make it easy.* (emphasis added)[99]

These observations seem to be supported by research, for Pech and Scheppele have been concerned with precisely the operation of 'rule of law backsliding' as a deliberate strategy pursued by public authorities in countries like Hungary and Poland to undermine pluralism and create a de facto one-party state/'dual state'. Changing the Government through fair and honest elections becomes 'all but impossible' following the capture of not only the political branches of the Government, but also 'the media, the judiciary, civil society, the commanding heights of the economy, and the security forces'. As Pech and Scheppele observed:

> These are states in which the rule of law had in fact been achieved and is now being systematically dismantled, which is a different sort of problem from not being able to achieve the rule of law in the first place. Backsliding implies that a country was once better, and then regressed. We are particularly concerned with cases where this retrogression is a deliberate strategy of a ruling party.[100]

And when voters and ordinary citizens realise that this is what is happening, it is usually too late; the damage has already been done, the proverbial 'frog' has lost the will and ability to jump out of the pot of broth.[101]

[98] *Farewell Sitting for the Honourable Mr Justice Tang PJ* (2018).

[99] See ibid.

[100] Pech and Scheppele, 'Illiberalism Within' (2017) 12.

[101] ibid 10; P Krugman, 'Boiling the Frog' *The New York Times*, 12 July 2009, available at www.nytimes.com/2009/07/13/opinion/13krugman.html.

Empirical research done by Karen Lee and Stephen Chiu in 2018 suggested that although Hong Kong residents generally have continued to have a high regard for the judicial system in Hong Kong, those in the younger generation between 18 and 29 register a lower score than others.[102] Lee and Chiu found them also to have low regard for Hong Kong's mechanisms of checks and balances of governmental powers and for governance by the social elite. And those with higher level of education also dislike governance by the elite and give low scores to the state of the rule of law in Hong Kong. Lee and Chiu thus postulated the existence of an interactive effect between the rule of law on the one hand and preference towards governance by the elite and checks and balances of governmental power on the other. Those who have lower level of education and generally prefer governance by the elite would not care much about checks and balances in the political system and might even consider the rule of law to be obstructive to governance of the selected 'able'. Those who have higher level of education and generally prefer a political system based on democracy and equality would have high expectations of the rule of law as a check and balance in the political system. And the young generation resent the courts sending students and social movement leaders to jail. All these, Lee and Chiu argue, will have long-term effects on the legitimacy of the Government and public attitudes towards compliance with laws and judgments.[103] Those apparently heartened by the research results should note the demographics: given the advances in living conditions and medical technology and the low birth rate, the age distribution in Hong Kong's population will remain like that of an inverted pyramid. The script for decline and decay remains valid, ready to be partaken by the privileged few in the citadel.[104]

This chapter began with the borrowed Germanic metaphor of the 'Twilight of the Idols' per Friedrich Nietzche. It is readily admitted that Nietzsche hammered as 'idols' the 'old truths' and their worshippers.[105] New truths have emerged for the New Era of Socialism with Chinese Characteristics. This chapter has examined idolatry of the institutions for the rule of law in Hong Kong and indeed 'hammered'

[102] See also the contribution of Wai-man Lam in this collection.

[103] KMY Lee and SWK Chiu, 'Rule of Law in the Hearts of the Public? The Scoring of Hong Kong Residents of the Judicial System' *Ming Pao*, 3 December 2018, available at news.mingpao.com/pns/%e8%a7%80%e9%bb%9e/article/20181203/s00012/1543775031208.

[104] The likelihood of a 'slow death' of Hong Kong has entered public discussion; see K Richberg, 'It took a while, but "The Death of Hong Kong" has arrived' *Inkstone*, 9 October 2018, available at www.inkstonenews.com/opinion/keith-richburg-expelling-foreign-correspondent-marks-beginning-hong-kongs-demise/article/2167594; P Bowring, 'A slow death for Hong Kong's separate identity in China' *South China Morning Post*, 24 October 2018, available at www.scmp.com/comment/insight-opinion/hong-kong/article/2169948/slow-death-hong-kongs-separate-identity-china; A Wu, 'Hong Kong isn't dead (yet), but it has lost its edge' *South China Morning Post*, 5 November 2018, available at www.scmp.com/comment/insight-opinion/hong-kong/article/2171449/hong-kong-isnt-dead-yet-it-has-lost-its-edge; H Davidson, '"The last fight for Hong Kong": activists gear up over extradition law' *The Guardian*, 7 June 2019, available at: www.theguardian.com/world/2019/jun/07/the-last-fight-for-hong-kong-activists-gear-up-to-protest-extradition-law.

[105] F Nietzche, *The Twilight of the Idols* (English translation, 1911), available at www.gutenberg.org/files/52263/52263-h/52263-h.htm.

them on their resilience as guardians of the rule of law and their capabilities as receptacles of, and instruments for furthering, the Party State's 'sovereignty, security and development interests'. This chapter shall end with another Germanic metaphor, again on the worshipper. It was Hannah Arendt who wrote:

> The ideal subject of totalitarian rule is not the convinced Nazi or the convinced communist, but people for whom the distinction between fact and fiction (ie the reality of experience) and the distinction between true and false (ie the standards of thought), no longer exist.[106]

[106] H Arendt, *The Origins of Totalitarianism* (Cleveland, Meridian Book, 1958) 474.

9

The Legislature as a 'Vetogate'

MARGARET NG

The 2002–03 attempt of the Hong Kong Special Administrative Region (Hong Kong SAR) Government to enact national security legislation to implement Article 23 of the Basic Law was thwarted by the resistance of democratic members of the Legislative Council (LegCo) and a massive civil society campaign culminating in a protest march of over half a million people on 1 July 2003.[1] LegCo has the constitutional function and responsibility to enact laws which are to Hong Kong's interest and to oppose legislative proposals that compromise Hong Kong's interests and the rights and freedoms of its people. The Basic Law has conferred upon LegCo important powers and privileges to perform its proper role and function. This paper analyses those powers and privileges, and the operation of LegCo, to show how they worked in the context of proposed Article 23 legislation in 2002–03, examines the changes since then that have steadily disarmed and weakened LegCo, discusses the prospect of reversing the erosion, and identifies the important factors which should be considered if Article 23 legislation or its like is brought back on the agenda.

I. The Nature of Hong Kong's Political System

A brief word on the nature of Hong Kong's political system is necessary to set our discussion in context. The Basic Law states from the start, in Article 2, that the Hong Kong SAR is authorised to 'enjoy executive, legislative and independent judicial power', and sets out the respective powers and function of each of them in separate sections within the chapter on political structure. However, conflicting views have persisted on whether Hong Kong's political system is that of an 'executive-led government' or one of 'separation of powers'. Neither term actually appears in the text of the Basic Law.

Underlying the conflicting views is the question of who calls the shots in the Hong Kong SAR: is it the executive branch, with all the top officials including the

[1] See also the contribution of Michael Davis in this collection.

Chief Executive appointed by Beijing, or the legislative branch which is constituted by election? If the former, ultimately Beijing has control; if the latter, then Hong Kong people do. Those who hold the 'executive-led government' view argue that pre-1997 the Hong Kong administration was executive-led, and must remain so post-1997 on the principle of continuity. Further, the Chief Executive and principal officials enjoy a special status as appointees of the Central People's Government, and the Chief Executive is accountable to Central Government and has the power and function to implement its directives. Those who uphold the separation of powers (in Chinese, 'three powers separate from each other', implying separate and equal status) point to the provisions of the Basic Law that grant the powers of the three branches to check against each other and the promise that Hong Kong will have democracy in which the executive authorities are accountable to an elected legislature. It is a basic precept in Western democracies that the three powers are separate and act as checks and balance against one another and not concentrated on an all-powerful executive.

This controversy is more political than legal. Notwithstanding repeated hints and statements of Chinese officials (for example, Xi Jinping's statement during a visit to Hong Kong in July 2008 that there should be solidarity within the governance team of the executive, legislature, and judiciary, and statement to similar effect in a White Paper published by the State Council in 2014[2]), Hong Kong courts have steadfastly made their rulings solely on the basis of the relevant articles of the Basic Law interpreted according to the courts' established common law principles of constitutional interpretation. In November 2014, in *Leung Kwok Hung v President of Legislative Council (No 1)* the Court of Final Appeal (CFA) held unequivocally, that the Hong Kong political system under the Basic Law is one of separation of powers.[3] This was notwithstanding the White Paper published by the State Council earlier that year which propagated a kind of 'co-operation of powers' in safeguarding the 'sovereignty, security and development interests' of the State.[4]

The divergence between the political and legal spheres is a fundamental source of conflict and tension permeating constitutional debates in Hong Kong.

II. Article 23: 'Shall Enact Laws on its Own'

Article 23 of the Basic Law states:

> The Hong Kong Special Administrative Region shall enact laws on its own to prohibit any act of treason, secession, sedition, subversion against the Central People's

[2] State Council, 'White Paper on the Practice of "One Country, Two Systems" Policy in the Hong Kong Special Administrative Region' (June 2014).

[3] *Leung Kwok Hung v President of Legislative Council (No 1)* (2014) 17 HKCFAR 689 [28].

[4] On 11 June 2014, the Hong Kong Bar Association issued a statement expressing serious concern on the views of the White Paper characterising judges as 'part of the governance team' upon whom a political requirement is imposed.

> Government, or theft of state secrets, to prohibit foreign political organizations or bodies from conducting political activities in the Region, and to prohibit political organizations or bodies of the Region from establishing ties with foreign political organizations or bodies.

The words 'shall enact laws on its own' are of central significance. They make it clear that, while the objective is to protect the state interest of China, the way by which this is to be achieved is not by the application of national laws to Hong Kong, but by laws enacted by the Hong Kong SAR 'on its own'. This means, first, that such laws must conform with common law principles which are in force in Hong Kong, as stated in Articles 8 and 18 of the Basic Law. These include the basic requirements of 'law' under the common law; ie it must be clear, certain and accessible to the public so that people may regulate their conduct accordingly.[5] Another principle of the common law is that penal provisions are not to be given retrospective effect.

Secondly, LegCo must enact such laws in accordance with established legislative procedure and practice.[6] An important feature of LegCo's procedure and practice is due process, an integral part of which is adequate consultation with the public, especially those who are likely to be directly affected by the proposed legislation. Openness, the timely submission of papers explaining or substantiating the Government's claims and proposals, are further examples of LegCo's standard practice and requirements.

Taken together, legislative procedure and LegCo practice preclude unclear and sweeping Article 23 laws to be rushed through on the nod without a full opportunity for legislators to examine the proposals in detail with the participation of the public, and to move amendments to the proposals as precondition of approval. These features played an important role in the successful opposition to the 2003 national security bill.

When compared to the central Chinese system, these features are distinctive to the Hong Kong system, largely inherited from the pre-1997 administration, which in turn was an adaptation of the Westminster parliamentary model, and sharply different from systems, law and practice in China.

III. LegCo's Constitutional Functions

Ironically, while LegCo formally became 'the legislature' of the Hong Kong SAR under the Basic Law (as opposed to being a merely 'advisory' body with whose views and agreement the Governor made laws for Hong Kong[7]), LegCo's

[5] *Shum Kwok Sher v HKSAR* (2002) 5 HKCFAR 381, 401–03.

[6] Under Art 75(2) of the Basic Law, LegCo has the power to make its own rules of procedures, provided that they are consistent with the Basic Law. The Rules of Procedure of LegCo adopted post-1997 followed the pre-1997 Standing Orders with only minor changes.

[7] Hong Kong Letters Patent 1917, Art VII.

legislative power became more restricted post-1997 in one central aspect. Notably, LegCo members have no power to introduce bills affecting public policy without the written consent of the Chief Executive, and no power at all to propose any bills 'relating to public expenditure or political structure or the operation of the government'.[8] Thus, in practical terms, the *legislative* role of LegCo is confined to passing legislative proposals (bills) introduced by the Government, amending such bills if it sees fit[9] and vetoing a bill or parts of it.

Ancillary to its legislative role, LegCo has the right and duty to consult the public and be consulted by the Government in the course of considering the Government's policy or legislative proposals. This process of consultation by LegCo has been formalised through practice, and can take place on large scale, as is appropriate for major issues like national security legislation. This would take the form of calling for deputations and setting up public hearings in the precincts of LegCo to receive oral and written representations. Special invitations may be issued to bodies with relevant expertise, such as the legal professional bodies, environmental protection organisations, educational institutes, and so on who might advise LegCo of their views on the proposed law. Also relevant is LegCo's power and function of making the executive account to it for the Government's action and policies.[10] In order to do so effectively, LegCo has the right to request information, and for officials to attend LegCo to answer questions and give evidence. Requests for information can take the form of oral and written questions at each LegCo meeting, and at the meetings of LegCo's panels set up to regularly monitor various areas of the Government's policies, of bills committees set up to examine Bills, or, most powerful of all, in select committees appointed by LegCo by resolution to enquire into special events of great public concern, exercising the powers of summoning witnesses to testify under oath.[11]

A function and effect of this ancillary role is to raise public awareness on issues relating to bills introduced by the Government, and to provide the public, and particularly the media, with important information on the implication of the Bill if passed into law, in terms of practical consequences, legal and constitutional principles, and fundamental rights and freedoms. This feature is particularly important for the success of a sustained public campaign by civil society bodies.

[8] Basic Law, Art 74.

[9] LegCo members' power to move amendments without Art 74 restrictions was disputed by the Government without success. This power turned out to be an important weapon in filibustering because members can move as many amendments as they like subject to the permission of the President, and make multiple speeches during the debate of these amendments. However, the pro-government groups of LegCo members succeeded to change the Rules of Procedure in December 2017 to limit this power.

[10] Basic Law, Arts 73(4), (5) and (6).

[11] Art 73(10) of the Basic Law, giving constitutional protection to the LegCo's power to summon witnesses to give evidence under oath provided in Part III of the Legislative Council (Powers and Privileges) Ordinance enacted in 1985 in the wake of the Sino–British Joint Declaration signed in September 1984. See *Cheng Kar Shun & Ano v Li Fung Ying & Or* [2011] 2 HKLRD 555 for a review of the legislative history and background of this LegCo power.

Often, LegCo members and civil society bodies are mutually dependent in order to be effective in checking the Government, as was dramatically demonstrated in the 2002–03 campaign against the proposed Article 23 legislation.

LegCo's powers can be used as bargaining chip to check unwelcome legislative proposals of the Government. Chief among them is the power to block the Government's application for financial approval.[12] However, this is not always practicable, especially when the funding applied for is for the purpose of improving public service. Blocking such applications will then come with a political price.

Last but not least, LegCo has control of the procedure of enactment, which takes place on the floor of LegCo.[13] The verbatim official record of proceedings means officials and members will be held responsible for what they say and do and how they vote or abstain from voting, not only to the public at the time but also to history. They will be judged with the benefit of hindsight, and will be held to their promises and undertakings. Equally, those in the minority, even though they cannot block the enactment, can point out the errors and wrongfulness of the Government. Such observations will be on permanent and accessible record, and may be vindicated at some future date. In other words, the *practice*, borrowed from Westminster since the inception of LegCo's, of keeping an official record[14] acts as sanction, restraint and empowerment.

The power of the record is most notable in its legal effect. The speech of the official introducing the Bill, the fact that clauses were deleted or inserted into the bill as a result of scrutiny at committee stage, are generally accepted by the courts as evidence in the process of interpreting legislative provisions.[15] Sometimes a Bill is passed only upon the Government's clarification or promise that it will not take advantage of ambiguity in its provisions.[16] False or misleading information given by an official on the floor of LegCo would expose him and the Government to censure.

Procedure can also be used as a weapon of delay or 'filibustering', which under special conditions can amount to veto,[17] as the public is becoming increasingly aware in recent years. Filibustering is a two-edged sword, and its indiscriminate

[12] Basic Law, Art 73(2) and (3).

[13] Basic Law, Art 73(1).

[14] The official record of LegCo's proceedings is nicknamed 'Hansard', after the official record of the House of Commons.

[15] The United Kingdom decision in *Pepper v Hart* [1993] AC 593 opened the way to using the official records of Parliament to ascertain the meaning of a statutory provision which is ambiguous. In Hong Kong, consultation of legislative materials especially the official record of LegCo debate is accepted as part of the exercise of purposive interpretation: see, eg, *HKSAR v Cheung Kwun Yin* (2009) 12 HKCFAR 568.

[16] eg, the promise given by Secretary of Security Lee Siu Kwong in the second reading debate of the Shenzhen Bay Hong Kong Port Bill that Art 20 would not be used to reduce Hong Kong people's rights and freedoms.

[17] One such situation is when the date is already fixed for LegCo's prorogation and there are a large number of Bills to debate.

use is seldom of advantage. Indeed, procedural delay is most powerful as a threat in the negotiation with a responsible government. Structurally, the constitutional arrangements favour checks and balances. From that perspective, veto is failure, to be regarded as triumph only because the alternative is far worse.

IV. LegCo in Operation: Vetoing the Veto

Constitutional powers are conferred on and exercised by LegCo as a body, not on individual members,[18] thus it is through resolutions passed by the House, in accordance with the Rules of Procedure (made by LegCo on its own) that these powers are exercised.[19] This means the composition of LegCo and the rules governing quorum and modes of voting are of critical importance. LegCo's composition is fixed by Article 68 and Annex II, Section I of the Basic Law,[20] quorum by Article 75(1) ('not less than one half of all [LegCo] members'), and procedure for voting by Annex II, Section II (Bills introduced by the Government requires a simple majority of members present, while motions introduced by a member requires a majority vote of each of the functional constituency and geographical constituency groups of members). These rules cannot be changed by the SAR on its own.

By Annex II, only half of the seats in LegCo are returned by geographical constituencies by direct election, on proportional representation. The remaining members are returned by functional constituencies. As from the 2012–16 term, there are 35 functional constituency seats. Five of them are nominated by District Councillors from among themselves and elected by voters who have no vote in any of the other 30 functional constituencies. Most of the remaining 30 are returned by a mere handful of corporate or individual voters. This process ensures that these members will be beholden to the Government and vested elite interests, and not accountable to the general public.[21] The combined result is that while the democrats hold a majority in the geographical constituency section, they can win no more than two or three seats in the functional constituency section. The end result is that government proposals can count on getting the simple majority of all members present for them to be passed, unless some of the pro-establishment groups choose to defect. On the other hand, proposals by the democrats are almost certain to be defeated for want of a majority in *both* the geographical constituency and functional constituency sections unless enough 'rebels' of the

[18] Judgment of Hartmann J in *Leung Kwok Hung v President of Legislative Council* [2007] 1 HKLRD 387.

[19] Basic Law, Art 75(2).

[20] The composition of LegCo can be changed from time to time in accordance with the procedure in Annex II. This has happened only once: in 2012 with the addition of five seats each for 'District Council (Second)' and for geographical constituencies.

[21] The functional constituencies and their respective electors are defined in Legislative Council Ordinance, enacted by the Provisional Legislative Council appointed by Beijing in 1996.

pro-establishment groups feel unable to support the proposals. Vetoing a government proposal is therefore an uphill task, as is moving LegCo to take positive steps to censure the Government or compel it to do anything.[22]

The two factors which can make the Government yield to its LegCo critics are persuasion and public pressure, and the two are of course inter-related. The views and support of well-regarded civil society organisations such as the Hong Kong Bar Association and Law Society,[23] and influential media still matter; political parties in so far as they control parcels of votes in LegCo, and outside LegCo, are important because they can rally support from the general public and organise significant campaigns and demonstrations.

As one can see from the 2002–03 experience of Article 23 legislation, nothing is certain; ineptitude in the way the Government handles an issue and responds to members and the public could lose or win support and tip the balance. Even pro-establishment political groups have to face their electorate. Government officials have been known to grumble about the difficulty of lobbying loyalist groups on issues which may cost they votes, while pro-establishment political parties have likewise grumbled about the difficulty of promoting certain government proposals to their voters. Logically, the more unpopular and indefensible the Government's proposal, the more room there is for democratic LegCo members to manoeuvre and ultimately succeed in bringing about a veto.

A. How the Factors Played Out in 2002–03

An illustration of how the above-analysed factors played out is the passing of the anti-terrorism Bill of April 2002.[24] The purpose of the Bill was ostensibly to fulfil Hong Kong's obligation to enact anti-terrorism law to implement the United Nations Security Council Resolution 1373, passed following the 9/11 terrorism attack. The Hong Kong SAR Government initially dragged its feet, and ultimately came up with a Bill that went much further than required by Resolution 1373. Among the most objectionable clauses was a schedule of draconian powers to be given to the police to question people and compel them to give information, to break into residential premises and search and seize things without a warrant, and so on: powers that were most convenient for the Government to have, but the use of which the police could justify in the name of anti-terrorism investigations. Supported by human rights groups, LegCo's democrats strongly opposed these extra powers while acknowledging Hong Kong's international obligation to comply with Resolution 1373. Because of the long delay, the Hong Kong SAR

[22] The democrat majority in the geographical constituencies section was broken for the first time in November 2018, when the democrats lost a by-election to replace a disqualified democrat legislator: see discussion below.

[23] See the contribution of PY Lo in this collection.

[24] United Nations (Anti-terrorism Measures) Bill, gazetted in April and passed on 11 July 2002.

Government came under international pressure to pass the legislation before the second anniversary of the 9/11 attack (or so LegCo was told). In exchange for LegCo's support to pass the Bill before the deadline, the Secretary for Security was forced to accept a number of important amendments, including shelving the schedule of extra powers for the police.

The Government published a consultation document on possible Article 23 legislation about two months later, in September 2002. Unlike the anti-terrorism bill, which was required by Resolution 1373, this was a political mission imposed on the SAR by China, to which the pro-establishment groups must pledge their loyalty and commitment. They were thus inclined towards passing an Article 23 law. It was also more important to the political career of the Secretary for Security that Article 23 law would be introduced. On the other hand, democrats were sworn to defend Hong Kong SAR residents against the erosion of their liberties through the applying of China's ideas of national security. Thus the divide in LegCo was deep and unbridgeable. In such a situation, the force of civil society was pivotal.

The history of the Article 23 legislation campaign is one of co-ordination between LegCo members and their civil society constituents and supporters on both sides. Notably at that stage, five years after the Handover, much of LegCo's practice was still functioning. Once the consultation document was released, the two policy panels most directly concerned[25] immediately embarked on a series of joint public meetings. Government officials were invited to explain the proposals to members in detail and to answer members' questions. A series of hearings was held to receive submissions and deputations from the public. Representatives of the Bar and the Law Society, academics and human rights organisations submitted detailed opinions on the legal issues and voiced their concerns.[26] The information provided to LegCo and the debates at these meetings stimulated social actions and political activities outside LegCo, such as signature campaigns and public forums. The media, which had their own concerns about potential erosion of press freedom and freedom of information, gave the issues sustained and substantial coverage. A novelty was the formation of the 'Article 23 Concern Group' of legal professionals who took to writing pamphlets and distributing them in street campaigns.[27] Meanwhile, supporters of the Government and patriotic organisations were no less active in rallying support and voicing their views in LegCo and in the community.

After the three-month consultation period, the Government made a cursory report on the result of the consultation, and announced that the public supported legislation to be introduced, and the National Security (Legislative Provisions)

[25] The Administration of Justice and Legal Services Panel and the Security Panel.

[26] A deputation of librarians was able to convince the Government that the proposed strict liability offence of 'possession of seditious material' would put every librarian at risk of prosecution.

[27] Declaration of interest: This author was a co-organiser of the Concern Group. See also the contribution of Michael Davis in this collection.

Bill was published a few weeks later and introduced into LegCo. This started the formal legislative procedure. A bills committee was set up to examine the details of the Bill. A large number of legislators joined the committee. The pro-government members ensured that they had the majority to elect a pro-government member as Chairman. The bills committee then took over as the central battlefield in LegCo, focusing on the actual contents and language of each of the offences to be created or reformed. The vast public campaign gathered momentum, and commentaries and representations to the bills committee followed the focus. The media continued to play an important role in keeping the public informed while journalists' associations took an active part as stakeholders whose vital interests were involved. Religious groups were deeply concerned, particularly because part of the Bill that proposed to proscribe Hong Kong organisations that have connection with proscribed organisations in mainland China. Thus, nearly all facets of civil society were mobilised and passionately engaged.

Two distinctive features should be recorded. One is the depth to which academics were engaged and the substantial contribution they made.[28] The other is the active participation of international legal experts including the English, American and Canadian Bar, and human rights organisations.[29] All were convinced that it was vital that LegCo should not allow the Bill to be passed without complete redrafting. The contributions were impressive both in quantity and quality. A total of 8,000 independent submissions were received, and a total of 369,374 people gave their views in one form or another during the consultation period of September to December 2002. Major comments and responses from chambers of commerce, foreign governments, parliaments, local and international legal professional groups and academics, commentaries published in local and international newspapers and journals, press releases and editorials exceeded 370.[30] LegCo's record shows that, at the stage of the Bill's scrutiny by the bills committee from March to July 2003, a total of 29 meetings were held, 117 papers were submitted by the Government and 194 representations were submitted by members of the public for the bills committee's consideration. This public engagement exercise set a model for how future major issues would be debated in LegCo.

[28] Scandalised by the slapdash way the Government dealt with opinions submitted by the public by simply putting them into the categories of 'support', 'oppose' and 'cannot be ascertained', a team of academics with expertise in survey analysis headed by Robert Chung of the University of Hong Kong volunteered to do a proper assessment of the material submitted to the Government. Their months of hard work resulted in a report entitled 'Doing Justice to Public Opinion' which was submitted to LegCo. The team's conclusion was in stark contrast to that of the Government. They held that public opinion was deeply divided, but with significantly greater opposed to the legislative proposals both in terms of quantity and quality.

[29] As just one example, a conference entitled 'Freedom and National Security – Has the Right Balance Been Struck?' was held on 14–15 June 2003 in the University of Hong Kong, sponsored by the law faculties of the University of Hong Kong and the City University of Hong Kong, and the Hong Kong Bar Association. Speakers and participants included lawyers, professors and public intellectuals from the United States of America, Canada, England and other parts of the world. The recent experience of anti-terrorism law in these jurisdictions was a valuable contribution.

[30] See 'Doing Justice to Public Opinion' (n 28).

The pro-government Chairman of the bills committee took advantage of the pro-government majority to sweep through the final stages of the examination of the Bill, and gave the green light to the Government to give notice for bringing the Bill back to LegCo to complete the legislative procedure. Contrary to practice, no committee time was given to consider proposals of amendments by members. In the event that did not matter, since before the legislative procedure could be resumed, the historic protest march of 1 July intervened and changed the entire course of the Government's attempt to introduce national security law, so indelible was the experience, for the Hong Kong SAR Government as well as for the Central Authorities who were watching closely off-stage.

The highhandedness of the Government and pro-government legislators actually backfired. The usually moderate Hong Kong public was provoked into action, and the huge number of people pouring into the street to march shook, if not the Chief Executive and his officials, certainly members of the conservative Liberal Party with their six members in LegCo who were usually firm supporters of the Government and business interests. The loss of these six votes finally broke the Government's spirit, and the passage of the Bill was first postponed and the Bill was finally withdrawn altogether. Thus, strictly speaking, LegCo did not veto the Bill. LegCo merely provided the focal point and information that made possible the mobilisation of civil society forces, which ultimately doomed the Bill to failure.

B. A New Policy: The Disarming of LegCo?

That was how it worked last time, but much has changed since the summer of 2003. Those changes raise doubts about whether LegCo will be able to repeat the exercise if new proposals of Article 23 legislation were to come before it. As discussed below, since then, China has become more powerful and confident of asserting its power in the world and over the Hong Kong SAR. As a result, LegCo has received many setbacks in the performance of its role. The governance of Hong Kong as a whole is now much more vulnerable to pressure exerted by the Central Government, and resisting its pressure in the field of national security is much more difficult. Of greatest relevance to the present discussion are three tactics to reduce the strength of democrats in LegCo: China's 'new policy' post 2004 in response to the 2003 march, taking action to disqualify unwelcome LegCo members and candidates, and the use of criminal prosecution against LegCo members.

Immediately after the events of July 2003, China embarked on an extensive reassessment of the Hong Kong situation, leading the Central Government to adopt a new policy of more direct and open participation in Hong Kong's governance.[31]

[31] J Cheng, 'The Story of a New Policy' (2009) 15 *Hong Kong Journal*; E Cao, 'Governing Forces under the Condition of "One Country, Two Systems"' (2008) 422 *Study Times*, English translation available at www.civicparty.hk/cp/media/pdf/090506_cao_eng.pdf.

It was pointed out that while the SAR Government is the most directly responsible for Hong Kong's administration under the Basic Law, it is by no means the only governing team. Many departments of the Central People's Government, by virtue of their responsibility over Hong Kong, also have a legitimate role in Hong Kong's governance. While the policy immediately after the handover was one of non-interference, under the new policy, this Central Government team would no longer shy away from making known their role in Hong Kong's governance, and from performing what they perceive as their role openly and actively.

The 'new policy' was pursued by the increasing influence of the China Liaison Office in Hong Kong over the Hong Kong SAR Government's administration, and the direct involvement of the Liaison Office in all levels of local elections to win more seats for pro-government groups and candidates of its liking. The active pursuance of this two-pronged strategy over the years has significantly changed the political landscape, most directly affecting the balance of powers in LegCo, and hence LegCo's ability to perform its function of holding the executive to account, shifting the political system from separation of powers to executive-led government.

However, in spite of the new policy, China was unable to prevent LegCo from rejecting the decision of the Standing Committee of the National People's Congress (NPCSC) of 31 August 2014 to fix the mode of election by 'universal suffrage' of the Chief Executive from 2017 onwards as one in which Hong Kong people could only vote for candidates pre-selected by Beijing.[32] Protest against this triggered the Umbrella Movement – the biggest and most sustained protest movement experienced in Hong Kong – in September 2014. Interestingly, LegCo has, through vetoing a proposal by the SAR Government that is based on the NPCSC's 2014 decision, the power to effectively reject the NPCSC's decision. By Annex II, Section II (3) of the Basic Law, a two-thirds majority is required for the Hong Kong SAR Government's resolution to be passed in LegCo. Democrats, though in the minority, still occupied more than one-third of the seats, and therefore collectively held the constitutional veto power. The Umbrella Movement galvanised the solidarity of the democrats, and the veto became a foregone conclusion.[33] However, that veto was done on the basis of special Basic Law provisions. It is another matter for ordinary legislative or financial proposals and resolutions in respect of which no such constitutional veto exists. It is here, where Hong Kong's internal governance is concerned, that the veto power can be taken away.

[32] The proposal falling from the NPCSC was that a nomination committee so composed as to ensure Beijing's control will be given the task of selecting a fixed number of candidates for the Chief Executive election, and the candidates will then be elected by universal suffrage. Democrats held that Hong Kong people should be given the right to freely choose their Chief Executive, and opposed the NPCSC model as a sham.

[33] The vote was taken on 18 June 2015 with 28 against with only eight in favour while 32 were absent. It was a big humiliation for the Government.

As discussed above, Article 23 legislation, being a government bill, requires only a simple majority to be passed into law. Thus what enabled LegCo's democrats to effect a veto in 2002–03 was not voting against the Bill, but preventing the Bill from coming up for a vote by sheer force of popular protest. That forceful popular protest was made possible and facilitated by the established practice of public consultation. If the pro-government majority can block or veto public consultation and confine the decision-making process within the four walls of LegCo, at the same time controlling the time table of the decision-making, then a repeat of the democrats' 2003 success seems more or less impossible.

Public consultation is a culture and a core value. Whether or not, and to what extent, LegCo should consult the public, or insist that LegCo itself be consulted, is solely the decision of LegCo itself. Indeed, whether and to what extent the Government is to be held to account for its acts and policies is a matter for LegCo itself. Thus, changing dynamics within LegCo can result in this culture and practice of consultation being undermined. The following examples illustrate this. On 30 September 2014, a request to invite the Government to explain in LegCo the police action in using tear gas on the protesters on 28 September, which sparked off the Umbrella Movement, was blocked by the pro-government members. On 6 November 2014 a proposal to appoint a select committee with coercive powers to inquire into Chief Executive CY Leung's non-disclosure of his acceptance of a large sum of money from UGL Limited was blocked by the pro-government majority. Later, in 2016, the democrats resorted to a little-used rule of procedure that allows 20 members to form a committee of inquiry on the matter, but a committee so established has no power to compel any witness to give evidence. The Chief Executive refused to co-operate, and the committee's inquiry was thus at a standstill. To put it in general terms, what these examples show is that when a majority of LegCo firmly blocks any proposal to hold the executive to account for failing to consult the public, the check-and-balance function of LegCo is disabled, and the powers conferred upon the legislature to perform that function lie unused.

This situation is plainly unacceptable, for it frustrates the LegCo's constitutional purpose and responsibility by the actions of a simple majority of the members. The argument that applies to a normal democratic system – that an act duly passed by a majority in accordance with the rules of procedure speaks the will and has the mandate of the electorate – does not apply to LegCo so long as its composition and methods of election remain unchanged, since the will of the electorate expressed by the popularly elected members of the geographical constituencies is systemically cancelled out by the protected functional constituency seats, the make-up of which is stipulated in the existing Legislative Council Ordinance passed in 1997 by a Beijing-appointed Provisional Legislative Council. By any measure of democracy, LegCo is not a democratically elected legislature. So long as this remains unchanged, the unequal balance of powers will be hard to change. While the Ordinance underpinning this is a local statute that can be amended by LegCo itself, Article 74 of the Basic Law provides that no amendment can be introduced without the written consent of the Chief Executive. Winning a majority in LegCo under these circumstances is a great challenge for democrats. Some of the difficulties can be seen from Table 9.1 below, illustrating the configuration of pro-government versus pan-democrat groups in past elections.

Table 9.1 Changes in configuration of pro-government v pro-democracy seats/vote share in the Legislative Council 2004–2016

2016 election results

	GC*		Traditional FC*		DC (2nd FC)*		Total no of seats
	Vote share	Seats	Vote share	Seats	Vote share	Seats	
Pro-government	40.17%	16	31.54%	22	41.98%	2	40
Pro-democracy	36%	13	59.13%	7	58%	3	23
Localists**	19%	6					6

2012 election results

	GC*		Traditional FC*		DC (2nd FC)*		Total no of seats
	Vote share	Seats	Vote share	Seats	Vote share	Seats	
Pro-government	42.66%	17	32.97%	24	49.28%	2	43
Pro-democracy	56.24%	18	62.28%	6	50.73%	3	27

2008 election results

	GC*		Traditional FC*		DC (2nd FC)*		Total no of seats
	Vote share	Seats	Vote share	Seats	Vote share	Seats	
Pro-government	39%	11	31.06%	26			37
Pro-democracy	59.50%	19	60.62%	4			23

2004 election results

	GC*		Traditional FC*		DC (2nd FC)*		Total no of seats
	Vote share	Seats	Vote share	Seats	Vote share	Seats	
Pro-government	37.40%	12	33.07%	23			35
Pro-democracy	62.44%	18	62.81%	7			25

* GC = Geographical constituencies
FC = Functional constituencies
DC (2nd FC) = District Council FC
Traditional FC = FC other than DC 2nd FC

** A school of pro-democrats so described because of their strong emphasis on local Hong Kong identity and interests.

Just as Beijing responded to the march of half a million in 2003 with a new policy of open and direct intervention, it responded to the Umbrella Movement and the rise of a younger generation of 'localist' activists by further tightening its control over the Hong Kong SAR. In the September 2016 LegCo election the Government introduced a new vetting system to prevent localists, including advocates of Hong Kong independence and other radical candidates, from standing for election by rejecting their nomination on the ground that they did not genuinely pledge allegiance to the Basic Law.[34] In spite of this, democrats including young 'localists' won a total of 29 seats. Following the election, the Chief Executive and Secretary for Justice sought court orders to disqualify two duly elected members[35] on the ground of their objectionable conduct and manner in taking the oath of office in LegCo. While judgment was still awaited (on 7 November 2016), the NPCSC of its own accord issued an Interpretation of Article 104. The contents of the lengthy Interpretation went further in interpreting a provision of the Basic Law than any previous Interpretation of the NPCSC, and in effect ruled that once a person has failed to make the oath 'sincerely' and 'solemnly', he or she instantly loses his or her seat without being allowed a second chance. The Interpretation also stated that loyalty to the Basic Law and the People's Republic of China was a pre-requisite for valid nomination to stand for election. On 15 November, the Court of First Instance gave judgment for the Government and disqualified the two legislators without relying on the Interpretation. On 30 November 2016, giving full and retrospective effect to the NPCSC Interpretation, the Court of Appeal (CA) dismissed the appeal.[36] The Government followed its success and further obtained the disqualification of four other duly elected members on 14 July 2017.[37]

In this way, within months of the new LegCo term, the democratic representation in LegCo was knocked down by six votes. The result is that for first time, pro-government members command a majority in both the geographical and functional constituency sections of LegCo, which would enable them to push through changes to LegCo's Rules of Procedure to make it even more difficult for any minority in opposition to block or delay government proposals or to inquire into the conduct of Government. This the pro-government groups proceeded to do. Taking advantage of the period before by-elections could be held to fill the vacated seats, in December 2017 pro-government members introduced amendments to the Rules of Procedure to make it more difficult for any member to question or veto government proposals, to form select committees of inquiry,

[34] In a by-election in January 2016, a university student Edward Leung Tin-kei representing a localist group won 66,000 votes. His nomination for the September election was rejected by the election officer on the ground that the officer did not believe he genuinely supported the Basic Law. In May 2018, Edward Leung, together with other activists, were charged with rioting for a clash between protesters and police in February 2016. Leung was convicted and sentenced to six years' imprisonment.

[35] Mr Sixtus Leung Chung Hang and Ms Yau Wai Ching, in HCAL 185/2016 and HCMP 2819/2016.

[36] *Chief Executive of HKSAR v President of the Legislative Council* [2017] 1 HKLRD 460.

[37] Nathan Law Kwun-chung, Edward Yiu Chung-yim, Lau Siu Lai and Leung Kwok Hung: See *Chief Executive of HKSAR v President of Legislative Council* [2017] 4 HKLRD 115.

or to delay LegCo's processes by filibustering or quorum-busting. All the amendments were passed as expected. This was in spite of the fact that, according to counsel's opinion obtained by the President, at least one of the amendments was unconstitutional.[38] It was believed that any challenge in court would simply be overruled by an Interpretation of the NPCSC which may go even further than the questioned amendment itself.

The democrats' loss of their one-third-minority veto might have even more serious consequences. Article 79(7) enables LegCo by a two-third-majority vote to censure a member for 'misbehaviour or breach of oath' and remove him or her from office. If this power is exercised successively, it is possible to reduce an opposition to a negligible level. The reality of this came a step closer when the Government used the NPCSC Interpretation of Article 104 to disqualify candidates who either advocated Hong Kong independence or expressed sympathy with advocating Hong Kong independence from standing in the by-elections held to fill the vacancies made by the disqualified members. This undoubtedly amounts to political censorship on thought and expression, but the returning officer's power to do so was unfortunately upheld by the Court of First Instance.[39]

In this grim situation for democrats, it is not easy to see what can be done to preserve, let alone strengthen, LegCo's resilience as an effective check against the erosion of freedom by the introduction of harsh laws to protect national security. Indeed, there are now worries about the disproportionate infringement of freedom of expression by the adoption of national anthem law, which imposes criminal liability on disrespectful behaviour in respect of the national anthem.

China is unlikely to change her mind and give Hong Kong democracy in the foreseeable future. The force for change may again be brought about by another unexpected massive civil society action at least comparable to the march in 2003 and even more powerful than the Umbrella Movement of 2014, but this cannot be planned or predicted. However, the continued growth of public awareness, and community-building and empowerment, are obviously important in giving LegCo the kind of support that contributes to its resilience as an institution. Meanwhile, LegCo's traditional parliamentary immunities which had been given statutory embodiment in 1985[40] are being challenged in a trend of prosecuting legislators for minor offences for their protests in LegCo proceedings. Some examples are: the prosecution of Wong Yuk Man for throwing a glass of water at the Chief Executive (incidentally, the glass shattered on the floor some distance behind

[38] The problem amendment was to reduce the quorum at the Committee Stage of the legislative procedure before LegCo to 20, when Art 75(1) of the Basic Law states that the quorum 'for the meeting of the Legislative Council of the Hong Kong Special Administrative Region shall be not less than one half of all its members'.

[39] *Chan Ho Tin v Lo Ying Ki Alan* [2018] 2 HKLRD 7. The decision was not appealed against when legal aid was refused. In another case concerning would-be candidate Agnes Chow, the rejection of her nomination has been challenged in judicial review and hearing is awaited.

[40] Legislative Council (Powers and Privileges) Ordinance, enacted in July 1985.

the Chief Executive);[41] Cheng Chung Tai being prosecuted for 'desecration' of the Hong Kong SAR flag; and Leung Kwok Hung being prosecuted for 'contempt of Legislative Council' for causing disruption in a committee meeting.[42] Under the Basic Law, a member who has been convicted of an offence and sentenced to imprisonment of one month or more may be removed from his office by resolution passed by a two-third majority. While so far there has been only one instance of success (and that was in 1998 against a member sentenced to three years' imprisonment for an offence involving dishonesty unrelated to LegCo), but the ease with which the Government can do so has disturbing potentials.

In this context, the independent judiciary is perceived as the last line of defence.[43] There are certain problems with such an expectation. In Hong Kong, with its weak political structure and huge democratic deficit, people (including LegCo members) increasingly look to the courts and the law to compensate, but the outcome is not always to their satisfaction. This is fundamentally because the court is an unsuitable arena for resolving political struggles, and also because of the limitations of the judicial process. This is especially so when the constitutional arrangements are challenged. In *Lee Mui Ling v AG*,[44] the court refused to grant leave in an application to review the Government's failure to abolish or reform the functional constituencies because they contravene Article 25 of the International Covenant on Civil and Political Rights; in *Leung Kwok Hung v President of Legislative Council*,[45] the court held that the rule in the Rules of Procedure under which the President refused to allow a member to move an amendment to a government bill on the ground that it engaged revenue did not contravene the member's right to participate in the legislative process; in *Leung Lai Kwok Yvonne v Secretary for Constitutional Affairs*,[46] the court refused to grant leave to challenge the Hong Kong SAR Government's promotion of the model for the selection of the Chief Executive in 2017 on the ground that it was unlawfully based on the NPCSC Decision of August 31, with Au J remarking that the SAR courts had no jurisdiction to question an act of the NPCSC. In *Kwok Cheuk Kin v Secretary for Constitutional and Mainland Affairs*,[47] the court refused leave to challenge the constitutionality of the Legislative Council (Amendment) Ordinance which prohibits a LegCo member who resigned voluntarily from standing in a by-election held within six months of his or her resignation, for the reason that the restriction of the voters' right to elect the representative of his choice was not disproportional, having regard to the political nature of the decision and principle of deference to LegCo as the most appropriate decision-maker. This deference to an unelected Executive that is not

[41] Wong's conviction was quashed on appeal on the facts.

[42] Leung successfully challenged the legality of the charge against him. The Prosecution is appealing on a Case Stated.

[43] See the contribution of PY Lo in this collection.

[44] *Lee Miu Ling v A-G* (1995) 5 HKPLR 585.

[45] *Leung Kwok Hung v President of Legislative Council* [2007] 1 HKLRD 387.

[46] *Leung Lai Kwok Yvonne v Secretary for Constitutional Affairs* (unreported, HCAL 31/2015, 5 June 2015).

[47] *Kwok Cheuk Kin v Secretary for Constitutional and Mainland Affairs* (2017) 20 HKCFAR 353.

accountable to a representative legislature, and to a LegCo that is a travesty of an elected legislature, has often been criticised, but so far to no discernible effect.

The decisions in the oath-taking cases are different and disturbing because, in these cases the court in effect summarily removed from office a duly elected member of the legislature upon the application of the executive, overriding the established principle of separation of powers without appearing to be particularly concerned or even aware that it poses fundamental challenges to constitutional principles and may merit deeper consideration. Furthermore, and even more disturbingly, the CA accepted the NPCSC's sweeping Interpretation of Article 104 and gave it retrospective effect as if it were a judgment of a superior court under the doctrine of *stare decisis*, while rejecting the submission that the Interpretation has exceeded the bounds of an interpretation under the Basic Law on the basis that a lawyer trained only in the common law is not qualified to speak on an Interpretation of the NPCSC under the 'civil law system' of China.[48] It may validly be argued that in these cases the courts conceded more autonomy than is necessary or appropriate.

Perhaps the CA did not have much room for manoeuvre given the previous decisions of the CFA, as it perceived them, on the unbounded power and categorically binding force of the NPCSC Interpretation.[49] However, it is not inconceivable for the CFA to correct itself and contain the most damaging effects of its earlier decisions, at least with respect to the issue of giving automatic retrospective effect to an NPCSC Interpretation.[50] It was disappointing that the CFA refused to grant leave to appeal from the CA's judgment in that case,[51] thereby missing an opportunity to do so. It is certainly within the power of the CFA to put some boundaries on the unquestioning implementation of the arbitrary exercise of naked power to undermine the Hong Kong SAR's constitutional system already promulgated in the Basic Law in China's discharge of her obligation under the Sino–British Joint Declaration to adopt the 'one country, two systems' policy in Hong Kong. Perhaps the *Leung* and *Yau* cases were unattractive on their facts, but the next opportunity is not far off to set down the principles much needed in this new situation at the next opportunity.[52]

Finally, a hitherto almost completely neglected area is the development of a principled parliamentary practice for LegCo.[53] In *Leung Kwok Hung v President*

[48] *Chief Executive of HKSAR v President of the Legislative Council* (n 36) [53]–[57].

[49] See *Yau Wai Ching v Chief Executive of HKSAR* (2017) 20 HKCFAR 390 [34]–[35].

[50] This possibility is suggested by the Hon Robert Tang, PJ in a Dr Mok Hing Yiu Memorial Lecture given in St Hugh's College Oxford on 22 February 2018. The text is available in the CFA website.

[51] *Yau Wai Ching v Chief Executive of HKSAR* (2017) 20 HKCFAR 390.

[52] Leung Kwok Hung's appeal was dismissed on 15 February 2019, see *Secretary for Justice v Leung Kwok Hung* [2019] HKCA 173.

[53] See generally, R Blackburn, 'The Politics of Parliamentary Procedure at Westminster' (2017) 4 *Journal of International and Comparative Law* 279 (for a discussion of parliamentary practice in the United Kingdom); EC Ip, 'Mapping Parliamentary Law and Practice in Hong Kong' (2015) 3 *The Chinese Journal of Comparative Law* 97 (for a discussion of the development of parliamentary practice in Hong Kong).

of Legislative Council (No 1),[54] the CFA decided in no uncertain terms that once the court has determined that the President has a certain power (in that case the power to terminate a debate), the court will not exercise its jurisdiction to intervene to assess whether the power was used rightly or wrongly, both as a matter of the non-intervention principle and as a matter of public policy. This unexceptionable ruling has unfortunately been taken by the President of LegCo to mean that he can do whatever he likes in exercising his powers under the Rules of Procedure, immune from any legal challenge. This cannot be right, because even if no legal remedy lies against his arbitrary or wrong ruling, the credibility and authority of LegCo as the legislature of the Hong Kong SAR will inevitably suffer, and with that, its ability to properly discharge its constitutional functions. *Erskine May's Parliamentary Practice* is an authority because of the fundamental principle and long tradition of impartiality and legality of the ruling of the Speaker who holds the respect of the House. Unfortunately, since the beginning of the 2016–20 term, LegCo practice has developed in the opposite direction. If the development of a proper set of principled parliamentary practice for LegCo cannot be expected from LegCo itself, then the task must fall to legal academics and practitioners, especially counsel who appear before the court on constitutional cases involving LegCo. The recently compiled *Companion* to LegCo's history, rules and practices published by LegCo[55] is only a first step. There is a long way to go.

V. Conclusion

This chapter is not the right place to discuss the future of Hong Kong's political development except as strictly necessary for the main issue of this chapter to be understood. However, one cannot ignore the real effect of politics on the rule of law, particularly in the context of Hong Kong under a sovereign state that is extremely sensitive to its national security and weak in its regard for basic rights and freedoms respected in modern democracies.

The danger is real and present enough for a Judge of the CFA to openly remark that Hong Kong can only claim to enjoy an approximation to the rule of law, and that what is needed to make up the deficit is the implementation of democracy as promised under the Basic Law.[56] A LegCo that cannot exercise a veto on the Hong Kong SAR Government's proposal of national security law – or *any* law for that matter – even if it undermines the core interests of Hong Kong and the rights and freedoms of its people, cannot defend the rule of law, and is worse than

[54] *Leung Kwok Hung v President of Legislative Council (No 1)* (2014) 17 HKCFAR 689.

[55] LegCo, 'A Companion to the History, Rules and Practices of the Legislative Council of the Hong Kong Special Administrative Region' (2016).

[56] The Hon Kemal Bokhary who retired as Permanent Judge in 2012 and now serving as Non-Permanent Judge of the CFA, in a recent speech at a forum of Project Citizens Foundation held on 8 December 2018.

dysfunctional as a legislature. Instead, such a LegCo would play the role of legitimising tyranny in the name of the rule of law. This subverts 'law' as required by the basic tenet of the common law, and allows such 'laws' to violate fundamental rights with impunity.

Twenty years after the Basic Law came into effect and 14 years after the government's failed attempt to enact national security legislation, Hong Kong can no longer pretend that it is a society in transition to full democracy.

One must admit that Hong Kong is now trapped in what some people call 'semi-authoritarianism'[57] or, in plain speech, authoritarianism with democratic trappings. What Hong Kong needs to actively explore now, as a matter of urgency, is the survival of the rule of law under the threat of such powerful and fast-moving authoritarianism.

[57] See, eg, M Ottaway, *Democracy Challenged: The Rise of Semi-Authoritarianism* (Washington DC, Carnegie Endowment for International Peace, 2003): *An Introduction.*

10

Popular Civil Society Resistance and the Survival of Hong Kong: A Clash of Civilisations

MICHAEL C DAVIS[1]

More than two decades after the Hong Kong handover a challenging dispute persists between the Chinese Central Government and Hong Kong civil society over 'one country, two systems'. This dispute implicates Hong Kong's political reform and any effort to enact legislation related to secrecy and national security as required by Article 23 of the Basic Law.[2] On the Chinese side of this dispute the Central Government promotes 'one country' and proclaims comprehensive jurisdiction over Hong Kong. Obsessed with control, the Beijing Government views any lack of control over political forces as a threat to national security. It worries that popular civil society actors, goaded by foreign interference, aim to undermine security or usurp Chinese sovereignty. On the Hong Kong side, in the absence of a strong local government voice willing to defend autonomy, Hong Kong civil society plays the dominant role as the chief guardian of Hong Kong's autonomy and rule of law.

An independent judiciary that has historically guarded the basic freedoms necessary to sustaining such civil society role has come under increasing pressure in a number of contentious cases.[3] Nevertheless, the combination of civil society engagement and judicial oversight has sustained Hong Kong's core liberal values in the early post-handover years.[4] The question now is whether such freedoms will survive growing Beijing interference and the increasing hardline public order enforcement efforts of the Hong Kong Government?[5] Or will Hong Kong be rolled

[1] Professor of Law and International Affairs, OP Jindal Global University; Global Fellow, Woodrow Wilson International Center for Scholars, Washington, DC.

[2] Basic Law of the Hong Kong Special Administrative Region of the People's Republic of China (1990).

[3] See also the contributions of PY Lo and Albert Chen in this collection.

[4] VT Hui, 'Hong Kong's Umbrella Movement: The Protests and Beyond' (2015) 26 *Journal of Democracy* 111.

[5] MC Davis, 'The Basic Law, Universal Suffrage and the Rule of Law in Hong Kong' (2015) 38 *Hastings International and Comparative Law Review* 275.

into the mainland system[6] and suffer the liberal retreat evident in other parts of Asia and around the world?[7]

This chapter seeks to unravel the key aspects that drive civil society's role in preserving Hong Kong's autonomy, considering, first, the importance of the rule of law and the Hong Kong Basic Law as a framework for social activism; second, the instrumental role of local civil society and its current roots in various political movements since the handover; third, government and pro-establishment responses to popular political demands; and fourth, some strategies going forward. I will argue that a vibrant civil society is Hong Kong's (and China's) greatest asset. By failing to deliver on core commitments to Hong Kong's autonomy and democratic self-rule, both Chinese and Hong Kong Governments have undermined Hong Kong's autonomy and put this important role at risk.

I. The Rule of Law and Basic Law Framework

Any effort to understand the expectations of Hong Kong civil society must contend with strikingly different views concerning the Basic Law that prevail in Beijing and Hong Kong. For Hong Kong people the Basic Law assures the continuance of international standards of liberal rule of law-based protections for human rights. In Hong Kong, the rule of law, as a core value, embodies the classic common law notion that nobody is above the law and everyone is subject to the law established in the ordinary manner before the ordinary courts.[8] To this can be added a thicker analysis of how the law is generated and its substantive application to protect human rights and basic equality in Hong Kong. For many Hong Kong lawyers and legal scholars, ensuring that the law made in Hong Kong fulfils these liberal values is critical, but Beijing accuses lawyers and scholars who promote this liberal common law notion of misleading society with a 'lopsided and confused view'.[9]

The Beijing view recently elaborated by Zhang Dejiang, Chairman of the Standing Committee of the National People's Congress (NPCSC), emphasises that Hong Kong's 'high degree of autonomy' is at the sufferance of the Central Government and subordinated thereto.[10] Posing a challenge to the

[6] F Tian, 'Hong Kong's legal system is undergoing "nationalization", and the opposition should realize this' *South China Morning Post*, 25 July 2017.

[7] MC Davis, 'Strengthening Constitutionalism in Asia' (2017) 28 *Journal of Democracy* 147.

[8] See R Cullen, 'The Rule of Law in Hong Kong' (Civic Exchange, 2005), available at www.academia.edu/5156780/Rule_of_Law_in_Hong_Kong.

[9] Information Office of the State Council, 'The Practice of the "One Country, Two Systems" Policy in the Hong Kong Special Administrative Region' (10 June 2014), available at www.fmcoprc.gov.hk/eng/xwdt/gsxw/t1164057.htm (White Paper).

[10] S Lau, 'Chinese state leader Zhang Dejiang announces Beijing's plans to tighten grip on Hong Kong' *South China Morning Post*, 27 May 2017, available at www.scmp.com/news/hong-kong/politics/article/2095923/chinese-state-leader-zhang-dejiang-details-beijings-plans.

legal institutions that protect basic rights, Zhang emphasised that Hong Kong's Government is executive-led and that there is no separation of powers, seemingly suggesting that there should be no meaningful institutional checks on executive power within the Hong Kong legal and political system itself. Calling Hong Kong's high degree of autonomy into question, he further emphasised that Beijing has the power to supervise Hong Kong officials.[11] He urged academics to devote time to study the Basic Law and instil a 'correct' view in Hong Kong's youth, and emphasised the need for Hong Kong to enact its own national security laws, referring to the Article 23 requirement that Hong Kong enact such laws 'on its own'. The Beijing version of the Basic Law was made even more explicit in the June 2014 State Council White Paper on 'one country, two systems'.[12] The White Paper reflected a distinct change of tone from the earlier injunctions to Hong Kongers to 'put your hearts at ease', now effectively indicating that 'Beijing is boss'. It emphasised in particular that the promised 'high degree of autonomy' is not 'full autonomy', and at the same time sought to undermine the international status of the Hong Kong Joint Declaration (which is an international agreement) by claiming that its 12 Articles, quoted verbatim in the White Paper, 'come solely from the authorization of the Central leadership'. The White Paper goes so far as to date the 12 principles to early 1983, nearly two years before the treaty. This overlooks the fact that, when leaked in Hong Kong in 1982, the original version of Beijing's principles caused great panic and they were not as generous as the 12 Articles that eventually emerged in the Joint Declaration after negotiations.[13] As if these representations were not a clear enough repudiation of the Sino–British Joint Declaration, Chinese diplomats in London made explicit their view that the Joint Declaration had been fulfilled and was no longer relevant.[14] This scepticism about the continuing vitality of the Joint Declaration was expressed again during the visit of President Xi Jinping in June/July 2017, although an official statement subsequently clarified that the Joint Declaration remains binding, even though that statement afforded Britain no role in interfering in or enforcing it.[15] These statements reflect the long-held Beijing view that foreign interest and oversight of the Hong Kong model is a form of improper interference that violates Chinese sovereignty.

[11] S Lau and K Chung, 'State leader Zhang Dejiang declares Beijing's power to "supervise" Hong Kong civil servants' allegiance' *South China Morning Post*, 27 May 2017, available at www.scmp.com/news/hong-kong/politics/article/2095957/state-leader-zhang-dejiang-declares-beijings-power-supervise?_=1495956457722.

[12] White Paper (n 9). See also the contribution of Albert Chen in this collection.

[13] See generally, S Tsang, *A Modern History of Hong Kong: 1841–1997* (London, LB Tauris & Co, 2007) 215–25.

[14] LG Crovitz, 'Beijing abrogates 1984 treaty it signed with Britain to guarantee the city's autonomy' *Wall Street Journal*, 15 December 2014, available at www.wsj.com/articles/gordon-crovitz-china-voids-hong-kong-rights-1418601004.

[15] J Ng, 'Beijing says Sino-British treaty on Hong Kong handover still binding but does not allow UK to interfere' *South China Morning Post*, 8 July 2017, available at www.scmp.com/news/hong-kong/politics/article/2101823/we-still-recognise-sino-british-joint-declaration-legally.

In extensive provisions on the rule of law the White Paper suggests that the NPCSC can interpret or amend the Basic Law as it sees fit. Within the White Paper the NPCSC is characterised as the 'guardian' of the rule of law. It is said to have 'comprehensive jurisdiction' and the power of 'supervision' over Hong Kong legislative acts. One can only wonder, if these assertions are true, whether there was a need for 'one country, two systems' at all. In reality the mainland legal practice reflects a different legal culture in which expediency prevails. In such a legal culture, the supplementation or amendment of legal texts to meet the exigencies of the moment is often presented as an exercise in 'interpretation'.[16] Law is generally viewed primarily as a tool of control – rule *by* law – not constraint on official action. This view is reflected in the White Paper.

The White Paper goes on to characterise judges as 'administrative' or 'governing' officials, quite at variance with the dominant conception of the judiciary in Hong Kong.[17] The Hong Kong Bar Association – supported by hundreds of lawyers protesting in a silent march – and current and former justices of the Hong Kong Court of Final Appeal (CFA) lodged a specific objection to this characterisation,[18] and its implication that judges must be patriots (notwithstanding the fact that some Hong Kong judges are foreign nationals). Any suggestions that judges and government servants should guard national security has been seen as an effort to promote enactment of the national security legislation specified in Article 23. That Hong Kong and Macau were named in a recently enacted mainland national security law lends credence to this view.[19] The White Paper does not address political reform to any great extent, except to say that the Chief Executive 'must be a person who loves the country and loves Hong Kong', language generally viewed in Hong Kong as code for exclusion of the more popular pan-democrats.

The Sino–British Joint Declaration by its language appears to envision a purpose and exercise of 'one country, two systems' that is quite different from the mainland vision reflected in these official statements and the White Paper.[20] For people in Hong Kong the affirmation of these commitments in an international treaty was quite important to establishing trust in the application of international standards.[21] In 1984 Deng Xiaoping specifically urged foreign

[16] H Fu, 'Guide to Legislative Interpretation in China' (HKU Legal Scholarship Blog, 2017), available at researchblog.law.hku.hk/2017/07/guide-to-legislative-interpretation-in.html.

[17] See the contribution of PY Lo in this collection.

[18] S Lau, A Chiu and B Yap, 'Hong Kong lawyers march to defend judiciary in wake of Beijing's white paper' *South China Morning Post*, 27 June 2017, available at www.scmp.com/news/hong-kong/article/1541814/hong-kong-lawyers-stage-silent-march-oppose-beijings-white-paper.

[19] National Security Law of the People's Republic of China (2015), English translation available at www.chinalawtranslate.com/2015nsl/?lang=en (PRC National Security Law).

[20] Joint Declaration of the Government of the United Kingdom of Great Britain and Northern Ireland and the Government of the People's Republic of China on the Question of Hong Kong (1984), available at www.cmab.gov.hk/en/issues/joint3.htm (Sino–British Joint Declaration).

[21] Tsang, *A Modern History of Hong Kong* (2007).

investors to 'put their hearts at ease'.[22] In order to secure such confidence the Joint Declaration provided that the common law system was to be maintained and that the courts were to remain independent and final. From the civil society perspective it is noteworthy that, of the approximately 16 rights listed in the Joint Declaration, about half relate to freedom of expression in one form or another. This is backed up by a continuing commitment to enforce the two international human rights covenants, the International Covenant on Civil and Political Rights (ICCPR) and the International Covenant on Economic, Social and Cultural Rights (ICESCR),[23] along with commitments for popular election of the future legislature and potentially the Chief Executive. It is hard to understand these guarantees as anything but a commitment to liberal constitutional government. That the socialist system was not to be practised in Hong Kong was made explicit as the essential purpose of the agreement. Without the local and international oversight that has ensued, the autonomy promised in the Joint Declaration may have been reduced to a pious statement, as is the case for autonomy guarantees elsewhere in China.[24]

The 1990 Basic Law offers further assurance of the seriousness of these liberal constitutionalist commitments.[25] It largely conforms to the Joint Declaration in respect of the human rights guarantees, providing in Article 39 for the application of the international human rights covenants. In accordance with common law practice, Hong Kong courts have used the power of constitutional judicial review to interpret Basic Law guarantees as consistent with both common law and international practice.[26] The courts have generally taken this role seriously, instituting a purposive approach to interpreting and protecting human rights.

However, judged against the spirit of liberal constitutionalism and the treaty commitments, the Basic Law has fallen short in two critical areas, which account for much of today's political contention. First, while the Joint Declaration promised that the courts would be independent and final and operate under common law principles, Article 158 of the Basic Law vests the final power of interpreting the Basic Law in the NPCSC. Second, the Joint Declaration promises a form of democratic rule in Hong Kong that has not been realised. This democratic commitment is elaborated in Articles 45 and 68 of the Basic Law, which articulate an ultimate aim of 'universal suffrage'. Foot dragging by Beijing and their efforts to interpret away this commitment have left Hong Kong's democratic development in tatters.

[22] ibid.

[23] ICCPR (1966), available at treaties.un.org/doc/publication/unts/volume%20999/volume-999-i-14668-english.pdf; ICESCR (1966), available at www.ohchr.org/EN/ProfessionalInterest/Pages/CESCR.aspx.

[24] See, eg, MC Davis, 'Tibet and China's National Minority Policies' (2012) 56 *Orbis* 429.

[25] Basic Law (n 2).

[26] See Davis, *The Basic Law* (2015).

In the popular view, the Chief Executive and leading establishment figures have failed to properly defend Hong Kong's autonomy.[27] Under Article 45 and Annex I of the Basic Law, the Chief Executive is still selected by a heavily pro-establishment Election Committee. This committee is under Beijing's manipulation and sway, leaving Hong Kong's top officials deeply dependent on and subordinate to Beijing. This is particularly significant when one considers the extensive powers that the Chief Executive possesses under the Basic Law.[28] Top officials have long dedicated themselves to representing Beijing concerns to the public and not much to representing Hong Kong concerns to Beijing. The Hong Kong Chief Executive now routinely uses Beijing terms to define Basic Law commitments, most recently degrading Hong Kong's promised 'high degree of autonomy' as 'semi-autonomy'.[29] This awkward circumstance has put Hong Kong's autonomy and its core values, especially the rule of law and basic freedoms, at risk.

Though always foot-dragging over democratic reform, Beijing was historically somewhat restrained with respect to the rule of law and the judiciary. That restraint is now in doubt as Beijing officials interfere more and more in local affairs.[30] As the White Paper implies, the gloves have come off both in words and deeds. The disappearances of booksellers and a businessman were a source of deep concern. Booksellers disappeared while visiting the mainland and in one case from the streets of Hong Kong.[31] The subsequent disappearance of a prominent businessman from a hotel in Hong Kong, who has yet to reappear, signals a rather brazen pattern of mainland interference. Clearly, the Hong Kong Government has not been up to the task of defending Hong Kong's autonomy. Rather, it appears increasingly to be a Beijing instrument in repressing Hong Kong opposition, most recently in banning a minor political party that advocated independence and in denying a visa to a foreign journalist who had hosted the Chairperson of that party, Andy Chan, for a talk at the Foreign Correspondents' Club.[32]

In 2017 the NPCSC elevated the level of interference by directly interfering in a pending court case where the Hong Kong Government was attempting to deny entry of newly elected legislators whose sarcastic oath of office was judged insufficient. At issue were the mocking efforts at oath-taking by protesting young activists

[27] MC Davis, 'Hong Kong Umbrella Movement and Beijing's Failure to Honor the Basic Law' (2014) *E-International Relations*, available at hub.hku.hk/bitstream/10722/207598/2/Content.pdf.

[28] See, eg, Basic Law, Art 48.

[29] K Ng, 'Hong Kong leader Carrie Lam says Beijing committed to City's semi-autonomy' *South China Morning Post*, 16 November 2017, available at www.scmp.com/news/hong-kong/politics/article/2120264/hong-kong-leader-carrie-lam-says-beijing-committed-citys.

[30] E Tong, 'HK20: Interview – Beijing's restraint with Hong Kong's rule of law has expired, says law prof. Johannes Chan' *Hong Kong Free Press*, 25 June 2017, available at www.hongkongfp.com/2017/06/25/hk20-interview-beijings-restraint-hong-kongs-rule-law-expired-says-law-prof-johannes-chan/.

[31] IM Sala, 'In Hong Kong book industry "everybody is scared"' *The Guardian*, 28 December 2016, available at www.theguardian.com/books/2016/dec/28/in-hong-kongs-book-industry-everybody-is-scared.

[32] A Lum, X Su, L Sum, and N Ng, 'British journalist Victor Mallet denied entry to Hong Kong as a tourist' *South China Morning Post*, 9 November 2018, available at www.scmp.com/news/hong-kong/politics/article/2172383/british-journalist-victor-mallet-denied-entry-hong-kong.

elected to the Legislative Council. While the case was pending the NPCSC issued an interpretation of Basic Law Article 104 effectively declaring such oaths to be invalid. In doing so it appeared to instruct the court on the favoured outcome of a pending case.[33] In the CFA, though the court attempted to apply local law to reach its result it also concluded that it was retroactively bound by the NPCSC interpretation.[34] That the Hong Kong Government was complicit in this intervention by bringing the cases to unseat the Government's political opponents caused great public concern. This concern arose not only over Beijing interference but also over dragging the courts into a political battle with Beijing that they could not win.

Further concerns arose over the dramatic government appeals of the community service sentences of the leading protesters of the Hong Kong Umbrella Movement and other protesters who opposed development projects in the New Territories. The Government appealed the sentences in two leading cases, sending 16 community activists to jail for between six and 13 months under new sentencing guidelines articulated by the Court of Appeal. The sentences for the three leading activists were subsequently overturned by the CFA, which accepted the new stricter guidelines in respect of civil disobedience, but held they could not be applied retrospectively.[35] The harsh sentencing of the three 'faces of democracy', had posed a direct challenge to civil society, as the new sentencing guidelines continue to do.[36] Added to this, the conviction in April 2019 of the 'Hong Kong Nine', including the three leading organisers of the Occupy Central movement and six others involved in popular roles in the movement. They were all convicted under various charges relating to the common law crime of nuisance, with the two most prominent leaders found guilty of conspiracy and incitement to nuisance and ultimately sentenced to 16 months in prison.[37] That the Government, as raised by the defendants, used the stick of a common law nuisance charge in place the ordinary statutory charges of unlawful assembly clearly sends a chilling threat to those inclined to engage in public demonstrations. Most recently, posing an even greater risk to the rule of law, the Hong Kong Government in 2019 proposed a new extradition law that would allow extradition of criminal defendants to face criminal prosecution on

[33] The Standing Committee of the 12th National People's Congress adopted the interpretation of Art 104 of the Basic Law at its 24th session. The interpretation is available at www.thestandard.com.hk/breaking-news.php?id=81866.

[34] *Chief Executive of HKSAR v President of the Legislative Council* [2017] 1 HKLRD 460 (CA) [55]–[58]; *Yau Wai Ching v Chief Executive of HKSAR* (2017) 20 HKCFAR 390 (CFA) [35]–[36].

[35] *Secretary for Justice v Wong Chi Fung* (2018) 21 HKCFAR 35 (CFA); C Lau and J Lam, 'Appeal ruling for democracy activist Joshua Wong could have a chilling effect on social activism' *South China Morning Post*, 7 February 2018, available at www.scmp.com/news/hong-kong/politics/article/2132321/appeal-ruling-hong-kong-democracy-activist-joshua-wong-could.

[36] MC Davis, 'With Hong Kong's young faces of democracy in jail, is civil society being put in chains?' *South China Morning Post*, 24 August 2017, available at www.scmp.com/comment/insight-opinion/article/2107915/hong-kongs-young-faces-democracy-jail-civil-society-being.

[37] *HKSAR v Tai Yiu* Ting [2019] HKDC 450.

the mainland.[38] Though the Bill was suspended the growing popular distrust of government from these many developments was evident from the massive civil society protest of up to two million protesters over that summer. Instead of listening to popular concerns to address the problem the Government launched an onslaught of aggressive police enforcement whose end is still awaited. Overall, what started out in 1997 as a rather positive legal roadmap for Hong Kong's future has become a roadmap for the political conflicts Hong Kong faces today, as Beijing increasingly interferes in Hong Kong. Added to this, the Hong Kong Government has proven a poor guardian of Hong Kong's autonomy, effectively shifting that burden to civil society.

II. Civil Society Demands and the Rule of Law

In the 20 years since the handover nearly all large-scale acts of popular protests have been aimed at securing Basic Law and rule of law commitments. That the methods used have also relied primarily on the liberal human rights guarantees entrenched in the Basic Law and enforced by the courts highlights the fundamental importance of free speech, press and associational guarantees both to Hong Kong's autonomy and its rule of law, as well as the continuing vital role of civil society in defending these values. Without the security of these Basic Law guarantees and the rule of law such civil society efforts would have proven futile. In this analysis, as defined by the United Nations, civil society should simply be understood as the non-governmental sector of the community, including non-governmental organisations and people linked by common interest.[39] The present analysis considers only those active sectors of civil society involved in prominent social activism related to the Basic Law issues addressed herein. Even activists who claim to have given up on the Basic Law – while advancing claims for self-determination or independence – rely primarily on its guaranteed freedoms of speech, association and the press, as well as the rule of law, to advance their concerns. They may judge that more extreme acts of civil disobedience are justified in the face of earlier more moderate demands for democracy being thwarted.[40] Such extreme demands would likely lose salience if full democracy were implemented and Hong Kong's promised autonomy under the Basic Law was secure. This section will consider some of the main protests and their

[38] MC Davis, 'Debate over Hong Kong's extradition law devolves into a scuffle in the Legislative Council' *Washington Post*, 11 May 2019, available at https://www.washingtonpost.com/politics/2019/05/11/debate-over-hong-kongs-proposed-extradition-law-devolves-into-scuffle-legislative-council/?utm_term=.b608d558bcd4.

[39] The United Nations refers to this as the 'third sector' beyond government and business. See United Nations, 'Civil Society', available at www.un.org/en/sections/resources-different-audiences/civil-society.

[40] R Yeung, 'Don't seek democracy under the Basic Law' *South China Morning Post*, 13 August 2017.

objectives, looking specifically at the 2003 Article 23 protests, the 2012 national education protests, and 2014 Umbrella Movement.

The first two of the noted protests, over Article 23 and national education, were more conventional in their objectives and methods. As noted elsewhere in this volume,[41] Article 23 of the Basic Law essentially provides that the Special Administrative Region must enact on its own laws on treason, secession, sedition and subversion, as well as laws relating to secrecy and foreign political organisations. The Article 23 protests, which with half a million protesters were then the largest since the handover, were the clearest case to date of activists specifically seeking full compliance with human rights and rule of law guarantees in the Basic Law. The emphasis was most evident in the make-up of the core members of Article 23 Concern Group leading the movement. The initial group's nine members included five leading barristers (Alan Leong, Gladys Lee, Audrey Eu, Ronny Tong and Margaret Ng), two prominent solicitors (Mark Daly and Christine Loh) and two legal academics (Johannes Chan and myself), with a couple of other lawyers joining as core members as the process evolved.[42] This team of lawyers, in a series of nine widely distributed pamphlets, offered an assessment of the proposed government bill under international legal and human rights standards, as such standards are called for in the Basic Law.[43]

The protests themselves were an exercise in using the freedom of expression and related rights secured under the Basic Law. This involved the distribution of pamphlets, elaboration of arguments in position papers, and a series of related press conferences. These were followed by a mobilisation effort by the Hong Kong Civil Human Rights Front,[44] which led the public information drive and carried out the legal notification and approval requirements for the massive marches that followed. When the Government, in the face of massive public opposition, lost the support of the pro-establishment Liberal Party in the LegCo the proposed bill was withdrawn.[45] Efforts to enact Article 23 legislation have not yet been restarted, although Beijing officials have increasingly sounded the alarm against radical acts of protests and calls for independence.[46] The importance of civil society engagement is born out by a legacy of government caution in attempting further

[41] See the introduction by Cora Chan and Fiona de Londras in this collection.

[42] See also the contribution of PY Lo in this collection.

[43] Submissions of the Article 23 Concern Group are available at www.article23.org.hk/english/research/research1.htm.

[44] The Civil Human Rights Front, an umbrella organisation that affiliates nearly all of the pan-democratic camp and numerous human rights related NGOs, was founded in late 2002 in conjunction with the Article 23 Concern Group. It has since expanded its focus across other human rights areas and has led annual marches for human rights on 1 July, the anniversary of the Hong Kong handover. See Civil Human Rights Front, NGO Submission to the Committee against Torture, February, 2015, available at https://tbinternet.ohchr.org/Treaties/CAT/Shared%20Documents/HKG/INT_CAT_ICO_HKG_19976_E.pdf

[45] See the contribution of Margaret Ng in this collection.

[46] T Cheung, 'Calling for an end to communist rule in China "is a crime against Hong Kong"' *South China Morning Post*, 6 April 2018, available at www.scmp.com/news/hong-kong/politics/article/2140649/calling-end-communist-rule-china-crime-against-hong-kong.

legislation in this area. The popular Article 23 Concern Group went on to push for democratic reform the next year, then formulated as the Article 45 Concern Group. The Group again enjoyed wide popular support, but had no practical success in moving democratic reform forward. Civil society actions seem to have been more effective at protecting basic civil and political rights than they have been at securing democracy. It appears that Beijing fears that its ability to control Hong Kong would be threatened by the fulfilling its Basic Law commitment to afford universal suffrage. Relinquishing such control has been off the table, though there is a good argument that allowing universal suffrage would help to reduce the level of contention in Hong Kong and normalise politics.

The 2012 protests against the Government plan to introduce moral and national education was primarily a youth movement, led by the student group Scholarism. Scholarism lasted about five years, taking a leading role in both the movement over national education and in the Umbrella Movement.[47] The movement over national education likewise aimed to protect freedoms provided in the Basic Law. Led by civil society activists as young as 14 years old, mostly from secondary schools (although also with strong parental support), this movement aimed to resist what was viewed as an attempt to brainwash Hong Kong students. The horror about alleged brainwashing was sparked by a 34-page government-funded booklet, *The China Model*, which was distributed to primary and secondary schools. The booklet described China's 'democratic centralism' as producing a 'progressive, selfless and united group', which was contrasted with a negative account of United States democracy as encouraging rivalry and suffering.[48] After massive protests these materials were withdrawn and schools were left free to pursue their own choice of curriculum in this area.[49]

The 2014 'Occupy Central' protests over democratic reform – the Umbrella Movement – has proven to be the most contentious and most sustained protest action since the handover, at least up until the current protest over the extradition Bill. Reflecting a growing scepticism about Beijing's intended compliance with Basic Law promises of universal suffrage, this movement employed civil disobedience. Under a non-violent civil disobedience campaign, activists occupied one of the busiest thoroughfares near central Hong Kong for 79 days,[50] causing significant disruption in the process. This movement likewise called for the Government

[47] J Lam, 'Hong Kong's Scholarism suspends its work ahead of the formation of a new "less politicized" student group' *South China Morning Post*, 20 March 2016, available at www.scmp.com/news/hong-kong/politics/article/1928100/hong-kongs-scholarism-suspends-its-work-ahead-formation-new.

[48] P Chiu, 'Is Chinese national education set to make a comeback in Hong Kong? It's not if, but how, experts say' *South China Morning Post* (Hong Kong, 4 August 2017), available at www.scmp.com/print/news/hong-kong/politics/article/2105343/chinese-national-education-set-make-comeback-hong-kong-its.

[49] Y Lai and J Tam, 'CE shelves national education guidelines after panel report' *South China Morning Post* (Hong Kong, 8 October 2012), available at www.scmp.com/news/hong-kong/article/1056353/panel-advises-against-dropping-national-education-classes.

[50] C Wong, '2 Years Later: A Look Back at Hong Kong's Umbrella Movement' *The Diplomat*, 29 September 2016, available at thediplomat.com/2016/09/2-years-later-a-look-back-at-hong-kongs-umbrella-movement.

to meet its Basic Law obligations to institute genuine democratic elections for Chief Executive. Basic Law Article 45 in relevant part provides: 'The ultimate aim is the selection of the Chief Executive by universal suffrage upon nomination by a broadly representative nominating committee in accordance with democratic procedures.'

Movement leaders demanded a nominating process that would ensure a genuine choice for the voters in full compliance with Basic Law requirements. Such requirements are elaborated in Article 39's incorporation of the ICCPR, with Article 25 of the ICCPR being particularly significant in this case. Because of its open embrace of civil disobedience, the movement faced government accusations that it was undermining the rule of law. But by openly violating the law in a non-violent civil disobedience campaign the Umbrella Movement protesters were, like many civil rights activists the world over who had come before them, in fact navigating the boundaries of free speech. Common law courts, mindful of the importance of free political speech, have long been loath to strictly enforce permit and other statutory violations against such activism. In Hong Kong, as well, law enforcement officials have complained about the difficulty of successful prosecution of such cases. Will such judicial restraint become a thing of the past? The decision in the CFA in the case of the three umbrella activists acknowledged judicial deference in respect of public protests, but still adopted the stiffer sentencing guidelines for future application.

Unlike the Article 23 and Scholarism movements, this campaign for implementation of promised universal suffrage – like the previous Article 45 Concern Group effort on the same issue – did not achieve its purpose, although it did successfully educate the public[51] and international community on these Basic Law commitments and highlight Beijing's problematic foot-dragging. The use of civil disobedience was particularly effective in educating the international community on the shortcoming of China's Hong Kong policy. While local social media were more instrumental in mobilising the protests and disseminating news of Hong Kong to mainland China (where the press is strictly controlled), the international press was instrumental in the wide dissemination of Hong Kong developments worldwide.[52]

An active civil society and the rule of law have been the core ingredients of Hong Kong's autonomy. For the Article 23 and national education movements that proved sufficient; for the Article 45 protests and the Umbrella Movement it was not. Civil society effectiveness in demanding the promised democratic reform appears to embody the very threat Beijing fears in withholding such reform. This reflects a level of mistrust that is mutual. The more repressive Beijing is the more civil society pushes back. Though Beijing, as the stronger party, has greater capacity to reduce this circle of mistrust by relaxing its repressive grip, it has shown little inclination to do so. Beijing apparently fears that a democratic society will be too

[51] See the contribution of Wai-Man Lam in this collection.
[52] E Parker, 'Social Media and the Hong Kong Protests' *The New Yorker*, 1 October 2014.

unruly and difficult to control, a concern that may seem to have been verified for Beijing by the massive civil society protests over Article 23 in 2003 and the unruly 2014 Umbrella Movement. The flaw in this reasoning is that liberal constitutional democracies generally prove to be more stable than moderately open societies under provocative authoritarian repression. Hong Kong, with an existing liberal constitutional system, is well suited for establishing a stable democracy.

A. Umbrella Movement Tactics

The Umbrella Movement, until then the high end of Hong Kong political protests, used the full panoply of modern social movement resources. Yet, in an autonomous region remote from the national capital, the movement faced a daunting challenge. With Beijing officials at great distance their rule was not directly under threat unless the protests in Hong Kong were to somehow spread to the mainland. With its extreme control over information on the mainland Beijing has long been able to curtail that threat. This has meant that the only tool available to Hong Kong civil society is the leverage to discredit the local government and shame the Central Government into compliance. For these purposes wide distribution of protest information both locally and globally is essential.

It is important to note some of the tools social activists brought to bear to disseminate information and encourage debate. Initially led by professors Benny Tai and Chan Kinman, and the Reverend Chu Yiu-ming, the civil disobedience campaign announced in 2013 as a planned occupation of Central Hong Kong's financial district by 10,000 supporters, was unique in Hong Kong experience for advocating civil disobedience – 'the active, professed refusal of a citizen to obey certain laws of the state, and/or demands, orders, and commands of a government'[53] – as a political strategy. 'Occupy Central in Love and Peace' adopted the widely accepted strategy of non-violence and would ultimately depend on such non-violent discipline for much-needed public support. Non-violent civil disobedience campaigns aim to impose burdens or shame on targeted elites, typically in the Government or business community, although in the Hong Kong context the business community did not appear particularly threatened.[54] The early announcement of the planned civil disobedience campaign over a year in advance may have contributed to its ultimate downfall, making the movement, instead of the Government, the chief target of accusations about undermining the rule of law.

To maintain non-violent discipline a series of deliberation days were used to generate and select three democratic proposals to be submitted to the voters

[53] For the classic discussion of civil disobedience see HD Thoreau, *On the Duty of Civil Disobedience*, available at https://www.gutenberg.org/ebooks/71.

[54] HS Toh, 'The Business Leaders Who Aren't Worried about Occupy Central' *South China Morning Post*, 29 August 2014, available at www.scmp.com/news/hong-kong/article/1581949/business-leaders-who-arent-worried-about-occupy-central.

in a planned civil referendum for June 2014. These deliberations also facilitated educating supporters on non-violent strategies and the reform issues. With the help of Beijing's untimely issuance of the June 2014 White Paper, participation exceeded expectations and nearly 800,000 voters voted in the civil referendum. It proved unfortunate that the three proposals ultimately presented to voters tended to be among the more radical proposals, calling for some form of civil nomination binding on the Nominating Committee. That the voters expressed a preference for the least radical of the three suggests that a more moderate compromise proposal would likely have won the most support.[55]

As is often the case with popular protests, the actual protests, launched in September 2014, were sparked by state action. The actions of the Umbrella Movement were triggered by the decision of the NPCSC on 31 August 2014. In that decision, the NPCSC outlined a model for electing the Chief Executive under 'universal suffrage' in which Beijing would effectively control the nomination.[56] Other government missteps further aggravated the situation, including police use of tear gas and pepper spray, government indifference to protester concerns, and aggressive actions to quell protests or clear streets. The protest movement remained largely non-violent with occasional shoving and pushing in confrontation with police. Although the Occupy Central leaders had planned for the protests to start on 1 October, students quickly got ahead of the Occupy plans with class boycotts and student marches, launching massive protests near government offices in late September so that Occupy Central was actually proclaimed on 27 September.[57] The Hong Kong Federation of Students (HKFS) and Scholarism, as a consequence, took up the leadership of what became the student-led Umbrella Movement – even representing the movement in a televised debate with the Government consultation committee head, Carrie Lam, in late October.[58] The protesters also occupied commercial districts in Mong Kok and Causeway Bay.[59]

B. The Role of the Press and Social Media

Beyond taking advantage of these state-driven aspects, the protest leaders were very effective in mobilising support through the mainstream press and social

[55] MC Davis, 'Promises to Keep: The Basic Law, the "Umbrella Movement," and Democratic Reform in Hong Kong' in M Monshipouri (ed), *Information Politics, Protests, and Human Rights in the Digital Age* (New York, Cambridge University Press, 2016) 239–66.

[56] NPCSC, 'Decision of the Standing Committee of the National People's Congress on Issues Relating to the Selection of the Chief Executive of the Hong Kong Special Administrative Region by Universal Suffrage and on the Method for Forming the Legislative Council of the Hong Kong Special Administrative Region in the Year 2016' (31 August 2014) (August 31 NPCSC Decision).

[57] 'Occupy is on: Benny Tai rides wave of student protests to launch movement' *South China Morning Post*, 27 September 2014, available at www.scmp.com/news/hong-kong/article/1601625/hong-kong-students-beat-us-it-benny-tai-declares-start-occupy-central.

[58] J Ng and G Cheung, 'Pan-Democrat Lawmakers Ready to Step Up after Student-Government Talks Stall' *South China Morning Post*, 31 October 2014.

[59] Davis, 'Promises to Keep' (2016).

media. The publisher of one of the leading Chinese language newspapers, Jimmy Lai of *Apple Daily*, actually joined in the occupation. Meanwhile other mainstream press such as the *South China Morning Post* published continuous updates on developments in the protest areas, and pro-establishment press took a more cautious view.[60] The international press arrived in droves and played a vital role in conveying the developing situation to the world. A later report by *PEN America* noted significant intimidation of local media through direct pressure on local editors and reporters, advertising boycotts and self-censorship.[61] Twenty-four journalists were reportedly assaulted by counter-protesters or the police.[62] International media pressure brought an element of caution about using heavy-handed tactics to suppress the movement. Initial fears that the People's Liberation Army might march in to clear the streets soon dissipated. Beijing did not want another 1989-like situation.

The social media options at hand during the protests were diverse, mostly reaching the local community. At the height of the protest Facebook-based news outlets attracted 100,000 subscribers. A web forum called HKGolden.com experienced a ten-fold jump in page views, logging about 300,000 hits per day in its current affairs chat room in October.[63] This was boosted to 2.9 million page views per day after the police used tear gas. Various social media were not just information sources but actually became tools to mobilise participants and devise strategies. That the police were monitoring these postings is verified by the arrest of a young man who was alleged to have used a social media site to advocate attacks on the police. It was feared that people using social media to advocate participation might be arrested for incitement. As a result coded language emerged. For example, when the Chief Executive asked people to support merchants in the protest areas, calls to join the protest would be coded as 'going shopping'.[64] Beyond mainstream press and social media other supporters became involved in memorialising the protests with documentaries or archival work.[65]

A pro-government anti-occupy movement also emerged, though it ultimately proved less effective in garnering popular support.[66] Mainland and pro-Beijing

[60] ibid 257–60.

[61] PEN America, 'Threatened Harbor: Encroachment on Press Freedom in Hong Kong', 16 January 2015.

[62] J Kaiman, 'Hong Kong Protests Bring Crisis of Confidence for Traditional Media' *The Guardian*, 29 October 2014.

[63] P Siu, 'How Social Media Shapes Occupy: Web Forum HKGolden.com Takes Off' *South China Morning Post*, 31 October 2014. When the phone system was overloaded offline apps such as FireChat were used. See P Shadbolt, 'FireChat in Hong Kong: How an App Tapped Its Way into the Protests' *CNN*, 16 October 2014. Popular blogs also arose. See, eg, 'Hong Kong's Umbrella Movement', available at victoriatbhui.wordpress.com.

[64] S Chan, 'The Game Changes: As Occupy Sites Are Cleared, Hong Kong's Democracy Protesters Go "Shopping"' *South China Morning Post*, 11 December 2014.

[65] A popular Netflix documentary on protest leader Joshua Wong even made it into the Sundance Film Festival. See *Joshua: Teenager vs Superpower*.

[66] P So, 'Anti-Occupy Group's Hotline for Reporting Student Strikes Branded "White Terror"' *South China Morning Post*, 8 September 2014.

forces were further reported to have done what they could to disrupt this broad public conversation through disruptive forms of cyber warfare against the civil referendum and against the activists directly – for example, an mRat was used to steal data when a user logs on to WhatsApp.[67]

Liberal freedoms afforded to mainstream and social media in Hong Kong have long proved critical to efforts to sustain the Hong Kong model. Without the airing of grievances both in the mainstream press and in social media it is doubtful the mass protests would have come to an end so peacefully. The sense that people can protest and, with their basic freedoms intact, live to fight another day seems to have been vital to the ultimate ability of each round of protest to wind down. While there is a great deal of cynicism as to the outcome of the 2014 protests, Hong Kong civil society remains viable and active. Whether recent government efforts to punish protest leaders with lengthy prison terms will encourage pushback or exit is yet to be determined.

III. The Government's Response to Popular Demands

In considering the three protest movements under discussion it becomes apparent that, where the Hong Kong Government was primarily left on its own to formulate a response, some degree of accommodation would usually be achieved. In this system where civil society plays such a vital role the local government ignores popular concerns at its peril. The Hong Kong Government backed down in both of the two earlier cases. For the Article 45 demands for political reform and the Umbrella Movement, in contrast, it was apparent that Beijing was calling the shots. Maintaining a government easily subject to control appears to be Beijing's imperative. Further, after the perceived failure to hold the line on the earlier protests, Beijing seems less inclined to leave critical decisions of substance or strategy to the Hong Kong Government. The kind of vibrant open society evident in the first 20 years after the handover is now under threat by increased Beijing interference. Increasing repression could see basic freedoms curtailed and the important role civil society plays in maintaining a viable autonomy in Hong Kong at risk.

In the first two protest movements, over Article 23 and over national education, the Hong Kong Government appeared to take the lead, though mainland pressure no doubt inspired those initiatives. For the Article 23 protests the ham-fisted government response was a major force in garnering popular support for the opposition. When the Article 23 Concern Group first sat down to formulate a response to the proposed government Bill, the widely shared perception was that the Government, confident it had the votes to pass the Bill, was indifferent

[67] KP Chow, KK Yau and F Li, 'Occupy Central and Cyber War: A Framework of Cyber-Attack in Political Events' Proceedings of Ninth IFIP WG 11.10 International Conference on Critical Infrastructure Protection (March 2015).

to popular objections. At that stage a win for opponents of the Bill would perhaps have been to make the enacted legislation highly unpopular. But as the protests unfolded the scathing response of the Government garnered public outrage. The then Secretary for Security, Regina Ip, was a lightning rod for the opposition. The poor timing of the initiative, during the SARS crisis, further aggravated public discontent and consequently gave the opposition the upper hand. The surprise withdrawal of support for the Bill by the pro-government Liberal Party ultimately doomed the Bill and it was withdrawn. New administrations since have generally disavowed any intention to take up the initiative again, though this may now be changing in the face of calls for independence.

The national education initiative followed a similar local pattern. The above-noted brazen language in the government-funded manual garnered a sharp public response the Government could never surmount. Earlier youthful protests had convinced Beijing that Hong Kong youth were ill-disciplined and not sufficiently patriotic. Whether the mainland Government or just local pro-Beijing supporters originally pushed this initiative is unclear. Again, the Government's ham-fisted efforts to ram this through spawned a pushback reaction from civil society, this time led mostly by secondary students. Eventually, Scholarism took the lead, accusing the Government of attempted brainwashing. Government indifference to popular concerns was again fatal and the initiative was withdrawn, though it has also again resurfaced.

When it comes to the democratic reform sought in the Umbrella Movement, Beijing appears to have been more directly calling the shots. This was evident in the Government's hardline lockstep with Beijing on basic principles and the nearly total absence of willingness to compromise. The local government was left to defend Beijing's very questionable interpretation of the Basic Law. This official threat to the rule of law was rooted back as far as the 2007 NPCSC decision denying political reform at that time. This decision promised that 'universal suffrage' for the Chief Executive could be permitted in 2017, and, if that was done, for the LegCo in 2020.[68] In that decision Beijing signalled its preference that such universal suffrage 'may' employ the form of the existing Election Committee as the required Nominating Committee. Since the Election Committee had always been a largely pro-Beijing committee, selected through various functional sectors, such Nominating Committee, selected on the same basis, would be sure to block pan-democratic candidates from nomination. The initiative to organise the Occupy Central campaign was largely driven by suspicion that Beijing was planning a vetted nomination, as has since proven accurate.

The first round Hong Kong Government consultation on political reform resulted in a consultation report submitted to the NPCSC in July 2014 and the

[68] NPCSC, 'Decision Relating to the Method for Selecting the Chief Executive of the Hong Kong Special Administrative Region and for Forming the Legislative Council of the Hong Kong Special Administrative Region in the Year 2012 and on Issues Relating to Universal Suffrage' (2007) (2007 NPCSC Decision).

decision on 31 August 2014.[69] Even before the consultation it seemed clear that Beijing would insist on the following requirements: that the nomination be by the Nominating Committee, that the loyalty of nominated candidates be assured, that the Nominating Committee formation follows that of the Election Committee and that a majority vote would be required for nomination. Pan-democrats and their supporters actively participated in the first round consultation, putting forth proposals that would relax these predicted requirements to allow a pan-democrat to be nominated. As noted above, Occupy Central even held a civil referendum where the majority of 800,000 participants favoured a form of civil nomination.

All of these public recommendations and even moderate proposals at compromise were ignored in the July 2014 consultation reports. In spite of wide public dissent, the first round report offered up conclusions that tracked Beijing's expressed preferences, finding that:

(1) 'mainstream opinion' favours exclusive power for nomination in the nominating committee;
(2) the 'community generally agrees' the Chief Executive should 'love the country and love Hong Kong' (code to exclude pan-democrats);
(3) 'relatively more views' agree the Nominating Committee composition should be like the Election Committee;
(4) 'considerable views' favour increasing the seats on the nominating committee with little attention to the constituent base;
(5) 'quite a number of views' suggest that candidates must obtain the support of a 'certain portion' (code for 50 per cent) of the Nominating Committee to show 'cross-sector support';
(6) that the views offered signalled support for limiting the number of candidates to two or three; and
(7) that there was popular agreement with the view that no reform regarding the LegCo was needed.[70]

This consultation report laid the foundation for Beijing to do exactly what it wanted, as it did in its 31 August 2014 decision, where electoral reform was approved on the basis of a nominating process that would block pan-democratic candidates from being presented to the voters. This involved the already signalled model where the nominating committee was to be formed 'in accordance with

[69] August 31 NPCSC Decision (n 56).

[70] Hong Kong Government, 'Report by the Chief Executive of the Hong Kong Special Administrative Region to the Standing Committee of the National People's Congress on whether there is a need to amend the methods for selecting the Chief Executive of the Hong Kong Special Administrative Region in 2017 and for forming the Legislative Council of the Hong Kong Special Administrative Region in 2016' (July 2014), available at www.2017.gov.hk/en/liberal/related.html; Hong Kong Government, 'Report on the Public Consultation on the Methods of Selecting the Chief Executive in 2017 and for Forming the Legislative Council in 2016' (July 2014), available at www.2017.gov.hk/filemanager/template/en/doc/report/consultation_report.pdf.

the number of members, composition and formation method' of the Election Committee, where a 50 per cent threshold would be required to nominate and where only two or three candidates would be allowed.[71] The second round consultation to prepare the legislation authorised by the 31 August decision was boycotted by the pan-democrats. In this round even compromise proposals offered by pro-Beijing forces were ignored as the Government marched in lockstep with Beijing to produce a Bill that would be vetoed by the pan-democratic legislators in the LegCo – holding just over one-third of the seats in the chamber, enough to block this sort of Bill.[72]

It is evident from this series of events and the lockstep between Beijing and the Hong Kong Government that the two public consultations were merely a formality to produce the result favoured by Beijing. It is apparent also that where Beijing is calling the shots civil society protests are likely to be much less effective and public frustration and resistance greater. Because of the failure of the Bill, the old method of selecting the Chief Executive by a Beijing-friendly Election Committee remains in place. Carrie Lam, who headed this sham consultation, was favoured by Beijing in the 2017 selection exercise and is now the Chief Executive. The sham consultation proved politically favourable to the pan-democratic camp, with blowback resulting in the election of several of the Umbrella Movement activists in the 2016 LegCo election. But several activists were barred from running and, as noted above, six of these elected legislators were removed at Beijing's bidding. Denied political participation, more radical civil society activists have been left largely to protesting such heavy-handed government actions, awaiting the next opportunity for effective mass mobilisation, which came in mid-2019.

IV. Going Forward

As it stands, the answer to the above-raised question whether Hong Kong is on its way to losing its promised freedoms and distinct way of life under growing Beijing interference is clearly 'yes'. This is clearly what motivated the massive protest in 2019. The above-noted policy initiatives to enact an excessive national security law, impose national education and hold back democratic development have served to further polarise Hong Kong society. A mix of Beijing and pro-Beijing intimidation of core institutions in Hong Kong, ranging from media to universities, to rule of law, have met with widespread disapproval. This has in turn, as noted above, encouraged the Hong Kong Government and pro-establishment figures to tow the Beijing line, leaving Hong Kong freedoms at risk. Local Beijing-friendly media and some sectors of the academy have likewise taken these pressures as cause for

[71] August 31 NPCSC Decision (n 56).

[72] M Forsythe and A Wong, 'Hong Kong Legislature Rejects Beijing-Backed Election Plan' *New York Times*, 18 June 2015, available at www.nytimes.com/2015/06/19/world/asia/hong-kong-votes-down-beijing-election-plan.html.

caution and in some cases self-censorship. At the same time civil society initiatives have often arisen to meet the threats: the Hong Kong Journalist Association has challenged media intimidation; the Hong Kong Bar Association and Law Society have attempted to guard the rule of law;[73] and academics have offered organised responses to pressure put on universities. The frustration of such efforts has seen the emergence of a localist camp that has included advocates for self-determination or independence. These activists have in turn been barred from holding political office. Efforts by young activists to mobilise youth would predict more efforts at pushback as we have seen in the summer of 2019.

After the umbrella movement it was clear, unless the Central and Hong Kong Governments are prepared to use extreme measures that would likely be destructive of Hong Kong, government moderation is essential. Such moderation has not been evident in responding to the continuing protests in 2019. As the local power holder, the Hong Kong Government stands in the best position to mediate these political tensions, though it has so far shown little willingness to do so. While nobody expects the Hong Kong Government to aggressively challenge Beijing there is hope that it will find its voice to reflect Hong Kong popular concerns to the Central Government. Successful autonomy depends on a local autonomous government's commitment to defending autonomy. It is widely believed that simply carrying out the democratic commitments contained in the Basic Law in a proper democratic spirit would deflate almost all civil society support for the radical pro-independence camp. The combination of repressive national security laws and withholding political reform only inflames things further. Repression invites a response. This circle of conflict can be expected to continue until a more enlightened approach is taken up. In such environment any new effort to draft Article 23 or other legislation threatening to autonomy may face difficulty garnering public support. Either the public may take to the streets again or, if a sense of futility sets in, the exit option may become more attractive.

[73] See the contribution of PY Lo in this collection.

11

Gentle into that Good Night?

Sources of Resilience in Hong Kong's Politico-Legal Culture

SURABHI CHOPRA

I. Introduction

National security laws across a range of constitutional democracies display similar, somewhat disquieting features. Security laws tend to enhance the Government's coercive powers, while diluting checks and balances on how these powers are deployed. As a result, national security laws raise a seemingly perennial dilemma for liberal constitutionalism. On the one hand, governments need to be empowered to pre-empt and confront increasingly sophisticated security threats. On the other, security powers can be deployed by the state to suppress debate, dissent and accountability.

A law implementing the imperative in Article 23 of the Basic Law is unlikely to be immune from this dilemma. Indeed, many in Hong Kong fear that Article 23 legislation will be the Trojan horse that brings authoritarian controls into the region's rights-respecting common law system. While the content of such a law remains to be seen, designing and implementing it will test the "one country, two systems" framework that structures Hong Kong's special politico-legal position within China.

The chapters in Part II of this book consider how Hong Kong's core political institutions could sustain fundamental rights and government accountability in the face of potentially expansive national security powers. Their arguments are sobering. Ng, Lo, Jhaveri and Davis reveal Hong Kong's bedrock institutions to be deeply constrained in their ability to check and balance the executive branch.

Below, I attempt to converse critically with the four chapters in Part II. I draw out themes from these chapters that I consider relevant to the resilience of liberal constitutionalism in Hong Kong. I discuss the decline of the Basic Law as a source of resilience. I then engage with arguments from the preceding chapters about the common law and civil society as liberal constitutionalist safeguards.

II. Institutional Decline

When considering how Hong Kong's core political institutions might preserve individual freedoms and state accountability in the region, Ng, Lo, Jhaveri and Davis appear to agree on an important point. Each author charts not simply institutional *constraints* but institutional *decline* in relation to liberal constitutionalism.

Interference with the judiciary and the resulting damage to judicial independence has been analysed in depth in prior chapters. Were Hong Kong's political branches more deeply and broadly representative, the judiciary might not find itself adjudicating socio-politically sensitive issues quite so often. As things currently stand, the 'judicialisation' of thorny political questions is unlikely to abate. Furthermore, this phenomenon is not simply the result of so-called 'cause lawyering'. It was the Hong Kong Government that initiated the landmark 'oath-taking' case, aiming to oust the Legislative Council's (LegCo) judgment on how to deal with presumptive members who staged a provocative protest while taking their oaths of office.[1] Ultimately this litigation harmed both legislative and judicial independence. As Davis notes, the Government enmeshed the courts 'in a political battle … they could not win'.

Ng's analysis draws our attention to worrying developments in the LegCo. It is well known that a number of politicians critical of the Chinese state have been barred from assuming elected office as well as standing for election. Ng also highlights quieter shifts that are deepening the LegCo's structural pro-establishment bias. She argues that changes such as the decline in pan-democrat legislators and amendments to rules of procedure are diluting due process, public consultation and meaningful debate on government policies and performance.

While I am persuaded by Ng's argument, I would have welcomed more analysis of the recent developments she highlights. What types of issues still lend themselves to co-operation across party lines? How have different reform-minded parties navigated exclusionary mechanisms such as the small-circle election for the Chief Executive and functional constituency elections? What synergies and tensions have emerged in recent years between public protest, litigation and work within the Legislative Council to promote accountability and rights protection? Research on such questions could help legislators, political parties and civil society groups on the strategy and substance of progressive reform efforts going forward.

As it stands, Ng's discussion has worrying implications. Open, respectful, cross-party and cross-institutional debate is essential for developing Article 23 legislation that provides for adequate checks and balances on the state's security powers. Once a law is in place, the Legislative Council should monitor how security powers are wielded. But legislators who are unquestioningly allied with the government or the Communist Party are very unlikely to query security-related government decisions.

[1] *Chief Executive of the HKSAR v President of the Legislative Council* [2017] 2 HKLRD 53 (CFI).

Pressure on the judiciary will also affect how national security initiatives play out in Hong Kong. Complex, evolving security threats might genuinely warrant heightened secrecy and wide powers to question, place under surveillance, investigate or punish. However, these conditions heighten the risk of government overreach or abuse. Counter-majoritarian, rights-protective judicial review is crucial both as individual recourse and as systemic safety net. If weakened and tentative, Hong Kong's courts might not be able to fulfil this need.

III. The Shaky Foundation

If Hong Kong's core institutions are weaker today than they were some years ago, what reserves can judges and legislators draw upon to preserve independence and strength in the national security arena? The analyses in Part II of the book suggest that Hong Kong's constitution, the Basic Law, will not be the bulwark that its relatively robust provisions on fundamental rights might lead us to expect.

The Basic Law's weakness is due not to flaws in the text, but to the fundamental instability of 'one country, two systems' as a political experiment. As Chan and De Londras note in the Introduction, Hong Kong's distinctive position as a reasonably liberal, rights-protecting region within a unitary, authoritarian state involves *sui generis* challenges. When the Basic Law was drafted, there was very limited comparative textual precedent or practice to draw upon that would have been directly relevant to operationalising 'one country, two systems'. The Basic Law includes creative mechanisms to share responsibility between central and regional state institutions for, inter alia, passing legislation, interpreting the constitution, reforming the electoral system, and amending the constitution. Unsurprisingly, perhaps, some of these mechanisms are textually ambiguous, and have proved awkward in practice.

Constitutional ambiguities and silences, whether accidental or strategic, can have profound effects. Some scholars argue that constitutional silences are not just inevitable but advantageous. Silence and ambiguity in a constitutional text can facilitate necessary flexibility in governance and politics.[2] Silence can also relegate destabilising political choices such as secession to the fringes of the collective political imagination.[3] By contrast, constitutional elucidation on extreme political scenarios might paradoxically render such outcomes more viable.

The text of the Basic Law allows us to imagine how constitutional silence might encourage resilient constitutionalism. Some silences in the Basic Law tend to favour a high degree of regional autonomy (for example, the lack of a deadline

[2] See, for example, MH Fadel, 'The Sounds of Silence: The Supreme Constitutional Court of Egypt, Constitutional Crisis, and Constitutional Silence' (2018) 16 *International Journal of Constitutional Law* 936.

[3] Richard Albert and David Kenny, 'The Challenges of Constitutional Silence: Doctrine, Theory, and Applications' (2018) 16 *International Journal of Constitutional Law* 880.

for passing legislation to implement Article 23). Other ambiguities and silences readily lend themselves to an understanding that would promote liberal constitutionalism. For example, Article 158 could be understood as placing a duty of self-restraint on the NPCSC, while also affirming the NPCSC's ultimate authority to interpret the Basic Law. Yet other ambiguities – the strategic phrasing of Articles 45 and 68 in relation to universal suffrage, for example – provide a platform for deliberation, negotiation and progressive reform.

Notwithstanding the rich potential of this constitutional text, ambiguities in the Basic Law have hurt rather than helped liberal constitutionalism. The chapters in Part II remind us that the central and regional governments, and the Standing Committee of the National People's Congress (NPCSC), have interpreted the Basic Law in ways that centralise decision-making power, constrain the representativeness of the legislature, weaken the independence of judicial review, and limit certain fundamental rights. This interpretive activity includes not just Article 158 Interpretations by the NPCSC, but also the understandings of the Basic Law reflected in government statements (on the disqualification of electoral candidates,[4] for example), government arguments advanced during judicial review proceedings, government actions (seeking the State Council's intervention after the CFA's *Ng Ka Ling* decision in 1999,[5] for example), and NPCSC Decisions (on the co-location arrangement,[6] for example).

Constitutional interpretation in Hong Kong is profoundly polyphonic, and the analyses by Ng, Lo, Davis and Jhaveri suggest that the judiciary is now the most embattled constitutional author in important respects. This will make judicial review based upon fundamental rights a loaded endeavour in relation to national security. It could trigger NPCSC Interpretations that whittle down the fundamental right at issue. Thus, the Basic Law might only be a weak constraint on the state's security apparatus in the future.

This also presents an urgent research task. We need better to understand the role of the Hong Kong Government as a generator of constitutional norms.[7] While the four preceding chapters critique the interpretive efforts of the NPCSC and the judiciary, they do not attend as closely to the Government's parsing of the Basic Law. Even if, as Davis argues, the Hong Kong Government has largely implemented

[4] Government of HKSAR, Transcript of Remarks by Acting CE at Media Session (27 January 2018) www.info.gov.hk/gia/general/201801/27/P2018012700399.htm, accessed 3 June 2019.

[5] The Chief Executive's letter of request (20 May 1999) is reproduced in J Chan, H Fu and Y Ghai (eds), *Hong Kong's Constitutional Debate: Conflict Over Interpretation* (Hong Kong, Hong Kong University Press, 2000) 474–77.

[6] Decision of the NPCSC on Approving the Co-Operation Arrangement Between the Mainland and the Hong Kong Special Administrative Region on the Establishment of the Port At the West Kowloon Station of the Guangzhou-Shenzhen-Hong Kong Express Rail Link For Implementing Co-Location Arrangement (Adopted at the Thirty-first Session of the Standing Committee of the Twelfth National People's Congress on 27 December 2017).

[7] I am grateful to Swati Jhaveri for helpful discussion in relation to this point. On the executive branch as a constitutional author more generally, see E Fisher, *Risk Regulation and Administrative Constitutionalism* (Oxford, Hart Publishing, 2010).

Beijing's diktats, we need to analyse the modes of argument and justification it uses, as well as the constraints it negotiates. This is particularly important in relation to national security decision-making, where secrecy, expertise and the persuasive force of security rhetoric are likely to give the Hong Kong Government a primary role in developing security-related norms for the region.

Finally, Hong Kong's experience poses a challenge for optimistic theorising about constitutional silence. It suggests that constitutional ambiguity and silence are risky[8] in a hybrid constitutional system such as Hong Kong's, and will tend to facilitate illiberal norms and outcomes. Hong Kong's experience would be instructive for future constitution-making efforts, particularly in hybrid, weakly democratic politico-legal contexts.

IV. The Safety Net

While Basic Law interpretation in relation to national security has the potential to be a minefield, the common law could serve as a stable source of institutional resilience in Hong Kong. Ng discusses, for example, how common law-based procedural norms strengthened the Legislative Council's ability to debate laws, monitor policies, promote transparency and consult the public. Lo, too, emphasises 'the rule of law under a common law system' as one of Hong Kong's deepest strengths.

How might 'the common law', as a body of legal norms, as a method, and as a strategic device, be deployed in the national security arena? Jhaveri's arguments are constructive and forward-looking in this regard. She proposes that the judiciary should interpret Article 23 legislation by drawing on common law principles, which would involve resolving textual ambiguities in favour of fundamental rights protection, specifying and narrowing the scope of vague and open-ended proscriptions, and drawing actively upon comparative common law jurisprudence when interpreting substantive and procedural statutory provisions.

Jhaveri's suggestions are a salutary reminder that statutory interpretation, adjudication and governance are iterative, adaptable enterprises. Even very expansive security legislation would be amenable to some measure of standard-setting and clarification by the judiciary,[9] and this could moderate government action over time. However, as Jhaveri herself notes, the Hong Kong judiciary's position, particularly if it attempts to interpret NPCSC Interpretations or Decisions on national security, is very delicate.

[8] For a discussion of the risks of constitutional silence and ambiguity, see A McHarg, 'Navigating without Maps: Constitutional Silence and the Management of the Brexit Crisis' (2018) 16 *International Journal of Constitutional Law* 952.

[9] F De Londras, 'Counter-terrorism judicial review as regulatory constitutionalism' in F Davis and F De Londras (eds), *Critical Debates on Counter-Terrorism Judicial Review* (Cambridge, Cambridge University Press, 2014).

With this in mind, Jhaveri's parallel discussion of administrative law as a source of resilience is helpful. While flagship, constitutionally mandated legislation might arouse particular interest and concern, it will operate within a wider system of law, policy and operational codes. Jhaveri advocates relying upon administrative law, rather than constitutional law, to challenge problematic security-related government decisions. Judicial review on common law grounds would mean that the fraught terrain of Basic Law interpretation can be avoided. Existing administrative law precedents in Hong Kong impose a higher standard of procedural fairness where core fundamental rights are at stake,[10] and could ameliorate harshness and injustice.

While Jhaveri explores various specific grounds of judicial review, her underlying argument is about tactics rather than technicalities. To my mind, she is arguing that the judiciary should couch its security-related interventions in a minor key. This is an argument not for judicial *restraint* – quite the contrary – but an argument for judicial *modesty*. It suggests that the judiciary should be jurisprudentially conservative, in the sense of hewing to well-trodden, technical modes of reasoning and argumentation, while being politically liberal. Jhaveri seems to suggest that jurisprudential conservatism is the most viable mode, and perhaps a necessary mode, for preserving liberal constitutionalism in the national security arena.

Two early, post-Handover cases support this argument. The judgment of the Court of Final Appeal ('the CFA') in the very controversial *Ng Ka Ling*[11] case can be contrasted with its judgment in *Chong Fung Yuen*[12] three years later. Both cases dealt with the scope of the right of abode in Hong Kong. Both were decided against the Government by the CFA. However, the Court's tone is markedly different in the two judgments. *Ng Ka Ling's* transparently creative interpretation and emphatic assertion of constitutional jurisdiction gave way to *Chong Fung Yuen's* technical rhetoric about a 'common law approach' to construing the Basic Law. But the CFA arguably interpreted the right of abode more generously in the latter, ostensibly more modest decision. Not only that, it took the risk of narrowly construing, and thereby somewhat limiting, the NPCSC Interpretation that had partially reversed *Ng Ka Ling*. While the aftermath of *Ng Ka Ling* was deeply bruising for the CFA, after *Chong Fung Yuen* it emerged largely unscathed.

This suggests that foregrounding the common law as normative source and interpretive method, and where possible avoiding constitutional law altogether, could help to sustain robust judicial scrutiny over security matters. However, a few caveats are important.

First, the standard health warning on common law rights and standards bears repeating: they can be overridden by legislation. That said, the diffuse nature of these standards protects them, and so does their image as shorthand for fairness.

[10] *Secretary for Security v Sakthevel Prabakar* (unreported, FACV 16/2033, 8 June 2004) (CFA).
[11] *Ng Ka Ling v Director of Immigration* (1999) 1 HKLRD 315 (CFA).
[12] Director of Immigration v Chong Fung Yuen (2001) 2 HKLRD 533 (CFA).

Common law principles are threaded through both public and private law jurisprudence. The impression that the common law framework is not as reliable as it once was, or the courts not as free, could harm Hong Kong's standing as a financial and trading hub.

Second, comparative common law jurisprudence on national security would be a decidedly mixed resource rather than a reliable buffer against security-related state excesses. Courts in long-standing constitutional democracies have often been deferential and avoidant when reviewing security-related laws, policies or decisions.[13] Given the pressure on the Hong Kong judiciary, judicial incentives might pull in the direction of institutional preservation rather than rights protection, and judges could justify extreme deference with reference to comparative precedents.

A third caveat comes from Lo's discussion of the judiciary. His analysis reminds us to think about 'the common law' not as a comforting abstraction but as embodied, negotiated, compromise-laced human endeavour. The mechanism for appointing judges has served Hong Kong well thus far, but Lo cautions that it could easily channel the informal veto of the central authorities (through the Chief Executive), and given the requirement for legislative assent for the senior-most judges,[14] will reflect the changing composition of the Legislative Council. An increasing proportion of legislators who believe that judges should defer to executive decisions could, over time, lead to appointments that dilute the counter-majoritarian capacity of the judiciary. This dilution would be felt particularly sharply on national security matters, where even ordinarily robust courts tend towards deference.

V. Civil Society: Champions of Liberal Constitutionalism … and Skeptics

All four authors, in different ways, position civil society as a force for liberal constitutionalism in Hong Kong. Lo reflects on the legal profession in Hong Kong, Ng on political parties. Jhaveri's arguments are about litigation strategy as much as approaches to adjudication, and are thus directed at lawyers and judicial review applicants. Davis analyses successful civil society campaigns against Article 23 legislation in 2003 and the 'national education' curriculum in 2012, as well as the unsuccessful campaign for electoral reform in 2013–14. Ng shows how different groups – lawyers, academics, political parties and NGOs – complemented and reinforced one another's efforts during these campaigns.

[13] K Lane Scheppele, 'The New Judicial Deference' (2012) 92 *Boston University Law Review* 89, 96–107; S Chopra, 'Judging the Troops: Exceptional Security Measures and Judicial Impact in India' (2019) *Law and Social Inquiry*, available at doi.org/10.1017/lsi.2019.3.

[14] Basic Law, Art 90(2).

Without a doubt, civil society groups in Hong Kong have advocated creatively and courageously to secure deeper democracy and protect fundamental rights. As they confront what Ng describes as 'powerful, fast-moving' and increasingly unapologetic authoritarianism, we need more nuanced analysis about the challenges they face. The arguments by Davis and Ng adopt a little too closely the narrative of a constitutionalism-loving polity being acted upon and let down by its government, both regional and central. This narrative, and its underlying assumptions about Hong Kong's politico-legal culture, should be queried more closely.

The authors in Part II treat 'civil society' as synonymous with politically progressive NGOs, informal groups, professionals, issue-based coalitions and other 'non-party political formations'.[15] But Hong Kong civil society encompasses politically conservative groups too. As scholars and practitioners committed to liberal constitutionalism, we need to analyse a broader spectrum of political civil society in Hong Kong. It is important to understand how pro-establishment political parties as well as other conservative groups are shaping grassroots aspirations for governance, social mobility and societal flourishing.

Hong Kong civil society's deep engagement with constitutional standards and legality has been rightly noted by Davis. University students confidently and rigorously debating senior civil servants on democratic reform during the Umbrella Movement protests is just one evocative example of this. However, sophisticated legal analysis is not solely the preserve of liberal civil society. The lead up to the 2014 political reform exercise saw groups across the political spectrum proposing how universal suffrage elections for the Chief Executive should be structured. Big constitutional moments have provided both progressive and conservative groups opportunities to hone and disseminate their visions of what the Basic Law means, how authoritative it is, and whether constitutional rights are binding constraints. And if we assume that the composition of Hong Kong's legislature distils societal sentiment, at least to a degree, then pro-establishment electoral success suggests that illiberal views on law and governance have considerable appeal. Davis warns that the Hong Kong Government's 'hardline lockstep' with the central authorities since 2014 could foster support for fringe secessionist views. Increased support for extra-constitutional exit strategies is one risk of the current impasse on democratic reform. But the greater danger in the coming years is likely to be the justification, selling and normalisation of authoritarian governance.

So, scholars and practitioners will need to analyse not just major state interventions (like a national security law), but also the wider political economy of authoritarian legality and governance. Lo exemplifies this in his forward-looking discussion of the legal profession. While highlighting how lawyers and professional legal bodies have criticised assaults on judicial independence, he also shows how this commitment might wane, due not just to political pressure but also increasing work opportunities for locally trained lawyers in mainland China.

[15] R Kothari, 'The Non-Party Political Process' (1984) 19 *Economic and Political Weekly* 216.

For many years after the handover, liberal civil society actively embraced the political opportunity structure created by the Basic Law and BORO to demand reform on various fronts. Ng, Lo, Davis and Jhaveri all indicate that the political opportunity structure in Hong Kong is less open and enabling today. Were an Article 23 law to be implemented, critical debate and advocacy will face new, possibly punitive, pressures. Liberal political groups will need to shore up the strategies that served them well in the past, while adding new tactics to their repertoire.

One fruitful strategy that different chapters in Part II raise is internationalisation, whether through the media, United Nations mechanisms, civil society networks, or academic forums. Indeed, Hong Kong's status as an international hub is itself a source of liberal resilience. The city's global connectedness renders certain types of controls, such as heavy Internet censorship, very difficult to implement. It also expands the range of powerful institutions, such as corporate actors, that are invested at least to some degree in the survival of baseline checks and balances on state power in Hong Kong. Another strategy these chapters highlight is close co-operation between activists, professional groups, academics and legislators.

Reflection on more recent tactical lessons would have been an interesting addition to Part II's discussions of civil society. It would have been useful, for instance, to consider how the strategies of a new generation of young politicians and activists – social media consciousness raising, performative protests, satire with Gen-Z characteristics – have expanded the liberal/left-liberal civil society repertoire, and how these strategies might be deployed in the coming years.

VI. Conclusion

Part II's exploration of resilience in Hong Kong's politico-legal culture suggests that liberal constitutionalist reserves in Hong Kong are thin. But the work by Davis, Jhaveri, Lo and Ng helpfully illuminates why institutions are frailer than they were some years ago. It also provokes questions and suggests directions for future advocacy, governance, lawyering and scholarship. I highlight some conclusions that flow from Part II's analyses.

The consensus amongst these authors on institutional decline points to a strong need for institutional diversification in Hong Kong. Section III of this volume consider this issue in depth.

In addition to building new mechanisms for state accountability, genuinely independent judicial review needs to be sustained. But particularly on national security matters, the Basic Law is likely to be a precarious resource. The approaches to litigation and adjudication discussed by Jhaveri offer some ways to negotiate this predicament. In addition, specificity in statutory language and rights-related provisos in relation to particular restrictions or offences within the text of Article 23 legislation could be helpful. Also important is the need to deepen knowledge of legislation and court judgments related to national security from a range of constitutional democracies.

Tacitly but unanimously, these chapters value Hong Kong's openness as a source of resilience. Multi-lateral, international networking and exchange among government officials, lawyers, judges, civil society activists and academics could support liberal constitutionalism intellectually and practically in the years to come.

Further, these chapters all, in different ways, point to the need for legal education in Hong Kong to shed its excessive positivism, and foster critical, creative, heterodox engagement with the law.

Finally, some of the absences in the preceding chapters highlight the need to transcend liberal blind spots. National security rhetoric can be powerfully persuasive, and dilute long-held, widely shared commitments to accountability. In responding to this, whether as scholars, practitioners, officials or simply as residents of a shared community, we need to be curious, critical, and take very little for granted.

PART III

Enhancing Resilience

12

Old Law in New Bottles

Reintroducing National Security Legislation in Hong Kong

SIMON NM YOUNG

It is unthinkable that any future legislative exercise to reintroduce national security legislation in Hong Kong would start from a clean slate. To do so would be to ignore the considerable amount of intellectual work and public debate that went into the 2003 proposals.[1] Those proposals had imperfections, but they also had some merit in proposing to modernise existing offences and abolish laws that, if used, would impinge on fundamental rights protected in the Basic Law. However, just as it would be foolhardy to disregard the 2003 proposals, it would be equally so to believe those proposals could be reintroduced without change; they are now old bottles for old wine. Important developments since 2003 in the legal and political contexts of China, Hong Kong and Macau need to be taken into account in any future exercise. Relevant international developments in anti-terrorism laws should also inform law-making deliberations.

This chapter considers the shape of new bottles for the old law of national security in Hong Kong. It identifies important local and international developments relevant to any future Article 23 legislative exercise, particularly two of the controversial proposals of 2003 concerning the offence of secession and the proscription mechanism for foreign political organisations. It will be argued there is no justification for reintroducing the proscription mechanism and its accompanying criminal offence. As for the secession offence, the 2003 proposal can be made legitimate by drafting the terms more clearly and keeping the scope within tighter limits. It is further argued that notwithstanding the rise in pro-independence sentiments amongst a small number of people in Hong Kong,

[1] National Security (Legislative Provisions) Bill 2003. See generally, H Fu, CJ Petersen and SNM Young (eds), *National Security and Fundamental Freedoms: Hong Kong's Article 23 Under Scrutiny* (Hong Kong, HKU Press, 2005); SNM Young, 'Guide to Basic Law Article 23: Hong Kong's Unresolved National Security Issue' (HKU Legal Scholarship blog, 15 March 2015), available at researchblog.law.hku.hk/2015/03/guide-to-basic-law-article-23-hong.html.

introducing an additional offence criminalising the advocacy of secession would be unjustified and highly problematic.

The chapter begins with a review of significant legal developments since 2003. First there is the case law of the Court of Final Appeal (CFA), from which can be derived a set of legislative guidelines for drafting national security offences. Next there are the legislative developments in mainland China and Macau related to national security. Finally, the consequences and experience of post-9/11 anti-terrorism legislation may shed light on the merits of adopting similar procedural mechanisms. Following this review, proposals for the secession offence, required by Article 23, and a proscription mechanism for individuals and bodies on national security grounds are discussed having regard to the developments since 2003 particularly the legislative guidelines proposed in this chapter.

I. Legislative Guidelines and Important Developments Since 2003

A set of guidelines for Article 23 legislative reform can be derived from the CFA's jurisprudence on criminal law and human rights.[2] Important developments in mainland and Macau law related to national security and in the comparative law of anti-terrorism should also be taken into account in any reform exercise.

A. Principles of Criminal Liability and Human Rights Developed by Hong Kong Courts

The CFA has developed a set of legal principles for the interpretation and constitutional review of criminal offences. Law drafters and legislators need to be fully apprised of these principles to understand how the courts are likely to apply them if laws introduced pursuant to Article 23 are later challenged. The main principles are discussed below and summarised in a set of legislative guidelines.

Statutory offences are to be interpreted purposively, meaning that 'context and purpose [are] considered in the first instance'[3] and 'Words are given their natural and ordinary meaning unless the context or purpose points to a different meaning.'[4] While a purposive interpretation can result in a broader or narrower construction, what is important is that the court will not follow a wide literal

[2] The 2003 consultation document also mentioned the need to comply with the Basic Law, protect the 'State's essential interests', and to ensure all offences were 'clearly and tightly defined'. See Security Bureau, 'Proposals to implement Article 23 of the Basic Law Consultation Document' (September 2002) [5], available at www.basiclaw23.gov.hk/english/download/reporte.pdf (Consultation Document).

[3] *HKSAR v Lam Kwong Wai* (2006) 9 HKCFAR 574 [63].

[4] *HKSAR v Cheung Kwun Yin* (2009) 12 HKCFAR 574 [12].

interpretation if to do so would overshoot the purpose of the law. A good example was seen in the money laundering case of *HKSAR v Li Kwok Cheung George*, in which the CFA considered the statutory definition of proceeds of an offence and whether 'any payment … received … in connection with the commission' of an offence included payments of clean money used to further a crime.[5] The CFA held it did not; the definition, when read purposively, included only payments received 'in the nature of a reward'.[6] This narrower construction was in harmony with the legislative purpose of 'stripping away the economic benefits obtained by defendant in connection with the commission of the predicate offence'.[7]

A more recent example is the case of *HKSAR v Fong Kwok Shan Christine*, concerned with a protest in a Legislative Council (LegCo) public gallery during sittings of a public works subcommittee.[8] LegCo administrative instructions did not allow persons in the public gallery to 'display any sign or message on any item of clothing'.[9] The CFA held that this provision could not be read literally as a blanket prohibition; it had to be read purposively, aiming at 'displays which entail the risk of disorder in public galleries and which may disturb LegCo sittings and the rights of others observing the proceedings'.[10] This narrower construction meant that a 'person in a public gallery wearing a T-shirt which happens to bear an innocuous message unconnected with the legislature's proceedings, not brandished intrusively, is not intended to be caught'.[11]

The CFA also recognises the principle of legality. This principle of construction holds that 'human rights and fundamental principles of law, even where derogable, cannot be overridden except by *express* words or *necessary* implication' (emphasis in original).[12] The principle involves a presumption against adopting the overriding interpretation, but it can be displaced if the court is 'satisfied that the legislature had its attention properly drawn to the abrogating provision and consciously enacted legislation to such effect'.[13] It is unlikely, however, that this principle will have much relevance to judicial interpretations of future national security legislation since the enactment of such legislation will most certainly only come after a full and heated legislative debate of the human rights implications of the proposed legislation.

The CFA has also developed a body of jurisprudence on the common law presumption of *mens rea* and the constitutional presumption of innocence.

[5] *HKSAR v Li Kwok Cheung George* (2014) 17 HKCFAR 319; Organized and Serious Crimes Ordinance (Cap 455), s 2(6)(a)(i).

[6] *HKSAR v Li Kwok Cheung George* (ibid) [74].

[7] ibid [68].

[8] *HKSAR v Fong Kwok Shan Christine* (2017) 20 HKCFAR 425.

[9] ibid [8], citing Administrative Instructions for Regulating Admittance and Conduct of Person, s 12(2).

[10] *HKSAR v Fong Kwok Shan Christine* (n 8) [105].

[11] ibid [107].

[12] *A v Commissioner of the Independent Commission Against Corruption* (2012) 15 HKCFAR 362 [24].

[13] *HKSAR v Yeung Ka Sing, Carson* (2016) 19 HKCFAR 279 [54].

Where an offence element is silent on its correlative *mens rea* element, the court fills the silence with the presumption of *mens rea*, thereby requiring the prosecution to prove a relevant subjective mental element. But if the court finds grounds for the displacement of the presumption, the offence is construed as one involving either strict or absolute liability. Where liability is found to be strict, the court reads in one of two possible halfway house defences of honest and reasonable belief, which either involve a legal burden on the defendant to prove the defence or only an evidential burden to raise it. These halfway house defences are important because, in the words of the CFA, 'To convict a person regardless of the mental state accompanying his conduct, even if he can show that he acted in a reasonable, diligent and socially unblameworthy manner is contrary to the fundamental values of the common law'.[14] Given the complexity and uncertainty involved in these issues, the main implication for legislative drafting is to avoid any silence as to *mens rea*. Being convicted of a national security offence will likely be punishable severely and carry a high degree of social stigma. If the presumption of *mens rea* is applied to fill any silence in the legislation, it is unlikely to be displaced and proof of full subjective fault will be required.

Given the mature jurisprudence on presumption of innocence from the Hong Kong courts, legislators would be wise to avoid any provisions that reverse the prosecution's burden of proof, requiring defendants to prove their own innocence, unless there are compelling reasons to justify the need for derogating from the presumption. The CFA has applied a rigorous approach to the constitutional review of reverse onuses that accords only modest weight to legislative deliberations. Where the reverse onus cannot be justified, the court will likely read down the legal burden to a less burdensome evidential one, which only requires evidence to raise the issue, whereupon the prosecution would need to disprove the issue beyond a reasonable doubt. Up to now, the CFA has read down a legal burden to an evidential burden in four decisions and in only one case has it upheld the legal burden.[15]

When the CFA decided its first constitutional presumption of innocence case in 2006, it also laid down a general test for assessing when restrictions on rights could be justified.[16] The three-step justification test required the Government to demonstrate that the measure engaging the right had a legitimate aim, the measure was rationally connected to the aim, and the measure was no more than necessary to achieve the aim. The third step, known as the proportionality test, results in the measure being disallowed if 'the Court is satisfied that a significantly less intrusive

[14] *Hin Lin Yee v HKSAR* (2010) 13 HKCFAR 142 [105]. See also *Kulemesin Yuriy v HKSAR* (2013) 16 HKCFAR 195; *HKSAR v Choi Wai Lun* (2018) 21 HKCFAR 167.

[15] See *HKSAR v Lam Kwong Wai* (2006) 9 HKCFAR 574; *HKSAR v Hung Chan Wa* (2006) 9 HKCFAR 614; *HKSAR v Ng Po On* (2008) 11 HKCFAR 91; *Lee To Nei v HKSAR* (2012) 15 HKCFAR 162, but the legal burden was justified in *Fu Kor Kuen Patrick v HKSAR* (2012) 15 HKCFAR 524.

[16] *HKSAR v Lam Kwong Wai* (ibid) [40].

and equally effective measure is available'.[17] In 2016, the CFA recognised a fourth step to the justification test requiring the Government to also show that 'a reasonable balance has been struck between the societal benefits of the encroachment and the inroads made into the constitutionally protected rights of the individual'.[18] The Court said this step involved making a 'value judgment',[19] and if the first three steps were satisfied, 'this will point towards the fourth step being satisfied as well'.[20] In matters of criminal law, where a person's liberty interest and other fundamental rights may be engaged, it is unlikely the court will apply a more deferential standard of proportionality, which the CFA has applied in cases 'involving implementation of the legislature's and executive's political, social or economic policies'.[21]

Although presumption of innocence challenges have generally been successful, freedom of expression challenges to criminal offences have been less so. In 1999, the CFA upheld the offences of desecrating the national and regional flags on the ground that they were necessary for *ordre public*, the flags were a 'unique symbol' of the principle of 'one country, two systems' enshrined in the Basic Law.[22] When a very similar challenge was raised again in 2014, the CFA refused leave to appeal because 'no real argument was mounted to suggest why the [1999 decision] should no longer be followed'.[23] More recently, the CFA upheld the LegCo administrative instructions that prohibited protest and disorderly conduct in the public gallery of LegCo conference rooms. The court said it was 'self-evident' that the restrictions could be justified as being 'necessary for respect of the rights of others and for the protection of public order'.[24] Similar to the flag case, the court also found justification for the restrictions in *ordre public*, 'to safeguard the proper functioning of the legislature'.[25] As the appellant was free to protest in designated places in the LegCo complex, on social media and other places, the restriction was no more than reasonably necessary to further the aim. However, the court also rejected a sweeping argument that the freedom of expression was inapplicable in certain government premises. Justice Ribeiro wrote that a 'rule presumptively excluding free expression at certain types of venues is too blunt an instrument' and that a 'proportionality analysis' was preferred because it enabled 'the court to take into account the dimensions of any particular exercise of [rights] and the exigencies of the intended venue'.[26]

[17] *Kwok Cheuk Kin v Secretary for Constitutional and Mainland Affairs* (2017) 20 HKCFAR 353 [136].

[18] *Hysan Development Co Ltd v Town Planning Board* (2016) 19 HKCFAR 372 [135].

[19] ibid [78].

[20] *Kwok Cheuk Kin* (n 17) [61].

[21] ibid [139].

[22] *HKSAR v Ng Kung Siu* (1999) 2 HKCFAR 442, 460–61. More recently, the Court of First Instance held that *ordre public* was a legitimate aim for requiring candidates seeking a Legislative Council seat to declare that they will uphold the Basic Law and pledge allegiance to the Hong Kong Special Administrative Region; see *Chan Ho Tin v Lo Ying Ki Alan* [2018] 2 HKLRD 7 [180]–[183].

[23] *HKSAR v Koo Sze Yiu* (2014) 17 HKCFAR 811 [8] (CFAAC).

[24] *HKSAR v Fong Kwok Shan Christine* (n 8) [113].

[25] ibid [114].

[26] ibid [45].

It is also well established that criminal laws must comply with the principle of legal certainty if they are to have the quality of being 'prescribed by law', and thus to be capable of restricting a fundamental right.[27] This means the law must be adequately accessible and the offence must be formulated with sufficient precision to enable persons to regulate their conduct. A person should be able to foresee (with the assistance of legal advice if needed) the consequences of one's action, though the requisite degree of foresight need not be that of absolute certainty and can vary according to the context of the law. Justice Bokhary in *HKSAR v Shum Kwok Sher* opined that if a law limited the exercise of a fundamental freedom, an 'exceptionally high degree of certainty of definition' would be required.[28] While there have been many legal certainty challenges heard in the CFA, the court has rarely invalidated laws on this ground. Where it has, the cases have generally concerned vague terms in executive powers rather than in criminal offences.[29] Many cases concern common law offences, where the CFA has opted to clarify the elements of the offence instead of invalidating it. The difficulty in complying with a law does not make it uncertain, general offences may have to be expressed in broad and abstract terms, and prescription by law inevitably may involve some degree of vagueness requiring clarification by courts. In *HKSAR v Fong Kwok Shan Christine*, the Court emphasised that reading provisions properly in the light of their context and purpose and with common sense can give them sufficient precision to satisfy the legal certainty requirement.[30]

Finally, criminal offences can be challenged on the basis that their prescribed elements or punishment give rise in a substantive manner to 'arbitrary imprisonment' contrary to Article 28 of the Hong Kong Basic Law. This is not a ground for courts to weigh in on whether they think certain conduct should or should not be the subject of criminal liability and punishment. Rather, the question is whether the law is arbitrary in the sense that it is 'capricious or unreasoned or without reasonable cause' or whether imprisonment will be imposed 'without reference to an adequate determining principle'.[31] Where the prescribed punishment is challenged, it must be shown that it is manifestly disproportionate, 'a disproportion so great as to reduce the law virtually to something capricious, unreasoned or without reasonable cause'.[32] The CFA has yet to invalidate an offence on this basis. The grievous bodily harm rule in murder (which accepts an intention to

[27] *Shum Kwok Sher v HKSAR* (2002) 5 HKCFAR 381 [60]–[65]; *Mo Yuk Ping v HKSAR* (2007) 10 HKCFAR 386.

[28] *Shum Kwok Sher v HKSAR* (ibid) [4]. This threshold was mentioned again in *Medical Council of Hong Kong v Helen Chan* (2010) 13 HKCFA 248 [78] by Justice Bokhary who wrote the unanimous judgment.

[29] See *Leung Kwok Hung v HKSAR* (2005) 8 HKCFAR 229; *Lau Wai Wo v HKSAR* (2003) 6 HKCFAR 624; *Leung Kwok Hung v Chief Executive* (unreported, HCAL 107/2005, 9 February 2006).

[30] *HKSAR v Fong Kwok Shan Christine* (n 8) [79], [91].

[31] *Lau Cheong v HKSAR* (2002) 5 HKCFAR 415 [48].

[32] ibid [112]. See also ibid [121], [130].

cause grievous bodily harm as sufficient *mens rea*), the mandatory punishment of life imprisonment for murder, and absolute liability in the offence of sexual intercourse with a girl under 16 years were held not to be arbitrary.[33]

The foregoing principles can be summarised in a set of legislative guidelines for drafting Article 23 offences:

(1) *Purposiveness*. The specific purpose of each offence should be identified and stated. The specification of offence elements should be targeted only at conduct, consequences, and circumstances that can further the offence purpose.
(2) *Specification of mens rea*. For each *actus reus* element (also known as physical or external elements), an appropriate subjective *mens rea* element (such as intention, recklessness, wilfulness, knowledge and belief) should be specified, unless it is wholly obvious from the nature of the element that an implicit mental element attaches. Leaving *mens rea* silent invites unnecessary legal uncertainty, wastage of judicial resources, and injustice where courts mistakenly apply strict or absolute liability. In case of doubt, the *mens rea* element should be specified.
(3) *Requiring proof of moral culpability*. Given the stigma attaching to Article 23 offences and the likely seriousness of the applicable punishment, the possibility of convicting a morally innocent person should be eliminated. Thus, the use of objective forms of *mens rea* and strict and absolute liability should be avoided unless there is compelling empirical and rational necessity for them.
(4) *Presumption of innocence*. Elements that impose a legal burden of proof on the defendant should be avoided unless there is compelling evidence they are needed and an evidential burden would be inadequate. Even where it is believed that the defendant would be better placed to prove a particular element, serious consideration should be given to imposing only an evidential burden on the defendant to raise the particular issue.
(5) *Justifying restrictions on fundamental rights*. If the offence is likely to engage a person's fundamental rights protected under the law, such as freedom of expression, there needs to be justification that the offence has a legitimate purpose, enforcement of the offence is rationally connected with that purpose, no significantly less intrusive measure of equal effectiveness could be enacted or applied instead, and a reasonable balance has been struck between the societal benefits of the offence and the inroads made to the fundamental rights. The burden is on the government to demonstrate this justification with evidence.
(6) *Principle of legal certainty*. Offence elements must be drafted clearly and precisely, to enable persons, with legal advice if needed, to foresee with reasonable certainty the legal consequences of their actions.

[33] ibid [49], [123].

(7) *Arbitrary imprisonment.* The offence elements should not be framed so broadly or absurdly as to be capricious, unreasoned or without reasonable cause. The prescribed punishment should not be manifestly or grossly disproportionate having regard to the nature and seriousness of the offence, culpability of the offender, and other legitimate sentencing objectives such as deterrence and denunciation.

B. Mainland Legal Developments

One might ask why mainland laws are at all helpful to the debate since Hong Kong is supposed to enact the law on its own within its separate common law legal system, which is fundamentally different from the civilian-law mainland legal system. It is noteworthy that the 2003 consultation paper only made brief references to national security offences in the Criminal Law of the mainland. Many of the mainland national security offences are punishable by the death penalty (which is abolished in Hong Kong[34]) if the conduct has caused grave harm to the state and the people, or the circumstances are especially serious. Given the differences in the two legal systems, the terms of the mainland law should not be transplanted in the same way as legislation from other common law jurisdiction is sometimes borrowed and incorporated in new Hong Kong legislation.

There are, however, at least two reasons why reference should still be made to mainland laws. The first is the salutary principle of minimal implementation: only that which is minimally required by Article 23 should be implemented. The relevant mainland laws may signpost what is *not* needed in a regional law to protect national security. For example, if a certain coercive measure or power is proposed for Hong Kong, yet such measure or power does not exist in the relevant mainland law, this would strongly suggest that the proposal is unnecessary to satisfy the implementation requirements of Article 23.[35] The second reason is the aim of having some degree of harmonisation between the national security laws at the national and regional levels. This is not to say that they should be the same but that they should at least be consistent and not diametrically opposed to each other. The Standing Committee of the National People's Congress (NPCSC) can return and invalidate Hong Kong legislation it determines to be inconsistent with Basic Law provisions 'regarding affairs within the responsibility of the Central Authorities or regarding the relationship between the Central Authorities and the Region'.[36]

[34] ibid [92].

[35] For example, John Kamm of Dui Hua Foundation, pointed out in 2003 that the Hong Kong proposal to blacklist groups on national security grounds had no equivalent under mainland law, and there were concerns that passage of the Hong Kong law would lead to the enactment of a blacklisting mechanism on the mainland that would threaten human rights groups there. See CJ Petersen, 'Hong Kong's Spring of Discontent: The Rise and Fall of the National Security Bill in 2003' in Fu, Petersen and Young (eds), *National Security and Fundamental Freedoms* (2005) 47–48.

[36] Basic Law, Art 17(3).

While this is not a power to invalidate Hong Kong laws for inconsistency with other mainland laws, if there were to be such inconsistency, the NPCSC may invalidate the regional law on the ground that it is not in conformity with Article 23, a provision 'regarding the relationship between the Central Authorities and the Region'.

Seen in this light, the two most important mainland legal developments since 2003 are the enactments of the Anti-Secession Law of 2005 and the National Security Law of the People's Republic of China (PRC) of 2015.[37] The Anti-Secession Law, adopted by the National People's Congress (NPC) on 14 March 2005, is concerned entirely with 'opposing and checking Taiwan's secession from China by secessionists in the name of "Taiwan independence"'.[38] The policy is to achieve 'peaceful national reunification' with Taiwan and to maintain 'peace and stability in the Taiwan Straits'.[39] The state must 'do its utmost with maximum sincerity to achieve a peaceful reunification'.[40] It is only if (a) the secessionist forces should 'cause the fact of Taiwan's secession from China', (b) 'major incidents entailing Taiwan's secession from China should occur', or (c) 'possibilities for a peaceful reunification should be completely exhausted' that the state would 'employ non-peaceful means and other necessary measures to protect China's sovereignty and territorial integrity'.[41] The law prescribes that the 'state protects the rights and interests of the Taiwan compatriots in accordance with law' even when non-peaceful means are being applied.[42] While it is provided that the 'state shall never allow … secessionist forces to make Taiwan secede from China under any name or by any means', the law does not create any new criminal offences, which are covered under the Criminal Law of mainland China.[43]

The National Security Law of the PRC was adopted by the NPC on 1 July 2015. 'National security' is defined comprehensively with reference to not only the 'State's political regime, sovereignty, unity and territorial integrity', but also 'the welfare of its people, its sustainable economic and social development, and other material national interests'.[44] National security in this sense is the 'status' of being 'relatively free from danger and international and domestic threats' and includes the 'ability to ensure the continuous status of security'.[45] The National Security Law delineates the organs responsible for national security, the duties to maintain

[37] The Cybersecurity Law of the PRC, effective from 6 January 2017, is also relevant but will not be discussed here.

[38] Anti-Secession Law 2005, Art 1, available at www.npc.gov.cn/englishnpc/Law/2007-12/13/content_1384099.htm.

[39] ibid Arts 5 and 6.

[40] ibid Art 5.

[41] ibid Arts 8 and 9.

[42] ibid Arts 6 and 9.

[43] ibid Art 2.

[44] National Security Law 2015, Art 2, available at eng.mod.gov.cn/publications/2017-03/03/content_4774229.htm.

[45] ibid.

national security, the multifaceted aspects of the national security system, the national security safeguards, and the related obligations and rights of citizens and organisations. The National Security Law does not provide for criminal offences, but states in several articles that the state shall punish specific offences 'pursuant to the law'.[46] In maintaining national security, it is 'imperative to abide by the Constitution and laws, uphold the principles of socialist rule of law, respect and safeguard human rights, and protect the rights and freedoms of citizens in accordance with the law'.[47] One also finds the principle of proportionality in the National Security Law:

> Where special measures that restrict the rights and freedom of citizens need to be taken during national security work, such measures shall be taken in accordance with the law, subject to the extent of the actual needs for maintaining national security.[48]

The scope of threats to national security mentioned in the National Security Law goes well beyond those mentioned in Article 23.[49] They include ethnic separatist activities, illegal and criminal activities carried out in the name of religion, illegal and criminal cult activities, terrorism and extremism, social conflicts, public health, public safety and other emergencies, environmental emergencies, nuclear power and nuclear technology, and war. Importantly, Article 23 does not contain the words 'national security'; rather its scope is limited to the seven specific acts that need to be prohibited by law.

Hong Kong and Macau are mentioned twice in the National Security Law. Once where it is provided that 'Maintaining national sovereignty, unity and territorial integrity is a shared obligation of all the Chinese people', and secondly where it provides that both special administrative regions 'shall fulfill the responsibilities for maintaining national security'.[50] The latter provision probably means not much more than implementing Article 23 and enforcing the implemented legislation. As the NPCSC did not add the National Security Law to Annex III of the Hong Kong Basic Law, the Law does not have direct application in Hong Kong. On 8 July 2015, Hong Kong's Secretary for Security stated that Hong Kong 'has the responsibility to safeguard national security, which is to be fulfilled by local legislation in accordance with the provisions of BL 23'; he confirmed that the National Security Law 'is not to be applied in the HKSAR'.[51]

[46] ibid Arts 9, 15, and 25–28.

[47] ibid Art 7.

[48] ibid Art 83.

[49] See also the contribution of Hualing Fu in this collection.

[50] National Security Law 2015 (n 44), Arts 11 and 40.

[51] Press Release of the HKSAR Government, 'LCQ5: National Security Law' (reply by Secretary for Security, Mr Lai Tung-kwok to a question by Hon Cyd Ho, 8 July 2015), available at www.info.gov.hk/gia/general/201507/08/P201507080755.htm. The same position is adopted in Macau; see Macau Government Spokesperson Office, 'Safeguarding National Security is Macao's Constitutional Responsibility' (2 July 2015), available at www.gov.mo/en/news/60363.

From this brief review of the Anti-Secession Law and National Security Law, a number of observations can be made. First, the approach to dealing with Taiwan secessionist activities is by peaceful means with sincerity in the first instance. Only when all peaceful means have been exhausted or major incidences towards secession have occurred should non-peaceful means be applied. Second, in dealing with Taiwanese secessionist activities or maintaining national security generally, it is imperative to abide by the law and to respect and safeguard human rights. Third, the two laws do not provide for criminal offences or purport to specify the elements of offences. Fourth, the legal mechanism of blacklisting is mentioned briefly only in the National Security Law but only in respect of banning cult organisations and terrorist organisations. Fifth, neither law has direct legal application in Hong Kong and Macau.

C. Macau's National Security Legislation

The Macau Government published its proposals for Article 23 legislation in October 2008, and within four months Article 23 legislation was passed with the overwhelming support of the Legislative Assembly members.[52] The law came into force on 3 March 2009.[53] It was more pressing for Macau to pass the law because after China resumed sovereignty in 1999 the Portuguese national security laws ceased to apply, leaving a 'legal void' in Macau.[54] By contrast, Hong Kong adapted its existing laws on treason, sedition, state secrets and societies to apply to the mainland and its institutions in partial fulfilment of Article 23.

The Macau National Security Law is a relatively neat and straightforward piece of legislation with only 15 Articles, the first seven corresponding to the seven prohibitions required by Article 23. As with mainland laws, there is a danger in trying to transplant Macau laws to Hong Kong given the two fundamentally different legal traditions. Nevertheless as the Macau authorities had the benefit of Hong Kong's 2003 Article 23 experience, there may be useful signposts in the Macau law of things that are unnecessary to the implementation of Article 23 and examples of more restrictive wording in the definition of offences.

Under the Macau law, those who commit treason, secession, or subversion are to be sentenced to a prison term of 10 to 25 years. Those who undertake 'preparatory acts' for these crimes can be punished by a prison term of up to three years.[55] A person commits sedition by 'publicly and directly inciting' one of the

[52] N Leung, 'Security bill put through with little hassle' *Macau Daily Times*, 26 February 2009. See also the contribution of Paulo Cardinal in this collection.

[53] National Security Law, No 2/2009.

[54] Government Information Bureau, 'Public Consultation on National Security Law Begins' (22 October 2008), available at www.gcs.gov.mo/showCNNews.php?DataUcn=33207&PageLang=E.

[55] National Security Law (n 53), Arts 1.2, 2.2 and 3.2.

first three crimes; the punishment is imprisonment between one and eight years.[56] The offence of theft of state secrets is specified in Article 5; the maximum punishment of the most serious offence is a prison term of five to 15 years. Article 5(5) defines 'state secrets' as

> documents, information, objects that must be kept secret *and are classified as such*, in the fields of national defence, foreign relations and other issues concerning the relationships between the Central Authorities and the Macao Special Administrative Region as set out in the Basic Law. (emphasis added)

When the agents of a foreign political organisation commit treason, secession, subversion, sedition or theft of state secrets in the name of the organisation and for its collective interest, the organisation can be convicted of offence under Article 6 and be subject to fines and supplementary penalties. Similarly when the agents of a Macau political organisation, which has established links with foreign political organisations and groups, commit the same offences in the name of the organisation and for its collective interest, the Macau organisation commits an offence under Article 7 and can be punished by fine, court ordered dissolution and other supplementary penalties. Articles 8 to 15, respectively, concern criminal responsibility of collective persons, supplementary penalties, extra-territorial scope, mitigation of penalty, public trial, changes to the Code of Criminal Procedure, supplementary application and entry into force. It is noteworthy the proscription or blacklisting mechanism proposed in Hong Kong's 2003 Bill was not included in the Macau legislation, although expulsion and banning of non-local residents from entering Macau for up to 15 years is available as a supplementary penalty after conviction.

The following observations can be made of the Macau legislation. First, it is obvious that reference was made to Hong Kong's 2003 Bill when the Macau law was drafted. There are similarities in the scope and text of the offences of treason, secession, subversion and sedition. Second, proposals in the 2003 Bill left out of the Macau law are instructive, suggesting that they are not essential to implementing Article 23. These include the offence of possession of seditious publications and the proscription mechanism for political organisations. Third, it is also instructive to note that in some places the Macau law uses clearer and more restrictive language in defining offences, eg incitement must be done 'publicly and directly' and definition of state secrets is restricted to those items kept secret and classified as secret.[57] Fourth, there are also less helpful ideas in the Macau law, either because offence elements are defined too broadly, such as the limb of the subversion offence that makes it an offence to use violence or other grave illegal acts to 'prevent or restrict' the functions of the Central People's Government, or legal concepts are unfamiliar to the common law system, such as crimes for mere preparatory acts.[58]

[56] ibid Art 4.1.
[57] ibid Art 5.5.
[58] ibid Art 3.1.

D. Experience of Anti-terrorism Laws

The same policy team that drafted Hong Kong's anti-terrorism legislation in 2002 also drafted the 2003 national security bill. The migration of ideas from the one to the other was obvious.[59] Kent Roach has observed that the 2003 Bill had a 'double dose' of security: the 'older vision of security based on betrayal of the state' and the new vision 'inspired by the United Kingdom's Terrorism Act 2000 and the post-September 11 anti-terrorism laws that have been modeled on that influential law in Canada, Australia, and Hong Kong'.[60]

Since 2003, there are now many judicial decisions, legislative reviews, policy reports and academic literature that shed light on the effectiveness and problems of anti-terrorism laws, particularly with proscription mechanisms.[61] The insights from this experience must be taken into account in deciding whether if anything should be borrowed from anti-terrorism law when drafting the next Article 23 Bill.

II. Implications for Reform

Two of the most controversial proposals in the 2003 Bill were the proposed offence of secession and the proscription mechanism for local organisations. This section considers the implications of post-2003 developments.

A. Secession

In 2003, a new offence known as secession punishable up to imprisonment for life was proposed. There were three forms of the offence defined as follows:

(i) a person withdraws any part of the PRC from its sovereignty by using force that seriously endangers the territorial integrity of the PRC;
(ii) a person withdraws any part of the PRC from its sovereignty by using serious criminal means that seriously endangers the territorial integrity of the PRC; and
(iii) a person withdraws any part of the PRC from its sovereignty by engaging in war.

[59] SNM Young, 'Security Laws for Hong Kong' in VV Ramraj, M Hor, K Roach and G Williams (eds), *Global Anti-Terrorism Law and Policy*, 2nd edn (Cambridge, Cambridge University Press, 2012) 377.

[60] K Roach, 'Old and New Visions of Security: Article 23 Compared to Post-September 11 Security Laws' in Fu, Petersen and Young (n 1) 120.

[61] See, eg, *Al-Dulimi and Montana Management Inc v Switzerland* [2016] ECHR 576 (Grand Chamber) and the decisions of the European Court of Justice, United Kingdom Supreme Court and Federal Court of Canada mentioned at [59]–[77]. At least two Canadians have been wrongly listed by a United Nations sanctions committee, see K Roach, 'Counter-Terrorism In and Outside Canada and In and Outside the Anti-Terrorism Act' (2012) 16 *Review of Constitutional Studies* 243, 260–61.

For Hong Kong permanent residents only, the offence was extra-territorial; their acts done outside Hong Kong were captured by the offence.

There are a number of drafting issues with the proposal. First, the two main elements of 'withdraws any part of the PRC from its sovereignty' and 'seriously endangers the territorial integrity of the PRC' are unclear. Second, there is no express *mens rea* element, leaving the matter unnecessarily for judicial consideration. Third, it is possible to commit the offence without actual or threat of violence because the definition of 'serious criminal means' included non-violent acts of damage to property and interferences with services and systems.

All of these issues, however, can be addressed with reference to the legislative guidelines set out above. For example, an express *mens rea* element of intention to secede (or, more appropriately, an intention to withdraw any part of the PRC from its sovereignty) should be included. This ensures the offence is not too readily used in cases of large-scale disruptive protests motivated by causes other than seeking secession. In defining the *mens rea* element, it should be made clear the aim of seeking greater democratic governance does not constitute the intention to secede. In other words, it is only the criminal pursuit of self-determination in its external dimension and not in its internal guise that should be made the subject of this offence.

There should also be refinement of the expression 'withdraws any part of the PRC from its sovereignty'. Limited assistance is gained from Article 103 of the Criminal Law of the PRC or Article 2 of the Macau national security law. These provisions use even less precise terms or attempt to impose inchoate liability. It is submitted that the following definition should be adopted. A person withdraws any part of the PRC from its sovereignty when he or she 'engages in conduct that precludes or frustrates the Central Government from exercising its lawful authority over a part of its territory'. This makes clear that the conduct must be sufficiently significant as to cut off the Central Government's exercise of lawful authority in the region. It approximates the act of 'splitting the State', the words used in Article 103 of the PRC Criminal Law.

The definition of 'serious criminal means' would lend greater confidence if it was limited to only means of a violent nature posing risks to human life or safety. The Macau national security law's definition of 'other grave illegal acts' in Article 2 did not include the 'damage to property' limb in the Hong Kong proposals. If interference with infrastructural systems and services is to be included within the definition, as it is under the Macau law, the drafters should include an exception for protest and other forms of expression.[62] This approach would be consistent with the definition of 'terrorist act' under Hong Kong law, which provides a similar kind of exception for 'advocacy, protest, dissent or industrial action'.[63]

[62] See Roach, 'Old and New Visions of Security' (n 60) 138–39; Young, 'Guide to Basic Law Article 23' (2015).

[63] United Nations (Anti-Terrorism Measures) Ordinance (Cap 575), s 2(1) (para (b) in the definition of 'terrorist act').

Making these relatively straightforward drafting improvements to the 2003 proposed secession offence would probably have settled most concerns at the time. But things have changed since 2003. The many political pro-independence developments within Hong Kong and abroad, such as in Catalonia, Spain in 2017, will complicate the Hong Kong proposal for a secession offence. The Central Government and pro-establishment politicians in Hong Kong have spoken out sharply against the rising pro-independence sentiments, especially amongst young people, promoting an independent Hong Kong polity. The 2016–17 legal actions brought by the Chief Executive and Secretary for Justice to disqualify two pro-independence legislators and four pro-democracy legislators, buttressed by an NPCSC interpretation on oath-taking, demonstrated the Central Government's determination to delegitimise any form of secessionist movement in Hong Kong.[64] This was followed by the 2018 proceedings brought under the Societies Ordinance to ban the Hong Kong National Party.[65] No doubt there will be pressure, whether from the Central or Hong Kong Governments, to enact one or more secession offence in wider terms than what was proposed in 2003.[66]

One critical issue will be whether as part of the implementation of Article 23 there should be an offence for advocating Hong Kong secession in a public place or on the Internet. Under the current law, if done without advocating violence or the commission of any other crime, this is not an offence, notwithstanding statements by government officials that such advocacy is 'totally contrary' to the Basic Law and the legal status of Hong Kong.[67] Mere advocacy would also not contravene the proposed 2003 offence as clarified in this chapter. Such advocacy without further action would not constitute withdrawing a part of the PRC from its sovereignty, although the intention to secede may be present. It would also be unlikely to constitute the inchoate offences of inciting or attempting to commit secession. For statutory attempt, there must be some act that is more than merely preparatory to the commission of the offence of secession. Although the full factual context is important, public advocacy would probably be counted only as part of the preparatory steps taken towards bringing about an actual withdrawal.

[64] See generally, PJ Yap and E Chan, 'Legislative Oaths and Judicial Intervention in Hong Kong' (2017) 47 *Hong Kong Law Journal* 1.

[65] See generally, CJ Petersen, 'Prohibiting the Hong Kong National Party: Has Hong Kong Violated the International Covenant on Civil and Political Rights?' (2018) 48 *Hong Kong Law Journal* 789.

[66] Note the Chief Executive's strong reaction to reports of Benny Tai's reference to Hong Kong independence at a seminar in Taipei organised by the Taiwan Youth Anti-Communist Corps in March 2018, see J Lam, 'Hong Kong government "shocked" by Occupy leader Benny Tai's independence comments at Taiwan seminar' *South China Morning Post*, 30 March 2018. On 26 February 2019, the Central People's Government issued a letter to the Chief Executive expressing its support for the HKSAR Government's decision to ban the Hong Kong National Party, see Press Release of the HKSAR Government, 'Opening remarks by CE at media session on letter issued by Central People's Government (with video)' (26 February 2019), available at www.info.gov.hk/gia/general/201902/26/P2019022600873.htm.

[67] Press Release of the HKSAR Government, 'Secretary for Justice on advocating independence of Hong Kong' (23 April 2016), available at www.info.gov.hk/gia/general/201604/23/P201604230805.htm.

For incitement, it was proposed in 2003 that a new offence known as sedition would replace any common law offences of inciting treason, secession or subversion. There would be additional hurdles to proving this new offence of sedition. The prosecution would need to prove that a person (or an ordinary person) incited was 'likely to be induced' to commit secession.[68] More significantly, it was proposed by the Government that there be a defence to the sedition offence if the sole purpose of the act was to persuade members of the public to attempt to procure, by lawful means, the alteration of any matter provided for in the law of the PRC or Hong Kong.[69] These hurdles make it difficult to prove sedition, especially if the person was advocating by lawful means to bring about a change in the basic policies of the Central Government in respect of Hong Kong's legal status.

If and when the time comes, the Hong Kong Government should resist any request to enact an offence criminalising the mere advocacy of independence or secession. First, such an offence would significantly undermine freedom of expression in Hong Kong. There is a fine line between advocating independence and discussing it. The criminal offence would chill any meaningful discussion of the topic for fear of being accused of advocating independence or organising an event during which someone advocates independence. Second, as it has been mostly students and young people who have engaged in such advocacy up to now,[70] the spectre of police officers policing university campuses for independence advocacy would be real and disastrous for academic freedom and the international reputation of Hong Kong's universities. Third, there is nothing in the 2005 Mainland Anti-Secession Law suggesting that the advocacy of peaceful secession should be criminalised. Rather the policy towards Taiwan independence advocates is to engage them peacefully and sincerely, using non-peaceful means only as a last resort or where concrete steps have been taken towards independence. Fourth, an offence that criminalises all forms of advocacy of independence would be a far greater impingement on the freedom of expression than the restrictions flowing from the offences relating to the national flag and national emblem (and shortly the offence relating to the national anthem).[71] These latter offences target a single mode of expression in the relevant context (eg flag, emblem, anthem) in order to uphold the dignity of a national symbol. However, an offence banning all forms of public expression advocating independence would serve a different kind of aim, one more questionable in its legitimacy. It would be to stop the spread of pro-independence sentiments. However, such sentiments could still arise from private gatherings and communications, including email. Perhaps the offence might be extended to advocacy in all contexts. An offence of such great width barring even the mere uttering of one's views of Hong Kong independence to another person would engage more than the freedom of speech; it would interfere with a person's

[68] Young (n 1).

[69] ibid.

[70] P Chiu, 'Students vow to revive pro-independence campaign on school campuses across Hong Kong' *South China Morning Post*, 14 November 2017.

[71] *HKSAR v Ng Kung Siu* (n 22); *HKSAR v Koo Sze Yiu* (n 23).

freedom of thought, including the right to hold opinions without interference, and the freedom of association. It is difficult to see how the advocacy offence (whether in its narrow or broad sense as described here) could satisfy the CFA's restriction test at all its stages.

B. Proscription

In 2003, the Hong Kong Government conceded that the Societies Ordinance already contained provisions to implement the final two prohibitions in Article 23 directed at foreign and local political organisations.[72] Yet the Government proposed giving the Secretary for Security an additional power to proscribe any local organisation on reasonable belief the proscription is 'necessary in the interests of national security and is proportionate for such purpose'.[73] The power would only apply to local organisations having an objective of engaging in treason, subversion, secession, sedition or committing the offence of spying, or local organisations that have committed or are attempting to commit one of these offences. An appeal mechanism to an independent tribunal, potentially holding in camera hearings to protect sensitive information, was also proposed.

Once an organisation was proscribed, existing offences relating to unlawful societies would apply to it and new proposed offences of participating in or aiding a proscribed organisation would also apply. As a late concession, defences to the criminal offence of participating in a proscribed organisation were added to remove liability if a person was participating in a legal proceeding, obtaining legal services, and making payment to discharge a liability.[74] There were other defences but they reversed the onus of proof and required the defendant to prove either the absence of relevant knowledge or reasonable belief.

The proposed proscription mechanism and participation offence were similar to (and even going further) than the procedures for specifying terrorists and related offences in the United Nations (Anti-Terrorism Measures) Ordinance.[75] Government's justification for introducing the proscription mechanism and offence was weak and unsupported by any empirical need. The Government acknowledged that the existing law was 'sufficient for the purpose of prohibiting foreign political organisations from taking part in the political process of the HKSAR' and provided 'effective sanctions against [organised political activities endangering the security of the state]'.[76] Yet, in a single sentence, the consultation paper asserted the rationale for the proposal as follows without justification:

> However, in view of the highly serious and reprehensible nature of activities damaging national security, together with the possibility that such activities would extend

[72] Security Bureau, Consultation Document (n 2) [7.11], [7.13].
[73] Proposed s 8A to the Societies Ordinance (Cap 151), see Young (n 1).
[74] Proposed s 8C(1A) to the Societies Ordinance (Cap 151), see ibid.
[75] United Nations (Anti-Terrorism Measures) Ordinance (Cap 575).
[76] Security Bureau, Consultation Document (n 2) [7.11], [7.13].

> beyond the HKSAR and have national-wide effects, more specific measures are needed to address national security concerns.[77]

Some were suspicious that pressure for the proposal came from the mainland because the initial proposal contained a ground of proscription to cover organisations affiliated with a mainland organisation proscribed in the mainland by the Central Authorities.[78] However, this ground was dropped as part of the package of final concessions made by the Government.

With the benefit of hindsight and experience, there are now many reasons why the proscription proposal and attendant criminal offence are unnecessary and misguided and should not be reintroduced when the Article 23 issue begins again. First, as mentioned, the proposals were not strictly speaking needed to comply with the duty in Article 23. Weak and unsupported reasons were given in 2003 for their need. Second, the absence of similar proposals in the Macau national security law, the mainland national security law, and Chapter I of Part Two of the Criminal Law of the PRC confirms that the proscription mechanism is not needed as a matter of national law and policy. The suspicion that the pressure came from the Central Government to enact these proposals is likely unwarranted; the relevant policy team at the time probably came up with the proposal on their own, drawing inspiration from their recent anti-terrorism work. Jorge Godinho wrote that the omission of the proscription mechanism in the Macau law was its 'most positive aspect'.[79] Third, criminal liability flowing from an executive proscription is fundamentally at odds with basic principles of criminal law. The rule against collateral attacks can make it nearly impossible for defendants to challenge the proscription decision made some time before the criminal proceedings.[80] In such circumstances, a person is convicted on the reasonable belief of the Secretary for Security rather than on the norm of a finding of fact proven beyond reasonable doubt. Fourth, proscription laws with attendant criminal penalties strike at fundamental freedoms, especially the freedom of association. In camera proceedings in the appeal mechanism are also inconsistent with rights to a public hearing and to make full answer and defence to the Government's case. Fifth, there has been no incidences or threats (at least not known to the public) in Hong Kong or anywhere in China to warrant the need for the proscription mechanism. Even the disturbances related to the 2019 anti-extradition reform protests, 2014 Occupy Central movement and the February 2016 unrest in Mongkok did not rise to the level

[77] ibid [7.13].

[78] See L Harris, L Ma and CB Fung, 'A Connecting Door: The Proscription of Local Organizations' in Fu, Petersen and Young (n 1) 303.

[79] J Godinho, 'The Regulation of Article 23 of the Macau Basic Law: A Commentary of the Draft Law on the Protection of State Security' (draft version 2, 28 November 2008) 18, available at papers.ssrn.com/sol3/papers.cfm?abstract_id=1303245.

[80] *Secretary for Justice v Ocean Technology Ltd* [2009] 1 HKC 271 (CA) [86], leave to appeal to CFA refused in [2009] HKCFA 54.

requiring these new measures. Sixth, it has not been shown that the powers under the Societies Ordinance to regulate and penalise local and foreign organisations and the specification mechanisms in the anti-terrorism legislation are inadequate to deal with any potential threats from local and foreign organisations. Indeed, controversially, the existing law has been used to ban the Hong Kong National Party, a pro-independence party.[81]

Finally, reference should be made to the many criticisms by courts, judges and scholars of proscription mechanisms in the anti-terrorism context. In addition to the above-mentioned challenges to basic criminal law principles and fundamental freedoms, there are also objections on constitutional and practical grounds. The main constitutional problem is executive usurpation of judicial power since the court's roles in making proscriptions and reviewing them are either removed or severely limited. Roach writes: 'Executive determination of proscribed organisations can usurp judicial powers in a prosecution by allowing the executive as opposed to the judiciary decide whether a group is a terrorist group or a threat to national security'.[82] Tim Legrand and Lee Jarvis discuss some of the practical problems with a system of designating or proscribing terrorist groups.[83] Groups labelled terrorist 'often lack anything approaching the institutional stability implied by such a designation'.[84] They also point out that these groups can often change their name or use different ones and tend to be short-lived. There are also challenges in identifying individual members of these groups. Citing a body of literature questioning the effectiveness of proscription, Legrand and Jarvis conclude that the proscription powers 'have dubious efficacy as a technique for countering terrorism' and 'may be used capriciously and politically for ends other than countering terrorism'.[85]

III. Conclusion

This chapter has highlighted some of the important legal and political developments since 2003 that should bear on Article 23 deliberations. One hopes that the passage of time will enable those in charge to see better ways of moving forward and shun the mistakes of the past. The process of reform will need careful attention. There should be adequate expertise employed in the formulation of options and proposals, ample time for consultation, public debate and legislative scrutiny

[81] See Petersen, 'Prohibiting the Hong Kong National Party' (2018).

[82] Roach (n 60) 141.

[83] T Legrand and L Jarvis, 'Enemies of the state: proscription powers and their use in the United Kingdom' (2014) 9 *British Politics* 450.

[84] ibid 458.

[85] ibid 466.

of proposals, and a consideration of whether a piecemeal, rather than omnibus, approach would be more effective.[86]

Since 2003, new complications and conflicts have arisen along the evolutionary journey of the 'one country, two systems' framework. Whatever those complications, one should not too readily assume that Article 23 provides the answer. New or additional measures, beyond what is strictly required to implement Article 23, must be justified with evidence of the need for the measure to further a legitimate aim, which cannot be achieved by a substantially less intrusive measure, existing or otherwise. As argued in this chapter, there is no justification for reintroducing the old proscription mechanism of 2003 or introducing a new offence of advocating secession. One also hopes that those in charge will find guidance in this chapter in drafting acceptable provisions to meet, minimally, the requirements of Article 23.

[86] See Petersen, 'Hong Kong's Spring of Discontent' (2005); Young, 'Security Laws for Hong Kong' (2012). Former Secretary for Justice, Ms Elsie Leung, spoke of adopting an incremental approach in 2017: see K Chung, 'Enact national security laws step-by-step former Hong Kong justice secretary' *South China Morning Post*, 17 June 2017.

13

Article 23 of the Hong Kong Basic Law

International Law and Institutions as Sources of Resilience

CAROLE J PETERSEN[1]

I. Introduction

In 2003, when the Hong Kong Government introduced the National Security (Legislative Principles) Bill, it listed international human rights law as one of the 'guiding principles' in the drafting exercise.[2] The Government also agreed to include clauses stating that any local ordinances implementing Article 23 of the Basic Law of the Hong Kong Special Administrative Region (HKSAR) should be interpreted and enforced so as to comply with Article 39, which incorporates the International Covenant on Civil and Political Rights (ICCPR) into Hong Kong's constitutional order.[3] Article 39 has its origins in the Sino–British Joint Declaration, a bilateral treaty that was duly registered with the United Nations (UN).[4] By agreeing that the ICCPR would be enforced in post-1997 Hong Kong, the People's Republic of China (PRC) made an important concession to the territory's autonomy and distinct identity. Since 1997, Hong Kong's Court of Final Appeal has consistently held that Article 39 incorporates the ICCPR into the regional constitution[5] and the local judiciary has regularly cited international and comparative

[1] Professor, William S Richardson School of Law and Graduate Chair, Matsunaga Institute for Peace, University of Hawaii at Manoa (carolep@hawaii.edu).

[2] HKSAR Government, 'Proposals to Implement Article 23 of the Hong Kong Basic Law, Legislative Council Brief: National Security (Legislative Provisions) Bill 2003', available at www.basiclaw23.gov.hk/english/resources/legco/legco_article/article9.htm.

[3] For discussion of these clauses, see CJ Petersen, 'Hong Kong's Spring of Discontent: The Rise and Fall of the National Security Bill in 2003' in H Fu, CJ Petersen and SNM Young (eds) *National Security and Fundamental Freedoms: Hong Kong's Article 23 Under Scrutiny* (Hong Kong, HKU Press, 2005).

[4] Joint Declaration of the Government of the United Kingdom of Great Britain and Northern Ireland and the Government of the People's Republic of China on the Question of Hong Kong 1399 UNTS 33 (19 December 1984), Annex I, s XIII (Joint Declaration).

[5] See, eg, *HKSAR v Ng Kung Siu* (1999) 2 HKCFAR 442; *HKSAR v Fong Kwok Shan Christine* (2017) 20 HKCFAR 425 [12]–[15].

jurisprudence when applying the ICCPR.[6] This link to international human rights law has helped Hong Kong to maintain a much higher standard of civil liberties than exists in mainland China.

Unfortunately, in 2019, the political climate has become far more confrontational and we cannot assume that the ICCPR will serve as a 'guiding principle' in the next effort to implement Article 23. Increased interference by the Central Government since the pro-democracy protests of 2014 gave rise to 'localism' and a tiny independence movement has emerged in Hong Kong.[7] In 2018, anxious to show Beijing that it can contain this movement, the local Government issued an order prohibiting the operation of the Hong Kong National Party (HKNP).[8] This was the first time that a political party had been banned in the HKSAR and the incident demonstrates how laws enacted to implement Article 23 may be applied in practice. The Secretary for Security relied upon the Societies Ordinance (a local law that already incorporates certain language from Article 23)[9] and cited 'national security' as one of the justifications for the order.[10] In February 2019, the Chief Executive in Council dismissed an appeal filed by Chan Ho Tin (the leader of the HKNP).[11] Beijing promptly expressed its support for the order and requested a written report, which the Chief Executive submitted in April of 2019.[12]

In this author's view, the order violates Hong Kong's obligations under the ICCPR because it fails to articulate how this tiny political party threatens China's national security.[13] However, the HKNP waived its right to challenge the order in court, citing the high cost of litigation and the uncertainty of success.[14] Indeed, the proportionality test is an inherently malleable standard[15] and local judges may apply Article 39 less robustly in cases involving pro-independence figures.[16] There is also a risk that the Standing Committee of the National People's Congress

[6] For examples, see CJ Petersen, 'Embracing Universal Standards? The Role of International Human Rights Treaties in Hong Kong's Constitutional Jurisprudence' in H Fu, L Harris and SNM Young (eds), *Interpreting Hong Kong's Basic Law: The Struggle for Coherence* (New York, Palgrave Macmillan, 2007).

[7] CJ Petersen and AYH Cheung, 'Academic Freedom and Critical Speech in Hong Kong: China's Response to Occupy Central and the Future of "One Country, Two Systems"' (2017) 42 *North Carolina Journal of International Law* 665.

[8] Societies Ordinance (Cap 151), Order under s 8(2), GN (E) 52 of 2018 (24 September 2018).

[9] See Societies Ordinance (Cap 151), ss 5, 5A, 5D and 8.

[10] Letter dated 24 September 2018 from the Secretary for Security to Daly & Associates, at Enclosure 2 (copy on file with the author).

[11] J Lam, T Cheung, L Sum, K Chung and A Lum, 'Beijing Backs city government's ban on Hong Kong National Party, leader Carrie Lam says' *South China Morning Post*, 26 February 2019.

[12] Press Release of the HKSAR Government, 'Report on the Prohibition of the Operation of the "Hong Kong National Party" Submitted by the CE to the CPG' (18 April 2018), available at www.info.gov.hk/gia/general/201904/18/P2019041800429.htm.

[13] See CJ Petersen, 'Prohibiting the Hong Kong National Party: Has Hong Kong Violated the International Covenant on Civil and Political Rights?' (2018) 48 *Hong Kong Law Journal* 789.

[14] A Lum, 'Hong Kong National Party waives right to legally challenge ban, paving way for more government crackdowns on independence groups' *South China Morning Post*, 22 May 2019.

[15] See C Chan, 'Rights, Proportionality and Deference: A Study of Post-Handover Judgments in Hong Kong' (2018) 48 *Hong Kong Law Journal* 51.

[16] There are signs of this in *Chan Ho Tin v Lo Ying Ki Alan and Others* [2018] 2 HKLRD 7, in which the High Court dismissed Chan Ho Tin's election petition against the Returning Officer's decision

(NPCSC) would issue an interpretation of Article 39 of the Basic Law, in order to pre-empt the local judiciary from declaring the order unconstitutional.[17]

In any event, the local Government has already used the order prohibiting the HKNP to discourage advocacy for independence. It has monitored demonstrators for signs of support for the party[18] and warned students that they risk criminal prosecution if they assist 'illegal' societies.[19] The Government also appears to have used its considerable discretion over immigration matters to punish the Hong Kong Foreign Correspondents' Club for hosting a talk by the leader of the HKNP, even before the party was banned.[20] In this highly charged political climate, it is almost certain that any legislation to further implement Article 23 will be less compliant with the ICCPR than the bill that was proposed in 2003.

The other worrying development is that China's Central Government is increasingly resistant to any suggestion that it has a binding obligation in international law to respect Hong Kong's autonomy. Beijing now regularly insists that Hong Kong is a purely domestic matter and sometimes characterises the Joint Declaration as a mere 'historical document' that no longer has relevance.[21] Beijing takes this position whenever the United Kingdom (UK) or another foreign government seeks to monitor China's compliance with the Joint Declaration.[22]

This chapter argues that the Central Government is mistaken: international law is at the very heart of Hong Kong's post-1997 constitutional order and must be considered in any legislative exercise to further implement Article 23.[23] Part I demonstrates this point by briefly reviewing Hong Kong's colonial history and its

to invalidate his nomination to stand for election to the Legislative Council. The court accepted the Government's argument that protecting principles that 'underpin the HKSAR's constitutional order' constitutes a legitimate aim and repeatedly referred to Hong Kong as an 'inalienable' part of China.

[17] The power to issue what are essentially legislative interpretations of the Basic Law derives from Art 158, which is arguably the single greatest threat to civil liberties in Hong Kong. See F Lin, 'The Duty of Hong Kong Courts to Follow the NPCSC's Interpretation of the Basic Law: Are There Any Limits?' (2018) 48 *Hong Kong Law Journal* 167; PY Lo, 'Enforcing an Unfortunate, Unnecessary and "Unquestionably Binding" NPCSC Interpretation: The Hong Kong Judiciary's Deconstruction of Its Construction of the Basic Law' (2018) 48 *Hong Kong Law Journal* 399.

[18] A Lum and C Lo, 'Hong Kong protesters channel Catalan spirit as they march for independence while testing limits of ban that saw separatist party in the city outlawed' *South China Morning Post*, 1 October 2018.

[19] T Cheung and X Su, 'Students who associate with outlawed Hong Kong National Party can face criminal sanctions, government tells schools as top Beijing Official Welcomes Ban' *South China Morning Post*, 26 September 2018.

[20] The work visa of the Vice-President of the Foreign Correspondents' Club (who served as host for the speech) was not renewed; the local government has refused to comment on the matter. See J Lam, T Cheung and X Su, 'Backlash as Hong Kong denies visa renewal for Financial Times journalist Victor Mallet' *South China Morning Post*, 5 October 2018.

[21] J Ng, 'Sino-British Joint Declaration on Hong Kong "no-longer has any realistic meaning" Chinese Foreign Ministry says' *South China Morning Post*, 30 June 2017.

[22] See Office of the Commissioner of the Ministry of Foreign Affairs of the PRC, 'Spokesperson of the Commissioner's Office Addresses Questions from the Press' (14 September 2016), available at www.fmcoprc.gov.hk/eng/gsxw/t1397525.htm (stressing that 'Hong Kong's affairs are China's domestic affair').

[23] I use the phrase 'further implement' because Hong Kong already has local legislation prohibiting much of what is listed in Art 23 of the Hong Kong Basic Law. See SNM Young, 'Guide to Basic

status, for 26 years, on the UN's list of non-self-governing territories. This created a legal presumption that residents would exercise their right to self-determination upon decolonisation. Although this did not occur (because Hong Kong was removed from the list in 1972 without public consultation), the Joint Declaration should be viewed as promising a form of internal self-determination and thus as a means of reconciling China's territorial claims with the rights of Hong Kong people.

Part II of the chapter then summarises the international norms that should be complied with in any new legislative exercise to further implement Article 23. In addition to the ICCPR itself, this section draws upon decisions of the UN Human Rights Committee (the treaty-monitoring body for the ICCPR), the Committee's General Comment 34,[24] and certain soft law instruments. It also references relevant decisions of the European Court of Human Rights (ECtHR), which has been recognised as a source of persuasive authority by Hong Kong courts.[25] Taken together, this body of law demonstrates that it is possible to protect China's legitimate security interests without violating the Joint Declaration.

Part III of the chapter will then briefly consider the role of the UN and foreign governments in monitoring China's compliance with the Joint Declaration. The success (or failure) of 'one country, two systems' has implications for the international community and any new proposal to further implement Article 23 will inevitably attract attention, just as it did in 2003.

II. The Joint Declaration as a Form of Internal Self-Determination

The term 'self-determination' was originally described as a principle rather than as a right.[26] Over time, it has been recognised as a right, both in multilateral treaties[27] and in the jurisprudence of the International Court of Justice (ICJ).[28] A right to *external* self-determination (which includes the right to choose independence) has been recognised primarily in the context of decolonisation[29] and

Law Article 23: Hong Kong's Unresolved National Security Issue' (HKU Legal Scholarship blog, 15 March 2015), available at researchblog.law.hku.hk/2015/03/guide-to-basic-law-article-23-hong.html.

[24] UN Human Rights Committee, General Comment 34, Art 19, Freedoms of opinion and expression, 12 September 2011, CCPR/C/GC/34.

[25] *Koon Wing Yee v Insider Dealing Tribunal* (2008) 11 HKCFAR 170 [27] (noting that decisions of the ECtHR are of 'high persuasive authority' in Hong Kong).

[26] UN Charter, Arts 1(2) and 55.

[27] ICCPR, Art 1; International Covenant on Economic, Social and Cultural Rights (ICESCR), Art 1; African Charter of Human and Peoples' Rights, Art 20.

[28] *East Timor (Portugal v Australia), Judgment*, 1995 ICJ 90, para 29; *Western Sahara, Advisory Opinion*, 1975 ICJ 12, para 162.

[29] *Legal Consequences of the Separation of the Chagos Archipelago From Mauritius in 1965, Advisory Opinion* (25 February 2019), paras 140–62 (recognising self-determination in the context of decolonisation as a crystallised norm of customary international law by 1960).

situations of foreign occupation.[30] Outside those two contexts, the state's right to territorial integrity has normally prevailed over any regional demands for independence.[31] However, a right to *internal* self-determination poses no threat to territorial integrity. In addition to the right of democratic participation, internal self-determination can also include the right of a people to exercise cultural, linguistic, religious, territorial or political autonomy within the larger state.[32] Autonomy is particularly appropriate in situations in which the inhabitants of a colonised territory were not permitted to hold a plebiscite to determine their political status upon decolonisation.[33]

As a British colony, Hong Kong was initially considered to fall within the decolonisation framework. This meant that the British Government undertook certain responsibilities with respect to Hong Kong. These duties were outlined in the Declaration Concerning Non-Self-Governing Territories, contained in Chapter XI of the UN Charter:

> Members of the United Nations which have or assume responsibilities for the administration of territories whose peoples have not yet attained a full measure of self-government *recognize the principle that the interests of the inhabitants of these territories are paramount*, and accept as a sacred trust the obligation to promote to the utmost, within the system of international peace and security established by the present Charter, the well-being of the inhabitants of these territories, and, to this end:
>
> (i) to ensure, with due respect for the culture of the peoples concerned, their political, economic, social, and educational advancement, their just treatment, and their protection against abuses;
>
> (ii) to develop self-government, to take due account of the political aspirations of the peoples, and to assist them in the progressive development of their free political institutions, according to the particular circumstances of each territory and its peoples and their varying stages of advancement; … (emphasis added)[34]

[30] *Legal Consequences of the Construction of a Wall in the Occupied Palestinian Territory, Advisory Opinion*, 2004 ICJ 136.

[31] *Katangese Peoples' Congress v Zaire*, African Commission on Human and Peoples' Rights, Comm No 75/92 (1995); *Reference Re: Secession of Quebec* [1998] 2 SCR 2017 (Canadian Supreme Court) (noting that a right to remedial secession would only arise in certain extreme cases). Although this argument was advanced to justify Kosovo's secession from Serbia, the ICJ avoided the issue of whether Kosovo had a right to secede. The ICJ interpreted the request from the General Assembly as asking only whether the declaration of independence violated international law and found no rule of international law prohibiting such declarations. See *Accordance with International Law of the Unilateral Declaration of Independence in Respect of Kosovo, Advisory Opinion*, 2010 ICJ 403 (especially paras 49–56).

[32] MC van Walt van Praag and O Seroo (eds), *The Implementation of the Right to Self-Determination as a Contribution to Conflict Prevention: Report of the International Conference of Experts held in Barcelona from 21 to 27 November 1998* (UNESCO Division of Human Rights Democracy and Peace and the UNESCO Centre of Catalonia, 1999), available at www.unpo.org/downloads/THE%20IMPLEMENTATION%20OF%20THE%20RIGHT%20TO%20SELF.pdf, p 12 (discussing the meaning of internal self-determination); P Hilpold, 'Self-determination and Autonomy: Between Secession and Internal Self-determination' (2017) 24 *International Journal on Minority and Group Rights* 302, 328 (noting the close relationship between autonomy and internal self-determination).

[33] M Pomerance, *Self-Determination in Law and Practice: The New Doctrine in the United Nations* (Leiden, Martinus Nijhoff Publishers, 1982) 74.

[34] UN Charter, Art 73.

Although the initial list of non-self-governing territories was created from information submitted by the colonial powers themselves, the UN also developed its own criteria for determining whether a territory should be considered 'non-self-governing'[35] and for determining the obligations of colonial powers.[36] Territories 'known to be of the colonial type' when the UN was formed were included on the list.[37] There was also a prima facie obligation to transmit information to the UN for any territory which was 'geographically separate' and 'distinct ethnically and/or culturally from the country administering it'.[38] Clearly, the British colony of Hong Kong met this definition.

The obligation of a colonial power to report to the UN on a dependent territory continues until the territory and its people have 'attained a full measure of self-government'.[39] This can be accomplished in one of three ways: (1) emergence as a sovereign independent state; (2) free association with an independent state (but only if it is the result of a free and voluntary choice by the peoples of the territory concerned, expressed through informed and democratic processes); or (3) integration with an independent state (but, again, only if it is the result of the freely expressed wishes of the territory's peoples, acting with 'full knowledge of the change in their status, their wishes having been expressed through informed and democratic processes, impartially conducted, and based on universal adult suffrage').[40]

Hong Kong was listed for 26 years as a non-self-governing territory under British administration, creating a legal presumption that the residents would eventually be given the right to choose among the three options: independence; association with an independent state; or integration with an independent state. By 1960, the right to self-determination was a crystallised norm of international customary law.[41] However, in 1972, soon after it replaced the Republic of China in the UN, the Government of the PRC requested that Hong Kong and Macau be deleted from the list, taking the position that the two territories were not colonies but rather 'Chinese territory occupied by the British and Portuguese' authorities.[42] This was in spite of the fact that Hong Kong's status as a colony had

[35] GA Res 742 (VIII), Factors which should be taken into account in deciding whether a Territory is or is not a Territory whose people have not attained a full measure of self-government (27 November 1953), available at www.un.org/documents/ga/res/8/ares8.htm.

[36] GA Res 1514 (XV), Declaration on the Granting of Independence to Colonial Countries and Peoples (14 December 1960); GA Res 1541 (XV), Principles Which Should Guide Members in Determining Whether or Not an Obligation Exists to Transmit the Information Called for Under Article 73e of the Charter (15 December 1960), available at www.un.org/documents/ga/res/15/ares15.htm.

[37] ibid, Principle I.

[38] ibid, Principle IV.

[39] ibid, Principle II.

[40] ibid, Principles VI–VII.

[41] *Legal Consequences of the Separation of the Chagos Archipelago From Mauritius in 1965, Advisory Opinion* (25 February 2019), paras 140–62.

[42] N Jayawickrama, 'Public Law', in Raymond Wacks (ed), *The Law in Hong Kong, 1969–1989* (Hong Kong, Oxford University Press, 2013) 50–51 (quoting from the Letter dated 10 March 1972, from Ambassador Huang Hua, Permanent Representative of the PRC to the UN, to the Chairman of the UN Special Committee).

been acknowledged by the PRC during the colonial period.[43] Bodies within the UN have also long recognised that the people of Hong Kong lived under colonial rule.[44] However, in 1972 the Committee on Decolonisation was chaired by an ambassador who was described as 'fiercely' pro-China.[45] He referred the matter to a small working group, which he also chaired, and it endorsed the PRC's request.[46] Although several members of the Committee believed that the issue required more consideration, this recommendation was adopted by the General Assembly without discussion.[47]

One might have expected the British Government to object to China's request or at least to insist on public discussion of such an important decision, one that would profoundly affect the future of the more than four million people who resided in Hong Kong in 1972. But the UK did not object; nor did it seek any public assurances that the Hong Kong people would be given an opportunity, at some future date, to vote on their political status. This is one of the reasons that Jayawickrama describes the UK's treatment of Hong Kong as 'perhaps the most shameful episode of British colonial history'.[48] However, in truth, the responsibility for Hong Kong's removal from the list of non-self-governing territories rested with all members of the UN's Committee on Decolonisation, who should have been sensitive to the fact that the British Government would not necessarily consider the interests of the Hong Kong people as its highest priority.

Of course, international law recognises that the right to self-determination is not absolute. In certain circumstances, it must yield to the norm of territorial integrity. This is often argued in the context of 'colonial enclaves' and other situations in which a neighbouring state has a competing claim to the colonial territory.[49] Clearly, China did have a competing claim, partly because the New Territories portion of Hong Kong had only been leased to the UK for 99 years (whereas Hong Kong Island and Kowloon were ceded 'in perpetuity')[50] and partly because China had long argued that all three treaties were 'unequal' and invalid. However, the treaties would have been considered valid transfers of territory according to the prevailing law and practice of the nineteenth century, when the

[43] For example, China recognised the right of the United Kingdom to issue currency in Hong Kong, an attribute of sovereignty. See R Mushkat, *One Country, Two International Legal Personalities: The Case of Hong Kong* (Hong Kong, HKU Press, 1997) 138.

[44] For example, the UN Human Rights Committee continued, for more than two decades after 1972, to call upon the UK to report on the implementation of the ICCPR in Hong Kong and the British Government did so.

[45] N Jayawickrama, 'The Right of Self-Determination – A Time for Reinvention and Renewal' (1993) 57 *Saskatchewan Law Review* 1, 16.

[46] ibid.

[47] ibid.

[48] ibid 15.

[49] J Trinidad, *Self-Determination in Disputed Colonial Territories* (Cambridge, Cambridge University Press, 2018) 157–235.

[50] See generally, P Wesley-Smith, *Unequal Treaty 1898–1997: China, Great Britain, and Hong Kong's New Territories*, revd edn (Hong Kong, Oxford University Press, 1998).

great powers commonly acquired territory by conquest and 'territories changed hands as if they were private property'.[51] Moreover, in 1972 there was no obvious reason why the PRC's right to territorial integrity had to override the right of a colonised people to exercise self-determination. Under the *uti possidetis* doctrine, borders drawn during the colonial period have generally been maintained[52] and the border between Hong Kong and the PRC was both longstanding and stable. Hong Kong is geographically minuscule, has no significant natural resources, and is adjacent to (rather than inside of) the PRC. There is nothing to indicate that the PRC would require this tiny bit of land in order to preserve its own territorial integrity. Thus, the UK (or, indeed, any member of the Committee on Decolonisation) could have argued, pursuant to Article 73 of the UN Charter, that Hong Kong had become a distinct community under colonial rule and that the interests of the *inhabitants* were now paramount rather than competing claims to land. This argument has been made in other contexts. For example, the residents' wishes have thus far prevailed over Spain's longstanding claim to the territory of Gibraltar.[53] Had the people of Hong Kong been consulted, there is little doubt that they also would have rejected integration with China, because a large percentage of the four million residents in 1972 had either fled Communist China or were descendants of those refugees.[54]

Once Hong Kong was removed from the list of non-self-governing territories the UK ceased reporting to the Committee on Decolonisation on progress towards self-government. This was convenient for the colonial Government and for Hong Kong's conservative businessmen, who feared that elected representatives would adopt more populist policies. It was also convenient for the Chinese Communist Party, which had no desire to see local democracy develop in the territory.

It was not until the Sino–British negotiations, in the 1980s, that the UK's obligations to Hong Kong began to attract international attention. The UK did not wish to be seen as forcing millions of people to be integrated with the PRC. Deng Xiaoping also wanted a smooth transfer of power and had good reason to fear that the people of Hong Kong might try to subvert the process, either through mass migration, transfer of capital or outright resistance.[55] Thus, it was in the interests

[51] Jayawickrama, 'The Right of Self-Determination' (1993) 15.

[52] *Frontier Dispute Case (Burkina Faso v Mali)*, 1986 ICJ 554, paras 20–26.

[53] Gibraltar remains on the UN's list of non-self-governing territories although it is now largely self-governing; the people have rejected integration with Spain in referendums. For a recent summary of the parties' respective legal arguments, see Special Committee on the Situation with regard to the Granting of Independence to Colonial Territories and Peoples, 'Gibraltar: Working Paper Prepared by the Secretariat' (UN Doc A/AC/109/2017/8, 7 March 2017).

[54] P Wesley-Smith, 'The Settlement of the Question of Hong Kong' (1987) 17 *California International Law Journal* 116, 117–19.

[55] Y Ghai, *Hong Kong's New Constitutional Order: The Resumption of Chinese Sovereignty and The Basic Law*, 2nd edn (Hong Kong, HKU Press, 1999) 76.

of both governments to give Hong Kong residents every reason to believe that they would enjoy at least a genuine form of *internal* self-determination after 1997.[56]

It is in this context that one must view the extensive promises that were made to the Hong Kong people in the Joint Declaration, including the detailed descriptions of the civil liberties they would enjoy as a Special Autonomous Region. Although the PRC itself is not a state party to the ICCPR (and therefore does not report to the UN Human Rights Committee), it notified the UN that the ICCPR would continue to apply to Hong Kong and that the Committee could continue to monitor Hong Kong's compliance with the treaty, just as it had done in the colonial era. This reporting relationship provides the UN with a mechanism for monitoring implementation of the Joint Declaration. It is also an important indicator of the high degree of autonomy that was promised to Hong Kong.

Indeed, on paper, the HKSAR was endowed with an extraordinary range of executive and legislative powers,[57] including some that we normally associate with an independent state.[58] For example, Hong Kong issues its own travel documents and maintains its own currency and monetary policy. It also maintains a separate customs regime and can join international organisations in its own name. Many of the initial assessments of 'one country, two systems' commented on this unusually high degree of formal autonomy.[59] Similarly, when Hong Kong was admitted as a separate member of the World Trade Organisation, Stephen Lam (Hong Kong's Secretary for Constitutional Affairs at the time) described the HKSAR's autonomy as surpassing that of states under many federal systems.[60] Lam also described Hong Kong's autonomy as a permanent feature, claiming that:

> 'One Country, Two Systems' is here to stay. The Basic Law and common law system will always be there to serve Hong Kong. They will underpin not just the Hong Kong economy, but also the rights and freedoms which Hong Kong residents enjoy.[61]

These remarks are representative of the image that the local Government likes to present to foreign investors and governments, of Hong Kong as a distinct common law jurisdiction, with a commitment to rule of law, clean government and civil

[56] Trinidad, *Self-Determination* (2018) 118–19 (noting that the Joint Declaration reflects 'a preoccupation with internal aspects of self-determination').

[57] See the contribution of Albert Chen in this collection.

[58] See, eg, H Hannum, *Autonomy, Sovereignty, and Self-Determination: The Accommodation of Conflicting Rights*, revd edn (Philadelphia, University of Pennsylvania Press, 1996) ch 7; H Hannum, 'The Foreign Powers of Autonomous Regions' (1988) 57 *Nordic Journal of International Law* 273 (comparing Hong Kong to other regions); R Mushkat, *One Country, Two International Legal Personalities: The Case of Hong Kong* (Hong Kong, HKU Press, 1997).

[59] See, eg, M Pei, 'Self-Administration and Local Autonomy, Reconciling Conflicting Interests in China' in W Danspeckgruber (ed), *The Self-Determination of Peoples: Community, Nations, and State in an Interdependent World* (Boulder, Lynne Rienner Publishers, 2001).

[60] S Lam, 'Speech by Secretary for Constitutional Affairs' (Seminar on Legal Landscape of China After Accession to WTO, 7 September 2002), available at www.info.gov.hk/gia/general/200209/07/0907233.htm.

[61] ibid.

liberties. But if the international community is to continue to view Hong Kong in that light, then the Government needs to draft any legislation implementing Article 23 in a manner that is fully compliant with the Joint Declaration and the ICCPR. The next section of the chapter argues that this is possible, drawing on jurisprudence from the UH Human Rights Committee and the ECtHR.

III. International Norms and National Security Laws

In some respects, Article 23 enhances Hong Kong's autonomy because it empowers the local legislature to enact its own laws defining the specified offences, with no obligation to adopt mainland Chinese legislation.[62] The one overriding obligation is that all local ordinances must comply with the ICCPR as it applies to Hong Kong. This section of the paper explores what that means in practice, focusing on the three civil liberties that are most likely to be at risk if legislation to implement Article 23 is drafted in an overly broad manner: freedom of expression (including access to information); freedom of peaceful assembly; and freedom of association. These rights are expressly protected by the Joint Declaration, the ICCPR (Articles 19, 21 and 22), and the Hong Kong Basic Law (Articles 27 and 39).

The ICCPR allows governments to place restrictions on freedom of expression, assembly and association if provided by law and necessary in a democratic society for certain legitimate purposes, including national security.[63] It is important to emphasise, however, that 'national security' is not synonymous with the security of a particular government or political party. The Human Rights Committee has frequently reminded governments that Article 19(3) of the ICCPR should not be relied upon as a justification for prohibiting advocacy for multi-party democracy or human rights.[64] The Committee has adopted this view even when the state argued that restrictions were necessary measures to achieve national unity or preserve public order.[65]

For example, in *Mukong v Cameroon*, the Government prosecuted a journalist for 'intoxication of international and national opinion' after he criticised the one-party system in an interview with the BBC. The Government argued that this was necessary to build national unity. The Human Rights Committee rejected this position, concluding that even if strengthening national unity were a legitimate aim, a government cannot lawfully pursue it by 'attempting to muzzle advocacy for multiparty democracy, democratic tenants, and human rights'.[66]

[62] See the contribution of Simon Young in this collection.

[63] ICCPR, Arts 19, 21 and 22.

[64] See, eg, *Mukong v Cameroon*, Comm No 458/91 (21 July 1994); *Sohn v Republic of Korea*, Comm No 518/1992 (18 March 1994), para 10.4.

[65] ibid.

[66] *Mukong v Cameroon* (n 64), especially para 9.7.

The Human Rights Committee has also determined that governments cannot use national security as a blanket justification for restricting the rights of expression and association. Rather, a government must demonstrate precisely how the restricted activities could threaten national security. For example, in *Tae-Hoon Park v Republic of Korea*, the applicant became involved in a student association that advocated for the peaceful reunification of North and South Korea. The association was highly critical of the South Korean Government and the student was later convicted under a national security law. The UN Human Rights Committee found that his conviction violated the ICCPR, in part because the burden was on the Government to 'specify the precise nature of the threat' to national security.[67]

The Human Rights Committee has applied a similar approach when reviewing complaints arising from restrictions on speech advocating for labour strikes or other forms of peaceful assembly.[68] Governments cannot simply assert that a local demonstration threatens national security. This is particularly relevant in the context of Hong Kong because a well-patrolled border separates it from the rest of China. Thus, any public assembly governed by Hong Kong law (even one as large as Occupy Central in 2014) is unlikely to spread to mainland China.

In addition to the decisions of the Human Rights Committee, Hong Kong can also look to 'soft law' instruments for guidance on the relationship between national security and civil liberties. For example, the *Siracusa Principles on the Limitation and Derogation of Provisions in the International Covenant on Civil and Political Rights* set parameters on the extent to which governments can rely on national security as a ground for restricting of freedom of expression and assembly.[69] Under the *Siracusa Principles*, national security may justify measures limiting these rights but only when taken to respond to a genuine threat to the existence of the nation, its territorial integrity or political independence. The *Siracusa Principles* have been cited by the Hong Kong Court of Final Appeal[70] and should be treated as persuasive authority in any future drafting exercise for legislation to further implement Article 23.

While not a UN publication, the *Johannesburg Principles* also provide detailed guidance regarding the relationship between national security laws and freedom of expression, including access to information.[71] Adopted in 1995 by a group of

[67] *Tae-Hoon Park v Republic of Korea*, Comm No 628/1995 (20 October 1998), para 10.3.

[68] See, eg, *Sohn v Republic of Korea*, Comm No 518/1992 (18 March 1994), especially para 10.4.

[69] UN Commission on Human Rights, The Siracusa Principles on the Limitation and Derogation of Provisions in the International Covenant on Civil and Political Rights (E/CN.4/1985/4, 28 September 1984), Part VI, National Security.

[70] See, eg, *HKSAR v Ng Kung Siu* (1999) 2 HKCFAR 442 [52]; *Leung Kwok Hung and Others v HKSAR* (2005) 8 HKCFAR 229 [32], [71].

[71] Johannesburg Principles on National Security, Freedom of Expression and Access to Information, Freedom of Expression and Access to Information (UN Doc E/CN.4/1996/39, 1996), Art 19 (Johannesburg Principles).

37 international experts, the *Johannesburg Principles* have arguably attained the status of the *Siracusa Principles* and should be used as a guide when drafting legislation. Indeed, in 2003, the Hong Kong Government agreed that the *Johannesburg Principles*, while not strictly binding, provided a 'useful benchmark against which the proposals [to implement Article 23] could be judged' and the Government therefore assured the Legislative Council that the proposals were broadly compliant with those principles.[72]

A foundational principle in the *Johannesburg Principles* is that a government should only seek to prohibit expression when it can demonstrate that the expression is intended to incite imminent violence and is likely to do so.[73] Moreover, a government that seeks to restrict freedom of expression on the ground of national security has the burden of first demonstrating that the restriction is necessary to protect a legitimate national security interest.[74] This means that the genuine purpose and demonstrable effect of the restriction must be to 'protect a country's existence or its territorial integrity against the use or threat of force, or its capacity to respond to the use of force'.[75]

If we apply these principles to Hong Kong, it is difficult to see how the Government could comply with international law if it attempts to use Article 23 offences to prohibit peaceful advocacy for independence.[76] Assume, for example, that a student posts a banner on a university campus endorsing 'peaceful negotiations for Hong Kong's independence'. It is inconceivable that such a banner would pose a genuine threat to the PRC's national security. If a banner of that nature is deemed a 'threat to territorial integrity' then so might an academic article disputing China's territorial claims in the South China Sea or a book proposing that Taiwan should be admitted to the UN. Yet publications of this nature are clearly protected by the ICCPR.

Peaceful advocacy for democratic reforms or other changes to the constitutional framework also should never be considered a threat to national security. Hong Kong cannot amend the Basic Law, but it does have the authority to propose amendments (via a rather complicated mechanism involving a vote by the local Legislative Council and Hong Kong's Deputies to the National People's Congress and consent of the Chief Executive).[77] Thus, by definition, Hong Kong residents must have the freedom to discuss and peacefully advocate for amendments to any provision in the Basic Law, including Article 1, which describes the territory as an 'inalienable' part of China.

[72] See Security Bureau, 'Proposals to Implement Article 23 Broadly Consistent with the Johannesburg Principles' (LC Paper No CB(2)1577/02-03(02), March 2003), available at www.legco.gov.hk/yr02-03/english/bc/bc55/papers/bc550325cb2-1577-2e.pdf.

[73] Johannesburg Principles (n 71), Principle 6.

[74] ibid, Principle 1(d).

[75] ibid, Principle 2(a).

[76] See also the contribution of Simon Young in this collection.

[77] Basic Law, Art 159.

The ECtHR reached a similar conclusion in the case of *Stankov and the United Macedonian Organisation Ilinden v Bulgaria*.[78] The Court held that the mere fact that a group of persons were likely to call for autonomy or request secession could not, by itself, justify a prohibition on that group's assemblies. This is because simply 'Advocating for territorial changes in speeches and demonstrations does not automatically amount to a threat to the country's territorial integrity and national security'.[79]

The ECtHR has also considered a number of cases arising from Turkey in the context of a violent separatist movement. For example, in *Sürek v Turkey*, the ECtHR accepted Turkey's argument that it was necessary to prosecute the applicant for commentary that described the actions of the PKK (a terrorist organisation) as a struggle for 'national liberation' and supported its use of armed force.[80] However, the ECtHR was far more sceptical when Turkey prosecuted individuals who simply used harsh language to criticise the Government. Thus, Turkey violated the Convention when it prosecuted the applicant for circulating a pamphlet that accused the Government of harassing Kurdish traders and urged citizens to oppose harassment through their neighbourhood committees.[81] The ECtHR rejected Turkey's assertion that the pamphlet threatened national security or territorial integrity. Similarly, when Turkey prosecuted a trade union president for writing an article that condemned acts of 'state terrorism' against the Kurdish people, the ECtHR found that the conviction was disproportionate because there was no evidence that he was encouraging violence against the state.[82]

The *Johannesburg Principles* also provide that a restriction on speech cannot be justified on grounds of national security if the 'genuine purpose or demonstrable effect' of the restriction is to entrench a particular ideology or protect a government from criticism.[83] This is a delicate matter in the context of Hong Kong because Beijing is accustomed to stifling criticism in mainland China. In contrast, under the Joint Declaration, the ICCPR and the Basic Law, residents of Hong Kong have a right to criticise both the local and national governments. The disappearance of Lee Bo from Hong Kong has already shaken the confidence of Hong Kong people.[84] It is essential that no local legislation be enacted that could further undermine the right to criticise public figures.

The *Johannesburg Principles* also provide guidance on access to information and the rights of journalists. For example, laws prohibiting 'theft of state secrets' must not be used to prevent politicians, journalists and the general public from

[78] *Stankov and the United Macedonian Organisation Ilinden v Bulgaria*, ECHR (First Section), Applications nos 29221/95 and 29225/95 (2001).

[79] ibid, para 97.

[80] *Sürek v Turkey (No 3)*, ECHR (Grand Chamber), Application no 24735/94 (1999).

[81] *Incal v Turkey*, ECHR (9 June 1998), in *Reports of Judgments and Decisions* 1998-IV, p 1569.

[82] *Ceylon v Turkey*, ECHR (Grand Chamber) (1999).

[83] Johannesburg Principles (n 71), Principle 2(a).

[84] See, eg, O Chou and P Siu, 'One year on: Hong Kong Bookseller saga leaves too many questions unanswered' *South China Morning Post*, 29 December 2016.

obtaining access to information about government operations. A government should not categorically deny access to information, but rather should designate only those 'specific and narrow categories of information' that must be withheld to protect a legitimate national security interest.[85] Journalists' sources must be protected,[86] and individuals who obtain information by virtue of government service should not be penalised for disclosure if the public interest outweighs the harm.[87]

Finally, under the ICCPR and the *Johannesburg principles*, an individual accused of a security-related offence must be given all of the normal procedural protections under international law.[88] If a government seeks extraordinary powers of investigation or detention then it must be able to show that these powers do not violate fundamental rights of due process and are truly necessary to respond to a genuine threat to national security.

In addition to the *Johannesburg Principles*, we now have the benefit of General Comment 34, which was adopted by the Human Rights Committee in 2011 to provide additional guidance on obligations under Article 19 of the ICCPR.[89] One of the topics that was discussed at length during the deliberations of General Comment 34 was the need to ensure that 'national security' and 'public order' do not become broad exceptions to the general duty to protect freedom of expression and access to information.[90] Rather, governments must ensure that 'treason laws and similar provisions relating to national security, whether described as official secrets or sedition laws or otherwise, are crafted and applied in a manner that conforms to the strict requirements' of the ICCPR.[91]

General Comment 34 is similar to the *Johannesburg Principles* in that it reiterates that limitations on freedom of expression and access to information are only consistent with the ICCPR if the restrictions meet the tests of necessity and proportionality; thus, the Government must adopt the least intrusive means to achieve the legitimate aim. In addition, any restrictions provided by law 'must be formulated with sufficient precision to enable an individual to regulate his or her conduct accordingly and it must be made accessible to the public'.[92] This is an important principle, particularly because some of the terms used in the 2003 Bill were rather vague. For example, the term 'intimidate the Central People's Government' (part of the definition of the offences of subversion and treason as proposed in 2003) is capable of many interpretations.

The legislation proposed in 2003 also contained vague language regarding theft of 'state secrets'. In fact, Hong Kong's Official Secrets Ordinance already contains

[85] Johannesburg Principles (n 71), Principle 13.
[86] ibid, Principle 18.
[87] ibid, Principle 16.
[88] ibid, Principle 20.
[89] UN Human Rights Committee, 'General Comment No 34. Article 19: Freedoms of opinion and expression' (CCPR/C/GC/34, 12 September 2011).
[90] ibid, para 34.
[91] ibid, para 30.
[92] ibid, paras 24–25.

several offences relating to espionage and protects a wide range of government information from unauthorised disclosure. The Bill proposed in 2003 sought to expand this by also prohibiting unauthorised and damaging disclosure of any information or document 'that relates to any affairs of the HKSAR which are, under the Basic Law, within the responsibility of the Central Authorities'. The problem is that this term is never definitively defined in the Basic Law. At one point, many of us assumed that this referred to the enumerated powers of the Central Government plus matters of defence and foreign affairs. But lately it appears that the Central Government has expanded the areas in which it can assume responsibility.[93] In any event, people need a more precise definition in order to protect themselves from potential legal liability.

The Human Rights Committee has also confirmed that the right to freedom of expression includes a right of public access to information that is in the public interest. Thus laws purporting to protect national security must not become a general vehicle for suppressing that access. General Comment 34 notes that:

> It is not compatible with paragraph 3, for instance, to invoke [national security] laws to suppress or withhold from the public information of legitimate public interest that does not harm national security or to prosecute journalists, researchers, environmental activists, human rights defenders, or others, for having disseminated such information. Nor is it generally appropriate to include in the remit of such laws such categories of information as those relating to the commercial sector, banking and scientific progress.[94]

This is an essential principle if Hong Kong is to continue to be viewed as a reasonably transparent government and one of the leaders in Asia in the campaign against corruption. Sadly, there is already less confidence in the ability of the Independent Commission Against Corruption to operate without political interference.[95] In that atmosphere, it is absolutely essential that no new restrictions are enacted that could hamper the ability of journalists to obtain information on possible wrongdoing by government officials.

IV. International Monitoring of Civil Liberties in Hong Kong

Critics of the 'one country, two systems' model of autonomy often complain about the lack of enforcement mechanisms in the Joint Declaration and the lack of

[93] For example, the NPCSC is using its power to issue legislative interpretations of the Hong Kong Basic Law more aggressively, so as to influence local legislation and even ongoing litigation. See, eg, Hong Kong Bar Association, 'Comments of the Hong Kong Bar Association on the Outline of the Third Report of the Hong Kong Special Administrative Region for the United Nations Human Rights Council Universal Periodic Review' (7 May 2018), available at www.hkba.org/events-publication/submission-position-papers/2018, especially paras 1–9.

[94] General Comment No 34 (n 89), para 30.

[95] See, eg, 'Hong Kong Loses a Corruption Watchdog: the Politicization of the ICAC Shows Beijing's Growing Political Control' *Wall Street Journal*, 14 July 2016.

remedies if the treaty is violated. Although it is true that the Joint Declaration has no express provisions for dispute resolution, that does not mean that violations have no consequences. At the UN, the Human Rights Committee (the treaty-monitoring body for the ICCPR) is the most relevant body because its mission is to monitor the rights that could be affected by Article 23 legislation. The Committee conducts a separate periodic review of the HKSAR and sends reminders to the local government if it does not comply with the Concluding Observations. The Committee's last review of Hong Kong occurred in 2013 and the Government's report for the next review is now more than one year late.[96] Although the Government's report may not even mention Article 23, the Committee can still seek information on plans, if any, for drafting legislation. Hong Kong's non-governmental organisations are also well versed in the international reporting process and regularly submit 'shadow reports' to the Human Rights Committee. This means that any proposed legislation to curtail ICCPR-protected rights will be swiftly brought to the attention of the Human Rights Committee.

The UN Human Rights Council also reviews the situation in Hong Kong whenever China undergoes Universal Periodic Review (UPR), which last occurred in November 2018. Although the Hong Kong Government's portion of China's report largely avoided discussing recent threats to civil liberties,[97] non-governmental organisations raised these issues in their 'stakeholder reports' and certain governments asked pointed questions concerning Hong Kong. For example, the Netherlands asked about threats to press freedom and Germany expressed concerns regarding the power of the NPCSC to interpret Hong Kong's Basic Law. The United States (US) asked for China's response to 'growing international concern' regarding Beijing's 'continued encroachment on Hong Kong's autonomy, the abduction of individuals from Hong Kong, and growing restrictions on the freedoms of expression, association, and political participation.'[98] The final report of the Working Group on Universal Periodic Review further highlighted human rights issues in Hong Kong, which was not done in previous reviews of China.[99] The Chinese Government 'accepted' the recommendations relating to

[96] Public consultation on Hong Kong's report (which was due on 30 March 2018) ended on 12 January 2018. For an outline of topics to be covered, see Constitutional and Mainland Affairs Bureau, 'An Outline of the Topics to be Covered in the Fourth Report of the Hong Kong Special Administrative Region in the Light of the International Covenant on Civil and Political Rights' (2017), available at www.cmab.gov.hk/doc/en/documents/policy_responsibilities/the_rights_of_the_individuals/ICCPR4_Outline_Full-e.pdf.

[97] See Constitutional and Mainland Affairs Bureau, 'Report of the Hong Kong Special Administrative Region for the United Nations Human Rights Council Universal Periodic Review' (2018), available at www.cmab.gov.hk/doc/en/documents/policy_responsibilities/the_rights_of_the_individuals/human/upr_3rd/UPR_3rd_report_full_e.pdf.

[98] See UN Human Rights Council, 'Universal Periodic Review – China', Advance Questions to China (First Batch), available at www.ohchr.org/EN/HRBodies/UPR/Pages/CNIndex.aspx.

[99] UN Human Rights Council, 'Report of the Working Group on the Universal Periodic Review: China' (UN Doc A/HRC/40/6, 26 December 2018); A Lum, 'In a UN First, Hong Kong's human rights situation singled out from China's, with city's global reputation at stake, 45 civil society groups say' *South China Morning Post*, 7 November 2018.

civil liberties in Hong Kong and claimed to have already implemented them.[100] Thus, China has implicitly acknowledged that the Human Rights Council has the right to assess Hong Kong's compliance with international norms.

If Article 23 is implemented in a manner that blatantly violates the Joint Declaration then I would argue that the UN Committee on Decolonisation and the General Assembly also have a duty to assess whether 'one country, two systems' is providing a meaningful form of internal self-determination. The General Assembly has the power to request an advisory opinion from the ICJ on whether China's actions in Hong Kong are in accordance with international law, including the Joint Declaration and the ICCPR. Given China's expanding economic power, it would be difficult, at this point, to obtain votes in the General Assembly for such a request. But states can lose their influence over time, as the UK discovered when the General Assembly requested an advisory opinion on the Chagos islands.[101] The ICJ has also made it clear that it will not decline to issue an advisory opinion simply because the request relates to a bilateral dispute and one of the parties has not consented to ICJ jurisdiction.[102] As long as the purpose of the request is to obtain the ICJ's guidance regarding discharge of the General Assembly's functions then the ICJ will likely provide the requested advice.[103] In this regard, it should be noted that the General Assembly has the power to re-inscribe a former colony on the list of non-self-governing territories if the process of decolonisation was not completed in accordance with international law.[104]

The UK also has a separate right, and indeed an obligation, to assess whether China is complying with the Joint Declaration and to protest if legislation implementing Article 23 conflicts with the treaty. Since 1997, the Secretary of State for Foreign and Commonwealth Affairs has reported every six months to the British Parliament on implementation of the Joint Declaration. The 44th Report, delivered in March 2019, details numerous controversies and notes that confidence in Hong Kong's ability to maintain civil liberties has declined.[105]

In fact, virtually every foreign government has a legitimate interest in monitoring civil liberties and the rule of law in Hong Kong. This is because foreign governments often treat Hong Kong differently from mainland China.

[100] UN Human Rights Council, 'Report of the Working Group on the Universal Periodic Review: China, Addendum: Views on conclusions and/or recommendations, voluntary commitments and replies presented by the State under review' (UN Doc A/HRC/40/6/Add.1, 15 February 2019).

[101] O Bowcott, 'EU members abstain as Britain defeated in UN vote on Chagos Islands: Mauritius supported by 94 nations in move to consult the Hague over colonial hold of Indian Ocean territory by British' *The Guardian*, 22 June 2017.

[102] See *Legal Consequences of the Construction of a Wall in the Occupied Palestinian Territory, Advisory Opinion* 2004 *ICJ* 136, paras 44–50; *Legal Consequences of the Separation of the Chagos Archipelago From Mauritius in 1965, Advisory Opinion* (25 February 2019), paras 83–90.

[103] *Legal Consequences of the Separation of the Chagos Archipelago From Mauritius in 1965, Advisory Opinion* (25 February 2019), para 86.

[104] The General Assembly re-inscribed French Polynesia in 2013, despite France's objections.

[105] Secretary for State for Foreign and Commonwealth Affairs, 'The Six-Monthly Report on Hong Kong: 1 July to 31 December 2018', available at www.gov.uk/government/collections/six-monthly-reports-on-hong-kong, p 18.

For example, the United States–Hong Kong Policy Act, which was enacted in 1992, provides that the US would continue to treat Hong Kong separately from mainland China for the purposes of trade and export controls, thus allowing Hong Kong to have access to sensitive technologies. However, the special treatment can be withdrawn if the US Government determines that Hong Kong is no longer sufficiently autonomous to justify being treated differently from the PRC.[106] The US State Department therefore produces annual reports on Hong Kong and has noted (in its 2019 report) numerous actions by the Central Government that 'appeared inconsistent with China's commitments' in the Basic Law and the Joint Declaration.[107] The US–China Economic and Security Review Commission has also expressed concerns regarding Beijing's increased encroachment on Hong Kong' autonomy and civil liberties.[108] It has recommended that Congress direct the US Department of Commerce and other relevant government agencies to prepare a public report, with a classified annex, examining and assessing the adequacy of US export control policy for dual-use technology as it relates to the US treatment of Hong Kong and China as separate customs areas. The Commission also recommended increased monitoring of China's adherence to the Basic Law, with specific attention to rule of law, freedom of speech and assembly and press freedom.[109]

Hong Kong also has its own extradition treaties with foreign governments, including many governments that would not be willing to enter into extradition treaties with mainland China because they do not trust its criminal justice system.[110] At present, Hong Kong does not have an extradition agreement with mainland China and thus foreign governments need not worry that a person surrendered to Hong Kong may be forcibly transferred to the mainland. However, the local government recently proposed a process for 'case-based' surrender to jurisdictions with which Hong Kong has no long-term agreement, including the mainland.[111] Although large-scale public demonstrations in the summer of 2019 compelled the Government to suspend the Bill, as of this writing the Bill had not

[106] United States–Hong Kong Policy Act of 1992, 22 USC Ch 66, ss 5701–5731.

[107] US State Department, Bureau of East Asian and Pacific Affairs, '2019 Hong Kong Policy Act Report' (21 March 2019), available at www.state.gov/2019-hong-kong-policy-act-report.

[108] US-China Economic and Security Review Commission, '2018 Report to Congress of the US-China Economic and Security Review Commission' (2018) 16. The Commission was created by Congress in 2000 to monitor, investigate, and submit to Congress an annual report on the national security implications of the bilateral trade and economic relationship between the US and the PRC and to provide recommendations to Congress.

[109] ibid 24.

[110] For a list of countries that have negotiated Mutual Legal Assistance Agreements with Hong Kong, see Department of Justice, 'List of Mutual Legal Assistance Agreements', available at www.doj.gov.hk/eng/laws/table3ti.html.

[111] For a critique, see Hong Kong Bar Association, 'Observations of the Hong Kong Bar Association on the Security Bureau's Proposal to Amend the Mutual Legal Assistance in Criminal Matters Ordinance, Cap 525 and the Fugitive Offenders Ordinance, Cap 503' (4 March 2019), available at www.hkba.org/events-publication/submission-position-papers.

been formally withdrawn. If this (highly controversial) proposal is ever enacted then Hong Kong's existing extradition agreements may be 'revisited by foreign countries'.[112]

V. Conclusion

Autonomy has long been considered a peaceful means of accommodating conflicting rights and 'one country, two systems' was initially viewed as providing a particularly high degree of autonomy. In theory, Article 23 of the Basic Law reinforces that autonomy by allowing Hong Kong to enact its own laws protecting national security. In practice, however, it will be difficult for Hong Kong to implement Article 23 in a manner that complies with international norms while also satisfying the demands of the Central Government. This makes it all the more important for the UN and foreign governments to continue monitoring civil liberties and the rule of law in the HKSAR.

[112] ibid paras 15–16.

14

Maintaining Institutional Strength: The Court, the Act of State and the Rule of Law

JOHANNES CHAN

Protection of national security and respect for personal liberty and the rule of law are not always on speaking terms. In the Hong Kong context, the conflicts between them are exacerbated by the diametrically opposing social and political values between Hong Kong and China. While an enlightened legislature and vibrant civil society are important in maintaining balance between rights and security in devising the legislative framework and monitoring its implementation,[1] the courts' role is crucial for they are the ultimate safeguard for human rights and the rule of law in the enforcement of national security legislation. This role is of particular importance in the sensitive area of national security which, in the Hong Kong context, refers to the security interest of the sovereign. The Hong Kong courts have to balance legitimate national interests and overzealous intervention by the Sovereign on the one hand and the integrity of the common law system and fundamental liberty on the other. This role may be seriously hampered by the vague concept of act of state under the Basic Law which restricts the jurisdiction of the courts. Unfortunately, the concept of act of state is equally elusive under the common law. The problem is further exacerbated by the power of final interpretation of the Basic Law being vested in a political organ of mainland China, the inherently secret nature of national security, and the weak adherence to procedural and evidential safeguards in the mainland legal system. This chapter will address the jurisdictional limits on the courts in handling national security matters, arguing for a narrow doctrine of act of state, fine-tuning the special advocate procedure, and strengthening the independence of the judiciary and the prosecuting authority.

[1] See also the contributions of Margaret Ng and Michael Davis in this collection.

I. Act of State and Fact of State

Under Article 19(3) of the Basic Law, the courts of the Hong Kong Special Administrative Region (HKSAR) shall have no jurisdiction over 'acts of state such as defence and foreign affairs'. Articles 13 and 14 further provide that foreign affairs and defence of the HKSAR shall be the responsibility of the Central Government. These provisions are clearly intended to identify 'forbidden areas' beyond the reach of Hong Kong courts, but a few questions arise. What is the meaning of an 'act of state'? Does it cover only defence and foreign affairs? Do matters of national security necessarily fall within the meaning of an 'act of state' so that they are outside the jurisdiction of the courts? The phrase 'such as', which exists in both the English and the Chinese versions, suggests that an 'act of state' may be wider than defence and foreign affairs; if so, what would it cover? And who should decide whether certain act is an 'act of state'?

As an archaic common law doctrine, 'act of state' is difficult to define and its scope is still evolving. Its origins lie in thirteenth-century powers to seize ships or cargoes at sea under letters of marque and reprisal issued on the authority of the Crown. By the eighteenth century, as a result of the expansion of British naval power, it became necessary to refine the concept so as to bring it in line with international and municipal law. Sir William Murray, later Lord Mansfield, the law officer of the Crown, opined in 1753 that the seizure of the property on behalf of the Crown gave rise to no right to damages or possession at the suit of the former owner.[2] The doctrine underwent further changes in the nineteenth century. In the celebrated decision of *Secretary of State in Council of India v Kamachee Boye Sahaba*,[3] Lord Kingsdown explained the doctrine as one of exercise of the sovereign power the effects of which

> may have been just or unjust, politic or impolitic, beneficial or injurious, taken as a whole, to those whose interests are affected. These are considerations into which their Lordship cannot enter. It is sufficient to say that, even if a wrong has been done, it is a wrong for which no Municipal Court of Justice can afford a remedy.[4]

Since then, it has been the position under the common law that the court has no jurisdiction over certain sovereign acts that were performed in the field of international affairs in the course of its relationship with another state or its subject. Most of these acts are prerogative in nature, such as 'the making of treaties, the defence of the realm, the prerogative of mercy, the grant of honours, the dissolution of Parliament and the appointment of ministers',[5] and 'the conduct

[2] *Mohammed v Ministry of Defence* [2017] 2 WLR 287 [101] (Lord Neuberger PSC): 'any attempt to define the precise nature and extent of the principle of Crown act of state is doomed to failure'. Unfortunately, there were only a handful of cases on this doctrine in the last two centuries.

[3] *Secretary of State in Council of India v Kamachee Boye Sahaba* (1859) 7 Moo Ind App 476, 540.

[4] ibid.

[5] *Council of Civil Service Unions v Minister for the Civil Service (CCSU)* [1985] AC 374, 418 (Lord Roskill).

of foreign affairs … making peace and war, conquering or annexing territories',[6] and recognising foreign states and diplomats.[7]

However, the fact that something is an exercise of prerogative power does not mean that it is automatically an act of state. The starting point, as recognised by the United Kingdom (UK) Supreme Court recently, is that

> English law does not recognise that there is an indefinite class of acts concerning matters of high policy or public security which may be left to the uncontrolled discretion of the government and which are outside the jurisdiction of the courts.[8]

Accordingly, the mere fact that a wrongdoing is an act done at the command of the sovereign is no defence. The enactment of the Crown Proceedings Act 1947, which abolished the general immunity of the Sovereign from tort liability, caused further erosion to the immunity. The act of the Crown and its agents are always in principle subject to the jurisdiction of the courts. Finally, while the Crown can do no wrong, and the Sovereign cannot be sued in tort, the person who did the wrongful act is liable in damages, as any private person would be.[9] Hence, a minister of the Crown could be found to be personally liable for contempt.[10]

A. The Crown Act of State

The modern doctrine of act of state comprises two distinct aspects: the Crown act of state and the Foreign act of state. The Crown act of state in turn comprises two aspects. The first is a principle of non-justiciability under which 'certain acts committed by a sovereign state are, by their very nature, not susceptible to adjudication in courts'.[11] Annexations and cessions of territory, or declarations of war and peace, are obvious examples. The second principle is a defence to an action in tort, under which 'a foreigner cannot sue the Government, or its servants or agents, in the courts of this country in respect of certain acts committed abroad pursuant to deliberate UK policy in the conduct of its foreign affairs'.[12]

[6] *Mohammed v Ministry of Defence* (n 2) [15] (Baroness Hale DPSC). An example of annexation of territories is *In re Wong Hon* [1959] HKLR 601, where the Full Court held that the New Territories Order in Council 1898 and the Kowloon City Order in Council 1899 declaring the extent of the jurisdiction acquired by the Crown under the second Peking Convention, which jurisdiction was extended to the Walled City, was an act of state binding on the court.

[7] *Carl Zeiss Stifung v Rayner & Keeler Ltd* [1967] 1 AC 853, 961. See also the *Congo* case (n 25 below) 483.

[8] *Mohammed v Ministry of Defence* (n 2) [4] (Baroness Hale DPSC), quoting H Street, *Governmental Liability: A Comparative Study* (Cambridge, Cambridge University Press, 1953) 50.

[9] *Johnstone v Pedlar* [1921] 2 AC 262, 271 (Viscount Finlay).

[10] *Re M* [1994] 1 AC 377.

[11] *Mohammed v Ministry of Defence* (n 2) [7] (Baroness Hale DJSC).

[12] ibid. See also *Burton v Denman* (1848) 2 Exch 167; *Attorney General v Nissan* [1970] AC 179.

These two aspects were best summarised by Lord Wilberforce in *Attorney General v Nissan*:[13]

> The first rule is one which provides a defendant, normally a servant of the Crown, with a defence to an act otherwise tortious or criminal, committed abroad, provided that the act was authorized or subsequently ratified by the Crown. It is established that this defence may be pleaded against an alien, if done abroad, but not against a friendly alien if the act was done in Her Majesty's Dominions …
>
> The second rule is one of justiciability: it prevents British municipal courts from taking cognizance of certain acts. The class of acts so protected has not been accurately defined: one formulation is 'those acts of the Crown which are done under the prerogative in the sphere of foreign affairs (Wade & Phillips's *Constitutional Law*, 7th ed, (1956), p 263). As regards such acts it is certainly the law that the injured person, if an alien, cannot sue in a British court and can only have resort to diplomatic protest. How far this rule goes and how far it prevents resort to the courts by British subjects is not a matter on which clear authority exists.

In the recent case of *Mohammed v Ministry of Defence*, the UK Supreme Court could not agree on whether the Crown act of state is comprised of one or two rules. The issue in that case was whether the British armed forces, acting as part of a multi-national force, established by a United Nations Security Council resolution and under NATO command, to maintain security in Afghanistan, was liable in tort for the arrest and detention for some months of the applicant, an Afghanistan citizen, in the first case, and the transfer of the claimants, who were citizens of Pakistan and Iraq and detained in Iraq by the British armed forces, to the United States armed forces pursuant to an agreement between the UK and the United States of America, in the second case. The Ministry of Defence pleaded the Crown act of state as defence, which was upheld by Baroness Hale DPSC, joined by Lord Wilson and Lord Hughes JJSC. They held that the act of state doctrine was a very narrow doctrine and 'cannot give *carte blanc* to the authorities to authorise or ratify any class of tortious acts committed abroad in the conduct of the foreign relations of the state'.[14] Its essential elements are: (1) the act should be an exercise of sovereign power, inherently governmental in nature. This is to be determined by the character of the act, and the nature of the act has to be an inherently governmental act that is capable of being authorised or ratified by the Crown. Thus, stationing a troop pursuant to an agreement with a foreign state would be an inherently governmental act, but the appropriation of a hotel was not a necessary act of implementation or an inherently governmental act;[15] (2) the act should be done outside the UK; (3) it was done with the prior authority or subsequent ratification of the Crown; and (4) it was done in the conduct of the Crown's

[13] ibid.

[14] *Mohammed v Ministry of Defence* (n 2) [33].

[15] *Attorney General v Nissan* (n 12) 216–17 (Lord Morris) and 227 (Lord Pearce); see also *Mohammed v Ministry of Defence* (n 2) [92]–[93] (Lord Sumption JSC).

relations with other states or their subjects.[16] The acts in question must be closely connected to and be necessary in pursuing the foreign policy.[17] They would be extended to cover the conduct of military operations which are themselves lawful in international law, but Baroness Hale DPSC expressly left open whether the defence could be extended to other situations outside military operations and whether the doctrine could ever be pleaded against British citizens.[18] Her Lady was attracted by the explanation of public policy as the basis of this aspect of an Act of State: it would be contrary to public policy to apply in an English court the tort law of the foreign state where the events took place. The attraction of public policy, as adopted by the Court of Appeal (CA) and explained by Baroness Hale DPSC, was that it would enable the court to consider the matter on a case-by-case basis. Therefore, while the deployment of armed forces in the conduct of international relations, and associated with it the inherent destruction or damage of property or the killing or detention or transfer of the prisoners would be an inherently governmental act, torture or maltreatment of these prisoners would be against English public policy and therefore not an inherently governmental act for the purpose of the Act of State doctrine.[19]

Lord Mance JSC considered that there was only one single doctrine of non-justiciability or, as his Lordship preferred, a principle of abstention or restraint.[20] Non-justiciability is not based on an absence of judicial or manageable standards, but on the basis that the nature and the subject matter are such that the appropriate forum for its control is Parliament (as in the case of the royal prerogative of making war and peace or treaties) or that 'representation and redress in respect of activities involving foreign states and their citizens may be more appropriately pursued at a traditional state-to-state level, rather than by domestic litigation brought by individuals'.[21]

Lord Sumption JSC regarded non-justiciability as a 'treacherous word' that is capable of causing confusion. While his Lordship also referred to an issue which

[16] *Mohammed v Ministry of Defence* (n 2) [37].

[17] Lord Sumption JSC cautioned that the policy might not have to be 'high policy' but may be extended to actions taken by the Crown's agents in the execution of those decisions, and these actions may be far below the level of policy-making, whereas decisions unauthorised but were ratified after the event would unlikely be taken in accordance with any high policy of the Crown: ibid [91]. His Lordship further warned that the court should avoid engaging in an assessment of political or tactical alternatives in considering whether the action was necessary: ibid [92].

[18] Lord Sumption JSC agreed and was, somewhat tentatively, prepared to restrict the defence to the situation where the tort was committed against a person not owing allegiance to the Crown: ibid [81]. Lord Mance JSC likewise agreed: ibid [72].

[19] ibid [35], but see Lord Sumption JSC, ibid [96], who had reservation that it would not be an inherently governmental act, but agreed that it would be contrary to English public policy and hence not a lawful exercise of the royal prerogative and therefore it could not be an act of state.

[20] ibid [47]. His Lordship considered *Buron v Denman* as an example of non-justiciability, and Lord Wilberforce's statement in *Nissan* was not intended to create a bifurcation of the doctrine and was not so regarded by other members of the House: ibid [69]–[70].

[21] ibid [57]. In this regard Lord Sumption JSC agreed that the two rules of Lord Wilberforce in *Nissan* have merged into one.

is inherently unsuitable for judicial determination by reason of its subject matter or its determination not falling within the constitutional competence of the court as, for example, it would trespass on parliamentary privilege, Lord Sumption JSC preferred to justify the doctrine on the nature of the rights involved:[22]

> The court is not disabled from adjudicating on a Crown act of state by virtue of its subject matter. *The acts of the Crown and its agents are always in principle subject to the adjudicative power of the courts.* They unquestionably have both jurisdiction and competence to determine the legal effects of a Crown act of state on the rights of those adversely affected by it. The real question is what are those rights. The rule of law relating to Crown acts of state defines the limits which as a matter of policy, the law acts upon certain categories of rights and liabilities, on the ground that they would otherwise be inconsistent with the exercise by the executive of the proper functions of the state. In principle an agent of the Crown is liable as a matter of English law for injury or detention of persons or goods without lawful authority. But that liability does not extend to a limited class of acts constituting Crown acts of state. It follows that the agent has a defence if his acts fall within that class. (emphasis added)

Thus, as Lord Sumption JSC reasoned, 'the reason why the liabilities of the Crown in municipal law do not extend to sovereign acts done in the course of military operation outside the United Kingdom is essentially a principle of consistency'.[23] The law has conferred on the Crown the power to conduct the UK's international relations, including the deployment of armed force in support of its objectives. Thus, it would be inconsistent, if not also illogical, that the Crown has such power which is beyond the competence of the judiciary and yet the inherent consequences of an exercise of that power would be regarded as civil wrongs.

Notwithstanding the disagreement among members of the Supreme Court on whether the Crown act of state comprises one rule with different aspects or two different rules, and the different justifications for the doctrine, the court was unanimous in holding that the Crown act of state is a narrow doctrine. Accordingly, it ought to be of limited use in excluding Chinese national security operations in Hong Kong from the jurisdiction of Hong Kong courts. For example, as it would be against public policy to arbitrarily deprive a person of his liberty, an abduction of a Swedish citizen in Thailand by the security force of China could not come within the doctrine of an act of state. Nor could the abduction of a Chinese citizen in Hong Kong to the mainland be an act of state, as the doctrine is not available to the subjects of the sovereign or to acts done within the sovereign state. Enforcement of domestic law (such as theft of state secrets or even secession or treason), which is a matter of law and order rather than an exercise of foreign affairs, should likewise be considered as falling outside the scope of an act of state and therefore within the jurisdiction of the domestic courts.

[22] ibid [79]–[80]. Lord Mance JSC disagreed: ibid [48].
[23] ibid [88].

B. Foreign Act of State

While Crown act of state deals with the liability of the Sovereign and its agents for conduct that took place on foreign soil as a matter of state policy, foreign act of state deals with the position of a foreign sovereign in a municipal court, under which the sovereign or governmental acts of one state are not matters upon which the courts of another state will adjudicate.[24] The doctrine operates purely as a rule of non-justiciability and is based on the international comity of equality among sovereign states. The difficulty is again what act would constitute a foreign act of state. This issue was raised in two local cases.

In the *Congo* case,[25] the issue was whether the Democratic Republic of Congo could claim immunity in an application of the applicant company before a Hong Kong court to enforce an arbitral award against Congo, pursuant to the New York Convention on Enforcement of Arbitral Awards to which Hong Kong is a party, by seeking an order to direct a People's Republic of China (PRC) state-owned enterprise to satisfy the arbitral award by fees that the state-owned enterprise was obliged to pay the Congo Government under a separate mining agreement. The Congo Government claimed sovereign immunity. The focus of the litigation was whether, under the law of Hong Kong, a sovereign state could claim absolute immunity or only restricted immunity in matters other than purely commercial transactions. Following a complex set of decisions at first instance and in the CA, the case came before the Court of Final Appeal (CFA) where it took an interesting turn. Under Article 158(3), the CFA is under a duty to refer a question of interpretation of a provision of the Basic Law to the Standing Committee of the National People's Congress (NPCSC) if the provision concerns affairs which are the responsibility of the Central People's Government and its interpretation is necessary for the resolution of the appeal. The focus of the litigation was thus shifted to the issue of whether the CFA should make a judicial referral. By a narrow majority, the CFA held that: (1) the extent of state immunity was a question of act of state under Article 19(3); (2) in light of the constitutional change, the common law principle on state immunity in Hong Kong was now an absolute immunity; (3) the Congo Government had not, by taking part in the arbitration proceedings, waived its immunity; and (4) it was necessary to interpret Articles 13 and 19 of the Basic Law for the resolution of the appeal, and therefore it should make a judicial referral. Four questions were drafted for the interpretation of the NPCSC, and not surprisingly, the NPCSC affirmed that the common law in Hong Kong was now one of absolute immunity.[26]

[24] *I Congresso del Partido* [1983] 1 AC 244, 262. See also, *Buttes Gas and Oil Co v Hammer (No 3)* [1982] AC 888; *Belhaj v Straw* [2015] 2 WLR 1105. See also, *Mohammed v Ministry of Defence* (n 2) [51] (Lord Mance JSC) and [89] (Lord Sumption JSC).

[25] *Democratic Republic of the Congo v FG Hemisphere Associates LLC (No 1)* (2011) 14 HKCFAR 95.

[26] *Democratic Republic of the Congo v FG Hemisphere Associates LLC (No 2)* (2011) 14 HKCFAR 395, 428 (where the Interpretation was annexed).

There is an element of contradiction in the decision of the majority of the CFA. If the extent of state immunity was an act of state under Article 19(3), it would be outside the jurisdiction of the Hong Kong court. It follows that it would not be for the Hong Kong court to determine whether the law in Hong Kong is absolute or restricted. Nor would it be relevant to decide whether state immunity was waived. The decisions of the majority on these issues would be relevant only if the extent of state immunity is not an act of state. Thus, of the four questions referred to the NPCSC for interpretation, three were probably misconceived. The fourth question on whether the common law on restricted state immunity previously in force in Hong Kong was inconsistent with the change of sovereignty and therefore should be modified or adapted was a wrong question. The common law to be changed is not whether state immunity is absolute or restricted, but whether the extent of state immunity is within the meaning of an act of state so that it is outside the jurisdiction of the Hong Kong courts. This is indeed the third question, which is the only relevant question. The second question whether the Hong Kong court is at liberty to apply the rule on restricted state immunity is irrelevant; it is only relevant if the extent of state immunity is not an act of state, but in that situation the extent of state immunity would be a matter of common law for Hong Kong and no referral on this question would be necessary. The first question on whether the Central People's Government has the power to determine the rule or policy of the PRC on state immunity is redundant. The answer must be yes. The question is whether such rule of policy shall apply to Hong Kong. If it is a matter of an act of state, which is the third question, then the matter would necessarily be a matter of foreign affairs and hence within the scope of Article 13.

This analysis leads to another issue: who should decide whether an act falls within the meaning of an act of state? If the determination of whether a matter falls within the meaning of 'act of state such as defence and foreign affairs' under Article 19(3) is necessarily a matter of defence and foreign affairs, the CFA will be obliged to refer the question to the NPCSC under Article 158(3) of the Basic Law. The net effect is that the court will no longer have a final say on what constitutes an act of state.

This takes us back to the central issue: is the extent of state immunity an act of state? The common law position is pretty clear: Whether an entity is a sovereign state is a matter of an act of state, as it is a matter of foreign relation that is beyond judicial assessment, but the determination of the extent of state immunity enjoyed by a sovereign state is always a matter for the courts. In the course of such determination, the court may take cognisance of or even defer to the views of the executive, but the final decision is always one of the court. Like the position of any common law principle, it can be changed or modified by the Legislature, and the Legislature in a number of jurisdictions has spoken. The UK Parliament enacted the Sovereign Immunity Act in 1978, which was extended to Hong Kong by the State Immunity (Overseas Territories) Order 1979, but this does not detract from the general principle that it is the court that decides the extent of state immunity unless Parliament intervenes. The prerogative order lapsed on 30 June 1997. There was no PRC law or any other applicable local statute on state immunity. Thus, the position, as argued by the minority, is that the extent of state immunity would remain a matter of common law for the court.

The majority did not really disagree with this position. What it decided was that this common law position should be modified in light of the changing constitutional environment. It is perfectly legitimate for the majority to take into consideration the policy and practice of the new sovereign, which adopts the principle of absolute immunity, and consider, whether as a matter of common law, the principle of state immunity should be changed or modified. If the Court decided that, which it did and held that the common law principle should be modified to one of absolute immunity, and stopped at that, the Central People's Government's concern would have been addressed. There would then be no need for an interpretation and the matter would be contained within the common law system. It is unnecessary for the court to go further to decide that the extent of state immunity is an act of state, which would result in a contradictory position of deciding on the content of state immunity and holding at the same time that it had no jurisdiction over the matter, and be led to the treacherous path of judicial referral which means unnecessarily giving up the common law position that the court has the ultimate say on what constitutes an act of state. This led Bokhary PJ, one of the two dissenting judges, to observe, in his extra-judicial writing, that 'what belongs to two systems has been instead assigned by the court to one country and that it is difficult to see how the loss can ever be recovered'.[27] It may be argued that the NPCSC would proceed to an interpretation if the minority prevailed, but this consequence is by no means inevitable if the majority decided that, in light of the changing constitutional framework, the common law principle is modified to one of absolute immunity and hence it is unnecessary to decide if the extent of sovereign immunity is an act of state. The Court did have an opportunity to preserve the common law system and avoid an interpretation from the NPCSC.

The consequence of the NPCSC interpretation is that no sovereign state would be subject to the jurisdiction of Hong Kong courts even when the sovereign state is engaged in purely commercial transactions. This may result in unintended consequences in private law. For example, a landlord who rents a premises to a state for use as its consular general's office or accommodation for its consular staff would have no judicial remedy for repossession or otherwise upon default of payment of rent. This highlights the risk of the NPCSC making final interpretation of the Basic Law for Hong Kong, as even with the best of intention, such interpretation made in the tradition of one legal system without the benefit of full arguments on the interpretation could have unfortunate and unintended consequences in another legal system, let alone that it may unjustifiably carve out

[27] K Bokhary, *Recollections* (Hong Kong, Sweet & Maxwell, 2013) 580.

the jurisdiction of an independent court of Hong Kong on matters of national security by an over-zealous Central Government adopting a broad meaning of act of state when it is precisely in such sensitive area that scrutiny of the court is most important in ensuring a proper balance of individual rights and legitimate state interest.

C. Fact of State

Another unsatisfactory aspect of the *Congo* case is the way evidence was presented to the Court. Three letters from the Ministry of Foreign Affairs were presented to the court through the Secretary for Justice at various stages of the litigation. The first letter, which was placed before Reyes J, stated that the doctrine adopted by the PRC was a doctrine of absolute immunity. The second letter, which was placed before the CA, replied to Reyes J's query on the position of the PRC when she had signed the United Nations Convention on Jurisdictional Immunities of States and their Property 2004, which adopted the position of a restrictive state immunity. The third letter, which was drafted in rather strong language, explained how the adoption of a divergent position by the Hong Kong court on state immunity would prejudice China's sovereignty and hamper its conduct of foreign affairs. The Secretary for Justice fairly pointed out that these letters were not intended to bind the court; they only served to provide evidence on what the foreign policy of China was. Under Article 19(3) of the Basic Law, the court is obliged to obtain a certificate from the Chief Executive 'on questions of fact concerning acts of state such as defence and foreign affairs whenever such questions arise in the adjudication of cases'. The certificate, which must be based on 'a certifying document from the Central People's Government', is binding on the courts. No such certificate has been obtained.

The Court avoided this evidential problem by construing the phrase 'whenever such questions arise in the adjudication of cases' to mean 'whenever there is controversy or doubt about such questions which need to be resolved in adjudicating a case'.[28] It found that the relevant facts 'have been authoritatively established and are not in dispute',[29] and therefore it could not have been intended that 'the Chief Executive should be troubled'.[30] This position is highly unsatisfactorily and factually wrong. One of the issues before the Court was whether it would cause any embarrassment to the PRC if the Hong Kong courts adopted a different doctrine of state immunity from the Central Government.[31] The applicant

[28] *Congo* case (n 25) [362].
[29] ibid.
[30] ibid.
[31] ibid [287]–[290].

company argued that a doctrine of restrictive state immunity would cause no prejudice to the state's sovereignty, and the Court held this argument was refuted by the third letter. Likewise, the second letter was a response to a query made by Reyes J. It would be most unsatisfactory that matters of such importance were to be left to be addressed by a letter. The purpose underlying the procedure in Article 19(3) is that important factual issues pertaining to questions of an act of state, which would have the effect of removing the jurisdiction of the courts, shall be certified in the most formal and serious manner by the state. It is not a matter to be addressed by consent, and the approach of the court will leave unsatisfactory questions of who could provide such evidence and when such evidence would be considered sufficient in the absence of a formal certificate from the Chief Executive. The dispensation, which was done purely on ground of inconvenience, was highly satisfactory, and the difficulty was graphically illustrated in the case of *Hua Tian Long (No 2)*.[32]

In *Hua Tian Long (No 2)*, a vessel, being the largest floating derrick crane-barge based in Asia, was arrested for an alleged breach of contract. The vessel was eventually released upon the payment of a substantial bond, and then the owner of the vessel, the Guangdong Savage Bureau (GZS), claimed sovereign immunity and alternatively Crown immunity before the Hong Kong courts on the basis that it was an entity of the Central People's Government. The factual basis for the claim for immunity was sought to be established by assertions, including hearsay evidence, made by an employee of GZS in successive affirmations, with conflicting expert evidence before the court. The court expressed dissatisfaction at such an approach and urged that a procedure for a certificate of the Chief Executive should be adopted in an important constitutional area involving the assertion of Crown immunity. It is more than a mere formality, as the evidential rule is to protect the right to fair trial and enables the parties to know and challenge what can or cannot be admissible in courts. The *Congo* and the *Hua Tian Long* cases highlighted the relatively under-developed understanding of procedural safeguards and evidential rules in the mainland. Given the inherent sensitivity and secrecy of national security, over which the courts have limited power of scrutiny, it is of singular importance that the Hong Kong courts should be vigilant in enforcing procedural and evidential requirements.

D. Crown Immunity

Hua Tian Long (No 2) gave rise to another serious issue. The Court of First Instance has no difficulty in rejecting the claim for sovereign immunity, which is based on equality among sovereign states and has no application between

[32] *Hua Tian Long (No 2)* [2010] 3 HKLRD 611.

different provinces within the same state. In contrast, Crown immunity has always been part of the common law. Notwithstanding the enactment of the Crown Proceedings Ordinance in 1957 which enabled the Hong Kong Government to be sued, the general position of the British Crown remained unaltered. Upon the change of sovereignty, it was held that the PRC in turn enjoyed similar 'Crown immunity' hitherto accorded to the British Crown. The claim eventually failed on the narrow ground that GZS has waived its immunity by taking part in the litigation.

This is a startling, if not also worrying, decision. Hua Tian Long was originally owned by a state-owned enterprise that was established in October 1989. Consequent upon a 2003 reform, it was owned by the Guangzhou Salvage Bureau of the Ministry of Communication of the PRC.[33] The dispute involved a failure to make available the vessel, contrary to an agreement between the plaintiff, a commercial enterprise and GZS, for two offshore oil development projects, and the reason for the failure was allegedly because the vessel was chartered to another commercial entity which refused to release the vessel for the plaintiff's use. There was conflicting evidence on the status, the nature and the organisational structure of GZS,[34] and yet the court made a far-reaching finding that a government bureau affiliated to and under the control of a Ministry of the Central Government would step into the shoe of the sovereign and became the *personam* of the sovereign. This requires a leap and would effectively mean any government entity of the PRC, even down to the provincial level, would be able to claim immunity from the jurisdiction of the Hong Kong courts in plainly commercial activities. This position is difficult to reconcile with Article 22 of the Basic Law, which provides that all offices set up by departments of the Central Government, provinces, autonomous regions or municipalities directly under the Central Government and their personnel shall abide by the laws of the HKSAR. Besides, and more fundamentally, the court has failed to distinguish between the Crown as the monarch and the Crown as executive, and therefore erroneously assumed that the British Crown means the British Government.[35] Crown immunity stems from the royal prerogative that the Sovereign can do no wrong. Since the Case of *Proclamations*, the courts have jealously guarded their jurisdiction to define the ambit of the Crown, and the absolute privilege of the monarch has been severely curtailed over the time, notably as a rise of parliamentary supremacy. The monarch cannot be sued in her own courts, but her servants and agents could. Prerogatives have been abrogated,

[33] ibid [30].

[34] ibid [98]–[126].

[35] As Lord Templeman pointed out in *Re M* (n 10), at 395: 'The expression "the Crown" has two meanings, namely the monarch and the executive. In the 17th century Parliament established the supremacy over the Crown as monarch, over the executive and over the judiciary …. Parliamentary supremacy over the judiciary is only exercisable by statute. The judiciary enforces the law against individuals, against institutions and against the executive. The judges cannot enforce the law against the Crown as monarch because the Crown as monarch can do no wrong but judges enforce the law against the Crown as executive and against the individual who from time to time represent the Crown.'

curtailed and subject to judicial review,[36] and ministers could be made personally liable for contempt of court.[37]

E. Some Observations

A core feature of the rule of law is that the executive is not above the law. The exception of an act of state is to an extent an anti-thesis of the rule of law and should hence be narrowly circumscribed. It is ultimately a doctrine based on public policy to delineate the boundary when the judiciary should decline to rule on the lawfulness of an act of the sovereign on the ground that any challenge to the act should be left to the executive, at least normally where the act is an exercise of royal prerogative. It is ironic that this doctrine, which has its origin in the exercise of royal prerogative power and which relies, to some extent, on the doctrine of separation of powers, which has repeatedly been rejected by the Central Government, should find its way in the Basic Law. The explicit reference to this doctrine in Article 19(3) seems to have unnecessarily elevated the importance of this very narrow doctrine; it is also probably redundant, as it forms part of the previous restrictions on the jurisdiction of the courts before the changeover under Article 19(2). Properly understood, this doctrine excludes from the jurisdiction of the court certain acts of the sovereign that was done abroad, and provided immunity of a foreign state in the domestic court. Foreign act of state is less relevant in the context of national security, whereas the Crown act of state is likely to be raised when the liability of an agent of the Central Government is in question. The Crown act of state doctrine could not be invoked against a subject; nor could it be relied upon to justify an act which is not lawful internationally, as it would not be an inherently governmental act to defy international law. Thus, an abduction of Hong Kong Permanent Residents in a foreign country to the mainland could not be defended as an act of state. Nor would the defence be available when a Hong Kong Permanent Resident in Hong Kong is abducted to the mainland by security force of the mainland.

While most of the acts of foreign affairs and defence would come within the scope of an act of state, not all acts of foreign affairs and defence would qualify. It is still an evolving doctrine under the common law, and hence, the words 'such as' in Article 19 should be so understood, rather than providing a springboard to enlarge the doctrine as one sees fit. The act of state doctrine also touches on sensitive issues between the Central Government and the HKSAR. The challenge of the court is to maintain a delicate balance between the interests of the sovereign and the integrity

[36] *CCSU* case (n 5). For a more detailed discussion, see J Chan, 'Prospect for the Due Process under Chinese Sovereignty' in S Tsang (ed), *Judicial Independence and the Rule of Law in Hong Kong* (Basingstoke, Palgrave, 2001) ch 6.

[37] *Re M* (n 10). See also *R v Home Secretary and Criminal Injuries Compensation Board, ex parte P* [1995] 1 All ER 870.

of the common law system. In *Congo*, the Court seems to have been too ready to give up common law principles, whereas in *Hua Tian Long*, the court is too ready to equate the new master with the old sovereign. Both cases involved commercial interest and are arguably wrongly decided. The balance may be even more difficult and sensitive when personal liberty is at stake, which is more likely to be the case when national security is in issue.

II. The Secretary for Justice and the Right to Fair Hearing

Most advocates for the enactment of national security law pursuant to Article 23 seem to suggest that national security could not have been safeguarded in the absence of such enactment. Nothing is of course further from the truth. The existing law of Hong Kong already prohibits treason, sedition, seditious libel, theft of state secrets and proscription of local political organisations or bodies from establishing ties with foreign political organisations or bodies.[38] The existing law on treason is wide enough to cover any act of secession and subversion against the Central People's Government. These laws were enacted before the changeover, and upon the change of sovereignty were adapted and adopted to become the laws of the HKSAR.[39] Thus, contrary to what has been repeatedly claimed, there is no dereliction of constitutional responsibility on the part of the HKSAR for not enacting national security law. That duty has already been discharged on 1 July 1997 when these previously colonial laws were adapted to apply to the Central People's Government. The real issue is whether the existing law is inadequate, and if so, in what way, *or* whether the existing law is too draconian so that revision is required in order for it to be compatible with the protection of fundamental rights in the Basic Law.[40]

The content of these laws has been adequately discussed elsewhere already.[41] It suffices to make two points here. The first observation concerns the office of the Secretary for Justice; the second is about the procedure of special advocate.

[38] See Crimes Ordinance, Cap 200, Parts 1 (Treason) and 2 (Other Offences against the Crown, including seditious libel, mutiny, incitement to disaffection); Official Secrets Ordinance, Cap 521, Part 2 (Espionage) and Part 3 (Unlawful Disclosure); Societies Ordinance, Cap 151, s 8(1) (proscription of society from establishing ties with foreign or Taiwan political organisations or bodies). The reference to Her Majesty, the Crown, the British Government has been modified to mean a reference to the Central People's Government: Interpretation and General Clauses Ordinance, Cap 1, Sch 8, para 1. See also the contribution of Simon Young in this collection.

[39] Hong Kong Reunification Ordinance; Interpretation and General Clauses Ordinance, Cap 1, Sch 8, para 1.

[40] Indeed, it appears that the real issue is whether peaceful advocacy for independence without any action or without any advocacy for the use of force should be prohibited and punished by law in Hong Kong. This question has nothing to do with the constitutional responsibility of the HKSAR under Art 23. It is simply a question how far Hong Kong is prepared to curtail freedom of speech.

[41] See, eg, H Fu, CJ Petersen and SNM Young (eds), *National Security and Fundamental Freedoms: Hong Kong's Article 23 under Scrutiny* (Hong Kong, Hong Kong University Press, 2005) and the contribution of Simon Young in this collection.

A. Secretary for Justice: Conflict of Roles

Upon the change of sovereignty, the post of Attorney-General was renamed as Secretary for Justice, and the Attorney-General's chambers as the Department of Justice. It is widely accepted that the change in nomenclature was not intended to involve any change in the nature of the office. However, in 2002, in an attempt to enhance political accountability of the Government and to foster political neutrality of the civil service, the Government introduced the Principal Officials Accountability System (POAS), under which heads of policy bureaus, who were civil servants, would be replaced by political appointees serving as ministers. As a result, the Secretary for Justice, alongside the Chief Secretary, the Financial Secretary, and another 11 ministers, became political appointees who would shoulder political responsibility and be politically accountable.

The office of the Attorney-General, which has a history of over 700 years, is an anomaly of the British constitutional history. The Attorney-General, or the current Secretary for Justice, is a politician, a minister, a member of the Government, a professional lawyer and the guardian of public interest. She is the principal legal advisor to the Government and government departments, providing legal advice in a confidential manner. She oversees all criminal prosecutions, and represents the Government in all civil matters. She is a member of the Executive Council, and participates in all major policy decisions of the HKSAR. As the most senior legal officer of the Government, she is involved in all discussions on legal matters with the mainland Government. In this regard, she may also have to represent the mainland Government's interests should the occasion arise, such as by intervening in the *Congo* case.[42] At the same time, she is also the guardian of the public interest. She has the duty to protect the due administration of justice, and if necessary to take out contempt proceedings or relator proceedings. She has by convention a duty to defend the judiciary when it is attacked, as it is improper for the judiciary to engage in public debates.[43] The multiplicity of functions make this post a curious one, and the basic problem is that the Secretary for Justice has to be a politician and a minister holding political responsibility and accountability on the one hand, and the guardian of public interest acting impartially and objectively under the law upholding the public interest on the other.[44] The conflict of interests, or at least the perception of a conflict of interests, is apparent. As Lord Woolf pointed out as early as in 1990, in politically sensitive cases involving the

[42] In the *Congo* case (n 25), the Secretary for Justice, who intervened in the litigation, was known to be in regular contact with, if not also taking instructions from, the Ministry of Foreign Affairs in Hong Kong in the process of litigation.

[43] She used to be the titular head of the Bar, but when Mr Jerome Matthews, a solicitor, was appointed as Attorney-General in 1988, the Hong Kong Bar Association decided to sever this link so as to maintain the independence of the Bar.

[44] Samuels described the office of Attorney-General as 'long standing and honourable but undeniably and irredeemably anomalous': A Samuel, 'Abolish the Office of Attorney General' [2014] *Public Law* 609.

Government or controversial criminal prosecution, it would be impossible for the public or the media to distinguish between the role of the Secretary for Justice as a politician and her role as the guardian of public interest.[45] Thus, when the first Secretary for Justice, Ms Elsie Leung, decided not to prosecute the newspaper proprietor Sally Aw Sian (whereas her subordinates in the newspaper were prosecuted for conspiracy to defraud the public/advertisers by fraudulently exaggerating the sales volumes of the newspaper) on the basis that the prosecution would not be in the public interest as it would bring down the newspaper resulting in a lot of unemployment, the public was bewildered. When the Secretary for Justice decided to take out disqualification proceedings against a number of popularly elected legislators for failing to take a proper oath of allegiance;[46] when she decided to review the lenient sentences imposed on three student leaders in a protest that the trial court has found to be restrained and out of public motives without any private gain;[47] and more recently, when she departed from the established practice of the Department of Justice to seek independent legal advice in deciding not to prosecute the former Chief Executive, the Secretary for Justice was widely criticised for doing so out of political motivation, if not also bowing to political pressure. Public confidence in the rule of law is essential in a democratic society, but how could the public have confidence in the Secretary for Justice's ability to separate and compartmentalise her different roles as a minister with her own political responsibilities, an adviser to the Government and other politically appointed ministers, and an independent guardian of public interest in such highly political decisions, particularly in times of political excitement?

There is a strong case for separating these conflicting roles. Article 63 of the Basic Law provides that the Department of Justice, as opposed to the Secretary for Justice, shall control criminal prosecutions, free from any interference. The rationale behind Article 63 is that decisions governing liberties of the persons should not be left to politics. The article was drafted against a strong tradition of the independence of the Attorney-General. The POAS eroded this tradition. Article 63 does not require prosecution decisions to be made by the Secretary for Justice personally, and there is nothing to suggest that such decisions could not be vested in the hands of the Director of Public Prosecutions. Indeed, none of the successive Secretaries for Justice since 1997 specialised in criminal practice, and yet the Secretary for Justice has the power to override the advice of the Director of Public Prosecutions who would invariably be an experienced and senior criminal practitioner. The same consideration applies to the taking

[45] Sir Harry Woolf, Hamlyn Lectures 1990; J Steyn, 'The Weakest and the Least Dangerous Department of Government' [1997] *Public Law* 84, 91–92; AW Bradley, 'Justice, Good Government and Public Interest Immunity' [1992] *Public Law* 514, 517.

[46] *Chief Executive of the HKSAR v The President of the Legislative Council* [2016] 6 HKC 417 (CFI); [2017] 1 HKLRD 460 (CA), (2017) 20 HKCFAR 390 (sub nom *Yau Wai Ching v Chief Executive of the HKSAR*) (1st oath case); *Chief Executive of the HKSAR v President of the Legislative Council* (2017) 4 HKLRD 115 (CFI) (2nd oath case).

[47] *Secretary for Justice v Wong Chi Fung* (2018) 21 HKCFAR 35.

out of civil proceedings. The Secretary for Justice decided not to take over or even participate in the application of taxi associations and mini-bus associations for an injunction to end the occupation of the protesters in the Occupy Central movement on the ground that the Government would remain neutral, and yet he decided to assist the enforcement of the court order by deploying over 5,000 policemen to clear the occupation site. These decisions are at best puzzling to many observers. Indeed, Sir Harry Woolf (as he then was) perceptively noted in his famous Hamlyn Lecture in 1990 that the public would not be able to differentiate the different roles of the Attorney-General in controversial cases; nor would they be convinced that the Attorney-General would be able to separate his different and conflicting roles. Woolf advocated for the creation of an independent Director of Civil Proceedings, a suggestion that is even more apt for Hong Kong today than for England 20 years ago. There is no reason why a politically appointed Secretary for Justice should oversee civil and criminal proceedings. She could remain a political and legal advisor to the Government, and entrust the power to enforce the law by civil and criminal proceedings to the Director of Public Prosecution and a Director of Civil Proceedings.

B. Special Advocate Procedure: An Inroad to Fairness?

A golden thread of the adversarial system is that a party to litigation is entitled to know the full case against him and to confront the evidence.[48] This principle of elementary fairness, which is further buttressed by the principle of open justice, is of particular importance in criminal cases, where the enormous weight of a state is brought to bear on an individual whose liberty is at stake. However, in recent years a trend has emerged, especially in the UK, of appointing a special advocate in closed materials proceedings when secret materials involving national security are relied upon in both civil and criminal proceedings.[49] As described by Lord Bingham in *R v H*,

> the procedure is to appoint a person, usually called a 'special advocate', who may not disclose to the subject of the proceedings the secret material disclosed to him, and is not in the ordinary sense professionally responsible to that party, but who, subject to those constraints, is charged to represent that party's interests.[50]

[48] *Re K (Infants)* [1963] Ch 381, 405 (Upjohn LJ); *Al Rawi v Security Service* [2012] WLR 531, 572 (Lord Dyson JSC); *Enrich Future Ltd v Deloitte Touche Tohmatsu* [2016] 3 HKLRD 827 [13]–[14] (Mimmie Chan J).

[49] The procedure was introduced as a result of comments made by the European Court of Human Rights in *Chahal v United Kingdom* (1997) 23 EHRR 413 [131]. It was initially confined to immigration and deportation cases, but was later extended to cover all types of civil litigation when disclosure of sensitive material might be 'damaging to the interests of national security' and when adoption of such procedure is 'in the interests of the fair and effective administration of justice': Justice and Security Act 2013, s 6.

[50] *R v H* [2004] 2 WLR 335 [21], adopted by Hartmann J in *PV v Director of Immigration* [2004] 3 HKC 637 [15].

The only case in Hong Kong in which this procedure has been invoked is *PV v Director of Immigration*.[51] In that case, the applicant, who was a Sri Lankan national, applied for leave to apply for judicial review against a removal order made against him, and upon leave being granted, applied for bail pending hearing. The removal order was made on the basis that the Director of Immigration considered him to be a 'threat to the peace, order and security of Hong Kong'. The Director's challenge to the court's jurisdiction to grant bail was rejected, and he opposed bail on the ground that the applicant 'had the intention to endanger life and property in Hong Kong' and had 'the training, capacity and experience' to carry out that intention. The Director further claimed public interest immunity for all the documents containing information upon which the Director had acted to detain the applicant. The court upheld this claim after having read the documents. This put the applicant's counsel in an invidious position as it would be difficult to advance the applicant's case for bail without knowing the reason or the evidence against his client. Upon consultation and consent of both parties, Hartmann J adopted the special advocate procedure on the ground that it was in the interest of justice to do so. The procedure is as follows. The special advocate has to be acceptable to both the Director and the applicant. The Secretary for Justice is responsible for appointing the special advocate and for meeting the necessary costs. In this regard, the court expressly stated that the Secretary for Justice is acting in his role as a guardian of public interest and not as a minister of the Crown or a minister having overall responsibility for criminal prosecution. The special advocate is likely to be security cleared. In that case, the Secretary for Justice approved a number of special advocates so that the applicant would be entitled to a choice. Once the special advocate is appointed, he would take instructions of a general nature from the applicant before he is shown the confidential materials that are subject to public interest immunity. He would not be permitted to further communicate with the applicant once he has seen the confidential material to avoid any confidential information being disclosed inadvertently. The special advocate and the Director would then appear before the court *in camera* and made submissions to the court. Neither the applicant nor his counsel would be present at that stage of the proceedings. After hearing the submissions, the court adjourned back into open court to allow the applicant, through his counsel, to make final submissions. The court eventually ruled that bail should be granted. As the reasons of his decision arose from the confidential material, he would not be able to disclose them, although his written ruling concerning the merits was made available to the Director and the special advocate, but was otherwise secured so as to be seen only by another court appraised of the matter.[52]

[51] ibid.
[52] ibid [47]–[49].

While Hartmann J took a bold step to introduce the procedure to Hong Kong, one must note that the procedure has its own ethical and practical problems:[53] there is a severance of lawyer–client relationship because such severance is the only basis on which the Government would accept appointment of the special advocate. One of the consequences is that the special advocate would not be able to communicate with or take further instructions from his client once he has seen the confidential information. This would necessarily hamper the special advocate to discharge his duty. Thus, if the confidential information is based on a source who may have a grudge with the applicant, the special advocate would not be able to discover the grudge without disclosing the identity of the source to the applicant.[54] At the same time, a party to the proceeding is excluded from the closed part of the trial. As Lord Dyson pointed out,

> he cannot see the witnesses who speak in that part of the trial; nor can he see closed documents; he cannot hear or read the closed evidence or the submissions made in the closed hearing; and finally he cannot see the judge delivering the closed judgment nor can he read it.[55]

The problem goes to the root of fundamental fairness and the due process.

In this regard, a distinction may have to be drawn between disclosure and representation cases. As there is an increasing demand for disclosure of information from the prosecution, not only in relation to inculpatory evidence but also exculpatory information, the prosecution has increasingly resorted to public interest immunity on the ground of protection of the safety of the informers and sometimes potential witnesses. Such a claim is invariably made in ex parte proceedings. While the Government is in general willing to disclose such information to the court, it is vehement not to disclose the same to the defendants. Since the celebrated decision of *Conway v Rimmer*,[56] the court has insisted that a claim for public interest immunity operated only as an exclusionary rule of evidence that could be overridden by other equally compelling public interest. In order to provide assistance to the court, independent counsel has been appointed to assist the court on the relevance of the undisclosed materials, the strength of the claim for public interest immunity, how helpful the materials might be to the defendant, and the risk of judicial error or bias. Jackson argued that the independent counsel

[53] *R v H* [2004] 2 WLR 335, 345 (Bingham LJ): 'Such an appointment does however raise ethical problems, since a lawyer who cannot take full instructions from his client, nor report to his client, who is not responsible to his client and whose relationship with the client lacks the quality of confidence inherent in any ordinary lawyer-client relationship, is acting in a way hitherto unknown to the legal profession.'

[54] These are examples cited by John Jackson: see J Jackson, 'The role of special advocate: advocacy, due process and the adversarial tradition' (2016) 20 *International Journal of Evidence and Proof* 343, 354.

[55] *Al Rawi v Security Service* [2012] 1 AC 531 [35]–[36].

[56] *Conway v Rimmer* [1968] AC 910. See also *Makanjuola v Commissioner of Police* [1992] 3 All ER 617.

is different from special advocates as the independent counsel is more akin to an *amicus* who is there, not to represent the defendant, but to represent the public interest in the due administration of justice.[57]

The purpose of ex parte public interest immunity application is fundamentally different from the closed materials procedure. In the public interest immunity procedure, if documents are disclosed as a result of the process, they are available to both parties and to the court. If they are not disclosed, they are excluded from the proceedings. Both parties are entitled to full participation in all aspects of the litigation. There is no unfairness or inequality of arms. In contrast, the effect of a closed material procedure is that closed documents are only available to the party which possesses them, the special advocate and the court. As Lord Dyson JSC described, the closed material procedure cuts across the fundamental principle of fairness and the right to fair trial in the common law system, and is the very antithesis of a public interest immunity procedure.[58]

Notwithstanding this reservation, Parliament has intervened in the UK, and the European Court of Human Rights has given its blessing to the special advocate procedure, at least when the applicant has been provided with sufficient information to give effective instructions to the special advocate.[59]

In light of the global concern in respect of terrorism, it is now difficult to turn the clock back and to reject the special advocate procedure. The fact that a special advocate is able to scrutinise the confidential materials and to test their internal reliability will still serve an important role when concern for secrecy dominates proceedings involving national security. The challenge is to fine-tune and improve the procedure. In the first place, while Hartmann J held that the court has an inherent jurisdiction to adopt the special advocate procedure without any statutory basis, it is better to have a statutory basis for the exercise of such a power. As Lord Dyson JSC pointed out, 'to allow a closed procedure in circumstances which are not clearly defined could easily be the thin end of a wedge'.[60] The history of how the special advocate procedure has developed from an exceptional procedure in immigration cases to become a general and widely used procedure in national security cases is itself a vivid illustration. Secondly, a statutory scheme would have to cater for the possible withdrawal of the special advocate from the proceedings when the special advocate finds that he could no longer discharge his duties, and for the court to make an appropriate order when no effective instructions could be given to the special advocate to an extent that this has hampered his ability to discharge his duties. Thirdly, consideration should be given to permit the special advocate, upon application to the court, to converse with counsel for the applicant upon an express undertaking of both counsel to the court that any sensitive information is to be kept confidential between counsel. It is important to maintain

[57] Jackson, 'The role of special advocate' (n 54) 355.
[58] *Al Rawi* (n 55) [41], [45].
[59] *A v United Kingdom* (2009) 49 ECHR 29.
[60] *Al Rawi* (n 55) [44].

public confidence in the due administration of justice, and it may be difficult to maintain such confidence if the special advocate is to be completely cut off from communicating with the defendant once the special advocate has been given sight of the confidential materials. If the special advocate system is to be accepted as a compromise between the need to maintain secrecy in the public interest and the protection of a fair hearing, there should be some element of trust in the counsel involved. In this regard, the Bar Association should be involved in further developing the practice and regulation of special advocate.[61] Fourthly, while the court is under great constraints to give reasons in its judgment regarding the closed material proceedings, the approach of Hartmann J in *PV v Director of Immigration* that written judgment should be made available to the government and the special advocate is to be commended.

III. The Judiciary

What has been discussed to this point mostly concerns external threats to the judiciary. This section will look at some internal problems of the judiciary in relatively brief terms. First, the legitimacy of the judiciary rests heavily on its open process, its fair procedure, the impartiality and independence of the judges in discharging their duties, and its provision of reasoned judgments. If a person is sufficiently aggrieved by a decision of a public authority that he is prepared to take out an application for judicial review, the public is entitled to know the reason if the court refuses to grant leave to apply for judicial review or if his or her application is unsuccessful. In recent years there have been criticisms that the court has spent too much time in giving lengthy judgments in plainly unmeritorious applications for judicial review.[62] While there is room for the court to be more succinct in its judgments, fairness and efficiency do not always sit well with one another. When it comes to questions of justice and public confidence in the judiciary, fairness should prevail over efficiency. The right to a reasoned judgment is an essential element of the right to fair hearing, and summary disposal of an application for judicial review should be adopted only in very clear cases. It is not just being fair to the litigants; a reasoned judgment also goes a long way to maintain public confidence in the judiciary.

Secondly, open justice means that judgments are open to public scrutiny. Judges are not infallible, and it is right that judgments should be subject to public criticism. The appeal system provides a means to correct judicial errors. Public criticisms are equally important and valuable. While constructive and rational criticisms would

[61] See also Jackson (n 54) 360.

[62] 'Hong Kong courts accomplices to abuses of judicial review', speech by the Hon Henry Litton, as reported in G Cheung, 'Hong Kong courts accomplices to abuse of judicial reviews, says former top judge Henry Litton' *South China Morning Post*, 17 December 2015), available at www.scmp.com/news/hong-kong/law-crime/article/1892247/hong-kong-courts-accomplices-abuse-judicial-reviews-says.

be valuable for the improvement of the law, it has to be accepted that 'not all public criticisms would be sweetly reasoned. Courts are not fragile flowers that would wither in the heat of criticism'.[63] The law of contempt, and notably contempt by scandalising the court, should limit such public outbursts and there should be no conviction for contempt without proof of an intention to scandalise the courts in a way to undermine public confidence in the due administration of justice.[64] At the same time, the strength of a judgment rests on its reasoning. A judgment is not to be assessed by the popularity or acceptability of the judgment according to one's political beliefs, and even less by attributing the judgment to unsound and speculative political inclination of individual judges. When the CA held that the offence of desecration of the national flag was inconsistent with the right to freedom of expression in *HKSAR v Ng Kung Siu*,[65] the three expatriate judges in that case were unfairly criticised on the ground of their race. More recently, judges have been subject to personal abuses when their judgments were found not to the liking of their critics.[66] When Judge Dufton sentenced seven police officers to two years' custodial sentence for assaulting an activist in the Occupy Central movement, the judge was subject to personal abuses and was criticised, without any foundation, for being politically motivated.[67] Likewise, when the CA substituted a jail sentence against three student demonstrators upon an application of review of sentences by the Secretary for Justice, it was alleged that the decision was politically motivated, again without any foundation, although the criticism now came from the opposite political camp. As former Chief Justice Andrew Li commented, such allegations are irresponsible and could have the effect of undermining public confidence in the judiciary.[68] The independence of the judiciary has to be carefully protected. Once it is gone, there will be nothing left to maintain the two systems in the 'one country, two systems' model.

Thirdly, an important guarantee of judicial independence lies in the process of appointment.[69] Under Article 88 of the Basic Law, judges are appointed by the Chief Executive on the recommendation of an independent commission composed of local judges, persons from the legal profession, and eminent

[63] *R v Kopyto* (1987) 47 DLR (4th) 213, 227 [Cory LJ].

[64] *Secretary for Justice v Choy Bing Wing* [2005] 4 HKC 416 (CFI), [2011] HKEC 235 (CA).

[65] *HKSAR v Ng Kung Siu* [1999] 2 HKC 10. The judgment of the CA was reversed by the CFA: [2000] 1 HKC 117. For the attack on the CA by members of the National People's Congress, see M Tam, 'Court crisis after flag row' *The Standard*, 25 March 1999.

[66] See also the contribution of PY Lo in this collection.

[67] *HKSAR v Wong Cho Shing* [2017] HKEC 255. The defendants have since lodged an appeal against both conviction and sentence: see *HKSAR v Lau Cheuk Ngai* [2018] HKCA 59, *HKSAR v Wong Wai Ho* [2018] HKCA 101; *HKSAR v Chan Siu Tan* [2018] HKCA 151; *HKSAR v Wong Cho Sing* [2017] HKEC 2704.

[68] C Buddle, 'Is Hong Kong's rule of law really under threat?' *South China Morning Post*, 27 Aug 2017, available at www.scmp.com/week-asia/politics/article/2108346/hong-kongs-rule-law-really-under-threat. The point was emphasised again by Geoffrey Ma CJ at the Opening of Legal Year in Jan 2019: www.info.gov.hk/gia/general/201901/14/P2019011400413.htm.

[69] See also the contribution of PY Lo in this collection.

persons from other sectors. By convention, the recommendation of the Judicial Officers Recommendation Commission (JORC) is always accepted by the Chief Executive. The JORC is chaired by the Chief Justice, and comprises two High Court judges, the Secretary for Justice, two representatives nominated respectively by the Hong Kong Bar Association and the Law Society of Hong Kong, and three lay persons appointed by the Chief Executive. Any recommendation of the JORC on appointment or promotion of a District Judge or above must not receive more than two dissenting votes. In other words, the three laypersons could join hands to veto a recommendation for judicial appointment or promotion even when the recommendation is unanimously supported by the members of the legal sector. While the voting procedure can be seen to be giving the public a real say in the appointment or promotion of judges, there is no criteria for the selection and appointment of the lay members on the JORC. It is unclear whether the lay members are recommended by the Government or whether the Chief Justice is consulted on the appointment. In the absence of clear criteria and procedure for the appointment of the lay members, it may be preferable to reduce the number of lay members to two, so that if a recommendation is not to be supported, the decision would require the endorsement of at least one member of the legal sector.

Fourthly, there is a serious structural problem of a shortage of judges in recent years.[70] As Professor Reyes pointed out, a large number of deputy judges can be sitting on any day, sometimes as many as 60 per cent of all sitting judges.[71] There are different reasons for the shortage of judges, though financial reward does not appear to be a major obstacle, as those members of the legal profession who are eligible for higher judicial appointment would be unlikely to regard financial reward as their major consideration. Article 92 of the Basic Law provides that judges shall be chosen on the basis of their judicial and professional qualities and may be recruited from other common law jurisdictions. Hong Kong has a small legal profession. The pool of people for potential judicial appointment is hence limited, and not every successful lawyer would have the temperament that is suitable for judicial appointment. While Article 92 expressly refers to the possibility of overseas appointment, it appears that there is little effort to recruit from overseas in recent years (apart from non-permanent judges at the CFA). The reason for this is unclear. An associated problem is the lack of diversity on the bench. It was only in 2018 that two lady judges were first appointed as non-permanent judges of the CFA, and all permanent judges are men. Three of the four existing permanent judges of the CFA come from the same set of chambers, which has also produced a number of judges on the High Court. While diversity should never be achieved at the expense of quality, the rather narrow and similar background of judges may

[70] See also the contribution of PY Lo in this collection.

[71] A Reyes, 'The Future of the Judiciary: Reflections on Challenges to the Administration of Justice in Hong Kong' (2014) 44 *Hong Kong Law Journal* 429.

hamper the ability of judges to be able to fully appreciate the variety of the different fabrics that make up our community.[72]

IV. Conclusion

'One country, two systems' is a highly asymmetrical model, the success of which rests entirely on self-restraint on the part of the sovereign power. The model was conceived at a time when Hong Kong had relatively strong economic but weak political power vis-à-vis the mainland. Twenty years down the road, the mainland has the upper hand both economically and politically. In the first decade after the changeover, the policy of China towards Hong Kong was marked by its decision to leave Hong Kong by and large on its own. With the emergence of China as a major global power in the last decade, she has adopted an increasingly intrusive approach to the internal affairs of Hong Kong. The non-compromising approach towards the nomination of the Chief Executive, the blatant interference with local election, the adoption of the fifth interpretation of the NPCSC, the stern approach towards discourse on localism and self-determination, the strengthening of stronger national education, and more recently, the adoption in the 19th Party Congress of the general principle of an exercise of comprehensive governance over Hong Kong, a vague principle that is open to any interpretation as the Central People's Government sees fit, are just some of the examples. There is no reason to doubt the sincerity of the Chinese leaders in maintaining 'one country, two systems', but it is equally clear that there is a shift towards 'one country' in the demarcation of 'two systems'.

There is very little the HKSAR can do in this context, except to adhere to the core values of Hong Kong and to commit to enhancing institutional strength. The two systems are distinguished by their core values, their institutional strengths, and their legal systems. This chapter has highlighted a few areas that could make Hong Kong's institutions more resilient. The reason to maintain two systems is that the co-existence of a capitalist system with its own distinct values, lifestyle, institutions and legal system is beneficial, not only to Hong Kong, but also to the development of China. The imposition of the mainland's ideology, values and ways of doing things would inevitably erode the boundary of the two systems. It should be realised that Hong Kong's contribution to China lies precisely in its social, economic, political and legal differences, all relating to systems that have earned the trust of the international community over the years. Hong Kong will be devaluating itself if it becomes just another mainland city. In that sense, retaining the differences and upholding the core values of Hong Kong are indeed the best contribution that Hong Kong can make to the social, economic and political development of China.

[72] See, eg, E Rackley, *Women, Judging and the Judiciary: From Difference to Diversity* (Abingdon, Routledge, 2013).

15

Building Rule of Law Resilience Through Institutions

A Proposed Institutional Infrastructure for National Security Legislation

CORA CHAN AND FIONA DE LONDRAS

Institutions can help to embed and protect the rule of law, even in the face of seemingly oppressive and worrying legislative moves to 'protect' security. Of course, many of those institutions – courts, the legal profession, the international human rights infrastructure – have already been canvassed in this collection as possible bulwarks against the encroachment of China's national security on Hong Kong's rule of law.[1] However, in this chapter we wish to propose the construction of a new institutional architecture that is designed systematically to build rights-based and rule of law concerns into the context in which an Article 23 law or similar legislation would operate and China's national security imperatives might 'leak' (formally or informally) into the law, politics and practices of governance in Hong Kong. As is well-known, Article 23 of the Basic Law provides that Hong Kong

> shall enact laws on its own to prohibit any act of treason, secession, sedition, subversion against the Central People's Government, or theft of state secrets, to prohibit foreign political organizations or bodies from conducting political activities in the Region, and to prohibit political organizations or bodies of the Region from establishing ties with foreign political organizations or bodies.

This is widely understood as an obligation to introduce national security law in Hong Kong, although that obligation has not yet been fulfilled.[2]

[1] See eg the contributions of PY Lo, Carole Petersen and Swati Jhaveri in this collection.

[2] An attempt to do this was made in 2003, but failed. See further the contributions in H Fu, CJ Petersen and SNM Young (eds), *National Security and Fundamental Freedoms* (Hong Kong, HKU Press, 2005).

In undertaking our task in this chapter, we recognise that institutions alone are not sufficient to reorient processes of law, policy and operation that have at their heart an oppressive approach to protecting national security that suppresses, among other things, political dissent and organising. However, neither is the text of a law itself, so that even if – as has been widely proposed[3] – an Article 23 law is drafted in a way that minimises its potential disruption to the ordinary criminal law and the rule of law, institutions will still be important as it is through them that the law will be interpreted, applied, reviewed, revised, resisted and realised. Institutions are the places where everything happens; state power flows through institutions (such as police forces, intelligence agencies and executive bodies), is formally constrained through institutions (such as courts and political institutions), and is called to account also through informal institutions (such as civil society and the electorate). Thus, we start from the intuition that institutions founded on sound principles, effectively constructed, and independent in their operations – that is, institutions that are 'strong' in the language of the Sustainable Development Goals[4] – have the capacity at the very least to inculcate participatory, reflexive, rights-based modes of working that in turn may temper the operation of repressive security laws and policies.

We start this chapter by considering the role of institutions in a system that is committed to sustainable security, and then consider the existing institutional infrastructure in Hong Kong in the light of this. That consideration reveals systemic concerns that, we argue, must be addressed if there is to be any chance of Article 23 legislation or the like being something less than a licence for oppressive governance by Beijing in Hong Kong. Some of those difficulties are reflections of broader challenges of constitutional infrastructure between Hong Kong and Beijing which take on a particular urgency and challenge in the context of security, while others are subject-specific, focused on the particular dynamics and anxieties of security as a rhetoric and a mode of governance. Having mapped the challenge around institutional infrastructure in these first two parts, we then go on to propose a new institutional architecture within which national security laws in Hong Kong might operate, arguing that it should be designed to achieve four key aims: effectiveness, accountability, transparency and participation.

In this exercise we are purposefully not constrained by concerns of what is politically likely or feasible; instead, we aim to map out an institutional model to which, we argue, Hong Kong should aspire if the 'one country, two systems' model of constitutional pluralism and accommodation that underpins the relationship with China is to sustain in the security context. However, this is not to suggest that we assume a benign or governance-oriented disposition on the part of Beijing to institutions within which a national security law might operate; we recognise that, to a government so inclined, 'strong' institutions might mean

[3] See eg the contribution of Simon Young in this collection.
[4] See especially Sustainable Development Goal 16.

institutions that bolster its power and approach to security. As clearly outlined by Hualing Fu in this collection,[5] China's approach to national security is one in which many of the fundamental elements of politicisation, resistance, dissent and protest that attempt to discipline state security power in other contexts are, themselves, susceptible to being seen as security risks that require suppression. In other words, we know that institutions have the capacity to compound oppressive and repressive regimes. They do not, in and of themselves, guarantee or even provide forms of transparency, accountability, reflection and participation that we will argue are the hallmark of the kinds of institutions that might provide resilience to the rule of law in Hong Kong or, indeed, elsewhere. Nor do they 'have minds of their own'.[6] Instead, institutions (just like laws and all other elements of governance) are deeply dependent on political commitment to their effective deployment towards the goal of maintaining security while respecting (and strengthening) the rule of law. We are acutely aware that such commitment cannot be assumed in the context of the China–Hong Kong relationship.

I. The Role of Institutions in Security

We take a very expansive approach to understanding institutions. Following North, we see them as 'the rules of the game in a society … that shape human interaction'.[7] In so doing, we do not subscribe to the view of institutions as 'constraints' *simpliciter* (as North himself did). Instead, we recognise that institutions can simultaneously be constraining, enabling and constitutive.[8] They are constraining because they regulate or constrain behaviours of power. They are enabling because the constraints placed on some actors or behaviours enable action by others. They are constitutive because 'all institutions have a symbolic dimension and therefore inculcate certain values, or world views, into the people who live under them'.[9]

This multiplicity of function hints at the problematic and challenging nature of institutions. Being humanly devised, institutions do not have their own innate values or 'natural' normative dispositions; instead, they are constructed pursuant to particular values and in order to achieve and incentivise certain kinds of behaviours and outcomes. The role and capacities of institutions, and what those desired outcome and underpinning normative commitment are, will vary

[5] See the contribution of Hualing Fu in this collection.

[6] M Douglas, *How Institutions Think* (Syracuse, Syracuse University Press, 1986) 9.

[7] DC North, *Structure and Change in Economic History* (New York, WW Norton & Company, 1981) 3.

[8] In this we are influenced by HJ Chang and P Evans, 'The Role of Institutions in Economic Change' in S de Paula and G Dymski (eds), *Reimagining Growth: Towards a Renewal of Development Theory* (London, Zed Books, 2005) 99.

[9] ibid 103.

across different contexts, including socio-political configurations; the ability to determine how power is distributed and, crucially, to disrupt that distribution should it lose its legitimacy or popular support will of course depend very much on the nature of the political context in which it operates (for example, democracy versus autocracy).

However, even if problematic, institutions matter, and they matter in the field of security.[10] At this time, this is not least because the Sustainable Development Goals have now firmly placed institutions into the realm of peace and security, enjoining states (in Goal 16), to 'strengthen'[11] institutions, and 'develop effective, accountable and transparent institutions at all levels'[12] in order to pursue the overall goal of peaceful and inclusive societies.[13] It is clear that these 'strong' institutions go beyond 'security institutions' conventionally understood,[14] but what 'strength' means here is undefined and, thus, the injunction within Goal 16 creates both an opportunity and a challenge. On the one hand, states are usually 'enthusiastic' about security activities, by which we mean that they tend to react quickly and often repressively to perceived security threats, including by introducing and 'strengthening' (including by resource expansion) security-related institutions such as police forces, armed services, intelligence agencies, and so on. However, unless carefully done and underpinned by a meaningful commitment to rights, the rule of law and constitutionalism, such institutional reinforcement may result in the exacerbation of conditions that underpin insecurity (such as repression, corruption, the use of violence by state agencies, impunity, and so on), as well as the 'hardening' of the rule of law into a tool of state force rather than of state limitation.[15] However, the linkage of institutions with the pursuit of inclusive and sustainable security – which underpins Sustainable Development Goal 16 – offers a new way for us to think about what a 'strong' institution might look like in that context. It is this opportunity that we pursue in this chapter.

Moving past the well-canvassed *problematique* of security per se,[16] and the ways in which transnational security discourses (especially transnational counter-terrorism) seem to license (if not endorse) repressive governance

[10] This has long been recognised on the international plane. See, eg, the contributions to H Haftendorn, R Keohane, and C Wallander (eds), *Imperfect Unions: Security Institutions over Time and Space* (Oxford, Oxford University Press, 1999).

[11] Sustainable Development Goal 16, Target 16.A.

[12] Sustainable Development Goal 16, Target 16.6.

[13] Sustainable Development Goal 16.

[14] See C Wallander and R Keohane, 'Risk, threat, and security institutions' in R Keohae (ed), *Power and Governance in a Partially Globalized World* (London, Routledge, 1999) 88.

[15] This is widely critiqued as one of the implications of the co-optation of the 'rule of law' within development agendas. See, eg, T Krever, 'The Legal Turn in Late Development Theory: The Rule of Law and the World Bank's Development Model' (2011) 52 *Harvard International Law Journal* 287; U Mattei and L Nader, *Plunder: When the Rule of Law is Illegal* (Oxford, Blackwell Publishing, 2008).

[16] The literature on the definition of security is voluminous. Useful starting points are found in MD Cavelty and T Balzacq (eds), *Routledge Handbook of Security Studies*, 2nd edn (Abingdon, Routledge, 2017) Part I.

impulses under the remit of 'security',[17] we can find within the Sustainable Development Goals a different way of thinking about security and of thinking about the role of institutions in the pursuit thereof. Building on previous work,[18] we argue that seeing security through the lens of sustainability can prompt us to start from everyday conditions of *insecurity* in order to envision the security to which we aspire, and then to build institutions that *constrain* behaviours exacerbating that insecurity, *enable* life in conditions of security including interpersonal and political security, and *constitute* a state disposition towards security that sees those constraining and enabling functions as reflective of the state of security to which we aspire.

What does this mean for Hong Kong? Leaving to one side considerations of personal and interpersonal security which, although important, do not manifest in the context of Article 23 per se,[19] there are at least three dimensions to insecurity that we argue should be taken into account when (a) articulating a vision for sustainable security in Hong Kong, and (b) designing an institutional infrastructure intended to enable that. These three dimensions are developed taking into account two sets of concerns: those of Hong Kong (including the concern to maintain the rule of law and the rights-based approach articulated in the Basic Law) and those of China (including the pursuit of its own national security strategy and maintenance of its desired government structure). While these two sets of framing concerns may seem irreconcilably at odds with one another, the reality of the 'one country, two systems' approach is that they must be reconciled for the overall constitutional settlement to sustain. Otherwise, as recent events in Hong Kong show only too well, it is the political will of Beijing that will almost certainly prevail.

The first dimension relates to those security risks that arise from Hong Kong's particular reliance on financial institutions for economic well-being and buoyancy, and its international significance as centre for international finance and trade. This raises the possibility that critical financial infrastructure may be vulnerable to, for example, cyber attacks or misuse in the course of terrorist financing or other kinds of financial crime. The second dimension relates to those security risks that arise from Hong Kong's status as part of China. These encompass the risk that internal actors may operate in Hong Kong to try to undermine China and Chinese political and legal infrastructure. The third dimension relates to Hong Kong's internal vulnerability flowing from its relationship with China, and in particular attempts to destabilise the political and legal infrastructure in Hong Kong in order to reduce

[17] See F de Londras, 'The Transnational Counter-Terrorist Order: A Problematique' (2019) *Current Legal Problems* (forthcoming).

[18] F de Londras, 'Sustainable Security: A Proposal' in D Akande, J Kuosamanen, D Roser and H McDermott (eds), *Human Rights and 21st Century Challenges: Poverty, Armed Conflict, and the Environment* (Oxford, Oxford University Press, 2020) (forthcoming).

[19] On the importance of interpersonal security in security and sustainable security more generally, see de Londras, 'Sustainable Security' (ibid).

its autonomy relative to Beijing, including by using law and policing to make meaningful participation in political life, dissent, protest and agitation difficult if not impossible.

Any approach to sustainable security in Hong Kong would take these three dimensions into account and try to address and accommodate all of them, sometimes having to strike a difficult balance between values or interests that seem to be in tension with one another. Our argument is that appropriate institutional design may enable this, although it cannot be expected to resolve all such tensions. However, if 'strong' institutions are constituted in order to try to ensure that, operating as a whole and in conjunction with the existing security institutions such as policing and the criminal law, these tensions can be mitigated and resolved in Hong Kong in a rule of law compliant way, then the occurrence of extraordinary interventions – including from Beijing – might be minimised. Achieving this is at the heart of the task of instantiating a sustainable approach to security in Hong Kong. What this means is that we must understand 'strong' institutions '[as] institutions that are effective, accountable, transparent and participatory … [and] committed to adherence to the Rule of Law'.[20] Effectiveness, accountability, transparency and participation are, thus, the benchmarks against which we assess the existing institutional infrastructure in Hong Kong for its 'preparedness' for the introduction of an Article 23 law (in section II), as well as the aspirational framework against which we propose a new institutional infrastructure (in section III).

II. The Existing Institutional Infrastructure in Hong Kong

There are five factors that, we argue, mean that the existing infrastructure is insufficient when considered against the benchmarks of effectiveness, accountability, transparency and participation.

First, there is no statutory obligation to create and retain records generally,[21] and no way of knowing how the Hong Kong Government treats national security assessments passed on from the Chinese Government. This leads to a lack of transparency as well as risks that the rule of law will be harmed. Even with a rigorous application of existing legal rules on disclosure, the courts may not be able to see the information that underlies the Government's national security judgements. The result is that national security assessments may go completely unchecked

[20] de Londras, 'Sustainable Security' (2020).

[21] There is a weakly enforced administrative scheme overseen by the Government Records Service. For inadequacies of existing arrangements, see, eg, Audit Commission, 'Report No 57: Records management work of the Government Records Service' (25 October 2011); Office of the Ombudsman, 'Direct Investigation Report – Public Records Management in Hong Kong' (March 2014).

and relatedly, there is no way of vetting whether the Hong Kong Government has accepted without independent verification security assessments from the Chinese Government.

These problems are exposed in the *Chu Woan Chyi* litigation.[22] The applicants were members of Falun Gong, a religious sect that is banned in China but legal in Hong Kong. They were refused entry into Hong Kong on 'security grounds', and physical force was used in the process of removal. Subsequently they brought judicial review to challenge the Government's decision to refuse them to enter. They argued, inter alia, that if the intelligence information for barring them came from the Chinese Government, the Hong Kong Government ought to treat it with scepticism and verify it independently, taking into account a number of considerations that would suggest that they were not a security threat.

Throughout the six years of litigation, the Government was unable to produce any facts to justify its assessment that the applicants posed a security risk. Not a single document was produced to support this assertion, nor was the degree or nature of the threat or the sources of information revealed. What was alarming was that only after nearly three years of litigation did the Government suggest for the first time that the documents that contained the information that formed the basis of their assessments were in fact *destroyed* in accordance with 'standard procedures' barely three weeks after the relevant decisions were made (and before the Government knew that judicial review proceedings were brought). The courts therefore had to adjudicate the claim purely on the basis of affirmations from government officials that stated conclusions – ie that the individuals would pose security risks – rather than reasons for the conclusions – ie why those individuals would pose security risks.

The Court of Appeal held that the Government breached the duty of candour. It expressed bewilderment and dissatisfaction with the 'coyness' and 'inconsistency' on the part of the Government.[23] It considered the clandestine situation a 'most extraordinary state of affairs'[24] and criticised the suggested 'standard practice' of destroying relevant documents.[25]

Nevertheless, despite finding that the Government breached the duty of candour, the court held that the substantive challenge failed, mainly because the burden of proving that the Government acted not on bona fide security grounds rested with the applicants, and clear evidence would be needed before it could find that a senior official has been deliberately untruthful in its affirmation – such evidence not available in the circumstances.[26]

This case exposed the limits of the court – or any organ or individual, for that matter – in guarding against abuses of power in the national security context when

[22] *Chu Woan Chyi and others v Director of Immigration* [2009] 6 HKC 77.
[23] ibid [119].
[24] ibid [118].
[25] ibid [157].
[26] ibid [151]–[152].

no or meagre information was available for its scrutiny. The applicants in this case wanted to know whether the Hong Kong Government had in place procedures to *meaningfully* and lawfully assess individuals accused of posing security risks and whether those procedures were followed in their case,[27] but no such information was forthcoming.

This problem is in fact part of a wider issue of the lack of transparency in and non-institutionalisation of the interaction between the Chinese and Hong Kong Governments. Much of such interaction is not governed by any formal rules. There are no statutory requirements on record-taking, keeping and disclosure of inter-governmental discussions. In the absence of legal rules regulating engagement between the two governments, such engagement is vulnerable to determination by politics. Given the power imbalance between the Chinese and Hong Kong Governments, and the Xi Jinping regime's clear will to suppress dissent in Hong Kong, the risk of the former imposing on the latter measures that harm Hong Kong's rule of law and autonomy is real.

The co-location controversy illustrates the difficulty of scrutinising interactions between the two Governments.[28] The controversy concerns the clearance arrangements for the high-speed railway linking Hong Kong and mainland China. Because the two jurisdictions practise different laws, it was necessary to have two checkpoints – one for Hong Kong, another for China. In order to facilitate speedy travels, the two Governments introduced a 'co-location arrangement' with both checkpoints at the Hong Kong terminus. This necessitated the application of Chinese laws in Hong Kong, and the Chinese and Hong Kong Governments proposed to do so in a way that apparently breached the arrangements under the Basic Law. The Governments argued that to ensure efficient travels, it would not be feasible to have passengers go through two checkpoints in two jurisdictions. An obvious alternative was to have passengers go through both checkpoints at a mainland terminus – this would have been the perfect solution as it would not require passengers to go through separate checkpoints at separate locations and would not involve the application of Chinese laws in Hong Kong.[29] It was revealed by the media that this option was tabled in the course of the negotiations between the two Governments.[30] However, it was not known why it was subsequently ruled out. There was no way of accessing and scrutinising the discussions between the two Governments.

The impression from this and other incidents (including in 2019 the Chinese Government requesting the Hong Kong Government to submit a report on the

[27] *Chu Woan Chyi and others v Director of Immigration* [2006] 4 HKLRD 280 [79].

[28] Guangzhou-Shenzhen-Hong Kong Express Rail Link (Co-location) Ordinance (Cap 632).

[29] This option has been suggested by members of the public. See, eg, K Cheng, 'Concern group proposes alternate plan for controversial Express Rail Link joint checkpoint' *Hong Kong Free Press*, 26 September 2017, available at www.hongkongfp.com/2017/09/26/concern-group-proposes-alternate-plan-controversial-express-rail-link-joint-checkpoint/.

[30] '福田站規劃興建均有預設海關口岸' *Cable News*, 18 August 2017, available at cablenews.i-cable.com/ci/videopage/news/510912/即時新聞/福田站規劃興建均有預設海關口岸.

latter's ban of a pro-independence political party in Hong Kong[31]) is that the Hong Kong Government was compelled to appear as a proponent of measures that harmed Hong Kong's autonomy and rule of law, in face of Beijing's overwhelming political power. In light of the power asymmetry between the two Governments, the lack of institutionalised mechanisms for inter-governmental interaction does not bode well for autonomy and the rule of law of Hong Kong.

This opaqueness in inter-government exchanges, compounded with the above-mentioned specific problem of not knowing how the Hong Kong Government treats intelligence information from the Chinese Government, can be exploited by the Chinese Government to export its idiosyncratic conceptions of national security to Hong Kong. It is necessary for the two Governments to share intelligence information on national security – and such sharing must already be taking place – but it is not known whether the relevant authorities in Hong Kong, such as the Security Bureau and the prosecutorial and law enforcement institutions, have in place procedures for screening out Chinese intelligence assessments that fall outside accepted understandings of security and human rights. If there are no such procedures, 'information-sharing' on crimes against the state might become a pretext for China to impose its draconian understandings of national security to Hong Kong.

Given all this it is not difficult to appreciate the widespread concerns against the Hong Kong Government's proposal to allow for case-by-case extradition to any jurisdiction with which Hong Kong currently does not have long-term extradition agreements, including mainland China.[32] Under the proposal, extradition to mainland China would take place after the Chinese authorities make a request for extradition, the Chief Executive certifies that the case should proceed, the court determines that the statutory requirements for extradition are met (eg the request for extradition was not made for punishing the individual by reason of his or her political views), and the Chief Executive makes a final order for extradition. Although political crimes are excluded from the proposed arrangement, there are worries that the Chinese Government might fabricate evidence to frame

[31] 'Beijing backs city government's ban on Hong Kong National Party, leader Carrie Lam says' *South China Morning Post*, 26 February 2019, available at www.scmp.com/news/hong-kong/politics/article/2187744/beijing-backs-city-governments-ban-hong-kong-national-party; HKSAR Government, 'Report on the Prohibition of the Operation of the "Hong Kong National Party" by the Hong Kong Special Administrative Region Government and Related Circumstances', available at gia.info.gov.hk/general/201904/18/P2019041800429_308626_1_1555572180892.pdf.

[32] The Fugitive Offenders and Mutual Legal Assistance in Criminal Matters (Amendment) Bill (gazetted on 29 March 2019 and being debated in LegCo at the time of writing). Under the current statutory regime, extradition to other parts of China is absolutely barred and that to other jurisdictions that Hong Kong has no long-term extradition arrangements with could only take place after vetting by LegCo. For a commentary on the proposed revision, see A Chen, 'A Commentary on the Fugitive Offenders and Mutual Legal Assistance in Criminal Matters Legislation (Amendment) Bill 2019 ("the Bill")' (*HKU Legal Scholarship blog*, 3 May 2019) http://researchblog.law.hku.hk/2019/05/albert-chens-commentary-on-proposed.html. At the time of writing, the Bill has been suspended due to widespread opposition.

political dissenters for committing non-political crimes: there is nothing that the courts could do to screen out such attempts if there are no apparent irregularities. Further, as the proposal stands at the time of writing, although courts do have a limited power to scrutinise whether the individual concerned would be prejudiced at his or her trial by reason of his or her political views, they are not expressly mandated to assess whether generally trials in the receiving jurisdiction meet international human rights standards,[33] a judgement that courts may prefer to leave to the political branches of the Government. Given the hold that the Chinese authorities have over the Chief Executive, it is difficult to envisage the latter refusing to certify the former's requests for extradition. The proposed extradition arrangement could be manipulated by the Chinese authorities to penalise Hong Kong people who performed acts that were perfectly legal in Hong Kong, but which were deemed by Beijing as threats to security.

A second and related hindrance to accountability, transparency and participation relates to the lack of an access to information law.[34] The complete absence of a positive legal obligation to declassify and release information allows the Hong Kong Government to withhold security information and exchanges with the Chinese Government even if they are objectively non-sensitive.[35] This weakens the public's ability to check against Chinese impositions of will, feeding into the power imbalance between the two jurisdictions. In addition, it weakens the ability of monitoring institutions to assess the reliability of the Government's national security claims. Around the world, courts tend to be highly deferential to the executive in national security matters because they feel that they lack the expertise and information in determining these issues. Hong Kong is no exception. The court in *Chu Woan Chyi* emphasised that 'security analyses and determinations are necessarily reserved for' the Government,[36] and the Court of Final Appeal (CFA) in *Hysan Development* listed national security as an example of a subject matter that would likely attract judicial deference.[37] In recent years, however, courts in some

[33] Hong Kong Bar Association (HKBA), 'Observations of the Hong Kong Bar Association ("HKBA") on the Fugitive Offenders and Mutual Legal Assistance in Criminal Matters Legislation (Amendment) Bill 2019' (2 April 2019), para 20. See also C Chan, 'Demise of "One Country, Two Systems"?: Reflections on the Hong Kong Rendition Saga', (2019) *Hong Kong Law Journal* 447; J Chan, '10 Days That Shocked the World: The Rendition Proposal in Hong Kong' (2019) *Hong Kong Law Journal* 431.

[34] Currently, there is a weakly enforced Code on Access to Information. For the inadequacies of the existing arrangements, see Office of the Ombudsman, 'Direct Investigation Report – The Access to Information Regime in Hong Kong' (March 2014).

[35] The absence of a freedom of information law also exposes journalists to the risk of being caught by Art 23 laws that impose further restrictions on the use of information that the government deems confidential. See D Weisenhaus, 'Article 23 and Freedom of the Press: Journalistic Perspective' in H Fu, CJ Petersen and SNM Young (eds), *National Security and Fundamental Freedoms* (Hong Kong, HKU Press, 2005) 299.

[36] *Chu Woan Chyi* (n 22) [141].

[37] *Hysan Development Co Ltd v Town Planning Board* (2016) 19 HKCFAR 372 [116]–[117].

jurisdictions have been able and willing to play a more active role,[38] partly because they have accumulated more expertise in assessing national security questions, and partly because public inquiries into national security blunders have exposed the fallibility of the executive's national security assessments,[39] leading them to view the Government's security claims with more scepticism. The unavailability of even non-sensitive security information in Hong Kong has handicapped the ability of the courts to build up the expertise for checking the Government's security decisions.

A third obstacle to building sustainable security is the absence of legal limits on the Chinese Government's powers over Hong Kong. Important decisions about Hong Kong could be made in Beijing without accountability and transparency and in defiance of the rule of law. The Chinese Government possesses what it calls 'comprehensive jurisdiction' over Hong Kong, manifested most prominently in its plenary and free-standing powers of interpreting the Basic Law.[40] Beijing may use these powers to export draconian concepts of national security to Hong Kong in numerous ways.[41] First, the Standing Committee of the National People's Congress (NPCSC) may control the content of national security legislation and the pace of enactment through issuing an idiosyncratic interpretation of Article 23 of the Basic Law, a suggestion that has been floated in some pro-China sections in early 2019.[42] Second, if the legislature passes a lenient Article 23 law, the NPCSC may veto it under Article 17(3) of the Basic Law, which grants it powers of returning laws passed by Hong Kong's legislature that relate to 'affairs within the responsibility of the Central Authorities'. Any doubt over whether national security laws relate to such affairs could be resolved by the NPCSC through an interpretation of Article 17 itself. Third, if issues arise in court over the compatibility of national security laws or the application of those laws with the Basic Law's human rights and other provisions (including Article 39 which entrenches the International Covenant on Civil and Political Rights (ICCPR)), the NPCSC may validate the national security acts in question by issuing an idiosyncratic interpretation of those provisions. Fourth, the NPCSC may apply Chinese national security laws to Hong Kong by adding them to Annex III

[38] See, eg, F de Londras, *Detention in the 'War on Terror': Can Human Rights Fight Back?* (Cambridge, Cambridge University Press, 2011) 230–79; A Kavanagh, 'Constitutionalism, counter-terrorism and the courts: changes in the British constitutional landscape' (2011) 9 *International Journal of Constitutional Law* 172.

[39] See, eg, C Chan, 'Deference, Expertise and Information-Gathering Powers' (2013) 33 *Legal Studies* 598, 615.

[40] See eg the contribution of Albert Chen in this collection.

[41] The following sets out what steps Beijing might take. We pass no judgement on whether these steps would be allowed upon a sensible reading of the Basic Law, although our tentative view is that they would not be. See also the contribution of Albert Chen in this collection.

[42] 'Cheng mum on potential NPC move to interpret Article 23' *The Standard*, 9 April 2019, available at www.thestandard.com.hk/section-news.php?id=206671&sid=11.

of the Basic Law pursuant to Article 18(3) of such Law. Any doubt over whether national security laws fall within 'defence and foreign affairs as well as other matters outside Hong Kong's autonomy as specified by this Law', areas covered by Article 18(3) may be resolved by the NPCSC through an interpretation. Finally, Beijing could declare Hong Kong to be in a state of 'turmoil … which endangers national unity or security and is beyond the control of the government of the Region' or in a 'state of emergency' and apply Chinese security laws pursuant to Article 18(4) of the Basic Law. Again, any doubts over the meaning of these phrases could be settled by an NPCSC interpretation.

As a matter of domestic constitutional law, there is no mechanism for enforcing the guarantees of autonomy and human rights in the Sino–British Joint Declaration and the Basic Law against the Chinese Government. In the early days of the handover, the CFA pronounced that Hong Kong courts had jurisdiction to invalidate legislative acts of the National People's Congress or NPCSC that violated the Basic Law,[43] but in recent years courts seemed to have retreated from this bold position.[44] Any argument that the courts can protect Hong Kong from draconian national security laws must be considered in this context.

The fourth obstacle in meeting the requirements of sustainable security and effectiveness lies in the lack of public accountability on the part of decision-takers (in security matters, but also more generally). This is the result of a combination of factors. First, the lack of genuine democracy. The existing way of returning functional constituencies, which take up half of the seats in the legislature, as well as the 1,200-person committee for the Chief Executive (who ultimately has to be appointed by the Chinese Government), is biased in favour of business elites and pro-China quarters. Second, various features of executive-led governance curtail the legislature's ability to check government powers. For example, under the split voting procedure, private members' Bills can only be passed by a majority of legislators from both functional constituencies and geographical constituencies while government bills need only be passed by a simple majority of both houses voting together.[45] Third, since 2016 the disqualification of pro-self-determination individuals from standing for election and taking office has also weakened the force of the opposition camp in the legislature. Fourth, the lack of an accountability culture as manifested in, inter alia, the absence of a convention of officials resigning upon losing the confidence of the public. The cumulative effect is that the Chinese Government will likely be able to control the content of any national security bill via the Chief Executive, and secure the passage of such bill via the pro-establishment legislators.[46]

[43] *Ng Ka Ling & Others v Director of Immigration* (1999) 2 HKCFAR 4, 26A–B.

[44] See, eg, *Leung Lai Kwok Yvonne v Chief Secretary for Administration* (unreported, HCAL 31/2015, 5 June 2015) [30]; *Kwok Cheuk Kin v Chief Executive of the HKSAR & Ors* [2017] 5 HKC 579 [41]; *Chief Executive of HKSAR v President of the Legislative Council* [2017] 1 HKLRD 460 [58]–[59]; *Yau Wai Ching v Chief Executive of HKSAR* (2017) 20 HKCFAR 390 [34]–[36].

[45] See eg the contribution of Margaret Ng in this collection.

[46] ibid.

The lack of public accountability plagues not just the legislative stage, but the subsequent stage of applying the law as well. In democratic jurisdictions, it could be said that the executive is to some extent accountable to the public for its national security judgements: if it makes wrong judgements, its key officials will be pressurised to resign and the public could vote out the ruling party at the next election. However, the same cannot be said of the executive in Hong Kong: there is no convention that officials that have lost the confidence of the public should resign, nor could the public penalise the head of the executive at the ballot box.

The fifth and final obstacle to fulfilling the requirements of sustainable security and effectiveness in institutional design is the lack of institutions dedicated to the periodic and comprehensive review of the necessity and desirability of national security measures. Although the court and legislature do play important roles to ensure that these measures do not jeopardise the rule of law, there are limits to what they could do as well. The court only comes into play when an individual dispute arises, is mandated to assess the legality rather than the desirability of national security measures, and cannot rewrite laws and policies from scratch. Whilst some requirements of sustainable and effective security, such as compliance with human rights, are legal requirements and may be overseen by courts, others, such as multi-facetedness, effectiveness, consideration of long-term impact, inclusivity, transparency and accountability, are not. The legislature can rewrite laws and policies, but it is not designed in a way that is conducive to the protection of individual (especially minority) rights and the long-term interests of the community. Given the complexity of national security issues, the far-reaching and significant impact of security measures, and the potential sensitivity involved, dedicated organs are needed for the scrutiny of such measures.

III. Towards a New Institutional Structure for National Security Legislation

In this Part of the chapter we sketch out seven key elements of a new institutional structure into which, we argue, an appropriately designed Article 23 law might be 'received' while maintaining to the extent possible the rule of law as part of Hong Kong's autonomy under the 'one country, two systems' arrangement. In doing so, of course, we outline only in thumbnail form the nature of these institutional innovations, some of which are of broader significance (because they relate to the maintenance of the constitutional relationship between Hong Kong and China) and some of which are very targeted in their scope (that is, relate only to the operation of an Article 23 law per se). The institutional structure that we propose aims to speak to the three different dimensions of security, contextualised by the Hong Kong–China relationship, as we outlined them in section I; to take into account and try to design solutions to the deficiencies in the status quo that we identified in section II; and to create an institutional infrastructure in which effectiveness, accountability, transparency and participation are valued as sustainable security goods. However, even if the institutional innovations we propose here were to be implemented *in toto* their ability to be constitutive of an approach to security that is built on commitments to the rule of law, rights and sustainable security could not be assured. That could be secured only by an effective mixture of institutional design and dispositional commitment in both Hong Kong and Beijing.

A. Limiting the NPCSC's Powers to Interpret the Basic Law

First, limits must be developed on the NPCSC's powers of interpreting the Basic Law. In this respect we have two, related proposals. Whilst the NPCSC is effectively unconstrained in exercising its interpretative powers in mainland China, this ought not to be the case in respect of the Basic Law. Thus, in order to preserve its guarantees, we propose that the NPCSC should follow a coherent set of principles for interpreting the Basic Law. Those principles need not replicate the common law purposive approach, but must at a minimum include a mandate to not deviate from the plain wording of and specified fundamental principles of the Basic Law.[47] Ghai argues that 'it is clearly necessary for the coherence of the Basic Law that some uniform and fundamental principles of and approaches to interpretation be adopted'[48] and that 'It is important to avoid a situation when the two systems are locked (or are seen to be locked) in a struggle for the soul of Hong Kong; instead the struggle must be towards coherence.'[49] Granted that coherence should be the goal, if the integrity of Hong Kong's common law system is to be preserved – and the 'one country, two systems' pledge meaningfully to be honoured – efforts to enhance coherence should not come from Hong Kong courts incorporating Chinese methods of interpretation in construing an NPCSC interpretation, but must instead come from the NPCSC.

Furthermore, there must be an institution to ensure that the NPCSC's decisions and interpretations do not stray from the requirements of the Basic Law. This is in essence the age-old suggestion that there should be an impartial body for resolving conflicts between the two jurisdictions. The Basic Law Committee, originally intended for this role, could be reformed to enable it to undertake it. For example, selection for the Hong Kong membership of this Committee could be made by the Judicial Officers Recommendation Commission (the body responsible for selecting judges in Hong Kong) rather than by Beijing, in order to guarantee independence from China. Also, the views of this body should be made binding rather than advisory, and the NPCSC should only be allowed to issue a decision or interpretation if it secures the endorsement of at least half of both of

[47] See, eg, EC Ip, 'Interpreting Interpretations: A Methodology for the Judicial Enforcement of Legislative Interpretations of the Hong Kong Basic Law' [2017] *Public Law* 552.
[48] Y Ghai, *Hong Kong's New Constitutional Order*, 2nd edn (Hong Kong, HKU Press, 2001) 191.
[49] ibid 212.

the Chinese and Hong Kong members. If the establishment of an impartial organ proves impossible, the courts of Hong Kong would be the most viable institution for taking up the role of overseeing the NPCSC's decisions and interpretations.[50] Courts' role as guardian of the Basic Law dictates that they maintain that Law not just against contravening Hong Kong organs, but against contravening Chinese organs as well.

B. Universal Suffrage for Election of the Chief Executive and the Legislative Council

Our second proposal is to introduce genuine universal suffrage in elections for both the Chief Executive and the Legislative Council (LegCo).[51] These are important institutions for the reception and development of an Article 23 law, not least because if it is to be revised or if it were found to contravene the Basic Law, it would be these institutions that would need to lead on that process of revision. However, as extensively considered elsewhere in this collection,[52] these institutions appear increasingly to be under the control of China, either because of Beijing's ability to appoint relevant office-holders, or because of interpretations of the Basic Law or legal interventions by China that effectively exclude dissenters from participation.[53] Questions of legitimacy, representation and participation thus clearly arise. As the possibility of rejection in free and fair elections is the most effective incentive for those holding parliamentary and other elected positions to act in a manner that maximises the common good of their electors, and that pursues sustainable security and the autonomy of Hong Kong, universal suffrage for these institutions is critical to ensure accountability and participation in the institutional infrastructure.

C. Procedures for Handling National Security Assessments

Moving on to institutional reform specific to the national security context, our third proposal is the establishment (if not already in existence) and disclosure in broad terms of procedures for filtering out national security assessments from Chinese authorities that are not in line with international human rights standards. The detailed procedures for scrutinising security assessments from

[50] See, eg, C Chan, 'The Legal Limits on Beijing's Powers of Interpreting the Basic Law' (HKU Legal Scholarship blog, 3 November 2016), available at researchblog.law.hku.hk/2016/11/cora-chan-on-legal-limits-of-beijings.html.

[51] See also the contribution of Michael Davis in this collection.

[52] See eg the contributions of Margaret Ng, Albert Chen, Hualing Fu, PY Lo and Michael Davis in this collection.

[53] ibid.

intelligence bodies would normally be considered too sensitive to be disclosed (as acknowledged by the Court of First Instance in *Chu Woan Chyi*[54]), but in the context of Hong Kong, rule of law imperatives require that there be effective procedures for independently verifying intelligence assessments from the Chinese Government. This is not least because of China's very broad approach to categorising security threats, covering within that category resistant political activity including secessionism.[55] However, as the ICCPR is embedded in the Basic Law,[56] and as Hong Kong has a different socio-political underpinning to China, such activities might not be considered sufficient to ground a national security assessment to which Hong Kong ought to accede. Thus, at the very least the public should know how such assessments are handled when received, what decisions are made in respect of them, how the rights-basis of the Basic Law is respected in making such decisions, and what the statistical overview of such assessment is, even if the details of individual cases might not be subject to public release. An Independent Reviewer, the establishment of which we propose below, might be empowered to review decision-making on a case-by-case basis.

D. Introduction of an Access to Information and Archives Law

Our fourth proposal is the enactment of the long-overdue access to information law and archives law. The enhanced transparency from such laws will enable the public and monitoring institutions more effectively to check the Government's national security decisions and guard against unwarranted impositions of will by Beijing. In 2018, the Hong Kong Law Reform Commission (HKLRC) released consultation papers on both access to information and archives law.[57] However, whilst the papers' proposal that legislation should be introduced is welcome, various proposals or assumptions in the papers raise concerns because they perpetuate 'secrecy' in the national security context, without putting in place a robust system for assessing the veracity and appropriateness of secrecy claims.[58] That this is so is evident from both papers.

The consultation paper on access to information defines 'information' as including only recorded information,[59] creating the risk that government officers would deliberately 'off-record' information to avoid disclosure requirements.[60]

[54] Above n 27.
[55] See also the contributions of Hualing Fu, Swati Jhaveri and Michael Davis in this collection.
[56] Basic Law, Art 39.
[57] HKLRC, 'Consultation Paper: Access to Information' (December 2018); HKLRC, 'Consultation Paper: Archives Law' (December 2018).
[58] On secrecy as deleterious of trust and accountability in the counter-terrorist context and, by extension, in security, see, eg, J Blackbourn, F de Londras, and L Morgan, *Accountability and Review in the Counter-Terrorist State* (Bristol, Bristol University Press, 2019) ch 4.
[59] HKLRC, 'Consultation Paper: Access to Information' (n 57), para 4.28.
[60] This criticism was raised in Hong Kong Journalists Association, 'HKJA Submission on Access to Information Consultation Paper' (5 March 2019).

This risk that is particularly acute in the national security context, where sensitive information is involved, and could be mitigated by implementing instead something akin to the approach in New Zealand, where non-recorded information held by a minister in his or her official capacity is covered.[61] It should be an offence to fail properly to create and maintain records,[62] and to alter, erase, destroy or conceal records with an intent to prevent disclosure.[63]

Furthermore, the HKLRC proposed a category of absolute exemptions,[64] including information on defence and security, intergovernmental affairs (including affairs between the Chinese and Hong Kong Governments) and immigration matters[65] – all areas in which national security matters arise. Information falling into this category would not be accessible under the legislation. This is in sharp contrast to a system of qualified exemptions, in respect of which the public interest for and against disclosure are balanced in deciding whether the information sought ought to be released. The justification given for introducing absolute exemptions is that the balancing exercise for information in these exempted categories would already have been accommodated by other access regimes, even though there does not seem to be any existing legal regimes that already incorporate a balancing exercise in relation to the three above-mentioned categories. Furthermore, experience from other jurisdictions shows that when it comes to security governments overclaim secrecy and security-sensitivity,[66] so that absolute exemption regimes are unlikely to be susceptible to mitigation in the way proposed. Even where there are limited exemptions, the 'balance' tends to be struck against disclosure,[67] so that it is difficult to avoid information black holes in respect of security even in limited exemption regimes. Thus, an access to information and archives law should have within it some kind of checking mechanism, ideally the Hong Kong courts, through which to challenge refusals of disclosure.

In this respect we do not agree with the view articulated in the consultation papers that Hong Kong institutions are 'in no position to decide whether or not the release of certain information … would harm or prejudice Hong Kong's

[61] HKLRC, 'Consultation Paper: Access to Information' (n 57), para 4.27.

[62] Similar suggestions have been made in: HKBA, 'Combined Views of the Hong Kong Bar Association on the Law Reform Commission of Hong Kong Archives Law Sub-Committee and Access to Information Sub-Committee Consultation Papers' (1 March 2019), para 15; Archives Action Group, 'Archives Action Group's Response to the Consultation Paper of the Law Reform Commission's Sub-Committee on Archives Law' (5 March 2019), para 22; Hon CP Mok, Hon T Chan and Hon D Kwok and the Archive Action Group, 'Draft Public Records Bill' (27 April 2017), s 23.

[63] This goes further than the HKLRC's proposal, which is that these activities should be an offence only when a request for access has been made (see HKLRC, 'Consultation Paper: Access to Information' (n 57), para 14.39). We argue that it should be an offence at any time, whether a request for access has been made or not.

[64] See HKLRC, 'Consultation Paper: Access to Information' (n 57), para 10.27.

[65] HKLRC, 'Consultation Paper: Access to Information' (n 57), para 10.28.

[66] See, eg, Blackbourn, de Londras and Morgan, *Accountability and Review* (2019) chs 3 and 4.

[67] Similar criticisms have been made in: HKBA, 'Combined Views' (n 62), para 41; Hong Kong Journalists Association (n 60).

defence and security'.[68] Interpretation and adjudication of local laws fall squarely within Hong Kong courts' jurisdiction.[69] Courts have powers to determine the validity of the Government's grounds for concealing information, including security grounds, and to determine whether the public interest for disclosure overrides such grounds.

E. A Human Rights Institution for Hong Kong

Our fifth proposed institutional reform is the establishment within Hong Kong of a human rights institution modelled on well-established international principles for national human rights institutions. The Basic Law protects individual rights[70] and expressly incorporates international human rights treaties.[71] However, in Hong Kong as elsewhere, the constitutional protection of human rights is no guarantee of their effective protection in the national security context. Instead, legislatures commonly pass laws that infringe disproportionately on constitutionally protected rights, and both civil society and independent institutions are instrumental in identifying potential violations at draft stage, in trying to have them redressed before the passage of the law, and in challenging them if they remain once a law has been passed.

While disproportionate infringements on rights are often ultimately a matter for courts to resolve, this is challenging in most jurisdictions[72] and the contours of the relationship with Hong Kong courts and the NPCSC adds a further layer of complexity in this context. Furthermore, just as in every jurisdiction, it is far preferable to address rights-related concerns at the policy- and law-formation stage, than to have to rely on individuals or groups taking on the burden of judicial review retrospectively. Hong Kong might, then, consider following many other jurisdictions in establishing an independent human rights institution that would be fully compliant with the Paris Principles Relating to the Status of National Institutions.[73]

According to those Principles, all such institutions should have a broad mandate including the capacity to advise on the rights-related implications of proposed legislation, the harmonisation of national measures with international human rights law, and the promotion of human rights including through human rights education. Members of the institution should be selected following an inclusive and transparent selection and appointment process (thus minimising the risk

[68] HKLRC, 'Consultation Paper: Access to Information' (n 57), para 10.28(6).

[69] A similar criticism has been made by the HKBA, 'Combined Views' (n 62), para 44.

[70] Basic Law, Ch III.

[71] Basic Law, Art 39.

[72] See generally, the contributions to FF Davis and F de Londras, *Critical Debates on Counter-Terrorism Judicial Review* (Cambridge, Cambridge University Press, 2014).

[73] Appended as an Annex to UN General Assembly Resolution 48/134 (1993).

of state 'capture' of the institution), be independent as a matter of both law and practice, and be adequately resourced. However, beyond these minimum standards there is no single defined model for a human rights institution; states can design a model that best suits their legal and social conditions. That said, there are some dominant models: more than half of the recognised NHRIs in the world are 'commissions', and a further third are 'ombudsmen'.[74]

Like many such institutions, a human rights institution for Hong Kong should have some kind of role in pre-legislative scrutiny, including by bringing to public attention the human rights implications of proposed laws. Such an institution – were it to be properly constituted and safeguarded in its independence – might be able to intervene at the stage of the design and implementation of a national security law, and to draw attention to any rights-related implications that such a law gives rise to in practice. Human rights institutions can also 'speak out' against human rights violations undertaken in pursuit of security, even in very difficult circumstances and when doing so might not be possible (or might be dangerous) for politicians or for civil society.[75] A human rights institution for Hong Kong might, then, straddle official state institutions and civil society in an interesting and potentially useful way.

A human rights institution of this kind has a wider and more proactive remit than a court (as it can intervene in an anticipatory sense before the law is passed), but feeds into government in an advisory rather than a binding way, thus enabling more reflexive law-making in the national security context. As part of a broader institutional redesign such a mechanism might well succeed in maintaining the Basic Law's commitment to individual rights as a central concern in the design and implementation of an Article 23 law, as well of course as having a broader rights-related impact and being able to report on Hong Kong specific issues in shadow reporting to United Nations treaty monitoring mechanisms.

F. An Independent Reviewer of Article 23 Legislation

Our sixth proposal is the establishment of an Independent Reviewer of Article 23 Legislation in the Article 23 law itself. In a number of jurisdictions – notably Australia and the United Kingdom[76] – strong independent review institutions

[74] UNHCHR, *National Human Rights Institutions: History, Principles, Roles and Responsibilities*, 4th rev (New York and Geneva, United Nations, 2010) 15.

[75] A good example is the Commission Nationale Consultative des Droits de l'Homme, which spoke out against the prolonged state of emergency in France following the 2015 attacks: CNCDH, 'Avis sur le suivi de l'état d'urgence et les mesures antiterroristes de la loi du 2 Juillet 2016' (26 January 2017).

[76] On Australia see, eg, J Blackbourn, 'The Independent National Security Legislation Monitor's First Term: an Appraisal' (2016) 39 *UNSW Law Journal* 975; on the United Kingdom see, eg, J Blackbourn, 'Evaluating the Independent Reviewer of Terrorism Legislation' (2014) 67 *Parliamentary Affairs* 955 and J Blackbourn, 'Independent Reviewers as Alternative; an Empirical Study from Australia and the UK' in Davis and de Londras, *Critical Debates* (2014).

have been established to ensure transparency about the operation and impact of counter-terrorism laws. In both cases the main role of the office-holder is to access data and information on the application of statutory powers in counter-terrorism legislation (the reviewer having high level security clearance) and then to report to the Government and to inform Parliament of the operation of the laws. These reports are usually reasonably evaluative, covering both operational matters (including valuable accounts of the frequency with which powers are used and the result of the use of such powers), and analytical reflection (for example, on the extent to which certain powers seem necessary, or where they seem to be having undesirable or disproportionate (including discriminatory) impacts).

Independent reviewers play a critical role in enhancing accountability in respect of such laws: because they have high level security clearance they get access to all relevant information, because they are independent they are largely seen as credible, and because they enhance the knowledge that is available in the public domain they enable effective parliamentary oversight of the use and operation of national security laws.[77] Reviewers cannot, of course, bring about a change in the law, but they can act as a focal point for the analysis of these laws, and cultivate trust and participation for a wide range of stakeholders, from security services to civil society to the general public.[78] An Independent Reviewer of Article 23 Legislation would, thus, create additional modes of accountability, transparency and participation, and generate evidence (both statistical and qualitative) of the (intended and unintended) consequences of that law, including societal and political consequences, on the basis of which revision and reform might be proposed and, at the very least, the LegCo might be empowered (within the constraints in which it operates[79]) to enact accountability for the law's use from the Chief Executive.

G. Inclusion of a Sunset Clause in Article 23 Law

Our final proposal is the inclusion in any Article 23 law of a sunset clause, providing that (all or some of) the law will lapse if they are not reconsidered and revalidated by the LegCo on a specified date (perhaps three years after its introduction) and periodically thereafter. Once more, this proposal borrows from the practice in other states, where sunset clauses are frequently used in national security law.[80] Sunset clauses have historically been used when highly contested legal changes are being introduced, sometimes as a matter of compromise and sometimes as a means of ensuring that experimental approaches to a

[77] See especially Blackbourn, de Londras and Morgan (n 58) chs 2 and 3.

[78] ibid, especially ch 3.

[79] See the contribution of Margaret Ng in this collection.

[80] On sunset clauses, see generally, A Kouroutakis, *The Constitutional Value of Sunset Clauses: An Historical and Normative Analysis* (Abingdon, Routledge, 2017); S Ranchordas, *Constitutional Sunsets and Experimental Legislation: A Comparative Perspective* (Cheltenham, Edward Elgar, 2014).

hard policy question can be trialled but can be revisited when a body of evidence about their operation is to hand,[81] although the ensuing debates have not always been robust or in fact subjected the law in question to meaningful challenge.[82]

However, in spite of their mixed record, in the case of Article 23 legislation, a sunset clause might well be appropriate especially if an Independent Reviewer of Article 23 Legislation is in place whose reports can inform the LegCo in any debate on whether the law should be allowed to lapse. Of course, sunset clauses are only as good as the parliaments that implement them, but if nothing else they create a firm and inescapable legislative process that in turn can trigger an intensive period of civil society activity and thus create as much political and popular pressure as possible to minimise the damaging impacts of an Article 23 law based on lived experience of its operation and its political and societal impacts.

IV. Conclusion

Our aim in this chapter has been to build on two imperatives – the imperative in Article 23 of the Basic Law to introduce 'national security' legislation in Hong Kong, and the imperative in Sustainable Development Goal 16 to create just, peaceful and inclusive societies including by strengthening institutions – first to articulate a set of benchmarks for institutions that might contribute positively to sustainable security in Hong Kong, second to assess the status quo against those benchmarks, and third to propose institutional reforms and innovations to bring the legal and institutional framework closer to those ideas and thus to minimise the risk of Article 23 legislation being a conduit for the undermining of Hong Kong's rule of law.

In undertaking this task we were, as we noted throughout the chapter, conscious that the success of any such reform could not be assured by simple institution building alone; instead a dispositional commitment to effectiveness, accountability, transparency and participation in building sustainable security would be required. We remain conscious that securing such a dispositional commitment will be challenging, not least because it is to many extents at odds with both the limited democracy of Hong Kong and the overall political system of China. However, notwithstanding this, we remind readers of three things. First, while the Basic Law requires Article 23 legislation it does not preclude the creation of rights-oriented, rule of law based institutions around that law. Those are within the gift of the Hong Kong Government and LegCo, which could establish a human rights institution or Independent Reviewer without in any way violating Article 23. Secondly, Article 23 is not the only constitutional imperative in action

[81] Kouroutakis, *The Constitutional Value of Sunset Clauses* (ibid).
[82] Blackbourn, de Londras and Morgan (n 58) ch 2.

here; there are also constitutional guarantees of rights protection and the overall constitutional settlement of 'one country, two systems' which institutional reforms of the kind canvassed here could help further to secure in a manner *harmonious* with the Article 23 requirement. And thirdly, while the ideal would be the implementation of all of these reforms, some are evidently beyond the power of the Hong Kong authorities to do alone. Instead, they require the willing participation of the Chinese Government, which recent events in Hong Kong suggest may not be forthcoming. The challenges of limiting the NPCSC's powers to interpret the Basic Law, for example, ought not to preclude or delay other, immediately realisable institutional reforms.

Meaningful commitment to the maintenance of the rule of law can readily be demonstrated by ensuring that in fulfilling its Article 23 obligation the Hong Kong authorities act to put in place an institutional infrastructure designed to ensure *sustainable* security in Hong Kong: security for Hong Kong's autonomy and rule of law, as well as for its financial and economic infrastructure, for the Hong Kong people and for China.

16

Unpalatable Realities and Hard Choices

DANNY GITTINGS[1]

The unmistakeable message running through the chapters in Part III of this book is that any fresh attempt to enact comprehensive Article 23 legislation is virtually certain to pose far greater challenges to Hong Kong's rule of law and freedoms than its 2003 predecessor. While that, ultimately abandoned, legislative effort was rightly seen as posing significant challenges at the time, for all its flaws many of the offences proposed during that earlier exercise were confined to conduct that endangered national security through the use of either force or serious criminal means, with the latter defined by reference to anti-terrorism legislation. Then Chief Executive Tung Chee-hwa's administration was careful to stress that the 'mere expression of views' would not have been outlawed under the National Security (Legislative Provisions) Bill 2003,[2] unless this incited others to use either force or serious criminal means.

That will not necessarily remain true during any renewed Article 23 legislative exercise. As Young points out in his contribution to this Part of the collection, things have changed since 2003 and there is certain to be pressure to enact one or more offences in wider terms that may prohibit purely peaceful conduct.[3] While any decision to introduce national security legislation is invariably portrayed in terms of implementing Hong Kong's constitutional responsibility under Article 23 of the Basic Law, in reality decisions on when to introduce such legislation – as well as on much of its content – are driven by political considerations. Judging from past experience, those political considerations invariably reflect the prevailing priorities of the Central Government at the time.

[1] Associate Professor, College of Humanities and Law, School of Professional and Continuing Education, University of Hong Kong.

[2] Security Bureau, Proposals to implement Article 23 of the Basic Law Consultation Document (September 2002) [14], available at www.basiclaw23.gov.hk/english/download/reporte.pdf (Consultation Document).

[3] See n 66 and associated text in Simon NM Young's contribution to this collection.

In 2003 those priorities included banning the continued operation in Hong Kong of the Falun Gong, the spiritual movement that had so badly embarrassed then still-influential Jiang Zemin by surrounding the Zhongnanhai leadership compound in Beijing while he was Chinese President. Despite strong pressure from the Central Government in Beijing, evidently unhappy that the Falun Gong continued to operate lawfully in Hong Kong four years after being outlawed on the mainland, it had proved impossible to ban its local affiliate under existing legislation.[4] So a proscription provision not required under Article 23 was slipped into the 2003 proposals, which would have allowed the banning of any local affiliate of a group outlawed on the mainland on national security grounds, and remained there almost to the bitter end – only being finally dropped after a huge public protest on 1 July 2003.

More than 15 years later, it seems unlikely the Central Government would consider it worthwhile to expend much political capital on trying once again to ban the local affiliate of a no-longer-influential spiritual group that angered a now long-departed Chinese leader. As Young notes, even in 2008, this proscription mechanism was left out of the Article 23 legislation enacted in Macau.[5] Instead, the prevailing political priority of the Central Government today, judging from its repeated statements on the issue, would be more likely to use any national security legislation as a vehicle to crack down on the growth in pro-independence sentiment in Hong Kong. Such sentiment did not exist during the last Article 23 legislative exercise in 2003, which may explain why Beijing was prepared on that occasion to see the proposed offence of secession largely confined to pro-independence activities involving the use of either force or serious criminal means.

From the Central Government's perspective, there would seem little point in Hong Kong going through all the political pain and controversy that any fresh Article 23 legislative exercise would inevitably entail unless new legislation was wide enough to tackle pro-independence activities in Hong Kong. As Johannes Chan points out, any proposal to outlaw peaceful advocacy of independence would have nothing to do with Hong Kong's constitutional responsibilities under Article 23.[6] But that misses the point since, as demonstrated by the experience of the 2003 exercise, any attempt to enact national security legislation in Hong Kong is not solely – or necessarily even primarily – about implementing constitutional obligations under Article 23. Rather, it would appear to be at least as much about using any such exercise as a vehicle for pursuing the prevailing political priorities of the Central Government at the time.

[4] Then Secretary for Justice Elsie Leung told the author she had examined the local affiliate's objectives and found that they did not breach any Hong Kong laws (personal conversation, 2000). See also CJ Petersen, 'Hong Kong's Spring of Discontent: The Rise and Fall of the National Security Bill in 2003' in H Fu, CJ Petersen and SNM Young (eds), *National Security and Fundamental Freedoms: Hong Kong's Article 23 Under Scrutiny* (Hong Kong, Hong Kong University Press, 2005) 27.

[5] See text before fn 57 in Simon NM Young's contribution to this collection.

[6] See fn 40 and associated text in Johannes Chan's contribution to this collection.

Young examines what form this likely major battleground in any fresh Article 23 legislative exercise might take, distinguishing between possible narrow and broad versions of any potential new offence outlawing peaceful advocacy of secession. Even Young's narrow – if it can be properly termed as such – version would have chilling implications for civil liberties, outlawing advocacy of Hong Kong independence in public places and on the Internet. But as Young points out, if the goal is to stop the spread of pro-independence sentiment, even such a draconian measure might be deemed insufficient as far as Beijing is concerned. Hence the possibility cannot be ruled out of a new secession offence being framed in much broader terms, possibly outlawing advocacy of independence in all contexts, including private gatherings and all forms of communication including email.[7]

But Young's analysis only scratches the surface in considering the potential ramifications of any expanded offence of subversion. In particular, the possible implications for other Article 23 offences also need to be considered. During the 2003 legislative exercise, the offences of secession and subversion were couched in very similar language, with both being largely confined to conduct that involved the use of force or serious criminal means.[8] So any fresh legislative exercise that sought to remove those qualifications in respect of the offence of secession would open the door to arguments that corresponding changes might need to be made to the offence of subversion as well, if only to maintain consistency between the two offences. In the most extreme scenario, any such changes could potentially lead to peaceful advocacy of the overthrow of the Chinese Communist Party being criminalised alongside peaceful advocacy of Hong Kong independence. Since Hong Kong's pro-independence forces are unlikely ever to pose any real threat that 'seriously endangers the territorial integrity of the People's Republic of China', to quote the language used to describe the offence of secession in the 2003 Bill,[9] that qualification might also need to be stripped from any fresh Article 23 legislative exercise if any new Bill was to achieve the objective of outlawing those currently advocating secession for Hong Kong. That, in turn, raises the question of whether one of the most important concessions made by government during the 2003 legislative exercise, in agreeing to restrict the offence of sedition to those circumstances where any incitement has some likelihood of inducing prohibited conduct,[10] might also be vulnerable to being reversed during any future legislative exercise. After all, it would seem self-contradictory and provide ammunition for government critics to propose outlawing advocacy of Hong Kong independence that has little likelihood of achieving such a result while continuing to retain such a likelihood test for the offence of sedition.

[7] See fns 66–71 and associated text in Simon NM Young's contribution to this collection.

[8] Compare the proposed amendments to ss 2A and 2B of the Crimes Ordinance (Cap 200) under the National Security (Legislative Provisions) Bill 2003.

[9] ibid s 2B.

[10] See H Fu, 'Past and Future Offences of Sedition in Hong Kong' in Fu, Petersen and Young, National Security and Fundamental Freedoms (2005) 247.

Viewed in that context, such troubling possibilities make Young's proposed guidelines for any renewed Article 23 legislative exercise all the more valuable.[11] Certainly, they represent a big improvement on the much vaguer guiding principles used by the Government during the 2003 exercise,[12] which may well make a reappearance in some shape or form during any renewed attempt to enact national security legislation. These government guidelines elevated 'the need to protect adequately the state's essential interests' – with what is adequate to achieve this goal left ambiguous – to a core drafting principle and one which, judging from the 2003 experience, is broad enough to allow for the addition of offences not specifically required under Article 23, such as proscription. While those government guidelines did make reference to fundamental rights and freedoms, as well as the provisions protecting them in the Hong Kong Basic Law, this was qualified by a principle that any Article 23 legislation need only be drafted 'as clearly and tightly defined *as appropriate*' (emphasis added) – a caveat probably broad enough to allow for the inclusion of vaguer advocacy-based offences during any fresh legislative exercise.

Judged against this admittedly low bar, Young's more specific guidelines are greatly to be preferred, particularly in their emphasis on need for legal certainty and the importance of fully justifying any restrictions on fundamental freedoms. As Young points out, it is difficult to see how any offence outlawing peaceful advocacy of secessionist sentiments could comply with all aspects of his proposed guidelines.[13] But that, to some extent, highlights the perhaps inevitable shortcoming of any such guidelines since the practical reality must be that the more successful they are in ruling out offences the Government may wish to introduce, the less likely they are to be adopted. Virtually any drafting exercise starts with preconceived notions about the preferred content of the proposed legislation and, as seems to have been the case in 2003, drafting guidelines tend to be fashioned in a way that ensures they will permit the inclusion of such content. So, if Young's guidelines are to play a role in informing any future Article 23 legislative exercise, it is less likely to be in restricting government drafters possibly under instructions to find a way of outlawing pro-independence activities, and more likely to be in providing a series of benchmarks that observers can use to judge what those drafters put forward. In particular, such benchmarks could potentially play an important role in influencing more moderate members of the pro-establishment camp, who in 2003 played an important role in forcing the shelving of the Government's legislative proposals.[14]

The unpalatable reality that the more successful Young's guidelines are in preventing the Government from achieving its objectives the less likely they are to be adopted, may also apply to Petersen's analysis of how any expanded

[11] See text between fn 33 and fn 34 in Simon NM Young's contribution to this collection.
[12] Security Bureau, Consultation Document (n 2) [1.7].
[13] See text before fn 72 in Simon NM Young's contribution to this collection.
[14] Petersen, 'Hong Kong's Spring of Discontent' (2005) 54.

Article 23 offences would probably fall foul of international human rights law. Petersen points out that any attempt to prohibit peaceful advocacy for independence would almost certainly contravene the foundational principle in the *Johannesburg Principles* that a government can only seek to prohibit expression when it can demonstrate such expression is intended to incite imminent violence and is likely to do so.[15] But even during the 2003 drafting exercise, the Government initially rejected the principle that Petersen cites as 'unnecessarily restrictive'[16] with the then Solicitor General complaining that 'compliance with this Principle would leave serious and unacceptable gaps in our law'.[17] So the perverse consequence of proving that a ban on pro-independence activities would contravene the *Johannesburg Principles* might well be to encourage the Government simply to abandon any effort to demonstrate compliance with those principles as a whole, including those it might otherwise have been prepared to adopt. That would mark another retrograde step from the 2003 legislative exercise when, even though it rejected adherence to the principle that Petersen cites, the Government made some effort to show that its proposals still complied with most other parts of the *Johannesburg Principles*.[18]

Petersen also suggests Hong Kong residents cannot be restricted from peacefully advocating secession because the Basic Law, by giving them the power to propose amendments to that document,[19] grants Hong Kong residents an absolute right to advocate any changes to their constitutional framework, including even stripping that document of the provision in Article 1 which describes the territory as 'an inalienable part of the People's Republic of China'.[20] While not without merit, that argument has already been rejected by the Government in its support for the disqualification over the past few years of several candidates in Legislative Council elections, simply because those candidates refused to rule out including independence as one possible option in any future referendum on Hong Kong's post-30 June 2047 future.[21] While Petersen is correct in stating that the Basic Law gives Hong Kong the power to propose amendments, under Article 159(4) this is qualified by an absolute ban on any amendments that contravene 'the established basic policies of the People's Republic of China regarding Hong Kong'.

[15] Johannesburg Principles, Principle.

[16] Security Bureau, 'Proposals to Implement Article 23 Broadly Consistent with the Johannesburg Principles' (LC Paper No CB(2)1577/02-03(02), March 2003) [7], available at www.legco.gov.hk/yr02-03/english/bc/bc55/papers/bc550325cb2-1577-2e.pdf.

[17] B Allcock, 'Freedom of expression is NOT under threat' (28 January 2003) [25], available at www.basiclaw23.gov.hk/english/focus/focus4.htm.

[18] Security Bureau, 'Proposals to Implement Article 23' (2003) [4].

[19] Under a complex procedure laid out in Basic Law, Art 159(2).

[20] See fn 77 and associated text in Carole J Peterson's contribution to this collection.

[21] eg the Government's support for the disqualification of Agnes Chow because her Demosisto political party supports a self-determination referendum on Hong Kong's future, which would include the option of post-2047 independence. See Press Release of the HKSAR Government, 'HKSAR Government responds to media enquiries regarding 2018 Legislative Council By-election' (27 January 2018), available at www.info.gov.hk/gia/general/201801/27/P2018012700291.htm.

Although the meaning of that latter term is not free from doubt,[22] judging from the bracketing together of Articles 1 and 159(4) in the confirmation form that electoral affairs officials began sending out to Legco election candidates from 2016 onwards, and which proved one of the grounds for disqualifying some candidates whom returning officers judged not sufficiently committed to upholding the Basic Law,[23] it appears the Government interprets Article 159(4) as barring any amendment to the Basic Law that would change Hong Kong's status as part of China, even after 30 June 2047. That interpretation has some very interesting implications, which could be usefully explored further. In particular, if it is really correct that Article 159(4) bars – in perpetuity – any change to Hong Kong's status as part of China because this is part of 'the established basic policies' that are now interpreted as remaining unamendable even after 30 June 2047, logically the same must also be true of other fundamental principles underlying Hong Kong's current constitutional structure, such as its high degree of autonomy and perhaps even the power of final adjudication, similarly preventing these from being taken away even after 30 June 2047.

Acknowledging her arguments are unlikely to prevail on the restrictions that international law places on the content of national security legislation, since it will be difficult for Hong Kong to implement Article 23 in a manner that complies with international norms while also satisfying the demands of the Central Government, Petersen puts forward the novel suggestion that if any national security legislation is implemented in a manner that blatantly violates the rights protected under the 1984 Sino–British Joint Declaration then both the United Nations (UN) Committee on Decolonisation and the General Assembly have a duty to take up the issue. This could include returning Hong Kong to the UN list of non-self-governing territories (commonly referred to as colonies) from which it was removed at Beijing's request in 1972,[24] a move which would suggest Hong Kong's continued legal status as part of China was open to review. While such a nuclear option – as it might aptly be termed, given Beijing's likely reaction to any such move – might be an interesting topic for academic discussion, whether it deserves any place in the realm of practical possibilities is a different matter. Petersen acknowledges that, given China's expanding economic clout, it would be difficult – some might say inconceivable – to gather the necessary votes in the UN for any such move at present.[25] Moreover the ramifications of encouraging a debate over such an unrealistic option merit careful consideration. Given that election candidates are already

[22] It has been generally taken as a reference to the 12 basic policies outlined by China in the 1984 Sino–British Joint Declaration. However, some statements by the Government suggest a more restrictive definition. See PY Lo, *The Judicial Construction of the Hong Kong's Basic Law: Courts, Politics and Society after 1997* (Hong Kong, Hong Kong University Press, 2014) 448–49.

[23] *Chan Ho Tin v Lo Ying Ki Alan* [2018] 2 HKLRD 7 [122]–[125], [140]–[143].

[24] See fns 100–04 and associated text in Carole J Peterson's contribution to this collection.

[25] She does however make the valid point that it is always possible for a currently powerful state to see its influence decline in future. See fn 101 and associated text in Carole J Peterson's contribution to this collection.

being barred from standing for Legco simply for refusing to rule out including independence as one option in any hypothetical referendum far into the future, it is not difficult to foresee the fate that would await any Hong Kong politician who follows Petersen's example and advocates reopening the issue of Hong Kong's legal status at the UN. In the most extreme scenario, if peaceful advocacy of secession is outlawed as part of any fresh Article 23 legislative exercise and – as was the case under the 2003 proposals – this offence is once again given extra-territorial effect, Petersen might even need to think twice about visiting Hong Kong, to avoid any possible risk of prosecution under the new law.

None of this is in any way intended to diminish the important role that international law and foreign governments can play in monitoring how national security legislation is implemented in Hong Kong and curbing its worst excesses. But, especially in the current political climate, some hard choices may have to be made. It may be strategically advisable to consider focussing on pressing for compliance with 'hard' international law such as the International Covenant on Civil and Political Rights, which the Government can hardly ignore given its incorporation into the Basic Law. This may be more fruitful than diverting too much time and effort into pursuing full compliance with 'soft' law such as the Johannesburg Principles, which is less likely to consider a receptive audience and may even end up backfiring if it prompts the Government to ignore these principles altogether. It may also be necessary to recognise that, while it is entirely practical and realistic to expect foreign governments with significant interests in Hong Kong – particularly the United Kingdom and United States – to continue to monitor the implementation of the Basic Law, it is questionable how practical or realistic it is to expect the UN General Assembly to perform a similar role.

Johannes Chan takes us into another area of the delicate balance between protecting the interests of the sovereign power and upholding the integrity of Hong Kong's common law system with his analysis of the courts' chequered record in performing this balancing act in two key cases involving mainland interests – *Hua Tian Long (No 2)*[26] and the Court of Final Appeal decision in the *Congo*[27] case. Criticism of these two judgments is not new, and he has strong grounds for concluding that both were wrongly decided.[28] But where Johannes Chan breaks new ground is in documenting procedural and evidential shortcomings in how the courts handled both cases that set a troubling precedent for how they may handle national security cases under any future Article 23 legislation. In particular, while the Ministry of Foreign Affairs' letters adduced as evidence during the *Congo* case have already been the subject of much criticism in respect of their content and threatening tone,[29] Johannes Chan points out that those letters

[26] *Hua Tian Long (No 2)* [2010] 3 HKLRD 611.

[27] *Democratic Republic of Congo v FG Hemisphere Associates LLC (No 1)* (2011) 14 HKCFAR 95.

[28] See the concluding paragraph of section I E in Johannes Chan's contribution to this collection.

[29] See, especially, ETM Cheung, 'Undermining Our Judicial Independence and Autonomy' (2011) 41 *Hong Kong Law Journal* 411, 412–13.

should probably never have been admitted as evidence at all since they essentially bypassed the proper procedure under the Basic Law for introducing evidence on questions of fact concerning foreign affairs, which requires a formal certificate from the Chief Executive based on a certifying document from the Central People's Government.[30] Similarly in *Hua Tian Long (No 2)*, the court relied partly on hearsay evidence from an employee of the mainland defendant company to settle an issue with constitutional implications, albeit while expressing dissatisfaction at the lack of any certification from the Chief Executive on the issue.[31]

The potentially troubling implications of a similarly informal approach to the admission of evidence in Article 23-related cases merits further consideration. Given the subject matter of these offences, it is quite possible the prosecution might sometimes seek to rely on evidence from mainland officials, even public security officers reluctant to expose themselves to scrutiny in open court. The Government has already indicated its preference for taking a deferential attitude towards mainland-related evidence on Article 23 matters, suggesting during the 2003 legislative exercise that it would sometimes be necessary to 'defer to the decision of the Central Authorities based on the comprehensive information that it possesses'[32] in relation to the then proposed offence of proscription. While that particular offence may not return as part of any future Article 23 legislative exercise, similar issues can be expected to arise in other contexts including in relation to any new advocacy-related offence. If the same language is used on sedition as in the 2003 Bill (and, if anything, the pressure will be to toughen it) then it is not difficult to envisage the Government arguing that it is similarly necessary to defer to the 'comprehensive information' that mainland authorities possess on what 'seriously endangers the territorial integrity of the People's Republic of China'. So Johannes Chan's analysis suggests that vigilance against any erosion of procedural and evidential requirements could usefully be added to the list of issues which will need to be monitored particularly closely during the enactment of any future Article 23 legislation. The conclusion from his analysis of the *Congo* and *Hua Tian Long* cases must be that the courts cannot necessarily be relied on rigorously to uphold procedural and evidential requirements without watertight legislative provisions requiring them to do so. More broadly, for all the importance of the judiciary's role in relation to any future Article 23 legislation, his chapter reminds us that it would be wrong to place too much emphasis on the courts alone as the guarantors of Hong Kong's rule of law and fundamental freedoms.

That raises the question of what can be done to strengthen Hong Kong's institutional infrastructure more generally – both within the courts and beyond – to prepare for national security legislation, the subject of Cora Chan and Fiona de Londras' chapter. With the authors declaring themselves purposefully not

[30] Basic Law, Art 19(3).
[31] *Hua Tian Long (No 2)* (n 26) [156]–[158].
[32] Security Bureau, Consultation Document (n 2) [7.16].

constrained by what is either politically likely or feasible, their proposals range from the utopian – at least in the short term – to the arguably more realistic. Those that fall in the former category would seem to include the early introduction of full universal suffrage for electing both the Chief Executive and Legco as well as the restrictions on the Standing Committee's power to interpret the Basic Law. More realistic proposals include the enactment of access to information and archives laws, as well as possibly the establishment of some form of human rights commission.

One very important point left unanswered by Cora Chan and de Londras' chapter is to what extent, if at all, implementation of some or all their proposed reforms would render more acceptable Article 23 legislation couched in terms that would otherwise be fiercely opposed? While the authors appear to envisage their proposed institutional structure as supplementing – rather than supplanting – the assurances provided by tight drafting guidelines and full compliance with international human rights principles, it is questionable whether the issue of possible trade-offs can entirely be avoided. Sometimes these choices would seem relatively easy to make. For instance, in the unlikely event Hong Kong was suddenly granted genuine universal suffrage for the election of the Chief Executive, without any of the screening mechanisms for candidates that have been previously proposed, it is not difficult to envisage that many would be willing to soften their opposition to national security legislation – and perhaps even tolerate content that would otherwise have been considered unacceptable – given the reassurance that this legislation would be implemented by a democratically elected administration. Similarly, from the Government's perspective, conceding some other elements of the Cora Chan and de Londras blueprint – perhaps even the human rights commission that successive administrations have long opposed – might well be seen as a small price to pay in the improbable event this was enough to secure the pro-democracy camp's support for Article 23 legislation drafted in harsher terms.

Since the issue of possible trade-offs is hard to ignore, if only because others are certain to raise it, it might be helpful to make some effort to quantify the impact of Cora Chan and de Londras' reforms. Some of these, such as the introduction of universal suffrage, are evidently on a vastly different scale to others, such as an archives law. So a useful first step might be to rank in order of priority the various different elements of their proposed institutional infrastructure reforms. A more ambitious goal would be to try and correlate these proposed reforms with specific issues that can be expected to arise during any drafting exercise, perhaps through some expanded version of Young's guidelines.

Finally, the breadth of Chan and de Londras' proposed reforms, taken together with the wide range of issues covered in these other chapters, serves as a useful reminder of one other very important point: the impact of Article 23 legislation, whenever it eventually comes, will be so far-reaching that it can be expected to pose challenges to almost every area of Hong Kong's civil society.

17

Conclusion: Security, Economy, Politics: The Chinese Agenda

YASH GHAI AND JILL COTTRELL GHAI

The story of Article 23 of the Basic Law governing, in part, the relationship between China and Hong Kong, is largely a reflection of the changes in China's perception of its standing at home and abroad. At first China accepted the Basic Law as governing its relationship with Hong Kong, and largely adhered to the commitment to ensure Hong Kong's autonomy for 50 years. The Chinese authorities had been greatly disturbed by the impact of the student rebellion in Tiananmen Square, and put it down with great violence including considerable loss of life. Seeing Hong Kong people's strong condemnation of the crackdown,[1] China worried that Hong Kong might become a base for subversion, and hence strengthened the wording of Article 23 of the Basic Law with an aim to desist foreign interventions. The situation is now somewhat different. China, on the whole, welcomes intimate relations with leaders of foreign states and enjoys greater international standing than it did in the 1990s. It also seems less inclined to treat itself as bound by the Joint Declaration and the guarantee of Hong Kong autonomy and, as other chapters in this collection have shown, seems quite willing to intervene in Hong Kong affairs,[2] including through interpretations of the Basic Law.

In this concluding contribution to the collection, we discuss the impact of China's economic and global policies on the development of close relationships with foreign states, in spite of the scepticism of citizens in those states as well as in Hong Kong. In particular, we will argue that China's global economic and investment approach – and especially the Belt and Road Initiative (BRI) – is strengthening its relative international position and, as a result, that the people of Hong Kong may find themselves less able to call on international solidarity to

[1] The crackdown attracted the largest public demonstration in the history of Hong Kong – one million people poured into the streets to protest against the Chinese Government. See, eg, JM Carroll, *A Concise History of Hong Kong* (Hong Kong, Hong Kong University Press, 2007) 191.

[2] See the Introduction and the contributions of Albert HY Chen and Michael C Davis in this collection.

ensure that China respects and gives effect to Hong Kong's autonomy, with potential negative implications for the Rule of Law. The discussion in this chapter reveals that China is coherent in its domestic and global policies through which it aims to extend control in political, security and economic terms (echoing the Chinese regime's priority on advancing 'sovereignty, security, and development interests'[3]). China's treatment of Hong Kong therefore makes for interesting comparisons with, and sheds light on, China's activities in the international political, security, and economic order.

China's local and global roles have changed greatly in the last 20 years, largely due to its phenomenal economic growth. China has been the world's fastest growing economy since the 1980s, with an average annual growth rate of 10 per cent. It has gradually moved to what can be described as a mixed market and socialistic economy. At the political level it is still a managed system, with strong penalties for those who defy the strict norms of the regime. Its transformation required a complex range of reforms in China's financial, enterprise, governance and legal systems, and the development of an ability to respond flexibly to the unintended consequences of these changes. This transformation has been accompanied by high levels of industrialisation and urbanisation, which in turn influence every aspect of China's society, culture and economy.

The improvements are often traced to the policies, termed 'socialist market economy', of Deng Xiaoping. This was also the period when China was considering the 'recovery' of Hong Kong. Its eyes were definitely on the wider economic world, although perhaps through the medium of Hong Kong. The Joint Declaration certainly opened up 'economic' or 'entrepreneurial' paths, both ways. While Hong Kong was at one time the route between China's economic enterprises and the world, now it is the BRI that fulfils this function although, as we shall show, this does not exclude Hong Kong, which is reinventing itself as the 'super-connector' in the BRI.[4]

The relationships that we sketch here are very different from that between Hong Kong and the mainland. Most obviously, Hong Kong does not need investment from China the way these other jurisdictions do. Outside Hong Kong there are genuine fears and unsurprising senses of rivalry about BRI investment, but in many BRI countries complaints are about the countries' own governments, not China as such.

In Hong Kong the relationship with China is structured around the Basic Law; in BRI countries it is around agreements. While Hong Kong views China as something of which it is a part (and ambivalently), something that tries to limit its

[3] See, eg, Xi Jinping's Report at the 19th National Congress of the Communist Party of China: J Xi, 'Secure a Decisive Victory in Building a Moderately Prosperous Society in All Respects and Strive for the Great Success of Socialism with Chinese Characteristics for a New Era' (18 October 2017), available at www.xinhuanet.com/english/download/Xi_Jinping's_report_at_19th_CPC_National_Congress.pdf.

[4] See HKSAR Government, 'Belt and Road' (video), available at www.beltandroad.gov.hk/videos.html.

identity and autonomy; and something trying to make Hong Kong part of itself, much of the rest of the world has a very different perspective. And while China views Hong Kong as somewhere that potentially harbours hostile forces, on the whole the rest of the world, at least that part linked by the BRI, is no positive threat. However, as former residents of Hong Kong, and now citizens of a BRI recipient country (Kenya), we have a particular perspective on this network of links between China and BRI countries and on their implications for and beyond Hong Kong. In offering these perspectives we are conscious – as Barry Sautman has written[5] – that at least some elements of racial prejudice are involved in criticisms of the BRI, and have noticed that a lot of 'evidence' is pedalled rather uncritically online without it being clear how reliable or representative it is. We have endeavoured to avoid such faults in our own analysis.

I. The Belt and Road Initiative

The BRI (or One Belt One Road, *yi dai yi lu*) was inspired by the historic route from China to the World, and comprises a land road, rail and pipeline 'belt', and a maritime 'road' of shipping lanes. As the original Silk Road was the route for Chinese silk, paper, gunpowder and spices to reach the Middle East and the West, so its modern successors are the routes for Chinese know-how, investment and influence.

The BRI represents a huge change, not only in China's economic growth, but even more in the manifestation of its relationship with other states, so significant that it has been enshrined in the Constitution of the Communist Party.[6] Even though the development of the BRI seems not much to be discussed among the general public in China or in the recipient countries of investment, the significance of the relationships supported by the BRI goes well beyond simple economics. This is clear from the 2015 'Vision and Actions on Jointly Building Silk Road Economic Belt and 21st-Century Maritime Silk Road' issued by the National Development and Reform Commission, which outlines the objectives of the BRI:

> Improving intergovernmental communication to better align high-level government policies like economic development strategies and plans for regional cooperation.
>
> Strengthening the coordination of infrastructure plans to better connect hard infrastructure networks like transportation systems and power grids.
>
> Encouraging the development of soft infrastructure such as the signing of trade deals, aligning of regulatory standards, and improving financial integration.

[5] B Sautman, 'The truth about Sri Lanka's Hambantota port, Chinese "debt traps" and "asset seizures"' *South China Morning Post*, 6 May 2019, available at www.scmp.com/comment/insight-opinion/article/3008799/truth-about-sri-lankas-hambantota-port-chinese-debt-traps.

[6] '"Belt and Road" incorporated into CPC Constitution' *Xinhua News*, 24 October 2017, available at www.xinhuanet.com//english/2017-10/24/c_136702025.htm.

> Bolstering people-to-people connections by cultivating student, expert, and cultural exchanges and tourism.[7]

China's motives and ambitions have been the subject of much speculation and analysis. It is only fair to present the Chinese view of BRI, which is broadly as follows:

> The BRI is an umbrella initiative which covers a multitude of investment projects designed to promote the flow of goods, investment and people. The new connections fostered by the BRI could reconfigure relationships, reroute economic activity, and shift power within and between states.[8]

President Xi has said, 'In pursuing the Belt and Road Initiative, we should focus on the fundamental issue of development, release the growth potential of various countries and achieve economic integration and interconnected development and deliver benefits to all.'[9] He also insists on integrity and service to the people (although his staff have been accused in some countries, particularly in Africa, of the exploitation of local workers). You could say that for a country which was isolated from most of the world for a very long time, it is wonderfully forthcoming and generous.

Many explanations of the BRI have been advanced, not necessarily complimentarily (particularly in Africa). Many commentators recognise that its functions are multiple and varied, from an attempt to gain global dominance to 'a Chinese Marshall plan',[10] an investment plan intended to 'mak[e] money, principally for [Chinese] banks'[11] and 'a Trojan horse for China-led regional development, military expansion, and Beijing-controlled institutions'.[12] As domestic growth slows down in China, the BRI offers a way for the leadership 'to open new markets for its consumer goods and excess industrial capacity'[13] in line with Xi's 'vision of a more assertive China'.[14] The economic BRI is complemented by a scientific BRI, intended

[7] China Power Project, Centre for Strategic & International Studies, 'How will the Belt and Road Initiative advance China's interests?', available at chinapower.csis.org/china-belt-and-road-initiative. For the full document, see National Development and Reform Commission et al, 'Vision and Actions on Jointly Building Silk Road Economic Belt and 21st-Century Maritime Silk Road' (28 March 2015), available at en.ndrc.gov.cn/newsrelease/201503/t20150330_669367.html.

[8] See ibid.

[9] See ibid.

[10] L Kuo and N Kommenda, 'What is China's Belt and Road Initiative?' *The Guardian*, available at www.theguardian.com/cities/ng-interactive/2018/jul/30/what-china-belt-road-initiative-silk-road-explainer.

[11] Comment made by H Kharas in an interview published in R Hass, B Jones and J Mason (eds), *China's Belt and Road: The New Geopolitics of Global Infrastructure Development: A Brookings Interview* (Washington DC, Brookings Institution, 2019) 5, available at www.brookings.edu/wp-content/uploads/2019/04/FP_20190419_bri_interview.pdf.

[12] A Chatzky and J McBridge, 'China's Massive Belt and Road Initiative' (Council on Foreign Relations Backgrounder, 21 May 2019), available at www.cfr.org/backgrounder/chinas-massive-belt-and-road-initiative.

[13] ibid.

[14] ibid.

'to restore China's place as one of the world's great civilizations, and that includes being seen by all other nations as a source of scientific power, too'.[15] Finally, China has also encouraged the training of government officers from Africa and Asia in Beijing, which raises for some the possibility that these public servants might absorb anti-democratic ideas, including for Kenyans, for example, fears that anti-terrorism training in Beijing will reinforce Kenya's already-oppressive approach to Kenyan Muslims, building on China's suppression of its Uyghur Muslim minority.

The United States (US) is certainly clear what it thinks of what it views as the global dominance motive behind the BRI in its multiple strands. It is hardly surprising that much critical analysis has emanated from the US. The US sees itself as the world's most influential, effective and popular nation in the world. China is the second largest economy. US resistance to what it sees as the growing hegemony of China has caused considerable tension between the two.[16] Maybe in the future they may settle down to a mutual acceptance of each other's positions in the world.

Foreign Affairs says:[17]

> In the Indo-Pacific region, China wants complete dominance; it wants to force the United States out and become the region's unchallenged political, economic, and military hegemon. And globally, even though it is happy to leave the United States in the driver's seat, it wants to be powerful enough to counter Washington when needed. As one Chinese official put it to me, 'Being a great power means you get to do what you want, and no one can say anything about it.'

Maybe it is – also – something more (or less). One source has suggested that it may be more about domestic political legitimacy for Xi Jinping.

> Every time a new bridge, railroad, port, or highway is built, Xi will receive his foreign partners' applause. Each headline that touts China's sweeping foreign policy will burnish Xi's claims to world leadership. With rewards like that, why worry if the bridges lead to nowhere?[18]

As the foregoing account suggests, the BRI as conceived by China, and its President Xi Jinping, is not simple. It has become a huge range of issues and mechanisms including monetary exchanges, transport (of different kinds, including mass transportation means), power and other forms of energy, including coal, as well

[15] E Masood, 'How China is redrawing the map of world science' *Nature*, 1 May 2019, available at www.nature.com/immersive/d41586-019-01124-7/index.html.

[16] See J Feffer, 'The Widening Rift Between the US and China: Worsening relations between the two largest economies in the world could lead to disaster' *The Nation*, 8 April 2019, available at www.thenation.com/article/china-us-xi-jinping-congagement.

[17] OS Mastro, 'The Stealth Superpower: How China Hid Its Global Ambitions' *Foreign Affairs* (January/February 2019), available at www.foreignaffairs.com/articles/china/china-plan-rule-asia.

[18] P Musgrave and D Nexon, 'Zheng He's Voyages and the Symbolism Behind Xi Jinping's Belt and Road Initiative' *The Diplomat*, 22 December 2017, available at thediplomat.com/2017/12/zheng-hes-voyages-and-the-symbolism-behind-xi-jinpings-belt-and-road-initiative.

as ports,[19] dams, fibre optic cables and security arrangements.[20] Energy and raw materials are major concern for China also, with the BRI including pipelines and canals conveying oil from the Middle East, without the necessity for it to be put to sea,[21] major oil sources in Africa (especially the Sudans and Angola[22]) and minerals required for digital equipment.[23]

But not all of the most ambitious Belt and Road projects are – or will be – about hard infrastructure. Recent reports have suggested a move away from the infrastructure emphasis, with industrial cooperation, poverty alleviation, business development[24] and artificial intelligence[25] cited as the next steps. The BRI also has a digital dimension, and is contributing to digital infrastructure being built 'across the developing world'.[26] There are apprehensions about the control this may give to authoritarian leaders in those countries, and indeed to China itself.[27] Huawei, the mammoth Chinese company that owns more 5G patents than any other in the world[28] and is deeply suspect in the US (and among some in the United Kingdom (UK)[29]), is at the spearhead of this digital plan, but China's digital interests go beyond that. In 2017 China launched an Artificial Intelligence Development Plan that anticipates that 'by 2030, China will "become the world's premier artificial

[19] Ports have been a major form of infrastructure. A major recent Chinese report said that Chinese companies have invested in 42 ports across 34 countries since 2013: J Zeng and D Kirton, 'Poor Planning Poses Threat to Some Belt and Road Port Projects, Report Finds' *Caixin*, 23 April 2019, available at www.caixinglobal.com/2019-04-23/poor-planning-poses-threat-to-belt-and-road-port-projects-report-finds-101407717.html.

[20] As well as the specific items cited here, it is worth noting the existence of a website devoted to the accumulation of BRI specific news items, focusing particularly on Asia and set up by two European residents of China, available at www.beltroad-initiative.com.

[21] P Mendis, 'From Taiwan to the belt and road, China's "grand plan" is to push the US out of Asia' *South China Morning Post*, 23 January 2019, available at www.scmp.com/comment/insight-opinion/united-states/article/2183127/taiwan-belt-and-road-chinas-grand-plan-push-us.

[22] A Scobell, B Lin, HJ Shatz, M Johnson, L Hanauer, MS Chase, AS Cevallos, IW Rasmussen, A Chan, A Strong, E Warner and L Ma, *At the Dawn of Belt and Road: China in the Developing World* (Santa Monica, RAND Corporation, 2018) 199, available at www.rand.org/content/dam/rand/pubs/research_reports/RR2200/RR2273/RAND_RR2273.pdf.

[23] 'Mining the Future: How China is set to dominate the next Industrial Revolution' *Foreign Policy*, 1 May 2019, available at foreignpolicy.com/2019/05/01/mining-the-future-china-critical-minerals-metals.

[24] E Zhang and G Wu, 'Reporter's Notebook: What's Next for the Belt and Road Initiative?' *Caixing*, 2 May 2019, available at www.caixinglobal.com/2019-05-02/reporters-notebook-whats-next-for-the-belt-and-road-initiative-101410969.html.

[25] 'Data: An Integral Part of China's New Belt and Road Initiative Strategy in Africa' *The Kenyan Wall Street*, 3 May 2019, available at kenyanwallstreet.com/data-an-integral-part-of-chinas-new-belt-and-road-initiative-strategy-in-africa.

[26] W Rahn, 'Belt and Road Forum: Will China's "digital Silk Road" lead to an authoritarian future?' *Deutsche Welle*, 26 April 2019, available at www.dw.com/en/belt-and-road-forum-will-chinas-digital-silk-road-lead-to-an-authoritarian-future/a-48497082.

[27] ibid.

[28] ibid, citing the *Wall Street Journal*.

[29] eg the Secretary of State for Defence, who was sacked for allegedly leaking National Security Council discussion on links with Huawei. See D Sabbagh, H Stewart, R Syal and P Wintour, 'Gavin Williamson hits back at "haphazard" Huawei leak inquiry' *The Guardian*, 2 May 2019, available at www.theguardian.com/politics/2019/may/02/gavin-williamson-hits-back-at-haphazard-leak-inquiry.

intelligence innovation center" which in turn will "foster a new national leadership and establish the key fundamentals for an economic great power"'.[30] When Chinese companies control the data-processing capacity of much of the world there are those who see that data will be a major export to China. 'Data colonialism' is a new buzzword, and its victims would not be restricted to developing countries.[31]

There is another dimension to this, at least in the view of analysts: security. Although *Foreign Affairs* accepts that 'China has no interest in establishing a web of global alliances, sustaining a far-flung global military presence, sending troops thousands of miles from its borders, leading international institutions that would constrain its own behavior, or spreading its system of government abroad',[32] the US Department of Defence's Africa Centre for Strategic Studies has said that in five states – Djibouti, Namibia, Pakistan, Sri Lanka and Greece – 'China's port investments have been followed by regular People's Liberation Army Navy deployments and strengthened military agreements. In this way, financial investments have been turned into geostrategic returns'.[33] Furthermore, the Pentagon has suggested that China may develop military bases around the world to protect its BRI investments.[34] So like Hong Kong, BRI countries may find themselves being host to the Chinese military. There is dispute over the accuracy of some of these statements, but a number of China's BRI recipient countries, especially sources of important raw materials, are notably unstable – the Democratic Republic of Congo is a particular example. In such cases a military presence might be foreseen and, of course, in this China would not be paving new paths: former colonial and other Western powers have considerable numbers of military bases around the world, and not just to protect investments.

A perhaps unexpected aspect of the BRI is the exportation of Chinese law and legal institutions. It is reported[35] that China plans to set up courts, in Shenzhen and Xi'an, the former hub of the original Silk Road, for BRI commercial disputes to be resolved and, according to the director of the Reconnecting Asia project at the Centre for Strategic and International Studies in Washington, the BRI is a vehicle for China 'to write new rules, establish institutions that reflect Chinese interests, and reshape "soft" infrastructure'.[36] It is expected that these courts will use Chinese

[30] Future of Life Institute, 'AI POLICY – CHINA', available at futureoflife.org/ai-policy-china/?cn.

[31] N Couldry and UA Mejias, 'Data colonialism: rethinking big data's relation to the contemporary subject' (2018) 20 *Television & New Media* 336, available at eprints.lse.ac.uk/89511.

[32] Mastro, 'The Stealth Superpower' (2019) (n 17).

[33] P Nantulya, 'Implications for Africa from China's One Belt One Road Strategy', 22 March 2019, available at africacenter.org/spotlight/implications-for-africa-china-one-belt-one-road-strategy.

[34] 'China will build string of military bases around world, says Pentagon' *The Guardian*, 3 May 2019, available at www.theguardian.com/world/2019/may/03/china-will-build-string-of-military-bases-around-world-says-pentagon.

[35] Kuo and Kommenda, 'What is China's Belt and Road Initiative?' (n 10).

[36] ibid.

judiciary together with arbitration and mediation agencies but apply international rules and also involve foreign legal experts.

The BRI is now enormous, involving countries with over half the world's population and 'a quarter of global GDP'.[37] The early countries to sign up were mostly in Asia, including Central Asia. Much of the attention has been on Africa, partly because of the levels of debt African states have accumulated, and a sense that their systems are less robust and less able to stand up to China. Some small Pacific nations are also involved – in fact, the Pacific has been for some time a major site of China/Taiwan struggle with small nations being courted by both for their United Nations (UN) votes. Now China is competing with Australia and New Zealand in their own backyard.[38] However, the BRI is now extending even further. Sixteen Central and Eastern European countries are firmly on the maritime road.[39] But one of the most recent countries to 'sign on' has been Italy, the first G7 country to do so. In Italy, China will invest in infrastructure for three ports.[40] This goes against a European Union commitment to put up a united front towards China on the BRI. Yet the UK also seems to be in danger of acting against that commitment, as the *Financial Times* implied when it reported on the visit of the Chancellor of the Exchequer to Beijing in April 2019. It said:

> Britain is among a number of [European Union] countries – including France and Germany – to have refused to sign a bilateral memorandum of understanding with China on Belt and Road, amid concerns about environmental issues, the debt burden on third countries and the openness of contracts to bids from western countries.[41]

What the brief account of the BRI offered here hopefully shows is that its vastness is substantive and geographic, and that ultimately what is sought through the BRI is the pursuit not only of international standing and power for China, but of a complete reconfiguration of geopolitical relations. As Bruno Maçães puts it:

> The new world the initiative will try to create is not one where one piece on the chessboard will be replaced, not even one where the pieces will have been reorganized. It will be a world built anew by very different people and according to very different ideas.[42]

[37] ibid.

[38] C Greenfield and C Packham, 'Making waves in West, China luring Pacific islands with Belt and Road' *Reuters*, 14 November 2018, available at af.reuters.com/article/worldNews/idAFKCN1NJ1C5.

[39] ET Gjorgjievska, 'The Chinese "silk road" of threats and opportunities in the void between the EU strategy, CEE interests and the citizens' (The Balkans in Europe Policy Advisory Group blog, 26 March 2019), available at biepag.eu/the-chinese-silk-road-of-threats-and-opportunities-in-the-void-between-the-eu-strategy-cee-interests-and-the-citizens/.

[40] A Chatzky, 'China's Belt and Road Gets a Win in Italy' (Council on Foreign Relations, 27 March 2019), available at www.cfr.org/article/chinas-belt-and-road-gets-win-italy.

[41] 'Hammond courts China economic ties on Beijing trip' *Financial Times*, 26 April 2019, available at www.ft.com/content/a791f700-6812-11e9-9adc-98bf1d35a056.

[42] B Maçães, 'What you need to know to understand Belt and Road' (World Economic Forum, 7 December 2018), available at www.weforum.org/agenda/2018/12/what-you-need-to-know-one-belt-one-road.

II. Resistance and Critique

As might be expected, there is significant concern about the BRI and China's accumulation through it of power and influence. The concerns voiced include: debt burden, consequent loss of control over assets, workers' rights, impact on local industry in receiving countries, impact on democracy, environmental impact, data abstraction and fair contracting terms. These concerns relate to the impact on the recipient countries, in addition to the concerns of countries like the US about their position in the global pecking order. Where the expression of concern emanates from also varies. In some countries that are party to the BRI there seems very little criticism – for example in the Pacific island nations. Issues like human rights and authoritarianism may emanate as much from Western countries as from the BRI participants themselves.

A. Workers' Rights

Frequent gatherings of other world leaders with Xi seem to pay little attention to workers (which tells us a good deal about the other world leaders). In developing countries, like Kenya, where scales of reward are sharply divided between Chinese experts and local staff, BRI takes on the character of worker exploitation. When the Chinese Government is involved in a transaction, negotiations are taken up between governments on both sides, with very little direct engagement with workers or their representatives including unions. There are some suggestions that China may not fully grasp the importance and power of workers' unions, especially in Europe;[43] perhaps not surprising for a country in which such organisations are 'virtually impotent when it comes to representing workers'.[44]

Sometimes the concern is that of jobs being taken from locals. In the past this has sometimes extended to labouring jobs, but China now seems at pains to ensure that locals do most such work. However, in Kenya there has been complaint about the number of Chinese working on the Chinese-built railway (discussed below). A newspaper alleged that 5,000 Chinese were working on running the railway, as engineers, accountants, dieticians, cooks, locomotive operators, welders and carpenters.[45] The figures were disputed, with the China Roads and Bridges

[43] See Zeng and Kirton, 'Poor Planning Poses Threat' (2019) (n 19).

[44] D Metcalf and J Li, 'Trade unions in China' (2006) *CentrePiece* 24, available at cep.lse.ac.uk/pubs/download/CP204.pdf.

[45] P Wafula, 'Revealed: The 5000- strong Chinese army powering the SGR' *The Standard*, 15 July 2018, available at www.standardmedia.co.ke/article/2001288060/revealed-the-5000-strong-chinese-army-powering-the-sgr.

Corporation saying that under 3,000 Chinese were working there and that 86 per cent of the workers are Kenyans.[46]

Unequal and degrading treatment of local workers is a further complaint.[47] It is impossible to tell how justified these complaints are in any systematic way. On the whole there is no particular prejudice against Chinese people in African countries. They do not have any colonial baggage, and surveys show generally positive attitudes towards them. But there are stories, including about a Chinese restaurant that refused to admit black people in the evening unaccompanied by people of other races,[48] as well as a tendency for Chinese workers to live apart from the rest of the community.

B. Debt and Loss of Assets

Some governments, including those of Malaysia, Pakistan and Sierra Leone, are starting to rethink the costs of the BRI projects to which they are committed.[49] The new President of Sierra Leone cancelled a deal for China to build a $400 million international airport;[50] and in Sri Lanka the Government was forced to lease a port to a Chinese company for 99 years after struggling to make repayments. The Centre for Global Development has analysed the debt-risk situation of 68 BRI countries and identified Mongolia, Kyrgyzstan, Tajikistan, Laos, Pakistan, the Maldives, Montenegro and Djibouti[51] as being at serious risk of not being able to repay their loans. Other countries at risk include Belarus, Bosnia and Herzegovina,

[46] L Mwiti, 'Confusion over number of Chinese workers under SGR' *The Standard*, 19 July 2018, available at www.standardmedia.co.ke/article/2001288597/confusion-over-number-of-chinese-workers-under-sgr.

[47] 'More Revelations of How Chinese Workers Continue to Mistreat Kenyan SGR Workers' *KTN News*, 9 August 2018, available at www.standardmedia.co.ke/ktnnews/video/2000159638/more-revelations-of-how-chinese-workers-continue-to-mistreat-kenyan-sgr-workers.

[48] J Okoth, 'Kenya must face up to rising claims of racial discrimination by Chinese against locals' *Quartz Africa*, 15 October 2018, available at qz.com/africa/1423930/kenya-must-deal-with-chinese-racial-discrimination. See also, J Goldstein, 'Kenyans Say Chinese Investment Brings Racism and Discrimination' *The New York Times*, 15 October 2018, available at www.nytimes.com/2018/10/15/world/africa/kenya-china-racism.html.

[49] Though Malaysia at least is not making a blanket rejection of BRI, but adjusting in the light of concerns including debt levels, see P Parameswaran, 'Malaysia's Evolving Approach to China's Belt and Road Initiative: the new government's evolving approach to the initiative continues to be much more flexible than some of the headlines may suggest' *The Diplomat*, 23 April 2019, available at thediplomat.com/2019/04/malaysias-evolving-approach-to-chinas-belt-and-road-initiative.

[50] Y Kazeem, 'One of Africa's poorest countries has pulled the plug on a $400 million China-funded airport' *Quartz Africa*, 10 October 2018, available at qz.com/africa/1419253/sierra-leone-cancels-400-million-china-airport-loan.

[51] J Hurley, S Morris and G Portelance, 'Examining the Debt Implications of the Belt and Road Initiative from a Policy Perspective' (Centre for Global Development Policy Paper 121, March 2018), available at www.cgdev.org/sites/default/files/examining-debt-implications-belt-and-road-initiative-policy-perspective.pdf.

Ethiopia and Kenya, although in those countries 'total public debt should remain low enough to mitigate the likelihood of default'.[52]

C. Contract Terms

Reports indicate that the contracts signed by China with loan-receiving countries normally require the details to be kept secret.[53] Chinese corporations are now increasingly active in some countries, particularly in Africa and Asia, where it is feared that there are few safeguards to protect national interests.

Some countries have managed to avoid having secrecy clauses – the Philippines is apparently one.[54] But that country did not escape another Chinese trap: waiver of sovereign immunity. The same source lists Guyana and Kyrgyzstan as other countries with similar clauses. Interestingly, the clause quoted has an interesting possible 'get-out':

> [E]xcept any other assets of the borrower located within the territory of the Philippines to the extent that the borrower is prohibited by the laws or public policies having force of law in the Republic of the Philippines, applicable and in effect at the signing date of this agreement from waiving such immunity.[55]

This applies only to (i) assets within the territory and (ii) protected by law. There is a certain irony in the use of these waiver clauses, in view of the Chinese law, and the case of *Democratic Republic of the Congo v FG Hemisphere Associates LLC* in which the Hong Kong Court of Final Appeal held that the Chinese law recognised absolute immunity even in commercial contracts, and Hong Kong had to apply the same rule.[56]

Another common provision relates to application of Chinese law and use of Chinese courts or arbitration. This is not unusual. Contracts with British companies or with the UK Government will usually provide that the governing law is to be that of England and maybe that disputes are to be resolved by the London Court of Arbitration, or possibly in Hong Kong. Indeed, sometimes contracts with China provide that arbitration will be at the Hong Kong International Arbitration Centre.[57] But, when contracts specify Chinese law and courts, it is hard to quiet concerns of those who look at the Chinese judiciary and its lack of the

[52] ibid 13.

[53] R Rivas, 'Made in China: Loan terms with waivers, shrouded in secrecy' *Rappler*, 27 March 2019, available at www.rappler.com/newsbreak/in-depth/226728-provisions-waivers-philippines-loan-agreements-with-china.

[54] ibid.

[55] ibid.

[56] *Democratic Republic of the Congo v FG Hemisphere Associates LLC* (2011) 14 HKCFAR 95. See also the contribution of Johannes Chan in this collection.

[57] Rivas, 'Made in China' (2019) (n 53).

usually-aspired-to tenets of judicial independence, with a Chief Justice who has said 'Bare your swords towards false western ideals like judicial independence'.[58]

D. Impact on Local Firms

It has been observed that 'China's dominance in the construction sector comes at the expense of local contractors in partner countries', suggesting that one motive for the BRI is to find work for domestic excess capacity.[59] Certainly industry in BRI recipient countries complains. In Kenya, China Roads and Bridges, China Wu Yi, and Sichuan Huashi Enterprises Corporation East Africa Limited are key actors in many new constructions. It is an issue that goes beyond BRI-funded projects to include those funded by the World Bank and African Development Bank. It has also been alleged that decisions to reserve a certain share of the work for local firms have been subverted by Chinese companies registering local subsidiaries and acquiring work through them.[60]

Similar complaints are found in many countries including within Eastern Europe[61] and Uganda, where Quartz Africa calculated that of 48 contracts for road building over ten years issued in the past decade, '70% of the funding went to Chinese contractors and only 4% to locally incorporated firms'.[62] In Jamaica there are complaints that 'We have handed our construction industry to the Chinese'.[63]

E. Corruption

There have always been concerns in Hong Kong that reunification with China might reignite corruption as an issue in Hong Kong which has, since the founding of the Independent Commission Against Corruption, had an enviable reputation as a corruption-free zone.[64] There have been various allegations of corrupt practices in the BRI agreements. Chinese money for the ill-fated Hambantota port was used to contribute to President Rajapaksa's election (see below). And the Malaysian state development fund, domestic corruption in which led to the fall of the Prime

[58] L Hornby, 'China's top judge denounces judicial independence' *Financial Times*, 17 January 2017, available at www.ft.com/content/60dddd46-dc74-11e6-9d7c-be108f1c1dce.

[59] Kuo and Kommenda (n 10).

[60] J Mwende, 'Chinese grip on Kenya projects upsets local builders' *Construction Kenya*, 21 January 2019, available at www.constructionkenya.com/2983/chinese-firms-dominate-kenyas-construction-industry.

[61] Gjorgjievska, 'The Chinese "silk road"' (2019).

[62] L Namubiru, 'Chinese contractors are going to keep dominating road construction in Uganda' *Quartz Africa*, 13 July 2018, available at qz.com/africa/1326618/china-is-building-expensive-roads-in-uganda.

[63] A Edwards, '"China Effect" hits Local Construction Industry' *Jamaica Observer*, 20 January 2019, available at www.jamaicaobserver.com/sunday-finance/we-have-handed-our-construction-industry-to-the-chinese-williams_154716.

[64] See M Yip, 'Can Hong Kong stay corruption-free under China?' *BBC News* (11 July 2013), available at www.bbc.com/news/world-asia-china-23223457.

Minister, was reported by the *Wall Street Journal* in 2019 to have been propped up by China by means of inflating the costs of BRI projects.[65] The author of the item cited points out that opaqueness in the BRI fuels perceptions of corruption.

The same article commented that China's enforcement of its law against foreign bribery has been weak. Now that President Xi has promised 'Everything should be done in a transparent way and we should have zero tolerance for corruption' in his speech at the 2019 BRI forum,[66] maybe things will change.

F. Environmental Risks

China's own record on environmental protection has not been stellar, but once it sets its mind to dealing with a situation it can be remarkably effective. However, its 'hands off' approach to the internal policy of countries it deals with – which is one of its virtues as far as recipients are concerned, but a cause for concern for other countries – may lead to its turning a blind eye to important issues including the environmental impact of projects undertaken under the auspices of the BRI, particularly notable as many elements of the BRI overlap with diversity hotpots.[67] Certainly UN Environment is concerned about this and has set up an initiative jointly with the Chinese Ministry of Ecology and Environment to support recipient countries in meeting environmental standards.[68]

There have been concerns about the environmental impacts of many big BRI project including high-speed trains and large dams.[69] Kenya is an example where environmental concerns seem to have been ignored. China is financing a coal-fired power project that is strongly resisted by the local community and would harm its inhabitants, and that evidence suggests is not needed in view of Kenya's renewable energy sources.[70] Since then the pressure on both China and the Kenya Governments has increased. Although neither government has made substantial public statements on the matter, proceedings are now before a judicial body, and

[65] See JE Hillman, 'Corruption Flows Along China's Belt and Road' (Centre for Strategic and International Studies commentary, 18 January 2019), available at www.csis.org/analysis/corruption-flows-along-chinas-belt-and-road, which discusses T Wright and B Hope, 'WSJ Investigation: China Offered to Bail Out Troubled Malaysian Fund in Return for Deals' *The Wall Street Journal*, 7 January 2019, available at www.wsj.com/articles/how-china-flexes-its-political-muscle-to-expand-power-overseas-11546890449.]

[66] 'Xi Jinping vows transparency over Belt and Road' *BBC News* (26 April 2019), available at www.bbc.com/news/business-48061951.

[67] Masood, 'How China is redrawing' (2019).

[68] United Nations Environment, 'International Coalition for Green Development on the Belt and Road', available at www.unenvironment.org/regions/asia-and-pacific/regional-initiatives/international-coalition-green-development-belt-and.

[69] B Gokkon, 'Environmentalists are Raising Concerns over China's Belt and Road Initiative' *Pacific Standard*, 18 July 2018, available at psmag.com/environment/environmental-concerns-over-chinese-infrastructure-projects.

[70] See Hurley, Morris and Portelance, 'Examining the Debt Implications' (2018) 10. The non-governmental organisation of which the authors are founding directors (Katiba Institute) is representing the community in this case before the National Environmental Tribunal.

the matter has attracted criticisms both locally and internationally, so that such silence cannot, we would think, be maintained for much longer. The controversial railway (see below) also has negative impacts for Kenya's wildlife – the second phase is to pass through the Nairobi National Park despite vigorous opposition from civil society, and litigation.[71] China takes a hands-off approach on this, as on other non-commercial issues; it is clear that the decisions on the railway's route are those of the Kenyan Government. In fact there is some perception that the Chinese are a negative influence on conservation in other ways.

G. Authoritarianism

Concerns about the BRI undermining democracy and civil space are multifaceted. On the one hand there is a fear that governments could simply feel that if China can govern in an authoritarian way and do so well, why shouldn't they? Secondly – as with many other states[72] – China's engagement at governmental level sometimes props up undemocratic regimes. African examples have included Bashir in Sudan, Mugabe in Zimbabwe and successive regimes in the Democratic Republic of the Congo. The *Guardian* has reported that 'African leaders are almost three times more likely to spend Chinese development aid in areas where they have ethnic ties'.[73] Chinese support for former President Rajapaksa in Sri Lanka is another example (see below). Another factor that may lead to support for undemocratic regimes is weapon sales; again, hardly a uniquely Chinese trait. However, in recent years 'China has become the top supplier of arms to sub-Saharan Africa, accounting for 27 per cent of the region's imports over the four year period from 2013–2017, an increase of 55 per cent over 2008–2012'.[74]

III. The Impact of the BRI: Three Illustrations

A. Sri Lanka

Some years ago, Yash Ghai was struck by a newspaper headline: 'Paying China with territory'. It was not, as he thought it might have been, April Fools' Day.

[71] Rulings have been on an interim basis so do not seem to be available online.

[72] F Wagner, 'EU is as comfortable as China with the African thugs and dictators' *EURACTIVE* (24 October 2018), available at www.euractiv.com/section/development-policy/opinion/wed-eu-is-so-comfortable-with-african-thugs-and-dictators.

[73] M Anderson, 'African presidents "use China aid for patronage politics"' *The Guardian*, 19 November 2014, available at www.theguardian.com/global-development/2014/nov/19/african-presidents-china-aid-patronage-politics.

[74] M Kovrig, 'China Expands Its Peace and Security Footprint in Africa' (International Crisis Group, 24 October 2018), available at www.crisisgroup.org/asia/north-east-asia/china/china-expands-its-peace-and-security-footprint-africa.

Apparently Sri Lanka had to forfeit a strategic northern port to China because it had not been able to pay for its construction. There were rumours that China had chosen that port because it would allow it to keep a close eye on southern India, given the considerable tension between the two states. Ghai found this all the more worrying when he learnt that China's management and control lasted for 99 years.

Sri Lanka is a small country and a victim of India/China rivalry.[75] China had established a special relationship with the Sri Lankan president, which enables it to use the port for strategic purposes, particularly targeting India – no doubt putting Sri Lanka in a difficult relationship with its long-term ally and close neighbour. The *New York Times* account relates the port story to China's relationship with former President Rajapaksa, victor of the country's civil war, and its rivalry with India for regional dominancc.[76] According to the *New York Times*, China contributed financially to Rajapaksa's electoral campaign, assisted the party in power in Sri Lanka to win the 2015 elections, lobbied voters and then started to tighten the screws to achieve its control over government policies.[77] Although the Hambantota Port project predates the BRI, it illustrates China's tendency to continue to provide loans and assistance even as doubts about feasibility arose, while other states refused, and Sri Lankan debt continued to grow.[78]

Such profligate financial support triggered suspicion as to motive, and as predicted the port project failed. By then a new government was in power in Sri Lanka. China declined easier repayment terms, essentially insisting on the port by means of repayment. A recent report by the Chinese Grandview Institution has explained, or justified, what happened:

> According to the report, the project entered difficulties because, after being conceived in 2012, Sri Lanka's subsequent 'change of government, swinging policies, insufficient management experience, [and] a lack of business and industry' gave passing vessels few good reasons to dock at the port. Problems arose largely because of poor planning and political uncertainty, it adds.[79]

In 2018 the new President tried to sack his Prime Minister and appoint Rajapaksa in his stead. The Supreme Court soon put a stop to this unconstitutional course of action,[80] but not before Rajapaksa had tweeted that he had received a congratulatory message from Xi Jinping, something the *Financial Times* suggested he would hardly have done if it had not been true.[81]

[75] See V Sridharan, 'What Rajapaksa's return means for China-India tug of war over Sri Lanka' *South China Morning Post*, 29 October 2018, available at www.scmp.com/week-asia/politics/article/2170621/what-rajapaksas-return-means-china-india-tug-war-over-sri-lanka.

[76] M Abi-Habib, 'How China Got Sri Lanka to Cough Up a Port' *The New York Times*, 25 June 2018, available at www.nytimes.com/2018/06/25/world/asia/china-sri-lanka-port.html.

[77] ibid.

[78] ibid.

[79] See Zeng and Kirton (n 19).

[80] *Rajavarothiam Sampanthan v Attorney General* (13 December 2018), judgment of the Supreme Court of Sri Lanka available at www.supremecourt.lk/images/documents/sc_fr_351_2018.pdf.

[81] 'Sri Lanka turmoil points to China's increasing role' *Financial Times*, 15 November 2018, available at www.ft.com/content/ccfb4d06-e807-11e8-8a85-04b8afea6ea3.

B. Kenya

In 2018, there was an exhibition at the National Museum in Nairobi, Kenya, comprising silk printed banners tracing the history of Chinese–East Africa relations from the great fifteenth-century admiral Zheng He to the BRI, an interesting example of a marketing campaign, though unlikely to have reached many people.

Many Kenyans are afraid that all the country's assets, within Kenya or abroad, are now subject to seizure by China if Kenya cannot repay its debts. This fear has arisen from wide belief that China is about to take over Mombasa, valuable to China as a military base, as Kenya has not cleared its debt to China. The great secrecy with which Kenyan and Chinese Governments have conducted their transactions has given the rise to these fears. Kenya has received more attention regarding BRI than many other states. The suspicion is that China has made more contracts, and more secret contracts, with Kenya than with any other state in Africa.

The fear about the failure to pay debts is hardly fanciful. This is not, however, solely because of debt owed to China. While Kenya owes to China 70 per cent of its bilateral debt, it owes China as such 'only' 21.3 per cent of its overall external debt. So though reports of China having some sort of stranglehold by holding 70 per cent of Kenya's external debt are exaggerated,[82] it is also important to take account of private debt (including, presumably, to Chinese banks). Kenya's debt to GDP ratio has been said to be 68.9 per cent.[83] The Kenyan–Chinese project demonstrates the secrecy that is common. The largest and the best known of the joint projects is the railway project, ie the Standard Gauge Railway now running from the coast to Nairobi and originally planned to go on ultimately to Uganda as the original, colonial railway did. This was funded by two separate $1.6 billion loans from China. The finance ministry played a key role in negotiating it, although on both sides the deal was made with heads of state. In fact it was reported that the Attorney-General of the time advised the Government that there was no legal basis for a government procurement of that sort, but this concern was brushed aside.[84] The contract itself has never been made public despite promises by government, recently renewed. The *Nation* newspaper claims to have seen the contract and that it also has a confidentiality clause 'gagging Kenya from making the deal public "without prior written permission of the lender [China]"'.[85] The debt was to be

[82] See C Mureithi, 'China owns 21.3% of Kenya's external debt – not 70% as reported' (Africa Check, 4 September 2018), available at africacheck.org/reports/no-china-does-not-own-more-than-70-of-kenyas-external-debt.

[83] S Bellows, 'Kenya's economic history and increasing public debt' *Business Daily* (Nairobi, 10 April 2019), available at www.businessdailyafrica.com/lifestyle/pfinance/economic-history-and-increasing-public-debt-/4258410-5065532-uyi94t/index.html.

[84] P Wafula and M Njagih, 'State agencies ignored AG's counsel on railway contract, MPs told' *The Standard*, 21 January 2014, available at www.standardmedia.co.ke/article/2000102836/state-agencies-ignored-ag-s-counsel-on-railway-contract-mps-told.

[85] E Okoth, 'SGR pact with China a risk to Kenyan sovereignty, assets' *Sunday Nation*, 13 January 2019, available at www.nation.co.ke/news/Hidden-traps-in-SGR-deal-with-China/1056-4932764-ebw46r/index.html.

repaid from revenue of the railway, but both the actual and foreseen revenues are inadequate for these purposes.[86] Under the basic agreement, the *Nation* says, 'Neither the borrower (Kenya) nor any of its assets is entitled to any right of immunity on the grounds of sovereignty or otherwise from arbitration, suit, execution, or any other legal process with respect to its obligations under this Agreement, as the case may be in any jurisdiction.'[87] It does not state that the clause goes on to include the get-out mentioned earlier in connection with the Philippines. This is potentially important because Kenyan law does prohibit the levying of execution against government property.[88] The effect of the clause on its face would be to risk the forfeiture of Kenya's rights, sovereign or otherwise, to any Kenyan national asset, whether the Port of Mombasa, another asset within Kenya, or a Kenyan asset abroad, if necessary to execute a judgment. China has denied that any of these assets is actually used as collateral,[89] but this does not prevent seizure in execution.

If the waiver is valid it is interesting to reflect on the remarks of Lord Haldane, quoted in Kenyan cases on immunity from execution:

> If execution and/or attachment against the Government were allowed, there is no doubt that the Government will not be able to pay immediately upon passing of decrees and judgments and it will be inundated with executions and attachments of its assets day in, day out. Its buildings will be attached, its plants and equipment will be attached, its furniture and office equipment will be attached, its vehicles, aircraft, ship and boats will be attached. There will be no end to the list of likely assets to be attached and auctioned by the auctioneer's hammer. No Government can possibly survive such an onslaught. The Government and therefore, the state operations will ground to a halt and paralyzed and soon the Government will not only be bankrupt, but its constitutional and statutory duties will not be capable of performance. This will lead to a chaos, anarchy and the breakdown of the Rule of Law.[90]

The standard clause on applicable law also applies. The secrecy clause certainly runs counter to the spirit of the Kenyan Constitution in which a national value is 'transparency' (Article 10). Some interesting constitutional dilemmas may arise. Article 35 recognises a right to access information held by any public body. The right is liable to be limited by law (Article 24), and indeed there is legislation that does so including allowing a refusal to supply information because it relates to foreign relations. However, there is an override – disclosure may be required if 'the

[86] The economist David Ndii has written a number of analyses including: 'SGR by the numbers – some unpleasant arithmetic' *East African Review* (21 July 2018), available at www.theeastafricanreview.info/op-eds/2018/07/21/sgr-by-the-numbers-some-unpleasant-arithmetic.

[87] Okoth, 'SGR pact with China a risk' (2019) (n 85).

[88] Now Government Proceedings Act, s 21(4).

[89] See the interview with the recently appointed Chinese ambassador to Kenya: M Gaitho, 'Chinese envoy: No Kenyan assets have been mortgaged for SGR loan' *Daily Nation*, 20 May 2019, available at www.nation.co.ke/news/Chinese-envoy--No-Kenyan-assets-have-been-mortgaged-for-SGR-loan/1056-5122688-2wsetu/index.html.

[90] *Auckland Harbour Board v R* [1924] AC 318, 326 quoted in *Kisya Investments Ltd v Attorney General & another* [2005] eKLR, available at kenyalaw.org/caselaw/cases/view/10865.

public interest in disclosure outweighs the harm to protected interests as shall be determined by a Court', and when deciding if this applies the court should take account of, inter alia, constitutional principles on the need to 'promote accountability of public entities to the public', 'ensure that the expenditure of public funds is subject to effective oversight' and 'promote informed debate on issues of public interest'.[91]

What is the status of the agreement with China vis-à-vis the Kenyan Constitution? Until recently, Kenya was a clearly dualist country: international law was not domestic law unless domesticated. But the 2010 Constitution provides that 'Any treaty or convention ratified by Kenya shall form part of the law of Kenya under this Constitution' (Article 2(5) and (6)). However, the phrase 'under this Constitution' clearly makes treaties subordinate to the fundamental law. Thus Article 35 on access to information must take precedence. When the status of the Act relative to the agreement comes to be considered, factors like whether the agreement is actually a 'treaty', and whether the phrase 'under this Constitution' places treaties subordinate to, equal to, or superior to statute will be critical to the determination of its legal force.[92]

Much concern has focused on the port of Mombasa, particularly since Yash Ghai informed civil society and the business community about the occupation by China of Hambantota. The county of Mombasa where the port is situated argues that the port is its property (this may be doubtful but ultimately be resolved in court). But in its efforts to raise money to pay off the Chinese, the national Government has compelled importers to send their goods by rail to Nairobi, depriving forwarding agents and others, and road transporters, of much business. This was apparently part of the agreement with the Chinese: '"This is a key issue for the Bank," Exim bank officials said during the negotiations in a strategy that put the port at the centre of the deal' according to the *Sunday Nation*.[93] Regardless of the ownership of the port, this measure has a significant impact on Mombasa County, and at least would seem to go against the constitutional requirement of cooperation between governments.[94] This is also likely to be resolved in court. If the land is vested in the Ports Authority (a separate legal personality as a state corporation under statute) – which seems likely – then there must be doubt as to whether the national Government could by contract effectively give it away.

Another irony is that on the side of the 2019 BRI forum the Kenyan Government sought funding for the next phase of the railway to Kisumu on Lake Victoria in the West. And it was refused – reportedly because China was not satisfied of

[91] Access to Information Act 2016, s 6.

[92] A Kenyan court recently held that an agreement between governments is not the same as a treaty: *Tax Justice Network v Cabinet Secretary for National Treasury* (15 March 2019). There are conflicting decisions on the relative status of a statute and a treaty.

[93] Okoth (n 85).

[94] Article 6(2).

its economic viability.[95] The Government sought to save face by denying it had even asked, but is not believed. The Chinese have said they would lend money to refurbish the old railway.[96] The end of the new line is 43 km from the nearest point of the old. Inevitably people are asking (again) why refurbishment was not the approach adopted from the beginning.

This takes us, finally, back to a constant Kenyan pre-occupation: corruption. There is an assumption that governments want to acquire new things rather than refurbish the old because there is more money to be made. This is not just because of kickbacks on contracts, but because of the pot of gold that opens for those who acquire land on the route from unsuspecting owners and then file for compensation. There are many media reports of Chinese companies or individuals being involved in transactions that smack of corruption at some level.[97]

Chinese individuals have also been implicated in corruption on a smaller scale, such as in a ticketing scam on the railway.[98] And there have been complaints about small-scale business people setting up, even selling roast corn on the streets or holding market stalls in a largely second-hand clothes market,[99] probably having obtained immigration papers by corruption.

The reflection earlier on the state of the Kenyan Constitution in relation to an agreement with China, gives rise to another issue: if there are legal differences that arise out of something like the SGR project, but are not bound to be dealt with by Chinese courts or arbitration, how reliable would Kenyan courts be? The Kenyan judiciary has been much strengthened under the 2010 Constitution, but is not always above suspicion, and is under pressure from the Government. There have been a few cases before the Kenyan courts challenging aspects of the SGR project. None has succeeded. Naturally this cannot taken as serious evidence that no case would succeed.[100]

[95] 'Why China refused to finance railway it initially backed' *Daily Nation*, 27 April 2019, available at mobile.nation.co.ke/news/Why-China-refused-to-finance-railway-it-had-initially-backed/1950946-5089900-item-1-ld90u0/index.html.

[96] A Olingo, 'Kenya fails to secure $3.6b from China for third phase of SGR line to Kisumu' *The East African* (27 April 2019), available at www.theeastafrican.co.ke/business/Kenya-fails-to-secure-loan-from-China-for-third-phase-of-SGR/2560-5090192-2o0y9j/index.html.

[97] See, eg, S Solomon, 'Chinese Officials Arrested for Bribery Amid Kenya's SGR Corruption Inquiry' *Voice of America*, 26 November 2018, available at www.voanews.com/a/china-kenya-bribery/4673798.html; B Ngugi, 'How Israel, China firms bribe Kenyan officials' *Daily Nation*, 25 September 2018, available at www.nation.co.ke/business/Israel-China-firms-bribe-Kenyan-officials/996-4776908-8j0d7j/index.html (citing Transparency International).

[98] Solomon (ibid).

[99] E Mutai, 'MPs push for deportation of Chinese hawkers after influx' *Business Daily*, 17 October 2018, available at www.businessdailyafrica.com/economy/deportation-of-Chinese-hawkers/3946234-4810730-uyaq7dz/index.html.

[100] In *Okiya Omtatah Okoiti & 2 others v Attorney General & 3 others* [2014] eKLR, available at kenyalaw.org/caselaw/cases/view/103808, the single source nature of a contract with China Roads and Bridges Corporation was challenged. The case failed because it relied on leaked or improperly obtained public documents. The Judge did warn that 'The public is watching [the respondents who included the government, the Chinese Corporation and the Kenya Railways] and this Court will not hesitate to uphold the Law where public bodies step outside its clear parameters'.

C. Djibouti

In spite of its very small size (23,200 km^2), Djibouti occupies a very strategic position as part of the Horn of Africa – that corner of Africa at the junction of the Arabian Sea (part of the greater Indian Ocean), and the route to the Mediterranean. Djibouti itself is at the very entrance to the Red Sea and thus on China's main maritime 'road' route to Europe. It is very much integrated into the BRI, with Chinese funding for major projects including the Doraleh Multipurpose Port, the Ethiopia–Djibouti Railway, and the Ethiopia–Djibouti Water Pipeline.[101] China's involvement with the Doraleh Multipurpose Port is considerable, but under US pressure the Djibouti Government said they would not hand it over to Chinese control.[102] However, it is the existence in Djibouti of the only Chinese overseas military base that causes most concern. Because of its strategic location, as well as because of operations against Somali pirates, Djibouti also houses not only a French military base (from its colonial connection), but the only permanent US military base in Africa, as well as troops from Italy, Germany, Spain and Japan.[103] Because of the closeness to Yemen, Saudi Arabia is developing a base there also.[104] China claims that its base is not for military purposes: '[It] has nothing to do with an arms race or military expansion, and China has no intention of turning the logistics center into a military foothold.'[105] Yet the size of the project, has caused apprehensions that it has wider implications, and the International Crisis Group comments that

> The [People's Liberation Army] describes it as a support base for naval anti-piracy operations in the Gulf of Aden, peacekeeping in South Sudan and humanitarian and other cooperation in the Horn of Africa, but has also used it to conduct live-fire military exercises.[106]

The US was never happy about this development and the *Diplomat* reports that the Pentagon has said that the Djibouti base, 'along with regular naval vessel visits to foreign ports, both reflects and amplifies China's growing influence, extending the reach of its armed forces.'[107] And in 2019 the Pentagon has repeated that 'China will seek to establish additional military bases in countries with which it has a

[101] T Headley, 'China's Djibouti Base: A One Year Update' *The Diplomat* (4 December 2018), available at thediplomat.com/2018/12/chinas-djibouti-base-a-one-year-update.

[102] 'AFRICOM Chief Warns of Chinese Control at Port of Djibouti' *The Maritime Executive*, 15 March 2018, available at www.maritime-executive.com/article/u-s-concerned-by-chinese-presence-at-port-of-djibouti.

[103] W van den Berg and J Meester, 'Ports & Power: the securitisation of port politics' (Life and Peace Institute, 14 May 2018), available at life-peace.org/hab/ports-and-power.

[104] J Aglionby and S Kerr, 'Djibouti finalising deal for Saudi Arabian military base' *Financial Times*, 17 January 2017, available at www.ft.com/content/c8f63492-dc14-11e6-9d7c-be108f1c1dce.

[105] Headley, 'China's Djibouti Base' (2018).

[106] Kovrig, 'China Expands Its Peace and Security Footprint' (2018).

[107] Headley (n 101).

longstanding friendly relationship and similar strategic interests, such as Pakistan, and in which there is a precedent for hosting foreign militaries', according to Al Jazeera.[108]

IV. Reflections on the BRI

If an important aspect of the whole BRI project is the enhancement of China's standing on the world stage, for both international and domestic audiences, it is hardly surprising that it has been responding to the barrage of criticism that the initiative has elicited. As Jane Golley, an Australian professor, has said: 'Rather than using their economic power to make friends, they've drummed up more fear that it will be about influence'.[109] While it is true that many of the criticisms are based on fears and perceptions, even an accumulation of 'friends' on such a scale is a matter for some concern. Within many developing countries, however, the criticisms expressed are not on a global scale; rather, they focus on national concerns.

China deals with governments. Arguably it does not have a good enough understanding of the nature of governance, and particularly of corruption, in many developing countries. It is perfectly possible to have corrupt deals associated with fundamentally useful projects. But the experience in some countries, including our own country of Kenya, is that the spoils of corrupt deals are so tempting that projects attracting BRI funding may be developed for their corruption potential and not for their intrinsic value to the country. A railway is useful and may be a trigger for development, indeed. But if there are no goods to be transported on it, maybe the project is not viable. On the other hand, it is also possible that China is taken by surprise by the extent of local criticism. Many BRI recipient countries may be imperfect democracies, but democracies to some extent they are, and free speech and a vigorous press is found in many – not to mention social media, of course.

China has shown that it is aware of some of the comments and concerns, and has responded to some with a degree of self-criticism. The Grandview Institution, mentioned earlier, is a government advisory research group. Its recent report has said that some projects in the BRI have suffered from a 'premature mentality' and the absence of adequate research on likely returns. This would seem to us to describe China's SGR project in Kenya.

Particularly interesting are its reported comments on 'a lack of information transparency' and 'a lack of evaluation on the impact of regional social culture', and that as well as being commercially unwise such projects may 'stimulate regional

[108] 'China to increase overseas military bases: Pentagon report' *Al Jazeera*, 3 May 2019, available at www.aljazeera.com/news/2019/05/china-increase-overseas-military-bases-pentagon-report-190503065146243.html.

[109] Kuo and Kommenda (n 10).

political conflicts and unfavorable public opinion, and at the same time trigger some social problems'.[110] Transparency would 'prevent the international public opinion and local people from having unnecessary imagination about the corruption of the projects'.[111]

At the 2019 BRI Forum, participants asked for more openness and environmental friendliness, 'so as to be better prepared for political risks in host countries'.[112] Aung San Suu Kyi said, 'The projects must not only be economically feasible but also socially and environmentally responsible and, most importantly, they must win the confidence and support of local communities.'[113] Chinese responses have included reassurances about encouraging state-owned companies to cooperate with local companies, establish 'joint ventures or industrial alliances based on market principles',[114] including beyond BRI countries. The Government had 'requested state-owned companies hire as many local employees as possible, and provide them with professional training'.[115] The Governor of the Central Bank said that China would 'strengthen the debt and risk control to ensure sustainable development'.[116] In November 2018, the 'Green Investment Principles' for the BRI were unveiled, and by 27 April 2019 global financial institutions were said to have signed up to them.[117]

To US criticism such as that 'China's infrastructure diplomacy activities ignore or weaken international standards and best practices related to development, labour protections, and environmental protection', China has been less emollient. The Communist Party's *Global Times* responded that critics 'have lost their abilities to use logic and common sense, and even rational thinking'.[118] Also interesting are foreign responses. The Brookings Institute report says that interviewees thought that,

> U.S. policymakers should adapt American strategy to respond to BRI. Some scholars believe that the right strategy is to multilaterize efforts, while others argue that it is to promote a race-to-the-top dynamic vis-à-vis China. Either strategy requires working

[110] See Zeng and Kirton (n 19).

[111] See ibid.

[112] Zhang and Wu, 'Reporter's Notebook' (n 24).

[113] B Blanchard and B Goh, 'RPT-China puts gentler face on Belt and Road, hits back at critics' *Reuters* (29 April 2019), available at www.reuters.com/article/china-silkroad/rpt-china-puts-gentler-face-on-belt-and-road-hits-back-at-critics-idUSL3N22A06U.

[114] Zhang and Wu (n 24).

[115] ibid.

[116] H Wu and F Wang, 'Central Bank Chief Says China Will Guard Against Belt and Road Debt Risks' *Caixing*, 25 April 2019, available at www.caixinglobal.com/2019-04-25/central-bank-chief-says-china-will-guard-against-belt-and-road-debt-risks-101408561.html.

[117] Hong Kong Trade Development Council, 'Twenty-seven Global Institutions Sign up to Green Investment Principles for the Belt & Road' (3 May 2019), available at beltandroad.hktdc.com/en/insights/twenty-seven-global-institutions-sign-green-investment-principles-belt-road.

[118] See Blanchard and Goh, 'RPT-China puts gentler face on Belt and Road' (2019).which discusses Editorial, 'BRI naysayers ridiculed by common sense and reality' *Global Times*, 26 April 2019, available at www.globaltimes.cn/content/1147523.shtml.

> proactively with allies and partners to regain the initiative on infrastructure programs, and to pre-emptively ring-fence areas of strategic concern from future Chinese investments. And there need to be increased efforts to foster an independent media in recipient countries that is capable of scrutinizing BRI projects.[119]

No doubt China is realising that it needs to be able to get its money back. In Kenya the media and civil society often criticise the Kenyan SGR by comparison with the Ethiopian rail project, arguing that the latter is much better value for money. But in 2018 Ethiopia obtained an extension for its repayment period from 10 to 20 years, leading the insurer (Sinosure, as contracts tend to require) to comment that 'the planning behind many of China's major infrastructure projects abroad has been "downright inadequate"'.[120] Such an experience may well lie behind its recent refusal to finance the next stage of Kenya's SGR project.

Suspicions that China was deliberately enticing countries into unrepayable debt may have been wrong, or of course China may simply realise that it does not want to take over non-viable projects. An important question is whether recipient countries will be pushed into more careful scrutiny of their own plans. That will depend on a combination of will and capacity, which are of course interrelated. In the Kenyan context at least it seems that politicians do not use to the full the capacities of their civil servants, and others, who are able to scrutinise the viability of projects. All too often the (corrupt) rewards of proceeding are very great, and the implications of failing will be borne by the unfortunate taxpayers and not by those who committed the country to the profligate expenditure. Whether China will change in terms of monitoring more carefully issues over environmental protection and workers' rights is questionable. It would require mechanisms like those of the World Bank (the Inspection Panel) and International Finance Corporation's equivalent for the mega-projects.

Complaints about the dominance of Chinese companies may reveal skewed playing fields. They also are testimony to the growing efficiency of Chinese business. The World Bank shows that 70 per cent of the contracts that it awards to Chinese construction companies are for projects outside China. And in Africa 42 per cent by value of the contracts awarded by the Bank are to Chinese companies, though it does seem that the percentage is higher for BRI projects. The problem about this is of course that it goes rather counter to any idea that the BRI is about improving local capacity. How far will China want to help local business to take over from it? A World Bank study shows that there are often possibilities for

[119] A Bhattacharya, D Dollar, R Doshi, R Hass, B Jones, H Kharas, J Mason, M Solís and J Stromseth, 'China's Belt and Road: The new geopolitics of global infrastructure development' (Brookings Institute Report, April 2019), available at www.brookings.edu/research/chinas-belt-and-road-the-new-geopolitics-of-global-infrastructure-development.

[120] A Olingo, 'China plans to sell off its African infrastructure debt to investors' *Daily Nation*, 5 November 2018, available at mobile.nation.co.ke/news/world/China-plans-to-sell-off-its-African-infrastructure-debt/3126396-4837516-owg3sm/index.html.

non-Chinese firms to be involved, albeit in a subsidiary capacity, in BRI projects.[121] But it comments in a footnote:

> Such partnerships may be more difficult to establish in developing countries, and especially in Africa, where a greater imbalance between Chinese and local firms has been observed. In Kenya, local firms have reportedly found it hard to compete with Chinese firms, and some have cut back their operations since the country opened up to Chinese projects.[122]

The Bank paper cites a source[123] that eventually leads us back to the Kenyan newspaper *Business Daily*.[124] The Bank paper concerns procurement procedures, but of course better procurement will not help less efficient local firms, and even less will it help when a contract is dealt with as government to government. The BRI is not of benefit to China alone. World Bank studies have shown that infrastructure developments will benefit other country players in global trade, by speeding up shipments, for example.[125]

V. Conclusions

Hong Kong institutions are involved, or potentially involved, in this whole BRI business. Funding hitherto has come from mainland government sources, but private finance is now being discussed. A forum was held in Hong Kong in the last quarter of 2018 on BRI financing, at which the chief executive of the Hong Kong Monetary Authority said 'A lack of structured, bankable infrastructure projects has created a huge gap between the financing needs of emerging markets and the "trillions" of dollars in capital looking for investment opportunities'.[126] And he said that the Hong Kong Mortgage Corporation was 'planning to securitise infrastructure loans and channel funds into' the BRI.[127]

[121] T Ghossein, B Hoekman and A Shingal, 'Public Procurement in the Belt and Road Initiative' (World Bank Group, Discussion Paper, MTI Global Practice No 10, December 2018), available at documents.worldbank.org/curated/en/143241544213097139/pdf/132786-MTI-Discussion-Paper-10-Final.pdf.

[122] ibid fn 15.

[123] Economist Intelligence Unit, 'Participation of foreign firms in the BRI' (19 June 2018), available at www.business.hsbc.com/belt-and-road/participation-of-foreign-firms-in-the-bri.

[124] V Juma, 'How China contractors drove Kenyan firms out of mega projects' *Business Daily*, 26 January 2017, available at www.businessdailyafrica.com/news/How-China-contractors-drove-Kenyan-firms-out-of--mega-projects/539546-3787626-48b2jy/index.html.

[125] M Ruta, A Mulabdic, S Murray, N Rocha, F de Soyres, 'How much will the Belt and Road Initiative reduce trade costs?' (World Bank blogs, 16 October 2018), available at blogs.worldbank.org/trade/how-much-will-belt-and-road-initiative-reduce-trade-costs.

[126] Y Liu and E Ng, 'To solve China's Belt and Road financing problem, Hong Kong looks to infrastructure loan-backed securities' *South China Morning Post*, 15 October 2018, available at www.scmp.com/news/article/2168671/solve-chinas-belt-and-road-financing-problem-hong-kong-looks-infrastructure.

[127] ibid.

But more than this, in 2016 Hong Kong set up its Belt and Road Office, intended to market Hong Kong as the best connector between China and the World. Together with projects from other parts of the world, the Hong Kong office highlights Djibouti as an example of its projects in Africa: 'A Hong Kong-based shipping and investment group takes part in the operation of the port, develops and manages a free trade zone at the port in joint venture with local enterprises'.[128]

Hong Kong is not what we have called a 'recipient' of BRI projects, but rather a beneficiary and an investor. This is not to say that the interactions that recipient countries have with China do not in various ways echo those of Hong Kong. The chapters in this book highlight the concerns that Hong Kong people have, including Hong Kong's sense that its own way of life and principles are subordinated to China's security needs,[129] a lack of transparency about inter-governmental relations,[130] a strong sense of inequality, vis-à-vis the sovereign power,[131] resentment at the notion that there might be a bit of Hong Kong that is Chinese-law territory,[132] and lack of understanding of democratic ideals, human rights and the justice system.[133]

Critics in many BRI countries might echo these concerns. On the issue of Chinese-law territory, some might observe that many developing countries have Special Economic Zones in which foreign investors, including China, can operate free from some of the protective laws of the surrounding state. In fact China has been developing a new type of SEZ: Overseas Economic and Commercial Cooperation Zones (OECCZ) – 'an enclave designed by a Chinese company appointed by China to create a haven in another country's territory to accommodate Chinese companies, which are de facto subject to Chinese law, and thus boost Chinese economic development'.[134] Ethiopia is the site of one such. The author of that description concludes that he wishes to 'warn countries of the danger of conceding any part of its territory to any foreign power, for there is no guarantee that the interests and ambitions of that foreign power will always converge with their own'.[135]

BRI countries (or their dissident minorities) have, as we have seen, many other concerns, including the undermining of local industry, debt burdens, the fear of losing control of their own assets, marginalising of other foreign voices, which – if not consistently – speak in support of human rights and a sense of losing control of their own data and destiny. What those other countries have, and Hong Kong

[128] Belt and Road Office, HKSAR Government, 'Belt and Road. Hong Kong: A key link for the Belt and Road' (2017), available at www.beltandroad.gov.hk/compendium.pdf.

[129] See the Introduction and contributions of Michael C Davis and Hualing Fu in this collection.

[130] See the contributions of Cora Chan and Fiona de Londras in this collection.

[131] See the contribution of Johannes Chan in this collection.

[132] See the contributions of Swati Jhaveri, and Cora Chan and Fiona de Londras in this collection.

[133] See the contributions of Hualing Fu and Michael C Davis in this collection.

[134] T Pairault, 'China in Africa: Phoenix nests versus Special Economic Zones' (CCJ Occasional Papers no 7, December 2018) 4, available at hal.archives-ouvertes.fr/hal-01968812/document.

[135] ibid 11.

does not, is their sovereignty. Yet critics feel that that sovereignty is being undermined. In a country like Kenya, the problem seems to be that the leaders do not value that sovereignty enough. Instead, those leaders look for short-term, often personal, advantage. China, as we saw from the playing out of the 99-year lease of Hong Kong, has patience. A parallel could be drawn here with Hong Kong, where government and many members of the public have become more willing to cede Hong Kong's autonomy in return for their (often personal) advantage – to businessmen, immediate economic gains; to politicians, advancement in their political careers. This judgment on the public should perhaps be qualified somewhat in the light of recent developments, namely weeks of demonstrations in which astonishing numbers of Hong Kong people have come out to protest against the Mainland's treatment of the Region.

A country like Kenya is sovereign, has its own constitution and has its own, not perfect but not totally cowed, judiciary. It does not need to turn, in our view, to international law, unlike perhaps Hong Kong[136] in order to assert itself in respect of China. Its Constitution already has a right of access to information and supporting law (unlike Hong Kong[137]), and it requires important decisions to have public involvement. It does have choices here: China is not a colonial power, taking over people who have no understanding of what is happening to them, as the UK did when it made so-called treaties with the Maori or the Maasai, or those who understood but had no effective choice, as with its unequal treaty over Hong Kong. Perhaps the problem is that the relationship between China and the elite in many of these countries is a symbiotic one in which both benefit. Can China come to view its relationship as one not just with the rulers, but with the people of the recipient countries, since the governments of those countries are all too often dismal failures in their responsibilities as trustees for their people?

A final reflection in the light of the general theme of this book: Hong Kongers may feel they need friends in order to help them negotiate the security relationship with China, including Article 23. However, although there may have been some missteps by China in its relationships with BRI recipient countries, and signs of dissatisfaction, reports of the demise of the BRI are definitely exaggerated. The reality is that China has won many friends with its BRI, friends that it does and can influence. The BRI and its success in building alliances and dependencies with other states may mean that friends for Hong Kong – if and when it needs their intervention and support vis-à-vis Beijing – are in short supply.

[136] See the contribution of Carole J Petersen in this collection.
[137] See the contributions of Cora Chan and Fiona de Londras in this collection.

INDEX

I

CPSIA information can be obtained
at www.ICGtesting.com
Printed in the USA
LVHW021616070520
655174LV00023B/1548

9 781509 928156